Harvey C. Knowles III
& Damon H.

The DIVIDEND *Investor*

A Safe and Sure Way
to Beat the Market
with High-Yield
Dividend Stocks

IRWIN
Professional Publishing®
Chicago • London • Singapore

ISBN 1-55738-892-X

Printed in the United States of America

BB

2 3 4 5 6 7 8 9 0

Dedication

To my children Tricia, Drew, and Katie.
H.K.

Special thanks to Priscilla Petty, interviewer, for her help in getting this project on the right track through the use of her unique interviewing talents and for her valuable assistance in editing the manuscript.
D.P.

Contents

Preface

Myths associated with investing abound. One myth holds that only certain enlightened professionals know the secrets of investing and therefore profit. Another myth is the novice's belief that if only he knew these secrets, he too could become rich. The truth is that achieving above-average investment returns requires discipline and information, not a degree from Harvard Business School. Much can be gained from listening to the sage advice of a successful professional or reading a book such as this. *The Dividend Investor* is intended to be a source of reliable data and objective analysis that helps investors with the decision-making process.

This book provides an in-depth analysis of one superior method of investing — dividend investing. The performance of the high-yield shares in the Dow Jones Industrial Average from 1957 to 1990 is set forth. The data are compelling. High-yield shares resist decline in bear markets and appreciate faster in bull markets. The portfolios produce exceptional income for income-dependent investors. The consistency of returns afforded by the Top Ten method described in Chapter 2 actually decreases risk relative to the stock market while increasing returns to the investor. Dividend investing can also be used with leverage to produce phenomenal results for the aggressive investor.

We do not claim to present all the answers here or to offer the ultimate truth about investing. But we *will* give you facts — not myths — on which you can rely. Dividend investing works.

Many people have contributed to the research and writing effort set forth in this book.

Elizabeth Armitage of Merrill Lynch, was a diligent researcher of the dividend phenomenon long before the first chapter of this book was written. Hours and hours of her time are buried in almost every table in the book. Likewise, Sue Dorger approached each research project with rigor. Lastly, Mary Ann Morgan has been very helpful updating statistics and dividend data weekly for the last two years.

We would also like to thank Michael Roberts for his editorial and research support.

Without the support of these committed individuals, we doubt this book would have been completed.

Harvey C. Knowles III & Damon H. Petty

1

Dividend Investing

Common investment wisdom holds that the best way to achieve capital gains is to purchase low-yield "growth" stocks. Our research shows that just the opposite is true: *dividend investing* produces both high income and superior capital gains. The high-dividend strategy is one of the most powerful investment tools available to both the individual and professional investor. For seventy years, study after study has shown that stocks with high dividend yields consistently outperform low-yield "growth" stocks. Remarkably, the high-yield issues both resist decline in bear markets and appreciate faster in bull markets. The dividend investor enjoys the best of all worlds—protection of capital in negative environments and superior returns in positive ones. The performance history of high-yield stocks refutes the widely held concept that the dividend investor must forego capital gains as he invests in high-yield shares. Thoughtful commentators have expressed the belief that corporate profits should be retained and reinvested by the companies themselves rather than paid out to shareholders. In theory, the company should earn a higher rate of return upon the

Table 1.1.

18-year Average Annual Total Returns

Years	Top Five	Bottom Five
1973 to 1990:	17.81%	4.87%

18-year Growth of a $100,000 Investment

Years	Top Five	Bottom Five
1973 to 1990:	$1,555,089	$148,743

capital than the shareholder. Our studies indicate the investor is far better off reinvesting his own dividends.

Thorough study of the high-yield shares within the Dow Jones Industrial Average and other prominent stock market indices undermines the compelling concept of "growth" stock investing. Over time, the high-yield issues outperform the low-yield issues by 50 percent and more *per year*. For example, the top five dividend payers in the Dow Jones Industrial Average have appreciated at 10.20 percent per year from 1973 to 1990. Meanwhile, the five lowest dividend payers provided a return of only 3.04 percent. With dividends included, the Top Five produced a 17.81 percent average annual total return; the Bottom Five provided just 7.18 percent.

When a $100,000 investment in the Top Five is compared to a $100,000 investment in the Bottom Five, the results are dramatically different. After 18 years, the Top Five portfolio is $1,406,346 richer than the Bottom Five (see Table 1.1).

Study after study of stock groups — the Dow Jones Industrial Average, the Standard and Poor 400, the Standard and Poor 500, the S&P Compustat II database (5,000 companies), and all New York Stock Exchange listed companies — have shown that the highest-yielding shares annually outperform the low-yielding shares as well as the group averages.

Our findings show that a portfolio designed for a widow with children is also suitable for the aggressive investor seeking growth.[1] The businessman pushing for capital gains should position his portfolio in shares that pay the best dividends. In every period studied, the high-yield issues have produced exceptional capital gains.

This concept was endorsed for decades by the father of modern securities analysis and one of this century's most successful investors, Ben Graham. Graham observed that companies with relatively high yields (2/3 of the AAA bond rate) and good balance sheets (where debt was less than tangible book value) consistently outperformed the market. Late in life, Graham began to work with Dr. James Rea, a California statistician. They screened the New York Stock Exchange from 1925 to 1975 for those companies that met the above criteria.[2] The average stock selected appreciated at an annual rate of 18.5 percent. By comparison, capital appreciation in the Dow Jones Industrial Average was 3.5 percent. Dividends brought the average DJIA total return up to 7.5 percent.

The original research in this book on high-dividend-yield issues focuses mainly on the Dow Jones Industrials for the years 1957 through 1990. The thirty industrials are segregated annually into four groups: the Top Five, the Top Ten, the Bottom Ten, and the Bottom Five. The Top Five are the stocks with the five highest dividend yields on the day of ranking; the Top Ten, the ten highest; the Bottom Ten, the ten lowest; and the Bottom Five, the five lowest. In the one-year periods following the day of ranking, the Top Five produced the highest average annual total return — 16.1 percent. The Top Ten were close behind at 15.0 percent. The Bottom Ten managed only 9.4 percent. The Bottom Five lagged behind with an 8.86 percent average annual return. The Dow Jones Industrials averaged 10.7 percent over these thirty-three years.

The power of the high-yield strategy is magnified when its higher return is compounded over a lengthy time period. For instance, investing in all thirty Dow Industrials managed to increase the value of a $10,000 portfolio to $194,409 from 1957 to 1990, while use of the Top Five high-dividend-yield strategy would have increased the portfolio value to $937,432. In the same time period, $10,000 invested in the Bottom Five compounded to $83,687 — less than one tenth the value of the Top Five portfolio.

To judge the performance of any investment strategy, one must measure its results against an appropriate benchmark. For instance, when evaluating the performance of a long-term Treasury bond portfolio, one should compare its performance to that of a long-term Treasury bond index

Chart 1.1.   The S&P 500 and the Dow Thirty Annual Total Returns

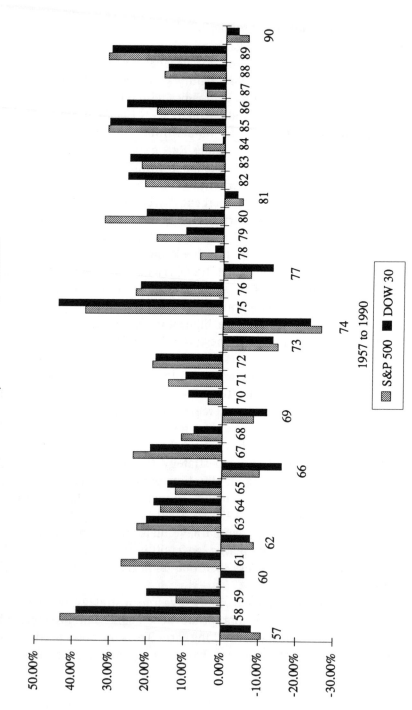

1957 to 1990

S&P 500   ■ DOW 30

such as the Lehman Brothers Long T-bond index. One should compare the performance of a stock portfolio to that of a stock market index such as the S&P 500, making the necessary calculations to include dividend income in total return.

The Dow Jones Industrial Average (DJIA) was used in this book instead of the S&P 500 as the benchmark against which portfolio results were measured. While the S&P 500 Index covers 500 issues and is generally considered by the investment community to be a more accurate indicator of the movement of common stocks overall, it tends to run in tandem with the Dow Jones Industrial Average to the extent that the deviation between the two indices is insignificant. Chart 1.1 shows just how closely the DJIA and S&P 500 returns are correlated.

Both the Top Five and Top Ten high-dividend yield portfolios significantly outperformed the market average as measured by the DJIA. To put this achievement in perspective, compare the following survey of the performance of professional money managers to that of the high-yield strategy.

MUTUAL FUNDS

The Merrill Lynch "Mutual Funds Research Commentary" for January of 1990 offers data on the total returns of approximately fifty mutual funds in each of four classes relevant to our topic. Listed from most aggressive management style to most conservative, they are:

(1) Capital Appreciation/Aggressive Growth Funds

(2) Growth Funds

(3) Growth/Income Funds

(4) Balanced Funds

Fund assets ranged from nine million to 2.5 billion dollars.

The fund groups were examined over various standard time periods ranging form one quarter to ten years. All four groups possessed average total returns that were substantially below the average return of the DJIA in all time periods. For instance, the group average for the Capital Appreciation/Aggressive Growth mutual funds was 305.1 percent over the ten-

Table 1.2.

Capital Appreciation/Aggressive Growth				
All periods end 12/89				
3 month	1 year	3 year	5 year	10 year
Failure Rate	96%	73%	74%	97%	82%
Group Average	-2.5%	25.9%	45.1%	95.6%	305.1%
DJIA Return	3.2%	31.6%	60.8%	173.1%	419.0%

Growth Funds				
All periods end 12/89				
3 month	1 year	3 year	5 year	10 year
Failure Rate	90%	80%	83%	97%	88%
Group Average	-1.0%	25.8%	46.4%	113.4%	328.4%
DJIA Return	3.2%	31.6%	60.8%	173.1%	419.0%

Growth/Income				
All periods end 12/89				
3 month	1 year	3 year	5 year	10 year
Failure Rate	90%	87%	95%	100%	86%
Group Average	0.8%	24.6%	46.4%	122.5%	352.6%
DJIA Return	3.2%	31.6%	60.8%	173.1%	419.0%

Balanced Funds				
All periods end 12/89				
3 month	1 year	3 year	5 year	10 year
Failure Rate	100%	100%	100%	100%	100%
Group Average	0.9%	19.7%	35.8%	105.7%	338.8%
DJIA Return	3.2%	31.6%	60.8%	173.1%	419.0%

year period beginning December 1979, while the total return of DJIA stocks was 419.0 percent. Table 1.2 is a complete summary of the data on all four fund groups.

The percentage of funds in a specific group that is unable to match or exceed the returns of the DJIA is known as the failure rate. Notice that failure rates decrease as the investment strategy of the fund category increases in aggressiveness. Capital Appreciation/Aggressive Growth funds possess the most aggressive strategies and have the lowest (albeit still embarrassing) failure rates, averaging 84 percent, while Balanced funds have the highest failure rates, actually failing to match or exceed the market return in all cases — a 100 percent failure rate. This trend is not indicative of better management among the more aggressive funds; rather, it is the result of more aggressive strategies that bring higher risk and higher variance between fund performances. In the aggressive categories, more funds occasionally will jut above the DJIA return because of their wider distribution around their group average. As aggressiveness decreases, the returns of the individual funds become more consistent, clustering more tightly around their group averages.

The average total return within a fund category actually decreases as aggressiveness increases. Capital Appreciation/Aggressive Growth funds had the lowest average returns, while Growth/Income funds had the highest. These results support the proposed strategy of choosing high-dividend-yield stocks for growth, as the Growth/Income fund portfolios are replete with high-yield issues which significantly outperformed the lower-yielding issues in the Aggressive Growth/Capital Appreciation funds.

Barron's conducted a three-year study comparing the performance of 2,190 mutual funds to the S&P 500. Of the funds tracked by *Barron's*/Lipper Gauge, only twenty consistently beat the market average as represented by the S&P 500 Index from January 1986 to December 1988. Their calculations did not include the effects of loads (up-front commissions that run as high as 8 3/4 percent) or other charges on total return. Of the twenty funds that beat the market, twelve were international funds that profited substantially from the devaluation of the dollar against foreign currencies.

Mutual funds are not alone. Research has shown that pension funds, bank trust departments, university endowment trusts, and stockbrokers all consistently underperform the market averages.[3] Even investment newsletters give advice that leads to sub-market performance 99 percent of the time.[4]

It is remarkable that such a large majority of professional investors find it so difficult to match the returns of the stock market itself. The most celebrated individual investor of our time, Warren E. Buffett, wrote in January 1965 on the puzzle of the tendency of professional investors to underperform the market. Mr. Buffett mused, "Why in the world does this happen to very intelligent managements working with (1) bright, energetic staff people, (2) virtually unlimited resources, (3) the most extensive business contacts, and (4) literally centuries of aggregate investment experience?" The answer may be that professional investors must battle all the obstacles that plague individual investors, plus a few more. All investors must master their emotions before they manage their money successfully. Fear and uncertainty tend to push individuals and professionals alike into a common mind set that is reassured by peer support. Thus, many investors wind up buying stocks that are over-priced but that nonetheless offer the security of popular approval. Collectively, these popular issues have limited potential for capital growth. They also pose the threat of a quick loss to the investor when popular opinion reverses itself.

Individual investors have one certain advantage over investment professionals: they don't have to cater to clients demanding constant, immediate results quarter after quarter. The clients' focus on quarterly performance has the detrimental effect of forcing many managers to assume short-term outlooks the attempt to score immediate profits. This unfortunate emphasis undermines long-run success and is one of the most prevalent money management mistakes. John Maynard Keynes held the opinion that a short-term perspective was a particularly American characteristic. He wrote, "Very few American investors buy a stock for the sake of something that is going to happen more than six months hence, even though its probability is exceedingly high; and it is out of taking advantage of this psychological peculiarity of theirs that most money is made."[5]

Comparative data from C.D.A. Investment Technologies ranks the performance of portfolios comprised of the Top Five and Top Ten stocks by yield in the Dow Jones Industrial Average with the top one percent of money managers. The poor showing of the professionals in particular shows how difficult it is for *anyone* to discover and implement a successful investment strategy.

The tendency of investors to underperform the market averages in the long run demonstrates the usefulness of the high-yield investment strategy outlined in this book. Dividend investing consistently beats the market, and provides the investor with a superior method for compounding capital.

Endnotes

1. This idea is attributable to David Dreman and his writings.

2. From the article "Ben Graham's Last Will and Testiment" published in *Forbes* Magazine, 1976.

3. From 1979 to 1988, only two-tenths of one percent of pension funds could produce returns that were higher than the S&P 500 + 1 percent in five or more individual years. No pension fund could beat the return of the S&P 500 + 1 percent in each of the ten years. In the period December, 1980 to June, 1989, an average of 80 percent of bank trust departments underperformed the S&P 500. Bank trust departments averaged 14.2 percent per year while the S&P 500 averaged 15.3 percent during this time. Between June 30, 1974 and June 30, 1987, university endowments underperformed the DJIA by an average of 27 percent per year, posting annual returns of 11.4 percent while the Dow gained 14.4 percent per year. A February 2, 1990 article in *The Wall Street Journal,* "Hot Stock Picks Burn 9 of 10 Major Brokers," pointed out that in a quarter when the DJIA picked up 3.2 percent, all the major brokerage house recommendations underperformed the market, with all but one losing money for its clients. Over the preceding 3 1/2-year period, 30 percent of the brokerage houses made buy recommendations that subsequently exceeded the return of the DJIA..

4. November 13, 1989 article in *The Wall Street Journal,* "Scoop on Newsletters May Be Bad News," states that performance based on investment newsletter recommendations fell below that of the market averages in all but one of ninety-seven cases observed. Ironically, newsletter proponents responded to the facts in the article by saying,

"Research shows that newsletter writers' performance hasn't been all that bad compared with mutual fund managers."

5.   The Collected Writings of John Maynard Keynes, XII, p. 78.

2

The Mechanics
of Dividend Investing

By following these six simple rules, you can consistently outperform the market average and 99 percent of the pros:

(1) Invest only in the thirty stocks comprising the Dow Jones Industrial Average. They make up your investment universe.

(2) Rank the DJIA stocks by dividend yield from highest to lowest. Dividend yield is defined as the stock's annualized cash dividend divided by its current share price.

(3) Purchase either the five highest-yielding stocks or the ten highest-yielding stocks from the universe.

(4) Hold these positions for one year.

(5) Re-evaluate your portfolio on its anniversary date by re-ranking all thirty Dow stocks by dividend yield as described in Rule 2.

> *Sell any stocks in your portfolio that no longer have one of the five or ten highest yields, and purchase those stocks which have replaced them in the high-yield group.*
>
> *(6) Do not deviate from this program.*[1]

Implementing a high-yield strategy is easy. Examining the historical data which follows in Chapters 3 through 7 will help you decide whether a Top Five approach or a Top Ten approach is more appropriate for your investment needs and temperament. The Top Five offers the highest returns, but those returns vary slightly more from year to year than do the returns of the Top Ten. Both portfolios represent conservative methods of equity investing as defined by high-yield issue selection, diversity, and consistent returns. After you decide which portfolio is right for you, refer to the most recent issue of *The Wall Street Journal,* a resource which will provide all the current investment data you need to make the calculations for selecting the stocks in your high-yield portfolio.

Since the dividend-based methods of investing advocated in this book use only stocks in the Dow Jones Industrial Average, you must first procure a list of these thirty stocks. An up-to-date list of the Dow Industrials can be found in a matter of minutes by looking in the "Money & Investing" section of the *Journal* (see Table 2.1).

The best companies are the best investments. The Dow Jones Industrials list is headed by companies like American Express and AT&T. Du Pont, General Electric, and IBM occupy the middle positions. More investment-grade issues like Westinghouse and Woolworth close the list. These companies represent the corporate muscle of America. The issue is not, "Will these companies be here ten years from now?" but rather, "When is it timely to purchase stock in one or more of these powerhouses?"

You now need to rank each stock in the DJIA by dividend yield. Look again in the "Money & Investing" section of the *Journal,* this time under "NEW YORK STOCK EXCHANGE COMPOSITE TRANSACTIONS." You will find each of the abbreviated Dow Industrial names listed alphabetically among the two thousand or so stocks on the NYSE. Circle the Dow Industrials as you find them. Be careful not to confuse the common stock with a preferred stock issued by the same company. Only common shares are in the DJIA, but some Dow companies also have preferred shares listed on the NYSE. These preferred shares are not relevant to this

Table 2.1.   As of January 1, 1991, the Companies in the DJIA

Name	WSJ Abbreviation		NYSE symbol
Allied-Signal	AlliedSgnl		ALD
Alcoa	Alcoa		AA
American Express	AmExpress		AXP
American Telephone & Telegraph	AmT&T		T
Bethlehem Steel	BethSteel		BS
Boeing	Boeing		BA
Chevron	Chevron		CHV
Coca Cola	CocaCola		KO
Du Pont	DuPont		DD
Eastman Kodak	EKodak		EK
Exxon	Exxon		XON
General Electric	GenElec		GE
General Motors	GenMotor		GM
Goodyear	Goodyear		GT
IBM	IBM		IBM
International Paper	IntPaper		IP
McDonald's	McDonalds		MCD
Merck	Merck		MRK
Minnessota Mining & Manufacturing	MinnMngMfg		MMM
Navistar *	Navistar		NAV
Philip Morris	PhilipMor		MO
Primerica *	Primerica		PA
Procter & Gamble	ProctGamb		PG
Sears, Roebuck	Sears		S
Texaco	Texaco		TX
USX *	USX		X
Union Carbide	UnCarbide		UK
United Technologies	UtdTech		UTX
Westinghouse Electric	Westnghse		WX
Woolworth	Woolworth		Z

* On Monday, April 29, 1991, three changes were made in the structure of the Dow 30.
Navistar, Primerica, and USX were removed from the group after being present for the entirety of our study. They were replaced by Caterpillar, Disney, and J.P. Morgan.

Figure 2.1.

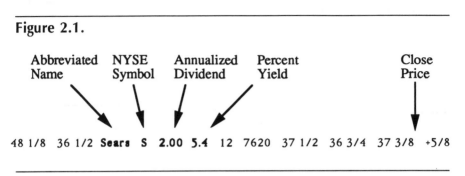

Abbreviated Name	NYSE Symbol	Annualized Dividend	Percent Yield								Close Price	

48 1/8 36 1/2 **Sears** S **2.00 5.4** 12 7620 37 1/2 36 3/4 37 3/8 +5/8

investment program. The abbreviated company names and stock symbols are included in Table 2.1 as they appear in the *Journal.*

The NYSE listings provide pertinent data on each stock. The annualized cash dividend for each company is printed after the company name and ticker symbol. The current dividend yield percentage follows the cash dividend per share. The close price is found in the next to the last column. Although *The Wall Street Journal* calculates a yield value for you, thoroughness requires the more serious investor to calculate the yield by hand in order to exclude the effects of any anomalies. Calculate the dividend yield for each stock by dividing the annualized dividend value by the close price, then rank the thirty Dow Industrials from highest to lowest by these dividend yield values.

Be sure to recognize the implications of any footnote. These are designated by letters following the cash dividend value. For instance, in Figure 2.2, "a" refers to the fact that there were additional dividends paid in the prior year above and beyond those reported in the 3.00 value listed below.

Occasionally an adjustment must be made which affects the stock's yield and rank when a dividend listed as an additional (or extra) dividend is actually a regularly paid dividend—which sometimes occurs when a

Figure 2.2.

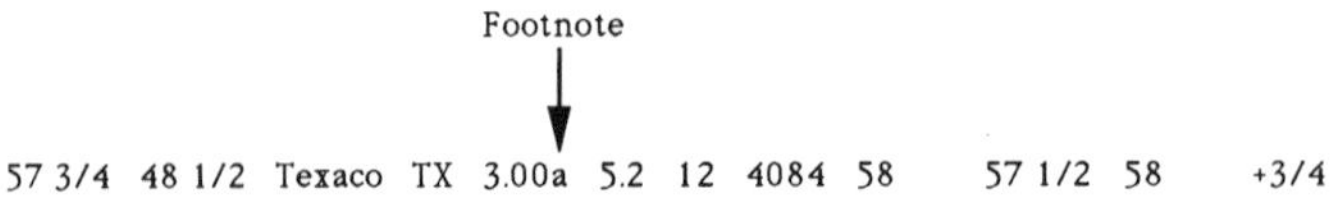

Footnote

57 3/4 48 1/2 Texaco TX 3.00a 5.2 12 4084 58   57 1/2 58   +3/4

company's dividend is growing rapidly—or after a split when a new dividend has just been declared.

While researching the historical data on the Dow Jones Industrials, we noticed a few years for which the dividend listed in *The Wall Street Journal* was inaccurate or mis-represented. All these "errors" were accompanied by footnotes. For instance, after a stock split one year, the new dividend quoted in the *Journal* for the split stock was only half of its actual value. The footnote in this case was "g," meaning "Indicates amount declared or paid after a stock dividend or split." In another case, dividend growth was grossly understated by the regular dividend declared in the *Journal*—to the extent that a $3.00 dividend was quoted as $2.00. Here the footnote read "a" (as in Figure 2.2), meaning "also extra or extras." An additional dividend was paid over and above the regular dividend. A good stock broker should be able to help you with questions about dividend irregularities.

After you have calculated the yields for all thirty stocks and arranged them from highest to lowest according to dividend yield, call your broker and purchase equal dollar amounts of each of the five or ten highest-yielding stocks, thus creating your Top Five or Top Ten portfolio.

Hold these positions for one year. This rule is simply stated but hard to obey. You needn't do anything related to the stock market for one year after purchase. Nonetheless, you will be inclined to monitor the performance of your portfolio throughout the year. Share prices will rise and fall. You will read newspaper articles or hear items on the news about your stocks. Your friends, family, and co-workers will also offer their opinions—but don't listen. It is critical for you to follow your program regardless of the doom prophesied by those around you. The great Ben Graham once observed that investors should worry more about their dividends than the short-term price changes of their stocks. Trust yourself, and history. And collect your dividends.

Re-rank the Dow Industrials on the anniversary date using the same process described above. Sell those issues in your Top Five or Top Ten portfolio that are not in the new group and purchase those stocks that have replaced them. Make an effort to maintain equal dollar values of each position. Because the issues in the portfolio grow at different rates, adjustments must be made in some years to prevent the portfolio from becoming too heavily weighted in any one position.

Table 2.2.   The Top Ten Portfolio: 1983

COMPANY	YIELD	INITIAL VALUE	ENDING VALUE	DIVIDEND PAID
Exxon	10.37%	$10,000	$12,629	$1,069
Texaco	9.80%	$10,000	$11,510	$980
American Can	9.43%	$10,000	$15,081	$943
American Tel & Tel	9.02%	$10,000	$10,438	$977
American Brands	7.69%	$10,000	$13,049	$781
Chevron	7.68%	$10,000	$10,920	$768
Allied Corp.	7.38%	$10,000	$17,115	$739
Woolworth	6.99%	$10,000	$13,786	$699
Du Pont	6.69%	$10,000	$14,286	$697
Union Carbide	6.62%	$10,000	$12,092	$662
			$130,906	$8,315

TOTAL: $139,221

The following is a step-by-step example of the creation and maintenance of a Top Ten portfolio from January 2, 1983 through December 31, 1985.

The ten highest-yielding stocks in the Dow Industrials in 1983 were as shown in Table 2.2.

Ten thousand dollars worth of each Top Ten stock was purchased. The capital increase and dividend income of the issues are shown in the table. The portfolio's value moved from $100,000 to $139,221 in 1983, for a total return of 39.22 percent. The dividend income was pooled in a checking or money market account and was used to purchase additional shares on the anniversary date.[2]

In January 1984, when the thirty Dow Industrials were ranked again, the Top Ten were as shown in Table 2.3.

Allied Corp. was not present in the new high-yield list. A 71.15 percent upsurge in its share price had reduced its yield from 7.38 percent to 4.31 percent. It could not make the yield cut in 1984, becoming a sell that was replaced by General Foods, with a 4.68 percent yield. The proceeds from the sale of the $17,115 position in Allied Corp. were pooled with the dividend income. A $14,000 position in General Foods was then purchased. The $11,430 remaining in the cash pool was used to make the

Table 2.3.   The Top Ten Portfolio: 1984

COMPANY	YIELD	INITIAL VALUE	ENDING VALUE	DIVIDEND PAID
American Tel & Tel	9.36%	$13,868	$14,797	$1,298
Exxon	8.74%	$13,629	$16,559	$1,247
Texaco	8.51%	$13,510	$13,030	$1,150
Chevron	7.03%	$13,420	$11,945	$944
American Can	6.25%	$15,081	$16,260	$943
American Brands	6.06%	$14,049	$15,084	$878
Union Carbide	5.47%	$13,592	$8,095	$744
Du Pont	5.46%	$14,286	$13,589	$808
Woolworth	5.07%	$13,786	$14,369	$699
General Foods	4.68%	$14,000	$15,025	$672
			$138,753	$9,383

TOTAL: $148,140

January, 1984 Portfolio Activity:

> SOLD: Allied Corp. -- $17,115
> BOUGHT: General Foods -- $14,000
> ADJUSTMENTS: BOT $3,430 AT&T; BOT $1,000 Exxon; BOT $2,500 Chevron;
> BOT $2,000 Texaco; BOT $1,000 American Brands;
> BOT $1,500 Union Carbide

necessary adjustments necessary to balance out the value of the portfolio's positions as shown in the table. In 1984, $139,221 grew to $148,140, for an average total return of 6.41 percent.

The thirty Dow Industrials were re-ranked again on January 2, 1985. The new Top Ten were as shown in Table 2.4.

Woolworth and General Foods moved out of the last two spots in the Top Ten and were replaced by Goodyear, which moved from the eleventh position on the yield list to the sixth, and General Motors, which moved all the way from the twentieth to the eighth. The proceeds from the sales

Table 2.4.   The Top Ten Portfolio: 1985

COMPANY	YIELD	INITIAL VALUE	ENDING VALUE	DIVIDEND PAID
Union Carbide	9.19%	$14,795	$29,290	$1,359
Texaco	8.82%	$14,630	$13,231	$1,291
Chevron	7.90%	$14,426	$17,810	$1,140
Exxon	7.64%	$14,959	$18,320	$1,160
American Tel & Tel	6.23%	$14,797	$18,928	$924
Goodyear	6.21%	$14,800	$17,818	$919
Du Pont	6.15%	$14,849	$20,217	$915
General Motors	6.12%	$14,800	$13,971	$953
American Brands	5.88%	$15,084	$15,499	$921
American Can	5.80%	$15,000	$18,038	$870
			$183,122	$10,452

TOTAL: $193,574

January, 1985 Portfolio Activity:

SOLD: Woolworth -- $14,369; General Foods -- $15,025
BOUGHT: Goodyear -- $14,800; General Motors -- $14,800
ADJUSTMENTS: SLD $1,260 American Can; SLD $1,600 Exxon
BOT $6,700 Union Carbide; BOT $1,600 Texaco; BOT $2,481 Chevron
BOT $1,260 Du Pont

---

of Woolworth and General Foods were pooled with the dividend income. Goodyear and General Motors were purchased in equal $14,800 lots. As described above, a number of moves were made within the portfolio to balance portfolio positions. The target value was $14,800 per position. Twelve hundred sixty dollars worth of American Can was sold and put into the Du Pont position. Sixteen hundred dollars worth of Exxon was sold. The proceeds were placed into Texaco. Sixty-seven hundred dollars from the cash pool was used to increase a shallow Union Carbide position. The remaining $2,480 from the cash pool was put into Chevron, completeing the adjustments.

The events concerning Union Carbide from 1984 to 1985 bear mentioning. Union Carbide was ranked seventh in 1984, where it posted a -35 percent total return. Due to the decline in its share price, it became the number-one-ranked issue in 1985. The now-famous disaster at Union Carbide's chemical plant in Bhopal, India, in December 1984 had decimated the share price. In 1985, however, Union Carbide shares rocketed up 107 percent as people realized that this unfortunate event would not materially affect the long-run profitability of the company. This turnaround is a good example of why not to sell a loser if it remains in the high-yield group. Fortunately, we actually bought more!

The value of our Top Ten portfolio has grown from $100,000 to $193,574 in these three years.[3]

Dividend investing actually forces one to sell high and buy low. This pattern is repeated year after year. Lawrence Pratt observed, "The Dow Jones companies, despite their financial strength, are subject to wide fluctuations in investor sentiment. The shares may rise or fall fifty percent depending upon common opinion. The core earnings of the companies as represented by the dividend rarely fluctuate. This constant affords the dividend investor a wonderful opportunity to purchase shares for both yield and appreciation."[4] When stocks rise 50 to 100 percent in a year, they leave the list. New companies appear on the Buy list as their yields rise through price depreciation, dividend increases, or some combination thereof.

It is amazing that so many professional investors ignore the dividend-yield indicator. Strategies involving it are both methodologically simple and statistically sound.

Endnotes

1. Exceptional returns are dependent upon consistent application of the rules.

2. The interest on the money market account is not considered in the total return figures. The actual total return figure is therefore slightly higher than the stated return.

3. Using premium, full service brokerage, the annual cost of commissions for all trades (buys, sell, and adjustments) never exceeded $1000 per year for this portfolio—that's less than 65 basis points

(0.65% per year). These transaction cost have not been subtracted from the final portfolio value mentioned here.

4. Lawrence Pratt, American Economics Institute.

3

The Foundations
of Dividend Investing

Dividend investing works. Data presented in this chapter prove the dependability and effectiveness of a high-yield strategy. Thirty-four years, 1957 through 1990, are covered in the tables and charts that follow. We compare the performance of the high-yield portfolios only to the Dow Jones Industrial Average — the most widely-followed benchmark of equity performance. A direct comparison between the dividend method and professional investment performance is not necessary in light of their consistent underperformance.

$547,000 or $1.6 MILLION?

One dramatic example will introduce you to the magnitude of the power of yield-oriented investing. Before we delve into the large body of data that follows, let's examine two hypothetical portfolios. The first we'll call

21

Chart 3.1.   Dividend Investing vs. The Market

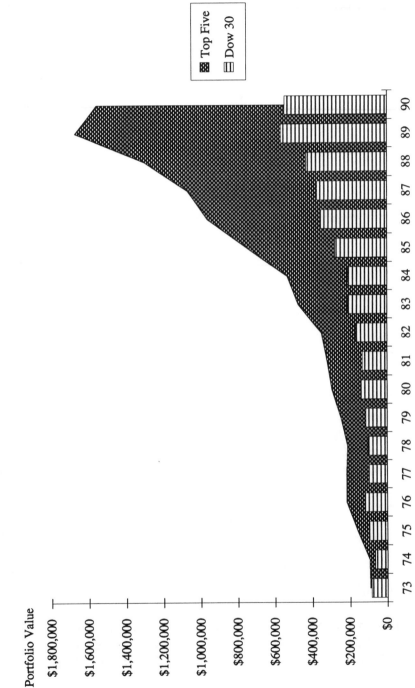

the DJIA Portfolio because it mimics the performance of the Dow Jones Industrials by buying all thirty DJIA stocks. All dividends are reinvested. The second portfolio is the Top Five Portfolio. It implements the high-yield strategy by buying the five highest-yielding Dow stocks each year. (This process is described in Chapter II, using the Top Ten as an example.)

If you had invested $100,000 in the DJIA Portfolio at the beginning of 1973, by the end of 1990 its value would have been $546,656. Your investment would have multiplied to five-and-a-half times its original value over eighteen years — not bad considering the institutional alternatives, where you would have been lucky to equal the DJIA return.

By placing your $100,000 in the Top Five Portfolio instead of the DJIA, the high-yield shares would have protected principal in down times and accelerated appreciation in rising markets. After the same eighteen years, your investment would have ballooned to $1,555,089 in the Top Five, making you more than one million dollars better off in the Top Five Portfolio than in the DJIA Portfolio.

THE SLATTER ARTICLE

The first set of data to examine appeared in *The Wall Street Journal* on August 11, 1988. The article presented a study done by analyst John Slatter, of Prescott, Ball & Turben, Inc., in Cleveland, Ohio. The data from that original article are presented in Table 3.1.

As you can see, the table compares the performance of the Top Ten to the performance of the Dow Thirty for the years 1973 to 1988, inclusive. It lists annual figures for appreciation, yield, and total return for both groups of stocks, as well as an overall average for each figure.

The Top Ten beat the Dow Industrials handily. The average annual total return shown for the Top Ten was 18.4 percent,[1] compared to 10.9 percent for the Dow Jones Industrials. Also note that in this time period the Dow Jones Industrials had three years with double-digit negative returns, plus another less catastrophic down year. The Top Ten, in comparison, had only one down year, falling 2.9 percent in 1974.[2] Not only did the Top Ten significantly outperform the thirty Dow Jones Industrials in rising markets, they also preserved capital in periods of decline.

Table 3.1.   Data from the Slatter Article
Capital Appreciation and Dividend-Yield Figures
for the Dow Thirty versus the Top Ten 1973 to
1988

	DOW 30			TOP TEN		
Year	Appreciation	Yield	Total Return	Appreciation	Yield	Total Return
1973	-16.60%	3.20%	-13.40%	-1.50%	4.80%	3.30%
1974	-27.60%	4.20%	-23.40%	-9.70%	6.80%	-2.90%
1975	38.30%	6.10%	44.40%	48.10%	10.80%	58.90%
1976	17.90%	4.40%	22.30%	28.70%	6.90%	35.60%
1977	-17.30%	4.10%	-13.20%	-4.80%	5.90%	1.10%
1978	-3.10%	5.50%	2.40%	-4.30%	7.60%	3.30%
1979	4.20%	6.00%	10.20%	4.50%	8.20%	12.70%
1980	14.90%	6.10%	21.00%	18.70%	8.60%	27.30%
1981	-9.20%	5.60%	-3.60%	-1.70%	8.00%	6.30%
1982	19.60%	6.40%	26.00%	15.40%	9.10%	24.50%
1983	20.30%	5.20%	25.50%	33.00%	8.10%	41.10%
1984	4.60%	4.40%	9.00%	2.70%	6.30%	9.00%
1985	22.80%	5.00%	27.80%	16.60%	6.70%	23.30%
1986	22.60%	4.00%	26.60%	21.30%	5.90%	27.20%
1987	2.30%	3.50%	5.80%	0.90%	5.40%	6.30%
1988	2.70%	3.70%	6.40%	11.70%	5.60%	17.30%
Average	6.03%	4.84%	10.86%	11.23%	7.17%	18.39%

Source: John Slatter

Note: These figures differ substantially from those found in our research in some cases.

THE NEW DATA

The data in Table 3.2 complement those presented in Table 3.1. The Top Ten portfolios, however, have been checked, revised and updated to 1990. There are some differences between our data and Slatter's findings. For instance, our research shows returns that are impressive, but slightly lower than those presented by Slatter. Again, there was only one down year, 1977, at -1.03 percent. Table 3.2 shows the course of a $100,000 investment made in each of the two groups through the same time period, 1973 to 1990, inclusive.

The early 1970's were terrible for the stock market. The Dow Jones Industrial Average plunged from 1050 in January 1973, to 580 in October 1974. Share prices of popular companies evaporated—Polaroid fell from 120 to 18; Avon from 150 to 25; Eastman Kodak from 150 to 50. Fortunes were lost; careers ended; brokerage houses went bankrupt.

As can be seen in Table 3.2, $100,000 invested in the Dow Thirty fell to $66,000 in just two years, with dividends reinvested. Notably, the Top Ten maintained their value. When the markets turned in 1975, a 44 percent rise couldn't get the Dow Portfolio back to its starting value. Meanwhile, the Top Ten portfolio leapt to $161,000. A 22 percent up-year in 1976 brought the Dow portfolio to $117,000, while the Top Ten rocketed to $214,000. Jimmy Carter then stepped into office in 1977. The Dow subsequently plunged 13 percent. The Top Ten again held their value.

After five years, the Dow Jones portfolio still hadn't advanced from its starting value. But at the same point in time, the value of the Top Ten portfolio had more than doubled, and was already $116,815 ahead of the lagging Dow portfolio. Due to a higher average rate of compounding, the discrepancy between the values of the Top Ten and Dow portfolios grew geometrically. By 1990, the value of the Top Ten stocks was $1,355,181; the thirty Dow stocks were worth only $546,656—a difference of over $800,000!

THE EMERGENCE OF THE TOP FIVE

The excellent returns offered by the Top Ten stocks prompted us to research the five highest-yielding stocks from the thirty Dow Jones Industrials. It seemed logical that if the Top Ten did so well, the Top Five

Table 3.2.   Revised Data for the Dow Thirty versus the Top Ten, 1973 to 1990. Average Annual Total Returns and Compound Values

Year	DOW 30	COMPOUND RETURN	TOP TEN	COMPOUND RETURN
Begin		$100,000		$100,000
1973	-13.40%	$86,600	3.88%	$103,880
1974	-23.40%	$66,336	1.02%	$104,940
1975	44.40%	$95,789	53.23%	$160,799
1976	22.30%	$117,149	33.21%	$214,200
1977	-13.20%	$101,686	-1.03%	$211,994
1978	2.40%	$104,126	2.40%	$217,082
1979	10.20%	$114,747	9.67%	$238,074
1980	21.00%	$138,844	27.53%	$303,615
1981	-3.60%	$133,846	2.68%	$311,752
1982	26.00%	$168,645	20.68%	$376,223
1983	25.50%	$211,650	39.22%	$523,777
1984	0.71%	$213,153	6.27%	$556,618
1985	31.14%	$279,528	31.20%	$730,283
1986	26.60%	$353,883	28.12%	$935,638
1987	5.80%	$374,408	6.89%	$1,000,104
1988	15.55%	$432,629	18.22%	$1,182,322
1989	30.75%	$565,662	27.37%	$1,505,924
1990	-3.36%	$546,656	-10.01%	$1,355,181
Average	11.41%		16.70%	

should have done even better. The data in Table 3.3 proved this assumption correct.

From 1973 to 1990, the average annual total return for the Top Five stocks was 17.81 percent, compared to 11.41 percent for the Dow Thirty, and 16.70 percent for the Top Ten. These figures show that the Top Five's average annual total return was 56 percent higher that that of the Dow Thirty. Once again we see that in bad times the high-yield group resists decline, while in good times it out-paces the Dow average.

The numbers in Table 3.4 demonstrate the efficacy of high-yield investing. The compounding of $100,000 in the Top Five over the eighteen-year period is shown.

In the first five years of the study period, $100,000 invested in the thirty Dow Industrials became $101,686 with dividends reinvested. During the same period, $100,000 invested in the Top Five became $219,607.

Table 3.3.   **Capital Appreciation and Dividend-Yield Figures for the Dow Thirty versus the Top Five 1973 to 1990**

Year	DOW 30 Appreciation	DOW 30 Yield	DOW 30 Total Return	TOP FIVE Appreciation	TOP FIVE Yield	TOP FIVE Total Return
1973	-17.09%	3.69%	-13.40%	-13.51%	5.86%	-7.65%
1974	-26.10%	2.70%	-23.40%	-2.72%	8.06%	5.34%
1975	35.86%	8.54%	44.40%	57.44%	7.66%	65.10%
1976	16.42%	5.88%	22.30%	28.60%	7.56%	36.16%
1977	-18.21%	5.01%	-13.20%	-6.64%	7.06%	0.42%
1978	-0.77%	3.17%	2.40%	-10.16%	7.77%	-2.39%
1979	1.62%	8.58%	10.20%	7.65%	8.80%	16.45%
1980	17.97%	3.03%	21.00%	10.52%	8.58%	19.10%
1981	-9.28%	5.68%	-3.60%	-0.41%	8.88%	8.47%
1982	16.38%	9.62%	26.00%	0.76%	8.48%	9.24%
1983	21.98%	3.52%	25.50%	25.42%	9.50%	34.92%
1984	-4.30%	5.01%	0.71%	4.30%	8.06%	12.36%
1985	28.26%	2.88%	31.14%	32.45%	7.98%	40.43%
1986	25.33%	1.27%	26.60%	21.39%	7.00%	28.39%
1987	4.56%	1.24%	5.80%	5.87%	5.35%	11.22%
1988	7.61%	7.94%	15.55%	15.16%	6.25%	21.41%
1989	26.96%	3.79%	30.75%	19.76%	8.78%	28.54%
1990	-7.10%	3.74%	-3.36%	-12.37%	5.42%	-6.95%
Average	6.67%	4.74%	11.41%	10.20%	7.61%	17.81%

After eighteen years, the Top Five portfolio was worth $1,555,089. The Dow Jones Industrials portfolio totaled only $546,656, for a bottom line difference of $1,008,433.

Long Run Reversion

A word of caution: it would be imprudent to expect such high returns to continue indefinitely because rates of return in capital markets have a tendency to revert to their mean. The period 1973 to 1990 was blessed with unusually good market performance, especially in the 1980's. The Dow's performance over this period is well above its long-run average,

Table 3.4.   The Dow Thirty versus the Top Five, 1973 to 1990
Average Annual Total Returns and Compound Values

Year	DOW 30	COMPOUND RETURN $100,000	TOP FIVE	COMPOUND RETURN $100,000
1973	-13.40%	$86,600	-7.65%	$92,350
1974	-23.40%	$66,336	5.34%	$97,281
1975	44.40%	$95,789	65.10%	$160,612
1976	22.30%	$117,149	36.16%	$218,689
1977	-13.20%	$101,686	0.42%	$219,607
1978	2.40%	$104,126	-2.39%	$214,359
1979	10.20%	$114,747	16.45%	$249,621
1980	21.00%	$138,844	19.10%	$297,298
1981	-3.60%	$133,846	8.47%	$322,480
1982	26.00%	$168,645	9.24%	$352,277
1983	25.50%	$211,650	34.92%	$475,292
1984	0.71%	$213,153	12.36%	$534,038
1985	31.14%	$279,528	40.43%	$749,949
1986	26.60%	$353,883	28.39%	$962,860
1987	5.80%	$374,408	11.22%	$1,070,893
1988	15.55%	$432,629	21.41%	$1,300,171
1989	30.75%	$565,662	28.54%	$1,671,240
1990	-3.36%	$546,656	-6.95%	$1,555,089
Average	11.41%		17.81%	

as is that of the Top Five. The average posted by this eighteen-year period can be expected to decline in a future period of lower rates of return, such as those seen in earlier decades.

THE LARGER SAMPLE

We expanded our research to include the sixteen years preceding our initial sample—1957 to 1972—in order to double-check the implications of the data in Tables 3.1 through 3.4. We assumed that if the dividend strategy were valid, the same relative performances would be seen in the broader time period—1957 to 1990—with regard to total return and protection against decline.

We also gathered the total return data on two new portfolios—the Bottom Ten and Bottom Five—comprised of the ten and five lowest-yielding Dow stocks. Since the high-yield stocks outperformed the Dow average, we expected to see a lower rate of return for these ignoble groups. We were not disappointed.

The data from this broader sample comparing the total returns on the Top Five, Top Ten, Dow Thirty, Bottom Ten, and Bottom Five portfolios are presented in Table 3.5.

Summarizing the data, the 1957 to 1990 average annual total returns were:

The Top Five	15.37%
The Top Ten	14.17%
The Dow Thirty	10.38%
The Bottom Ten	8.87%
The Bottom Five	7.89%

These figures solidly confirm the findings of our initial research. The pattern is exactly the same for the expanded thirty-four-year period. The average return is highest for the Top Five; the Top Ten follow; the Dow Thirty are next; and the Bottom Ten and Bottom Five bring up the rear. There were fewest down years in the Top Ten—seven. The next fewest were in the Top Five—eight. The Dow Industrials had ten. The low- yield Bottom Ten had eleven. And the lowest-yielding group, the Bottom Five, had twelve down years.

Table 3.6 shows the compounding of four portfolios with $100,000 placed into each of the four groups. The money was invested over the entire thirty- four-year period 1957 to 1990. The differences in final values are staggering. Once again the returns follow the same progression from highest to lowest: Top Five, Top Ten, Dow Thirty, Bottom Ten, Bottom Five. The final values:

Top Five	$8,498,740
Top Ten	$6,360,419
Dow Thirty	$1,927,868
Bottom Ten	$1,025,306
Bottom Five	$659,680

The difference between the value of the Top Five portfolio and the Bottom Five portfolio is $7,839,060, or 1,188 percent. The substantial differences

Table 3.5.   Average Annual Total Returns, 1957 to 1990

Year	TOP FIVE	TOP TEN	DOW 30	BOTTOM 10	BOTTOM 5
1957	-8.72%	-7.53%	-8.17%	-6.05%	-6.37%
1958	50.88%	45.78%	38.92%	36.24%	39.46%
1959	11.81%	9.52%	19.83%	27.89%	25.10%
1960	-9.74%	-1.45%	-6.29%	-14.26%	-23.37%
1961	24.10%	24.16%	22.16%	22.96%	25.15%
1962	1.55%	-0.15%	-7.70%	-7.71%	-12.27%
1963	23.27%	22.73%	20.10%	32.39%	43.66%
1964	26.25%	23.07%	18.11%	15.56%	21.75%
1965	29.98%	20.42%	14.45%	14.56%	16.51%
1966	-11.94%	-15.66%	-15.99%	-13.73%	-6.75%
1967	31.71%	26.86%	19.26%	20.57%	13.21%
1968	20.85%	13.11%	7.60%	0.65%	-2.01%
1969	-11.24%	-12.78%	-11.90%	-6.02%	3.75%
1970	-0.10%	3.48%	9.10%	1.64%	0.77%
1971	3.98%	5.75%	9.90%	18.62%	16.77%
1972	19.35%	23.85%	18.10%	16.46%	25.39%
1973	-7.65%	3.88%	-13.40%	-23.03%	-7.67%
1974	5.34%	1.02%	-23.40%	-34.30%	-34.77%
1975	65.10%	53.23%	44.40%	44.58%	41.53%
1976	36.16%	33.21%	22.30%	28.09%	1.75%
1977	0.42%	-1.03%	-13.20%	-18.70%	-22.70%
1978	-2.39%	2.40%	2.40%	8.92%	11.78%
1979	16.45%	9.67%	10.20%	2.81%	0.09%
1980	19.10%	27.53%	21.00%	30.78%	10.31%
1981	8.47%	2.68%	-3.60%	-14.77%	-14.83%
1982	9.24%	20.68%	26.00%	13.43%	3.08%
1983	34.92%	39.22%	25.50%	28.70%	39.70%
1984	12.36%	6.27%	0.71%	-9.47%	-18.69%
1985	40.43%	31.20%	31.14%	24.26%	23.46%
1986	28.39%	28.12%	26.60%	3.50%	-14.56%
1987	11.22%	6.89%	5.80%	27.74%	55.76%
1988	21.41%	18.22%	15.55%	11.75%	20.68%
1989	28.54%	27.37%	30.75%	26.50%	10.32%
1990	-6.95%	-10.01%	-3.36%	-8.85%	-17.59%
Average	15.37%	14.17%	10.38%	8.87%	7.89%

Table 3.6.   Compound Return on $100,000 from 1957 to 1990

Year	TOP FIVE	TOP TEN	DOW 30	BOTTOM 10	BOTTOM 5
Begin	$100,000	$100,000	$100,000	$100,000	$100,000
1957	$91,280	$92,470	$91,830	$93,950	$93,630
1958	$137,723	$134,803	$127,570	$127,997	$130,576
1959	$153,988	$147,636	$152,867	$163,696	$163,351
1960	$138,990	$145,495	$143,252	$140,353	$125,176
1961	$172,486	$180,647	$174,997	$172,578	$156,658
1962	$175,160	$180,376	$161,522	$159,272	$137,436
1963	$215,920	$221,375	$193,988	$210,860	$197,440
1964	$272,599	$272,447	$229,119	$243,670	$240,383
1965	$354,324	$328,080	$262,227	$279,149	$280,071
1966	$312,018	$276,703	$220,297	$240,822	$261,166
1967	$410,958	$351,025	$262,726	$290,359	$295,666
1968	$496,643	$397,045	$282,693	$292,246	$289,723
1969	$440,820	$346,302	$249,053	$274,653	$300,588
1970	$440,380	$358,354	$271,716	$279,157	$302,902
1971	$457,907	$378,959	$298,616	$331,136	$353,699
1972	$546,512	$469,341	$352,666	$385,641	$443,503
1973	$504,703	$487,551	$305,409	$296,828	$409,487
1974	$531,655	$492,524	$233,943	$195,016	$267,108
1975	$877,762	$754,695	$337,814	$281,954	$378,038
1976	$1,195,161	$1,005,329	$413,146	$361,155	$384,654
1977	$1,200,180	$994,974	$358,611	$293,619	$297,337
1978	$1,171,496	$1,018,854	$367,217	$319,810	$332,364
1979	$1,364,207	$1,117,377	$404,674	$328,797	$332,663
1980	$1,624,771	$1,424,991	$489,655	$430,000	$366,960
1981	$1,762,389	$1,463,181	$472,028	$366,489	$312,540
1982	$1,925,233	$1,765,766	$594,755	$415,709	$322,166
1983	$2,597,525	$2,458,300	$746,417	$535,017	$450,066
1984	$2,918,579	$2,612,435	$751,717	$484,351	$365,949
1985	$4,098,560	$3,427,515	$985,801	$601,854	$451,801
1986	$5,262,141	$4,391,332	$1,248,024	$622,919	$386,018
1987	$5,852,554	$4,693,895	$1,320,410	$795,717	$601,262
1988	$7,105,585	$5,549,123	$1,525,734	$889,214	$725,603
1989	$9,133,520	$7,067,918	$1,994,897	$1,124,855	$800,486
1990	$8,498,740	$6,360,419	$1,927,868	$1,025,306	$659,680

in portfolio values offer strong evidence of the positive correlation between dividend-yield and total return within the Dow Thirty.

Parallel Studies

Numerous parallel studies of dividend investing have been done by investment experts such as Cleveland analyst John Slatter, David Dreman, Michael O'Higgins, Ernest Widmann (an investment advisor in Bryn Mawr, Pennsylvania) and Economist Lawrence Pratt; and by firms such as Prudential Bache, Merrill Lynch and Dean Witter. They all confirm our findings. A study dated March 20, 1981, by Widmann, Blee & Co. looked at the performance of the Ten High-Yield stocks versus the Ten Low-Yield stocks and Dow Thirty. It found that between 1954 and 1980, the Ten High-Yield issues averaged an annual total return of 13.0 percent, beating the Ten Low-Yield issues (7.8 percent) and the Dow Thirty (10.0 percent).

Another study by Mr. Widmann using the S&P 400 stocks showed that high-yield issues outperformed low-yield issues through the period 1973 to 1980. His findings offer evidence that the yield indicator maintains its efficacy outside the Dow universe.

Research findings by Prudential Bache are almost identical to those presented in Table 3.1 (see Appendix 2). Also, many people have recently noticed that income oriented stock funds, curiously enough, tend to outperform aggressive growth equity funds. The income funds make larger gains in good markets and demonstrate good protection of principal in falling markets.

THE RETIREMENT PLAN

Table 3.7 depicts the performance of four hypothetical retirement funds, such as Keogh or 401(k) plans, into which $10,000 is placed at the beginning of each year from 1973 to 1990. The advantage given the investor by the Top Five and Top Ten portfolios is evident: their respective final values of $1,136,529 and $967,332 trounce the Dow Thirty portfolio's $693,835. The laggard Bottom Ten and Bottom Five once again post the worst showings, with final values of $460,465 and $304,385, respectively.

Table 3.7.   Hypothetical 401(k) Plan with $10,000 per year contribution
Annual Compounded Portfolio Values

Year	TOP FIVE	TOP TEN	DOW 30	BOTTOM 10	BOTTOM 5
	$10,000	$10,000	$10,000	$10,000	$10,000
1973	$9,235	$10,388	$8,660	$7,697	$9,233
1974	$20,262	$20,596	$14,294	$11,627	$12,546
1975	$49,963	$46,882	$35,080	$31,268	$31,909
1976	$81,645	$75,773	$55,133	$52,860	$42,642
1977	$92,030	$84,889	$56,535	$51,106	$40,693
1978	$99,592	$97,167	$68,132	$66,556	$56,664
1979	$127,620	$117,530	$86,102	$78,707	$66,724
1980	$163,905	$162,639	$116,283	$116,012	$84,634
1981	$188,635	$177,265	$121,737	$107,400	$80,600
1982	$216,989	$225,992	$165,988	$133,166	$93,391
1983	$306,253	$328,548	$220,865	$184,255	$144,437
1984	$355,342	$359,775	$232,504	$175,859	$125,572
1985	$513,049	$485,144	$318,020	$230,949	$167,378
1986	$671,543	$634,379	$415,274	$249,382	$151,551
1987	$758,012	$688,777	$449,939	$331,334	$251,633
1988	$932,444	$826,094	$531,460	$381,441	$315,738
1989	$1,211,417	$1,064,933	$707,959	$495,173	$359,354
1990	$1,136,529	$967,332	$693,835	$460,465	$304,385

Chart 3.2 depicts a truly remarkable scenario. If a 32-year-old wage earner had set up a Top Five portfolio in 1957 by investing $10,000 in a tax-deferred retirement plan and made an additional $2000 contribution in each subsequent year, the value of his protfolio at the time he was ready to retire in 1989, at the age of 65, would have been $2,375,000.

The Top Ten would have done almost as well, providing him with a 1989 portfolio value of $1,883,000. The Dow Thirty would have produced only $625,000. If he had invested in the Bottom Ten, he would have only $375,000. The Bottom Five would have turned out even worse, amassing only $225,058 in 33 years — a pittance compared to the returns of the high-yield portfolios.

Chart 3.2. The Top Five versus the Bottom Five

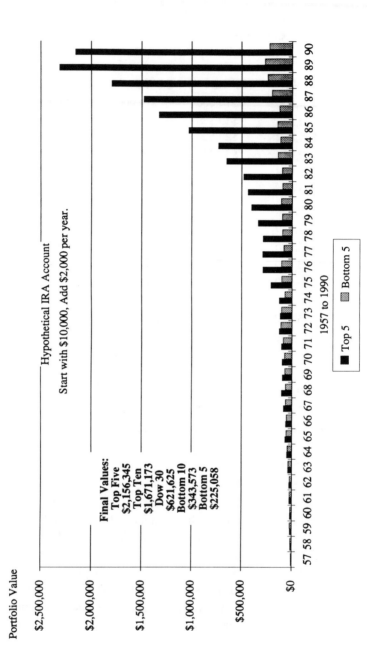

Portfolio Value

Hypothetical IRA Account

Start with $10,000, Add $2,000 per year.

Final Values:
Top Five
$2,156,345
Top Ten
$1,671,173
Dow 30
$621,625
Bottom 10
$343,573
Bottom 5
$225,058

$2,500,000

$2,000,000

$1,500,000

$1,000,000

$500,000

$0

57 58 59 60 61 62 63 64 65 66 67 68 69 70 71 72 73 74 75 76 77 78 79 80 81 82 83 84 85 86 87 88 89 90

1957 to 1990

■ Top 5   ▨ Bottom 5

Endnotes

1. Our research showed the actual Top Ten average annual total return value for the period 1973-1988 was 17.70 percent.

2. Our research showed that the only down year in the Top Ten was actually 1977, at -1.03 percent, and that the Top Ten posted +1.02 percent in 1974.

4

Why Are Dividends Important?

Most growth investors don't think much about dividend income, as evidenced by their general lack of interest in high-yield issues. A fixation on capital gains — for both psychological and monetary satisfaction in their investment endeavors — motivates many people to overlook the importance of dividends. They spend or ignore dividend income instead of reinvesting it.

Table 4.1 depicts the importance of regular reinvestment of dividend income. In this example, dividends have been stripped out of the Top Five, Top Ten, Dow Thirty, Bottom Ten and Bottom Five portfolios, leaving only capital gains to provide growth. Notice the effect of non-reinvestment of dividends on the final values of our five portfolios.

The final value of the Top Five portfolio suffered a substantial drop when dividends were excluded. The growth of $10,000 over the 34-year period declined from $849,874 to $108,586 when dividends were left out. Reinvestment of dividends was responsible for 87.22 percent of the final dollar value of the portfolio. Squandering dividends cost the investor $741,288, reducing the portfolio value by seven times.

Table 4.1.   No Dividends Reinvested

	Top 5		Top 10		Dow 30		Btm. 10		Btm. 5	
Year	Capital Return	Portfolio Value	Capital Return	Portfolio Value	Capital Return	Portofilo Value	Capital Return	Portfolio Value	Capital Return	Portfolio Value
Begin		$10,000		$10,000		$10,000		$10,000		$10,000
1957	-14.39%	$8,561	-12.83%	$8,717	-11.44%	$8,856	-9.31%	$9,069	-9.43%	$9,057
1958	44.87%	$12,402	40.26%	$12,226	33.77%	$11,846	32.87%	$12,050	36.27%	$12,342
1959	5.17%	$13,044	4.20%	$12,740	15.57%	$13,690	25.24%	$15,091	22.51%	$15,120
1960	-16.04%	$10,951	-6.58%	$11,902	-10.13%	$12,303	-16.58%	$12,589	-25.50%	$11,265
1961	18.43%	$12,970	19.01%	$14,164	18.76%	$14,610	20.59%	$15,181	23.04%	$13,860
1962	-3.33%	$12,538	-4.64%	$13,507	-10.75%	$13,039	-9.81%	$13,692	-14.14%	$11,900
1963	17.70%	$14,757	17.66%	$15,892	18.44%	$15,444	29.77%	$17,768	41.37%	$16,823
1964	21.10%	$17,871	18.38%	$18,813	13.54%	$17,535	13.15%	$20,105	19.63%	$20,126
1965	24.69%	$22,283	15.85%	$21,795	11.35%	$19,526	12.16%	$22,549	14.35%	$23,014
1966	-16.53%	$18,600	-20.02%	$17,432	-18.80%	$15,854	-15.91%	$18,962	-8.65%	$21,023
1967	25.77%	$23,393	21.22%	$21,131	15.31%	$18,282	17.83%	$22,343	10.98%	$23,331
1968	15.53%	$27,026	8.11%	$22,845	4.51%	$19,106	-1.70%	$21,963	-4.13%	$22,368
1969	-16.53%	$22,558	-17.54%	$18,838	-14.62%	$16,314	-8.41%	$20,116	1.71%	$22,750
1970	-6.63%	$21,063	-2.09%	$18,444	2.64%	$16,744	-0.83%	$19,949	-1.27%	$22,461
1971	-1.07%	$20,837	0.60%	$18,555	7.07%	$17,928	16.15%	$23,171	14.64%	$25,749
1972	13.52%	$23,654	18.49%	$21,985	16.01%	$20,799	14.18%	$26,456	23.61%	$31,829
1973	-13.51%	$20,459	-1.48%	$21,660	-17.09%	$17,243	-25.22%	$19,784	-9.37%	$28,847
1974	-2.72%	$19,902	-6.35%	$20,285	-26.10%	$12,742	-37.16%	$12,432	-37.19%	$18,119
1975	57.44%	$31,334	44.94%	$29,400	35.86%	$17,312	40.14%	$17,423	37.76%	$24,960
1976	28.60%	$40,296	26.17%	$37,095	16.42%	$20,155	24.93%	$21,766	-0.95%	$24,723
1977	-6.64%	$37,620	-7.33%	$34,375	-18.21%	$16,486	-22.01%	$16,975	-25.81%	$18,342
1978	-10.16%	$33,798	-4.99%	$32,660	-0.77%	$16,358	4.38%	$17,719	7.62%	$19,740
1979	7.65%	$36,383	1.42%	$33,124	1.62%	$16,623	-2.03%	$17,359	-4.25%	$18,901
1980	10.52%	$40,211	19.07%	$39,441	17.97%	$19,611	25.46%	$21,779	5.82%	$20,001
1981	-0.41%	$40,046	-5.22%	$37,382	-9.28%	$17,792	-19.00%	$17,641	-18.55%	$16,291
1982	0.76%	$40,350	12.52%	$42,062	16.38%	$20,705	9.14%	$19,253	0.14%	$16,313
1983	25.42%	$50,608	30.91%	$55,063	21.98%	$25,255	25.32%	$24,128	37.04%	$22,356
1984	4.30%	$52,784	-0.49%	$54,794	-4.30%	$24,169	-12.17%	$21,192	-20.61%	$17,748
1985	32.45%	$69,912	23.99%	$67,939	28.26%	$31,001	21.28%	$25,701	21.09%	$21,491
1986	21.39%	$84,866	21.94%	$82,844	25.33%	$38,855	1.46%	$26,076	-15.62%	$18,134
1987	5.87%	$89,848	1.78%	$84,319	4.56%	$40,628	25.72%	$32,783	54.76%	$28,065
1988	15.16%	$103,469	12.57%	$94,918	7.61%	$43,719	9.35%	$35,849	18.77%	$33,333
1989	19.76%	$123,914	20.38%	$114,262	29.58%	$56,653	24.10%	$44,488	8.71%	$36,236
1990	-12.37%	$108,586	-14.91%	$97,226	-7.10%	$52,631	-10.91%	$39,634	-18.86%	$29,402
Average	8.70%		8.09%		6.29%		5.95%		5.46%	

The Top Ten also showed a dramatic decrease in performance when dividends were removed. Here the final value dropped from $636,042 to $97,226. Dividend reinvestment would have multiplied the final value more than sixfold.

Without dividends, the Dow Thirty offered an average annual return of only 6.29 percent. This rate of growth turned an initial investment of $10,000 into a mere $52,631 over the thirty-four-year period from 1957 to 1990. Comparing this final value with the final value of the Dow Thirty with dividends reinvested — $192,787 — we see that the reinvestment of dividend income was responsible for $140,156, or 72.70 percent, of final dollar return in the Dow Thirty portfolio.

Failure to reinvest the meager dividends provided by the Bottom Ten cut the final value of this lowly portfolio by 60 percent. The Bottom Ten multiplied the initial $10,000 investment to only $39,634 over the 34 years without dividends.

Without the Bottom Five's spare dividends, it could muster a final value of only $29,402 at the end of the 34 years.

To recap, the results of non-reinvestment of dividends on $10,000 over the 34 years from 1957 to 1990 are:

Top Five	$849,874	dropped to	$108,586
Top Ten	$636,042	dropped to	$97,226
Dow Thirty	$192,787	dropped to	$52,631
Bottom Ten	$102,531	dropped to	$39,634
Bottom Five	$65,968	dropped to	$29,402

The power of dividends is obviously enormous. Any long-range investment strategy should address the issue of dividend reinvestment. Even though dividend income added only about 3 to 6.5 percent to total returns annually, the effect of this marginal addition on total return was gargantuan due to the effects of compounding. Over time, that additional 3 to 6.5 percent per year provided by dividends makes all the difference in the world.

A FAIR PRICE FOR THE ISLAND?

Peter Minuit, Governor of the Dutch West India Company, purchased the island of Manhattan in 1624 from the Manhattan Indians. For this land he paid $24 worth of cloth, beads and trinkets. Many people tout this real estate deal as a disgraceful example of how the European immigrants took advantage of the Native Americans. Minuit is generally considered to have stolen the property from an naive people who didn't have an understanding of the island's real value. Perhaps he did.

If, however, the Manhattan Indians had invested the proceeds of the land sale in enterprises that appreciated at an average compound rate of 8 percent, their holdings today would be worth $75,979,380,000,000 — 76 trillion dollars. They would now have had enough to buy back Manhattan, and then buy with the change Tokyo as well as all of the companies in the S&P 500. But had the Manhattan Indians failed to reinvest just 2 percent per year, their portfolio would have been worth only about 44 billion dollars ($43,869,010,000). Squandering dividends would have cost more than seventy-five trillion dollars.

5

How to Beat a Bear

The point has been made that high-yield portfolios resist decline in bad markets. The resiliency of high-yield portfolios is demonstrated further in what is perhaps this book's most important table, Table 5.1. The time period 1966 to 1981 was chosen for its inimical nature.

The year 1966 was a very bad time to start a portfolio in the stock market. In this year, the total return for the Top Five was -11.94 percent — their worst year in the 34-year study period. The Dow Thirty fared even worse, posting a -15.99 percent return. The Dow Jones Industrial Average cycled between 600 and 1100 for the following sixteen years, starting 1966 at 968.54 and ending 86 points lower in 1981 at 882.52.

By 1974, the halfway point of the bear market, $100,000 invested in the Dow Thirty had become $89,214 with dividends reinvested. But in 1974, the undaunted Top Five stood at $150,048.

Over the full sixteen-year bear market period, $100,000 invested in the Dow Thirty became $180,007, with an average total return of only 5.2 percent — roughly equal to a passbook savings account. The Bottom 10 did even worse, averaging only 3.91 percent per year. The Bottom Five

Table 5.1. "Bear Market" 1966 to 1981
Total Return Figures and Compound Values

Year	D.J.I.A.	TOP FIVE	COMPOUND RETURN	TOP TEN	COMPOUND RETURN	DOW 30	COMPOUND RETURN	BTM.10	COMPOUND RETURN	BTM.5	COMPOUND RETURN
Begin	968.54		$100,000		$100,000		$100,000		$100,000		$100,000
1966	786.41	-11.94%	$88,060	-15.66%	$84,340	-15.99%	$84,010	-13.73%	$86,270	-6.75%	$93,250
1967	906.84	31.71%	$115,984	26.86%	$106,994	19.26%	$100,190	20.57%	$104,016	13.21%	$105,568
1968	947.73	20.85%	$140,166	13.11%	$121,021	7.60%	$107,805	0.65%	$104,692	-2.01%	$103,446
1969	809.20	-11.24%	$124,412	-12.78%	$105,554	-11.90%	$94,976	-6.02%	$98,389	3.75%	$107,326
1970	830.57	-0.10%	$124,287	3.48%	$109,227	9.10%	$103,619	1.64%	$100,003	0.77%	$108,152
1971	889.30	3.98%	$129,234	5.75%	$115,508	9.90%	$113,877	18.62%	$118,624	16.77%	$126,289
1972	1031.68	19.35%	$154,241	23.85%	$143,057	18.10%	$134,489	16.46%	$138,149	25.39%	$158,354
1973	855.32	-7.65%	$142,441	3.88%	$148,607	-13.40%	$116,467	-23.03%	$106,333	-7.67%	$146,208
1974	632.04	5.34%	$150,048	1.02%	$150,123	-23.40%	$89,214	-34.30%	$69,861	-34.77%	$95,372
1975	868.71	65.10%	$247,729	53.23%	$230,034	44.40%	$128,825	44.58%	$101,005	41.53%	$134,979
1976	999.75	36.16%	$337,307	33.21%	$306,428	22.30%	$157,553	28.09%	$129,377	1.75%	$137,342
1977	817.74	0.42%	$338,724	-1.03%	$303,272	-13.20%	$136,756	-18.70%	$105,184	-22.70%	$106,165
1978	811.42	-2.39%	$330,629	2.40%	$310,550	2.40%	$140,038	8.92%	$114,566	11.78%	$118,671
1979	824.57	16.45%	$385,017	9.67%	$340,580	10.20%	$154,322	2.81%	$117,785	0.09%	$118,778
1980	972.78	19.10%	$458,555	27.53%	$434,342	21.00%	$186,730	30.78%	$154,040	10.31%	$131,024
1981	882.52	8.47%	$497,395	2.68%	$445,982	-3.60%	$180,007	-14.77%	$131,288	-14.83%	$111,593
Average		12.10%		11.08%		5.17%		3.91%		2.29%	

had the hardest time, averaging only 2.3 percent per year and gaining only $11,593 on the initial $100,000 investment. In contrast, the average annual total return for the Top Five was 12.1 percent. The power of the Top Five's annual 6.9 percent advantage over the Dow Thirty was enormous when coupled with sixteen years of compounding, turning $100,000 into $497,395 by the end of 1981.

THE INFLATION RACE: DIVIDENDS VERSUS THE C.P.I.

Inflation is a lethal enemy. Chart 5.1 shows the competition between inflation and the high-yield investment groups. The average annual returns of the Top Five, Top Ten and S&P 500 Index, as well as the average rate of inflation, are displayed in five overlapping ten-year periods from 1960 to 1989.

From 1965 to 1974 inflation averaged 5.2 percent per year while common stocks gained only 1.2 percent. If you were talented enough to match the average market return, *you effectively lost 4.0 percent on your money every year for ten years.* A $100,000 initial investment was diminished to $66,761 in real terms during this brutal time.

The ten-year block starting five years later, 1970 to 1979, proved to be no better for most equity investors. Inflation raged at an average compound rate of 7.37 percent throughout the decade, while the S&P 500 Index grew at returned less than 6 percent. Once again, investors watched helplessly as the purchasing power of their portfolios was consumed by the relentless pace of the Consumer Price Index (C.P.I.).

The high-yield portfolios, in contrast to the market itself, fared well against inflation in both of these difficult time periods. In fact, both the Top Five and Top Ten outpaced inflation in every time period studied. For instance, while inflation was devastating most portfolios during the 1965-1974 period, the Top Five and Top Ten had average total returns two to three precentage points higher than inflation, and four to five times higher than the average return on common stocks. During the 1970 to 1979 period, the high-yield portfolios offered annual total returns that were almost twice the C.P.I. and more than two times higher than the S&P 500 Index. Dividend investing helps the investor win the inflation war.

Chart 5.1. Dividend Investing versus Inflation

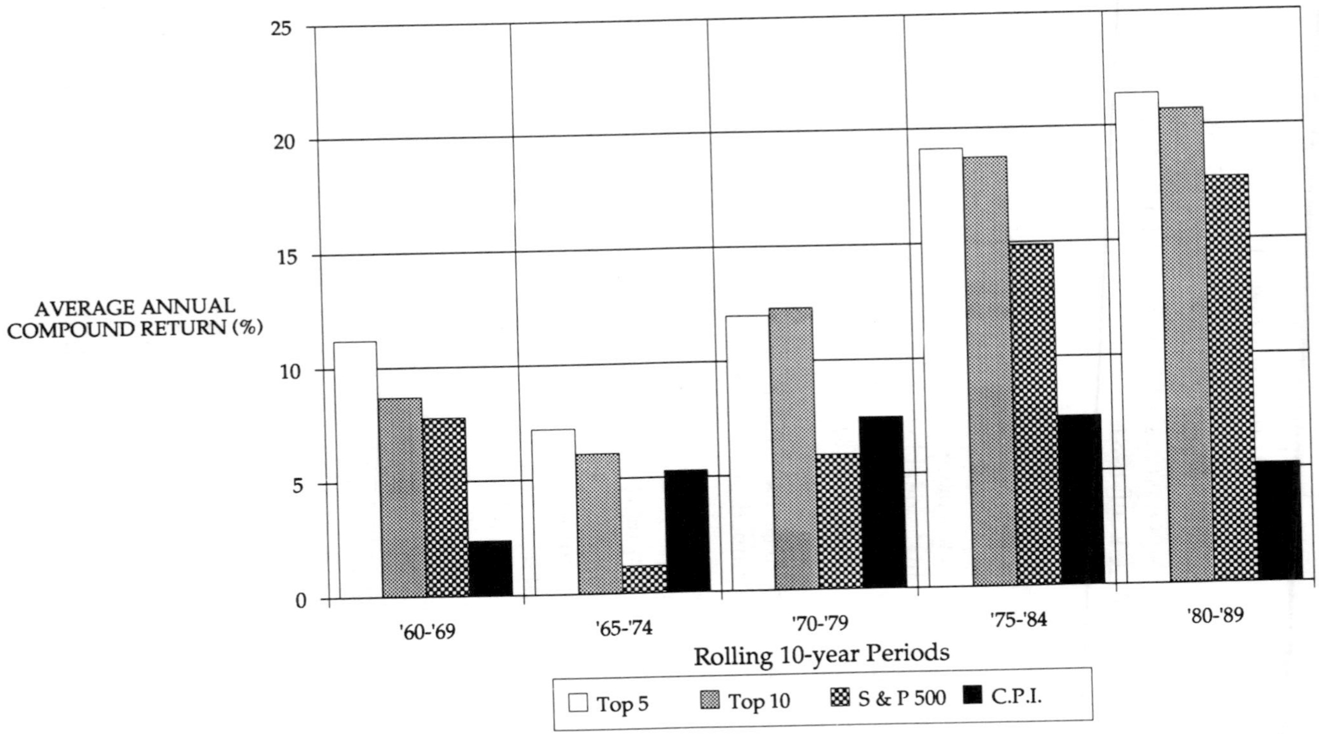

AVERAGE ANNUAL COMPOUND RETURN (%)

Rolling 10-year Periods

'60-'69 '65-'74 '70-'79 '75-'84 '80-'89

☐ Top 5 ▨ Top 10 ▦ S & P 500 ■ C.P.I.

BULLS ARE EASY TO MANAGE

Almost any portfolio will do well in a bull market. Therefore, starting a new strategy in a bull market can be deceiving. Investors beguiled by recent and instant success think they've found the answer to investing, only to be annihilated in the next market reversal. When the market turns bearish, most investors are lucky to keep what they have. An individual needs a successful strategy—like dividend investing—to maintain a steady, high rate of growth.

Chart 5.2a displays the performances of the five groups in both a bull market (1980 to 1989) and a bear market (1966 to 1981). Notice that all the portfolios did well during the bull market; the lowest performer, the Bottom Five, logged a ten-year average close to 12 percent. In the bear market, however, only the high-yield groups (the Top Five and Top Ten) could muster double-digit returns. *An investor could certainly live with the high-yield returns in a bear market while waiting for better times.*

Chart 5.2b shows the performances of the Top Five, Top Ten, Bottom Ten and Bottom Five relative to the Dow Thirty for both the bull and bear market periods. The Top Five and Top Ten had nearly a 50 percent advantage over the Dow Thirty during the bear market. Dividend investing is more important during bear markets than during bull markets. *If one is going to take the risk of the market, the data indicate that one should do it with high-yield shares.*

DIVIDEND INVESTING VERSUS THE PERFECT MARKET TIMER

Some investors try to hedge their portfolios against decline by using a technique called market timing. They hope to sidestep market losses by selling out before they occur, with the intention of buying back in as prices bottom out. In almost all instances, efforts to time the market detract from, rather than add to, investment performance.

Table 5.2 shows what would have happened if a certain timid investor had tried market timing in a attempt to allay his fears concerning the erratic stock market. Our special investor is prescient when it comes to predicting down years in the Dow Thirty. Since issue selection isn't his forte, he buys a Dow Thirty portfolio. He is out of the market in every one of the ten years from 1957 to 1990 in which the Dow posted a negative total

Chart 5.2a. Average Annual Total Return in Bull ('80–'90) and Bear ('66–'81) Markets

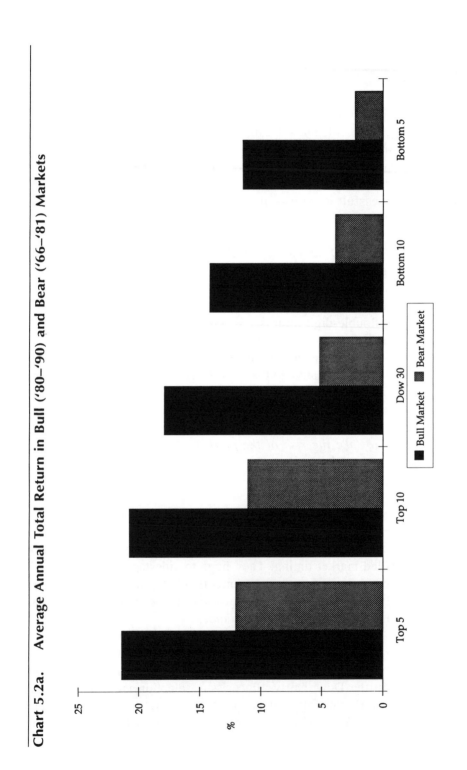

Chart 5.2b. Performance of the Top Five, Top Ten, Bottom Ten, and Bottom Five relative to the Dow Thirty in Bull ('80–'89) and Bear ('66–'81) Markets

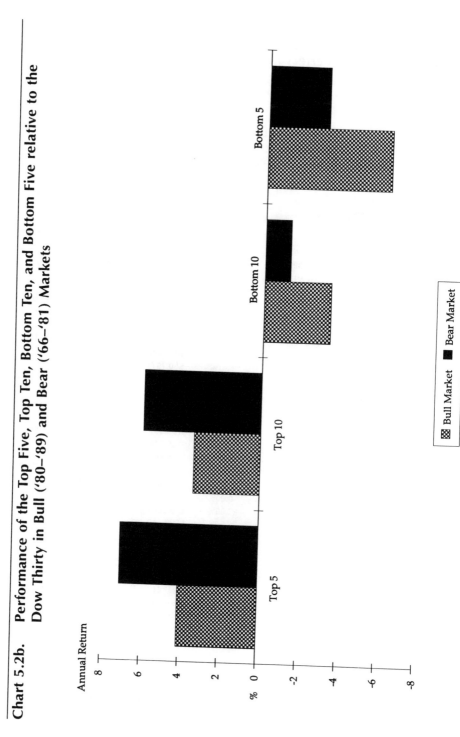

Table 5.2.   The Perfect Market Timer

Year	DOW 30	PORTFOLIO VALUE	DOW 30: OUT IN DOWN YEARS	PORTFOLIO VALUE	DOW 30: T-BILLS IN DOWN YEARS	PORTFOLIO VALUE
Begin		$10,000		$10,000		$10,000
1957	-8.17%	$9,183	0.00%	$10,000	3.10%	$10,310
1958	38.92%	$12,757	38.92%	$13,892	38.92%	$14,323
1959	19.83%	$15,287	19.83%	$16,647	19.83%	$17,163
1960	-6.29%	$14,325	0.00%	$16,647	2.70%	$17,626
1961	22.16%	$17,500	22.16%	$20,336	22.16%	$21,532
1962	-7.70%	$16,152	0.00%	$20,336	2.70%	$22,114
1963	20.10%	$19,399	20.10%	$24,423	20.10%	$26,558
1964	18.11%	$22,912	18.11%	$28,846	18.11%	$31,368
1965	14.45%	$26,223	14.45%	$33,015	14.45%	$35,901
1966	-15.99%	$22,030	0.00%	$33,015	4.80%	$37,624
1967	19.26%	$26,273	19.26%	$39,373	19.26%	$44,870
1968	7.60%	$28,269	7.60%	$42,365	7.60%	$48,281
1969	-11.90%	$24,905	0.00%	$42,365	6.60%	$51,467
1970	9.10%	$27,172	9.10%	$46,221	9.10%	$56,151
1971	9.90%	$29,862	9.90%	$50,797	9.90%	$61,710
1972	18.10%	$35,267	18.10%	$59,991	18.10%	$72,879
1973	-13.40%	$30,541	0.00%	$59,991	6.90%	$77,908
1974	-23.40%	$23,394	0.00%	$59,991	8.00%	$84,140
1975	44.40%	$33,781	44.40%	$86,627	44.40%	$121,499
1976	22.30%	$41,315	22.30%	$105,944	22.30%	$148,593
1977	-13.20%	$35,861	0.00%	$105,944	5.10%	$156,171
1978	2.40%	$36,722	2.40%	$108,487	2.40%	$159,919
1979	10.20%	$40,467	10.20%	$119,553	10.20%	$176,231
1980	21.00%	$48,966	21.00%	$144,659	21.00%	$213,239
1981	-3.60%	$47,203	0.00%	$144,659	14.70%	$244,585
1982	26.00%	$59,475	26.00%	$182,270	26.00%	$308,178
1983	25.50%	$74,642	25.50%	$228,749	25.50%	$386,763
1984	0.71%	$75,172	0.71%	$230,373	0.71%	$389,509
1985	31.14%	$98,581	31.14%	$302,111	31.14%	$510,802
1986	26.60%	$124,803	26.60%	$382,473	26.60%	$646,675
1987	5.80%	$132,042	5.80%	$404,656	5.80%	$684,183
1988	15.55%	$152,574	15.55%	$467,580	15.55%	$790,573
1989	30.75%	$199,491	30.75%	$611,361	30.75%	$1,033,674
1990	-3.36%	$192,787	0.00%	$611,361	7.25%	$1,108,616
Average	10.38%		13.53%		15.35%	

return. His remarkable ability raises his average annual total return from 10.38 percent to 13.53 percent.

Sadly, no one has the ability to time the market for 34 straight years. But even if someone had met with the incredible success described above, the high-yield portfolios still would have offered better returns, at 15.37 percent for the Top Five and 14.17 percent for the Top Ten, compared to the market timer's 13.68 percent. Had the clairvoyant market timer invested in T-bills during his years out of the market, his average annual total return would have been 15.35 percent. Perfection put him one percent ahead of the Top Ten, but still left him 0.02 percent short of the Top Five. As you can see, dividend investing meets the objective of what market timers try to do, without the need for a crystal ball.[1]

THE WORST CASE SCENARIO

Now we come to the ugliest period described by our data – Table 5.3. What if an investor had started his portfolio in the Dow Thirty in 1966, at the precipice of the worst market downturn in this half-century? He was instantly robbed of 10 to 20 percent of his portfolio's value. He then suffered through the misery of 1969. His resolve to continue investing ebbed with the 1973-1974 slaughter during which he lost 34 percent of his capital, prompting him to sell out at the end of '74. He was devastated. The Dow Thirty had depreciated his assets at the average rate of -0.08 percent per year, nine years in a row, dropping the value of his $100,000 portfolio to $89,214. The Bottom Ten depreciated even faster during these troublesome nine years, at -2.13 percent, leaving him with $69,861.

Dividend investing would have provided a lifeboat that would have carried the investor through this brutal time. The Top Five had an average annual total return of 5.59 percent turning $100,000 into $150,048. The Top Ten's average return of 5.50 percent compounded $100,000 to $153,123. While the market printed negative numbers for nine years, the high-yield portfolios turned a profit.

Table 5.3. Worst Case Scenerio
1966 to 1974

Year	D.J.I.A.	DOW 30	COMPOUND RETURN	TOP FIVE	COMPOUND RETURN	TOP TEN	COMPOUND RETURN	BTM.10	COMPOUND RETURN	BTM.5	COMPOUND RETURN
Begin	968.54		$100,000		$100,000		$100,000		$100,000		$100,000
1966	786.41	-15.99%	$84,010	-11.94%	$88,060	-15.66%	$84,340	-13.73%	$86,270	-6.75%	$93,250
1967	906.84	19.26%	$100,190	31.71%	$115,984	26.86%	$106,994	20.57%	$104,016	13.21%	$105,568
1968	947.73	7.60%	$107,805	20.85%	$140,166	13.11%	$121,021	0.65%	$104,692	-2.01%	$103,446
1969	809.20	-11.90%	$94,976	-11.24%	$124,412	-12.78%	$105,554	-6.02%	$98,389	3.75%	$107,326
1970	830.57	9.10%	$103,619	-0.10%	$124,287	3.48%	$109,227	1.64%	$100,003	0.77%	$108,152
1971	889.30	9.90%	$113,877	3.98%	$129,234	5.75%	$115,508	18.62%	$118,624	16.77%	$126,289
1972	1031.68	18.10%	$134,489	19.35%	$154,241	23.85%	$143,057	16.46%	$138,149	25.39%	$158,354
1973	855.32	-13.40%	$116,467	-7.65%	$142,441	3.88%	$148,607	-23.03%	$106,333	-7.67%	$146,208
1974	632.04	-23.40%	$89,214	5.34%	$150,048	1.02%	$150,123	-34.30%	$69,861	-34.77%	$95,372
Average		-0.08%		5.59%		5.50%		-2.13%		0.97%	

OVERCOMING THE RISK/RETURN TRADE-OFF

During our research we remarked at the amazing consistency of the Top Ten's performance. Its pattern of stability prompted us to measure the amount by which the returns of the four portfolios fluctuate year by year. This measure of fluctuation is called variance. To get an intuitive feeling for what variance is in this case, picture two lines: a straight line and a sawtooth line that has many high peaks and low valleys. The straight line has no variance; the jagged line has a high variance.

Through simple statistical analysis of the data, we ascertained that the variance of the Top Ten was actually lower than that of the thirty Dow Industrials for the 34-year study period. Since variance is used as a proxy for risk, we can conclude that *the Top Ten strategy actually reduces risk to the investor while increasing return.*

The Top Five portfolio had a higher variance than the Dow Thirty. This was not surprising since the returns on the Top Five seemed to fluctuate more than the thirty Dow Jones Industrials. In this case, a higher rate of return was traded for less stability from year to year in the classic risk/reward trade-off.

The Bottom Ten and Bottom Five portfolios proved to possess the most despised combination of qualities in an investment—higher risk and lower return. The variance of the Bottom Ten was higher than the Dow Thirty and Top Five, while the Bottom Five had the highest of the five groups studied. Its returns were also the lowest.

Endnotes

1. John Maynard Keynes had a similar experience after abandoning his "Credit Cycle" approach to investing, which was essentially a market-timing approach, in deference to a contrarian investment philosophy. After creating a hypothetical portfolio for a perfect market timer, Keynes found that over the trial period his contrarian approach had earned "almost exactly double that earned by the credit cycle genius, 82 percent." Keynes achieved a return of 162 percent.

6

More Proof for the High-Yield Strategy

Dividend investing consistently outperforms the market. However, the magnitude of the advantage offered the investor by a high-yield strategy varies from one time period to another and is dependent upon the market personality prevalent for the period. For instance, dividend investing was remarkably successful throughout the period 1973 to 1990, protecting the investor from any significant down years. While the dividend method was still effective at both limiting down-side risk and increasing return in the earlier years of the study, 1957 to 1972, the same claim of invincibility cannot be made. While dividend investors avoided the late 1973-1974 bloodbath, both 1966 and 1969 left dividend investors with double-digit negative returns in both the Top Five and Top Ten.

Table 6.1 shows the annual total return figures and the compounded values of $100,000 portfolios for the Dow Thirty, the Top Five, the Top Ten, the Bottom Ten and the Bottom Five for the early years, 1957 to 1972. Table 6.2 shows data on the same portfolios for the later years, 1973

Table 6.1. Total Return Figures and Dollar Compounded Values 1957 to 1972

Year	DOW 30	COMPOUND RETURN	TOP FIVE	COMPOUND RETURN	TOP TEN	COMPOUND RETURN	BOTTOM 10	COMPOUND RETURN	BOTTOM 5	COMPOUND RETURN
		$100,000		$100,000		$100,000		$100,000		$100,000
1957	-8.17%	$91,830	-8.72%	$91,280	-7.53%	$92,470	-6.05%	$93,950	-6.37%	$93,630
1958	38.92%	$127,570	50.88%	$137,723	45.78%	$134,803	36.24%	$127,997	39.46%	$130,576
1959	19.83%	$152,867	11.81%	$153,988	9.52%	$147,636	27.89%	$163,696	25.10%	$163,351
1960	-6.29%	$143,252	-9.74%	$138,990	-1.45%	$145,495	-14.26%	$140,353	-23.37%	$125,176
1961	22.16%	$174,997	24.10%	$172,486	24.16%	$180,647	22.96%	$172,578	25.15%	$156,658
1962	-7.70%	$161,522	1.55%	$175,160	-0.15%	$180,376	-7.71%	$159,272	-12.27%	$137,436
1963	20.10%	$193,988	23.27%	$215,920	22.73%	$221,375	32.39%	$210,860	43.66%	$197,440
1964	18.11%	$229,119	26.25%	$272,599	23.07%	$272,447	15.56%	$243,670	21.75%	$240,383
1965	14.45%	$262,227	29.98%	$354,324	20.42%	$328,080	14.56%	$279,149	16.51%	$280,071
1966	-15.99%	$220,297	-11.94%	$312,018	-15.66%	$276,703	-13.73%	$240,822	-6.75%	$261,166
1967	19.26%	$262,726	31.71%	$410,958	26.86%	$351,025	20.57%	$290,359	13.21%	$295,666
1968	7.60%	$282,693	20.85%	$496,643	13.11%	$397,045	0.65%	$292,246	-2.01%	$289,723
1969	-11.90%	$249,053	-11.24%	$440,820	-12.78%	$346,302	-6.02%	$274,653	3.75%	$300,588
1970	9.10%	$271,716	-0.10%	$440,380	3.48%	$358,354	1.64%	$279,157	0.77%	$302,902
1971	9.90%	$298,616	3.98%	$457,907	5.75%	$378,959	18.62%	$331,136	16.77%	$353,699
1972	18.10%	$352,666	19.35%	$546,512	23.85%	$469,341	16.46%	$385,641	25.39%	$443,503
Average	9.22%		12.62%		11.32%		9.99%		11.30%	

to 1990. This grouping of the data should help to display the differences in the characters of the early and late time periods (1957 to 1972 versus 1973 to 1990). One can see that the average annual total returns for all groups were substantially lower in the earlier time period.

Nevertheless, the effect of the high-dividend approach is consistent between the early and late periods. Once again, the Top Five and Top Ten groups gained a significant advantage over the Dow Thirty and the low-yield groups, with the Top Five group offering the most lucrative returns.

Charts 6.1 and 6.2 illustrate the data presented in Tables 6.1 and 6.2. The compounded portfolio values for the four groups are represented in graph form.

The numbers show that the high-dividend approach has had a greater impact on investment return in recent times. In the period 1957 to 1972, the Top Ten portfolio delivered an approximate 23 percent increase in average annual total return with respect to the thirty Dow Industrials. But in the 1973 to 1990 period, the advantage was doubled, increasing average annual total return 46 percent.

The same trend of increasing potency is equally apparent in the Top Five. In the period 1957 to 1972, the Top Five had a 37 percent advantage over the Dow Thirty. But in the years 1973 to 1990, the Top Five beat the Dow Thirty by 56 percent per year with respect to average annual total return.

RELATIVITY: BUILDING CITIES OVER THE DOW THIRTY

Charts 6.3a through 6.3d present another comparison of the performance of the high-yield program with that of the Dow Thirty. The total return of the Dow Thirty (as a percent) is subtracted from the total return of the Top Five, Top Ten, Bottom Ten and Bottom Five for each year. The horizontal line represents the normalized performance of the Dow Thirty. Bars projecting above the line represent the amount by which one of the other four portfolios outperformed the Dow Thirty in a given year. Bars below the Dow Thirty line show the amount by which a portfolio under-performed the market.

As you can see, the Top Five and Top Ten portfolios build skyscrapers above the line, indicating superior performance by the high-yield groups. The Bottom Ten and Bottom Five, however, seem to be preoccupied with

Table 6.2. Total Return Figures and Dollar Compounded Values 1973 to 1990

Year	DOW 30	COMPOUND RETURN	TOP FIVE	COMPOUND RETURN	TOP TEN	COMPOUND RETURN	BOTTOM 10	COMPOUND RETURN	BOTTOM 5	COMPOUND RETURN
		$100,000		$100,000		$100,000		$100,000		$100,000
1973	-13.40%	$86,600	-7.65%	$92,350	3.88%	$103,880	-23.03%	$76,970	-7.67%	$92,330
1974	-23.40%	$66,336	5.34%	$97,281	1.02%	$104,940	-34.30%	$50,569	-34.77%	$60,227
1975	44.40%	$95,789	65.10%	$160,612	53.23%	$160,799	44.58%	$73,113	41.53%	$85,239
1976	22.30%	$117,149	36.16%	$218,689	33.21%	$214,200	28.09%	$93,651	1.75%	$86,731
1977	-13.20%	$101,686	0.42%	$219,607	-1.03%	$211,994	-18.70%	$76,138	-22.70%	$67,043
1978	2.40%	$104,126	-2.39%	$214,359	2.40%	$217,082	8.92%	$82,929	11.78%	$74,941
1979	10.20%	$114,747	16.45%	$249,621	9.67%	$238,074	2.81%	$85,260	0.09%	$75,008
1980	21.00%	$138,844	19.10%	$297,298	27.53%	$303,615	30.78%	$111,503	10.31%	$82,741
1981	-3.60%	$133,846	8.47%	$322,480	2.68%	$311,752	-14.77%	$95,034	-14.83%	$70,471
1982	26.00%	$168,645	9.24%	$352,277	20.68%	$376,223	13.43%	$107,797	3.08%	$72,641
1983	25.50%	$211,650	34.92%	$475,292	39.22%	$523,777	28.70%	$138,734	39.70%	$101,480
1984	0.71%	$213,153	12.36%	$534,038	6.27%	$556,618	-9.47%	$125,596	-18.69%	$82,513
1985	31.14%	$279,528	40.43%	$749,949	31.20%	$730,283	24.26%	$156,066	23.46%	$101,871
1986	26.60%	$353,883	28.39%	$962,860	28.12%	$935,638	3.50%	$161,528	-14.56%	$87,038
1987	5.80%	$374,408	11.22%	$1,070,893	6.89%	$1,000,104	27.74%	$206,336	55.76%	$135,571
1988	15.55%	$432,629	21.41%	$1,300,171	18.22%	$1,182,322	11.75%	$230,581	20.68%	$163,607
1989	30.75%	$565,662	28.54%	$1,671,240	27.37%	$1,505,924	26.50%	$291,684	10.32%	$180,491
1990	-3.36%	$546,656	-6.95%	$1,555,089	-10.01%	$1,355,181	-8.85%	$265,870	-17.59%	$148,743
Average	11.41%		17.81%		16.70%		7.89%		4.87%	

**Chart 6.1.   The Top Five versus the Dow Thirty versus the Bottom Five
1957 to 1972
The Early Period**

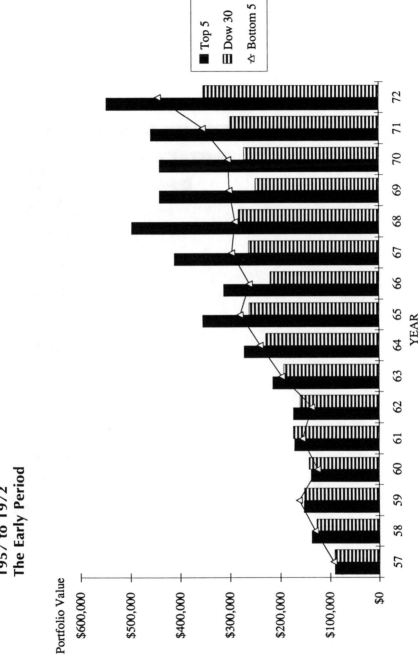

Chart 6.2. The Top Five versus the Dow Thirty versus the Bottom Five 1973 to 1990

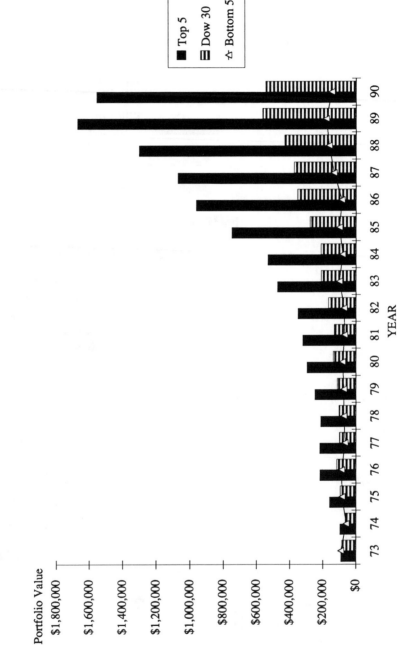

Portfolio Value

YEAR

Chart 6.3a. Top Five versus the Dow Thirty

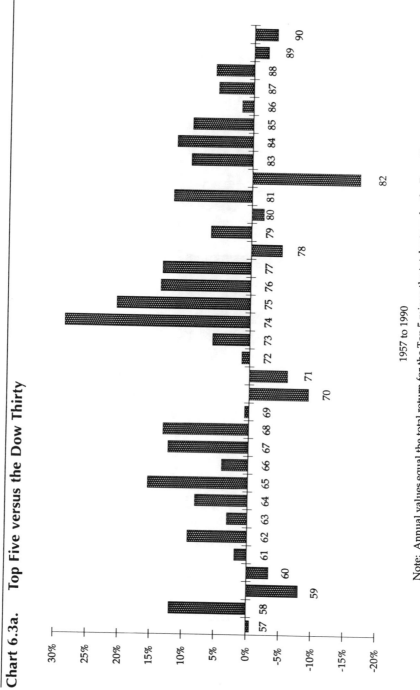

1957 to 1990

Note: Annual values equal the total return for the Top 5 minus the total return for the Dow 30.

Chart 6.3b. Top Ten versus the Dow Thirty

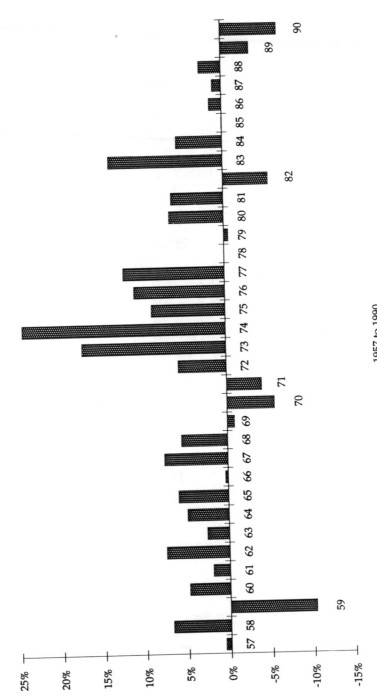

1957 to 1990

Note: Annual values equal the total return for the Top 10 minus the total return for the Dow 30.

Chart 6.3c.   Bottom Ten versus the Dow Thirty

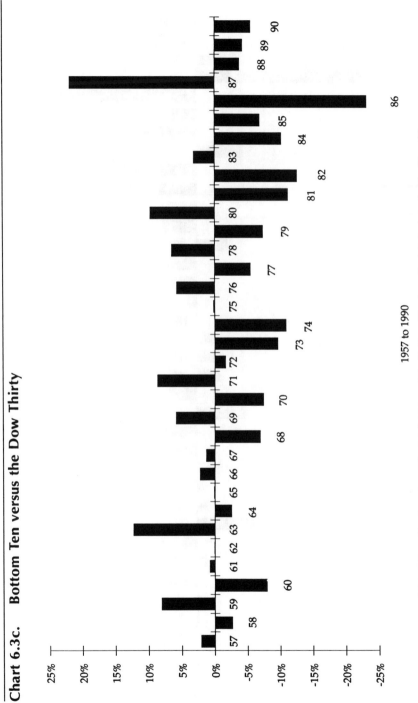

1957 to 1990

Note: Annual values equal the total return of the Bottom 10 minus the total return for the Dow 30.

Chart 6.3d. Bottom Five versus the Dow Thirty

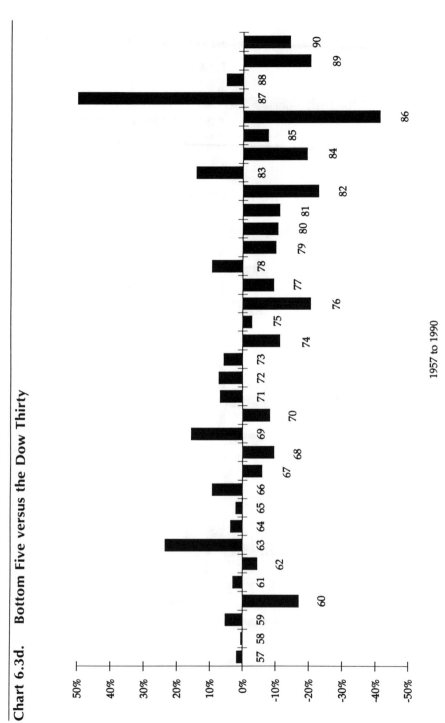

1957 to 1990

Note: Annual values equal the total return for the Bottom 5 minus the total return for the Dow 30.

Table 6.3a.   "Average" Market (1959 to 1968)
                Total Return Figures

Year	TOP FIVE	TOP TEN	DOW 30	BOTTOM 10	BOTTOM 5
1959	11.81%	9.52%	19.83%	27.89%	25.10%
1960	-9.74%	-1.45%	-6.29%	-14.26%	-23.37%
1961	24.10%	24.16%	22.16%	22.96%	25.15%
1962	1.55%	-0.15%	-7.70%	-7.71%	-12.27%
1963	23.27%	22.73%	20.10%	32.39%	43.66%
1964	26.25%	23.07%	18.11%	15.56%	21.75%
1965	29.98%	20.42%	14.45%	14.56%	16.51%
1966	-11.94%	-15.66%	-15.99%	-13.73%	-6.75%
1967	31.71%	26.86%	19.26%	20.57%	13.21%
1968	20.85%	13.11%	7.60%	0.65%	-2.01%
Average	14.78%	12.26%	9.15%	9.89%	10.10%

oil and gas exploration, as time and time again the bars sink well below the Dow Thirty line.

CONTRASTING THREE DECADES

Tables 6.3a through 6.3c segregate the performance of the five groups into three recent decades. This grouping displays the gamut of market personalities — average, bear and bull. Dividend investing performs admirably in all these types of markets.

In the period 1959-1968 (Table 6.3a), the Dow Thirty performed in line with their historical average, at 9.15 percent. The Top Five portfolio beat the Dow Thirty by a 50 percent margin; the Top Ten outperformed the Dow Thirty by 30 percent; the Bottom Ten matched the Dow Thirty; and, surprisingly, the Bottom Five surpassed the Dow Thirty by almost a percent.

The greatest strength of dividend investing is its ability to offer excellent returns while the market as a whole performs miserably. This

Table 6.3b.   "Bear" Market (1969 to 1978)
Total Return Figures

Year	TOP FIVE	TOP TEN	DOW 30	BOTTOM 10	BOTTOM 5
1969	-11.24%	-12.78%	-11.90%	-6.02%	3.75%
1970	-0.10%	3.48%	9.10%	1.64%	0.77%
1971	3.98%	5.75%	9.90%	18.62%	16.77%
1972	19.35%	23.85%	18.10%	16.46%	25.39%
1973	-7.65%	3.88%	-13.40%	-23.03%	-7.67%
1974	5.34%	1.02%	-23.40%	-34.30%	-34.77%
1975	65.10%	53.23%	44.40%	44.58%	41.53%
1976	36.16%	33.21%	22.30%	28.09%	1.75%
1977	0.42%	-1.03%	-13.20%	-18.70%	-22.70%
1978	-2.39%	2.40%	2.40%	8.92%	11.78%
Average	10.90%	11.30%	4.43%	3.63%	3.66%

attribute allows the investor to continue compounding at high rates through both bull and bear markets. The period 1969-1978 was a bear market horror, even more severe than that of 1966 to 1981 (see Table 6.3b). During these ten years, the Dow Jones Industrial Average moved from a start of 947.73 to a close of 811.42. The average annual total return for the Dow Thirty was only 4.43 percent. The investor had to accept 3.63 percent in the Bottom Ten, and 3.66 percent in the Bottom Five. The returns on the high-yield portfolios were both approximately 120 percent greater than those of the Dow Thirty — 10.9 percent for the Top Five and 11.3 percent for the Top Ten. This superior performance comes largely from the resiliency in bad markets of high-yield stocks.

The final decade, 1979-1988 (Table 6.3c), saw a tremendous bull market. All five groups posted double-digit returns. Here the advantage of the high-yield portfolios over the Dow Thirty was only 33 percent — still a substantial divergence, but not as striking as during the bear market. Even so, the 80 percent spread between the total returns of the Top Five and the low-yield groups was enough to dishearten those investors in the Bottom Ten and Bottom Five.

Table 6.3c.   **"Bull" Market (1979 to 1988)**
              Total Return Figures

Year	TOP FIVE	TOP TEN	DOW 30	BOTTOM 10	BOTTOM 5
1979	16.45%	9.67%	10.20%	2.81%	0.09%
1980	19.10%	27.53%	21.00%	30.78%	10.31%
1981	8.47%	2.68%	-3.60%	-14.77%	-14.83%
1982	9.24%	20.68%	26.00%	13.43%	3.08%
1983	34.92%	39.22%	25.50%	28.70%	39.70%
1984	12.36%	6.27%	0.71%	-9.47%	-18.69%
1985	40.43%	31.20%	31.14%	24.26%	23.46%
1986	28.39%	28.12%	26.60%	3.50%	-14.56%
1987	11.22%	6.89%	5.80%	27.74%	55.76%
1988	21.41%	18.35%	15.55%	11.75%	20.68%
Average	20.20%	19.06%	15.89%	11.87%	10.50%

While dividend investing gives a distinct advantage to the investor in any type of market, it proves to be most helpful in grim times. The best time for the wary investor to be invested in a high-yield portfolio is when he is skeptical about the future performance of the market. While skittish market timers get shaken out of stocks and into CD's, the intrepid dividend investor can hold his ground, often collecting over 10 percent in the worst market periods.

7

The Individual Companies

The preceding data have shown you that dividend investing is extremely effective throughout both happy and angry markets. The Top Five and Top Ten portfolios consistently outperform the market average and the low-yield groups, notably trouncing them in bear market periods. The mechanical reason behind the success of dividend investing is that it forces the investor to buy low and sell high. Comparing the track records of the Dow companies when they are in the high-yield groups to their long-term average returns proves this.

Table 7.1 segregates the data by company for all those that have been present in the Dow Jones Industrial Average during the 34-year study period. The total number of participants is 42 due to changes in the structure of the Dow Thirty list over time. The table lists data on each company's Average Yield Rank, Average Annual Total Return for all years in the study, Years in the Top Ten Portfolio, Average Annual Total Return while in the Top Ten, Years in the Top Five Portfolio, and Average Annual Total Return while in the Top Five.

Table 7.1

1957 to 1990 Company Name(s)	Avg. Yield Rank	Avg. Total Return	Yrs. in Top 10	Avg. Return in Top 10	Yrs. in Top 5	Avg. Return in Top 5
1 Allied-Signal (A. Chemical/A. Corp.)	13.4	9.08%	11 of 34	20.75%	3 of 34	3.18%
2 Aluminum Co. of America	24.1	7.65%	1 of 31	20.29%	0 of 31	n/a
3 American Brands (American Tobacco)	6.5	15.21%	23 of 29	14.87%	16 of 29	12.08%
4 American Express	21.6	10.17%	0 of 8	n/a	0 of 8	n/a
5 American Smelting	6.0	11.19%	2 of 3	11.13%	2 of 3	11.13%
6 American Telephone & Telegraph	9.4	10.92%	23 of 34	12.41%	10 of 34	13.91%
7 Anaconda	9.2	10.44%	12 of 17	4.37%	10 of 17	12.91%
8 Bethlehem Steel	13.1	6.64%	17 of 34	8.75%	11 of 34	9.28%
9 Boeing	21.3	42.43%	0 of 3	n/a	0 of 3	n/a
10 Chevron (Standard Oil CA)	11.4	13.71%	17 of 34	19.78%	6 of 34	20.90%
11 Chrysler	18.3	10.27%	6 of 23	8.78%	4 of 23	17.54%
12 Coca-Cola	23.7	37.54%	0 of 3	n/a	0 of 3	n/a
13 Corn Products Refining	11.3	31.27%	1 of 3	22.22%	0 of 3	n/a
14 Du Pont	17.0	7.78%	4 of 34	35.70%	0 of 34	n/a
15 Eastman Kodak	25.4	13.57%	2 of 34	0.57%	0 of 34	n/a
16 Esmark (Swift & Co.)	17.7	8.93%	2 of 17	17.09%	0 of 17	n/a
17 Exxon (Standard Oil NJ)	7.9	13.57%	26 of 34	15.02%	11 of 34	21.84%
18 General Electric	22.4	11.91%	0 of 34	n/a	0 of 34	n/a
19 General Foods	17.1	16.07%	4 of 29	11.43%	0 of 29	n/a
20 General Motors	6.6	10.14%	27 of 34	7.72%	18 of 34	5.47%
21 Goodyear	17.1	10.06%	9 of 34	14.57%	4 of 34	19.19%
22 IBM	18.1	11.97%	1 of 11	19.36%	1 of 11	19.36%
23 INCO (International Nickel)	22.5	8.50%	1 of 31	36.35%	0 of 31	n/a
24 International Paper	16.9	10.18%	6 of 34	16.58%	0 of 34	n/a
25 Manville Corp. (Johns-Manville)	12.0	5.29%	10 of 26	4.63%	4 of 26	-9.37%
26 McDonald's	27.6	13.43%	0 of 5	n/a	0 of 5	n/a
27 Merck	26.5	25.34%	0 of 11	n/a	0 of 11	n/a
28 Minnesota Mining & Manufacturing	20.9	14.09%	0 of 14	n/a	0 of 14	n/a
29 National Distillers	14.0	16.73%	0 of 3	n/a	0 of 3	n/a
30 National Steel	6.0	17.80%	3 of 3	17.80%	1 of 3	47.20%
31 Navistar (International Harvester)	13.4	4.66%	19 of 34	16.29%	11 of 34	12.40%
32 Owens-Illinois Glass	21.1	12.23%	0 of 28	n/a	0 of 28	n/a
33 Philip Morris	10.8	42.16%	2 of 5	46.86%	0 of 5	n/a
34 Primerica (American Can)	8.0	7.81%	25 of 34	11.16%	14 of 34	14.64%
35 Procter & Gamble	23.6	15.25%	0 of 34	n/a	0 of 34	n/a
36 Sears, Roebuck	20.9	10.81%	8 of 34	10.83%	2 of 34	-5.21%
37 Texaco (Texas Corporation)	12.1	12.55%	16 of 34	15.88%	13 of 34	13.40%
38 USX (U.S. Steel)	10.0	7.58%	18 of 34	11.57%	10 of 34	17.34%
39 Union Carbide	13.3	7.56%	13 of 34	14.73%	4 of 34	39.59%
40 United Technologies (United Aircraft)	15.6	13.04%	10 of 34	19.83%	6 of 34	25.29%
41 Westinghouse Electric	19.1	14.81%	3 of 34	29.41%	2 of 34	39.90%
42 Woolworth	11.9	16.40%	15 of 34	24.91%	6 of 34	44.87%

Dividend selection had a greater impact on the performance of some issues than others. For instance, the high-dividend indicator increased returns substantially with companies like Woolworth, Westinghouse, Union Carbide, USX and more. But a high dividend didn't lead to higher average returns with General Motors and Manville Corp. It's difficult to draw conclusions from this data, however, because of anomalies like GM's 90-percent gain in 1975 from the number three position on the yield list. An investor would be loath to have excluded GM in this year even though GM performed poorly most other years.

The average annual total return for a participating company over the entire 34-year period was 12.4 percent.[1] When among the Top Ten, the return increased to 16.9 percent. The average return of a company when in the Top Five was 17.7 percent. An investor looking to purchase one of these companies would be foolish not to look at its dividend yield before making a decision.

Endnotes

1.   This figure excludes companies that have never been in the Top Ten.

8

The Forces Behind
Dividend Investing

Our 34-year study shows that portfolios of the highest-yielding Dow Jones Industrial stocks significantly outperform the average. One cannot help but wonder why the yield issues do so well.

The first and most obvious answer is the superior cash yield. For the eighteen-year period 1973 to 1990, the average yield of the ten highest-yielding Dow Jones Industrial stocks was 7.4 percent, compared with only 4.7 percent for the thirty in the average. Assuming equal capital appreciation, the ten highest-yielding issues would have an advantage of nearly 3 percent per year. Notably, the yield issues appreciated faster by 4 percent as well. Therefore, one has to conclude that cash yield is only half the story.

Dividend investing produces superior capital returns because it takes advantage of the inefficiency in short-run market pricing by pointing the investor to companies that are currently out of favor with the investing public. Investors tend to exaggerate the demand for up-front cash yield when they are not optimistic about a company's prospects for capital appreciation. In fact, it is this lack of expectation of performance that allows you to buy a bargain. High relative yield frequently is a signal that a stock's price is temporarily depressed by either a corporate event to which investors have over-reacted, or through investor disinterest in a particular company or industry.

For instance, after the December 1984 explosion at the Union Carbide plant in Bhopal, India, the price of Union Carbide shares fell from 60 to a year-end close of 37. Investors essentially threw the stock away in reaction to this event, driving the price down 40 percent. The yield on Union Carbide stock rose from 5 percent to 9 percent during this round of selling, placing Union Carbide in the number-one position on the high-yield buy list. Union Carbide stock subsequently rose 98 percent in 1985 to close the year at 73 1/4.

You don't always need an event to put a Dow Jones company on the buy list. USX Corporation was having one of the best years in its history during 1988, but no one cared. Investors weren't interested in the stock, although the company's fundamentals were improving dramatically from quarter to quarter. In the 1988 Annual Report, USX Chairman David M. Roderick issued the following "Chairman's Message":

> In this, my last message to you, I am pleased to report that 1988 was one of the best years in the Corporation's history. Net income was $756 million on sales of $16.9 billion. Operating income reached $1.4 billion, one of our highest levels ever. And discretionary cash flow, after meeting the requirements for dividends and capital expenditures, totaled $1.5 billion, exceeding our objective of $1 billion.

> All of our major business segments were profitable in 1988, with Steel recording the most dramatic improvement.

All the while, USX was overlooked in the marketplace. USX shares fell from their first-quarter high of 34 to a low of 26, notwithstanding this exceptional year. This downward price movement combined forces with an increased dividend to put USX in the Top Ten for 1989, where it gained 27.86 percent.

MEDIA INSULATION

The power of current media coverage is enormous. It drives entire industries and markets into periods of enormous valuation error and back out again. The disciplined application of dividend investing creates rigid guidelines for the investment process which insulate the investor from the daily pressures of newspaper headlines and peer pressure. No matter what the current wisdom, and no matter how strong the vision of imminent Armageddon, the process does not allow you to stray from the path by selling in a panic. Further, the process will force you to buy low over and over again.

HAVE CONFIDENCE IN THE TURNAROUND

A turnaround in stock price precipitates capital gains for the dividend investor. A Dow company's lack of performance is usually front-page news. The negative publicity creates an abundance of concern and worry among those shareholders afflicted with short-term perspectives. The company may be changing, but the change in the actual company is rarely as extreme as the change in investor perception of the company. Pessimistic investors start dumping the stock, and as the share price plummets negative sentiment snowballs.

Eventually the sellers are gone. The long period of liquidation has used them up. The stage is set for a significant upward move in price when the company's operations improve. As soon as a story about the "impressive fundamental recovery" appears, investors again begin to pay attention to headlines. Their interest initiates a recuperation in share price as well. Since the sellers have already sold, there is nothing to hold down the price and prevent the turnaround. The C.E.O. is interviewed in *Forbes* magazine; *The Wall Street Journal* praises the recovery; and the publicity cycle is complete. Portfolio managers who sold the stock at $8 a year or two before can't get enough now at $18. Ironically, the tendency of investors to overreact to short-term events and temporal market concerns starts both the price decline and the recovery.

Dividend investing works while other strategies fail because it's based on discipline, not on what's hot today. It makes use of predictable human weaknesses like the herd mentality, fear, greed, short-term perspective and a lack of discipline. Other programs are flawed by the very human weaknesses that propel dividend investing.

Some skeptics argue that if this method were so productive, surely countless people would start using a high-yield technique and thus eliminate its advantageous properties. Many people have seen the data on dividend investing, yet most ignore it. The fact that 99 percent of pros underperform the returns offered by the Top Five implies many are unimpressed. This lack of participation, however, is good for dividend investors. Dividend investors need someone to sell to them at market bottoms — they can't get a bargain otherwise.

9

Academic Support
for Dividend Investing

THE ACADEMICS AND AN EFFICIENT MARKET

Two decades ago, many academics would have dubbed the claims about high-yield investing poppycock. Their resistence was due primarily to their belief that the stock market was "efficient," and that this efficiency precluded the possibility of success for such a simple and obvious tactic as buying high-quality, high-yield stocks. Their notion of an efficient market came mostly from a popular topic of research and debate, the Efficient Market Hypothesis (EMH).

The EMH claimed that stock market prices reflect a rational estimation of the fundamental value of the companies whose stocks are traded in the marketplace. New information was also assumed to be instantaneously assimilated into current prices. These proposed conditions led many academics to the conclusion that *portfolio managers cannot outperform the market by trading on publicly available information.*

The existence of a truly efficient market would indeed render professional money management useless as no investment strategy could provide above-market returns in the long run. The professional investment industry would be a sham, offering no more real value to its consumers than the miracle tonics and elixirs that were sold in the nineteenth century.

Years ago, the eminent investor Warren Buffett wrote of these academics. They disagreed with his views on the wisdom of fundamental analysis, holding fast instead to their view of market efficiency. Buffett observed that they always told him the same thing in regard to his phenomenal success through the use of fundamental methods: "Well, Mr. Buffett, it may work in practice... but it'll never work in theory."

While some still hold to the idea of an efficient market, the foundations of the EMH are crumbling. Recent studies by leading economists from America's most prestigious universities point to a market which is not efficient. The research shows that today's stock market is replete with over-valued and under-valued securities—just as were the markets of yesterday.

A number of noted academics now harbor tremendous skepticism about the validity of the EMH. Harvard economist Lawrence Summers notes that "despite the widespread allegiance to the notion of market efficiency, a number of authors have suggested that certain asset prices are not rationally related to economic realities." Summers argues that existing evidence cannot prove that the stock market is efficient in regard to representing the fundamental values of its component companies. Summers also writes, "The data in conjunction with current methods provide no evidence against the view that financial market prices deviate widely and frequently from rational valuations... thus the results here call into question the theoretical as well as the empirical underpinnings of the EMH."

A study done by Summers and James M. Poterba, of the Massachusetts Institute of Technology, led them to conclude that stock prices, which are often excessively high or low, tend to return to their average values—a phenomenon known as reversion to mean. These findings refute the EMH and the notion of an efficient market.

The analysis of Summers and Poterba pointed to positive short-run serial correlation and long-run negative serial correlation in stock prices.[1]

This statement can be interpreted to mean that trends in stock prices persist in the near term, but the long-run tendency is for the trend to reverse and bring prices back to their average values. The findings of Poterba and Summers imply that valuation errors are temporary in nature and tend to be corrected by a reversion to mean. Poterba and Summers concluded, "The presence of transitory price components also suggests the desirability of investment strategies. . . involving the purchase of securities that have recently declined in value." We like this advice.

Dividend investing leads the investor to stocks with relatively low prices because these stocks have recently declined in value. It is effective because these stocks have usually entered the buy list through a temporary depression in price. When their prices revert back to normal or average levels, capital gains are realized. In this way the yield indicator works in tandem with the tendency of prices to revert to their mean values. The use of Dow Jones Industrial companies for one's investment universe contributes to the creation of a stable system in which reversion to mean is swift and reliable.

Some investors don't need Lawrence Summers to tell them the market isn't efficient. They reject the EMH on intuition derived from their first-hand market experience. Common sense tells them that the market couldn't possibly be efficient. The extreme daily, weekly and even annual fluctuations in stock prices don't agree with the notion of efficiency in their minds. Such excessive fluctuation, it seems, would not be produced solely by true economic dynamics in an efficient market. What news or economic variation could have caused the supposed change in fundamental values reflected by the difference in the open and close prices of stocks on the NYSE on October 19, 1987? The intrinsic value of a stock doesn't often change so substantially in a day, but public perception does.

The notion of stock market price fluctuations being excessive is also supported in academia by the research of Robert Shiller.[2] Shiller implies that price movements are too big to be explained by an EMH model which attempts to justify changes in stock prices only in terms of information about future real dividends. Shiller found that stock prices moved with a volatility that was five to thirteen times too high relative to the movement of real dividends around their long-run means. He also suggests that the stock market, far from being efficient, is irrational and subject to fads. This notion corresponds to the ideas behind yield-oriented investing.

Notably, Shiller uses dividends as the determinant of a company's future value. *Price* is deemed to be the expected value of future dividends — not earnings, which he refutes as realistic expressions of a company's true performance. "Earnings models are correct only insofar as earnings are indicators of future dividends," writes Shiller. "Earnings, by contrast (to dividends) are statistics conceived by accountants which are supposed to provide an indicator of how well a company is doing, and there is a great deal of latitude for the definition of earnings." This perspective on dividends helps to explain why relative dividend yield is often a more powerful indicator than its cousin, price/earnings ratio. The latter is a longstanding, warhorse indicator of many pros, but is dependent on an element (reported earnings) that is misleading in Shiller's view.

Another example that sets off many investors' "common sense alarm" is the enormous change in share price that accompanies a corporate buyout or takeover. It is not uncommon for a share price to jump 50 percent to 75 percent following the announcement of a takeover. How can an efficient market miss the fundamental value of a company by such a wide margin? The discrepancy between the value of a company to the takeover artists and the market price is a strong indication of market inefficiency.

Union Carbide serves as an example of typical market behavior. The Bhopal, India disaster was an event that only temporarily depressed the price of Union Carbide stock. It rose 98 percent while occupying the number one yield position the year after the catastrophe. Erratic and extreme price movements for both individual companies and the market as a whole tend to be transitory.

The market may not be efficient in the short run, but when values get too far out of line tremendous pressure is created that eventually pushes prices in the direction of a more rational equilibrium. In the short run, fads, events and other short-term forces dominate investor choices, allowing price levels to become distorted. But in the long run, rational values carry more weight in price determination. Trends of investor favoritism and disapproval will create frequent valuation errors, but the market will always find its way home again. This is why extreme situations don't last forever, and why we have confidence that the depressed price of a Dow stock as it enters the Top Five or Top Ten will recover to provide a profit. The Union Carbide situation was a typical example of the correction of a depressed price.

The EMH loses more credibility through its proposition that all new information is rapidly and correctly assimilated and its consequences reflected in share prices. This claim gives too much credit to market participants. The average investor is not a genius. More broadly, the market is comprised of individuals who are not capable of analyzing and interpreting all available data. There is simply too much information for all parties to perceive and comprehend. It is therefore not realistic to assume that all information is instantly and properly integrated into share prices.

The propensity for exaggerated investor reaction was pointed to in the January 1981 issue of *Science* magazine. An article entitled "The Framing of Decisions and the Psychology of Choice," by Tversky & Kahneman, discussed how "subjects overreact to new information in making probabilistic judgments." The research of Tversky & Kahneman showed how it is possible for investors to consistently overreact to new information, causing stock prices to make exaggerated moves. Sometimes investors misinterpret a corporate event as a terminal disease.[3] Other times their emotions amplify the perceived magnitude of the impact of the change. They overestimate both the benefits of good news and the detrimental effects of bad news. This overreaction can be harnessed by more level-headed investors to provide above-market returns through a method such as dividend investing.

The body of logic and evidence against the EMH establishes the theoretical viability of investment methods such as dividend investing. Since market prices deviate from rational fundamental values, and since those deviations tend to be corrected through reversion to mean, a technique which points out these valuation discrepancies can be used to garner above-market investment returns. Dividend investing is such a technique.

Endnotes

1. James M. Poterba & Lawrence H. Summers, *Journal of Financial Economics* 22, 1988, 27-59.

2. See "Do Stock Prices Move Too Much to be Justified by Subsequent Changes in Dividends?," *American Economic Review* 71, June 1981, 421-436.

3. See Chapter II.

10

The Income Investor

Dividend investing is a versatile investment tool. Both the Top Five and Top Ten portfolios produce satisfying results for the growth investor. What may have gone unnoticed thus far, however, is the power of dividend investing to provide substantial income as well as capital gains. Dividend investing's high-yield focus causes income to grow even faster than principal in the Top Five and Top Ten portfolios. This characteristic allows dividend investing to meet the long-term needs of income-dependent investors, such as retirees, or educational and artistic endowments. Since income investors also frequently are risk-averse, the inherent resistance of high-yield issues to decline in bad markets is particularly valuable.

The usefulness of a high-dividend strategy to the income investor is demonstrated by the example of Mr. and Mrs. Greenwood, a hypothetical couple just moving into retirement at age sixty-five. Mr. Greenwood is given a roll-over check from his firm's 401(k) plan for exactly $200,000 in January of 1980. This money represents the bulk of Mr. and Mrs. Greenwood's savings, and will have to supply them with income for the rest of their lives.

Mr. Greenwood has a sixty-day roll-over window within which he must decide how to invest his life savings. He is unsure of how to proceed in this matter. The magnitude of the decision frightens him, as his family's future security is at stake.

Mr. Greenwood turns to Mr. Nihles, a bank trust officer and longtime friend. Mr. Nihles urges him not to take any "unnecessary risks." He recommends that Mr. Greenwood be "safe" and put the $200,000 into thirty-year Treasury bonds. Mr. Nihles explains that they presently offer the highest current yield in their history, 9.75 percent. "The principal should be secure for two reasons," says Mr. Nihles. "The Treasury never defaults, and the high coupon will protect against a decline in the bond's principal value because it is unlikely that interest rates will ever go much higher."

The idea of locking himself into a thirty-year bond troubled Mr. Greenwood. He talked with a stockbroker to get another perspective. The broker, Mr. Widmann, had researched the performance of the five highest-yielding stocks in the Dow Jones Industrial Average and was aware of the potential they offered Mr. Greenwood. He recommended that Mr. Greenwood use a high-dividend-yield strategy. After a lengthy conversation with Mr. Widmann, Mr. Greenwood decided that both ideas had merit, and split the $200,000 evenly between them, creating a Top Five portfolio and a Treasury Bond portfolio. The Greenwoods spent all dividend income, rather than reinvesting it. The results are shown in Table 10.1.

Mr. Nihles was right to some extent. The U. S. Treasury didn't default and, while Treasury Bond yields spiked up to 14 percent in 1982 (when the bond he bought for $100,000 was worth $72,170), the lower current yield on Treasury Bonds in 1990 gave Mr. Greenwood a modest $17,320 gain in principal value as well.

Breaking down the results of the two component strategies shows which advisor gave better advice to the Greenwoods in 1980. The principal value of the Top Five portfolio grew from $100,000 to over $350,000 in these ten years, increasing at an average compound rate of 13.38 percent. As shown above, the value of their Treasury Bond portfolio increased in value $17,320 — an average annual rate of compounding of only 1.6 percent. The income produced by the Top Five was more than two-and-a-half times that of the T-Bond portfolio by the final year. So while both may have been "right," Mr. Widmann was *more* right.

Table 10.1.   Performance of a Top Five Income Portfolio versus Thirty-Year Treasury Bond

Year	TOP FIVE Capital Value	TOP FIVE Income	% of Original Capital	T-BOND Capital Value	T-BOND Income	% of Original Capital
Begin	$100,000	n/a	n/a	$100,000	n/a	n/a
1980	$110,520	$8,580	8.6%	$84,660	$9,750	9.75%
1981	$110,067	$9,814	9.8%	$72,620	$9,750	9.75%
1982	$110,903	$9,334	9.3%	$93,310	$9,750	9.75%
1983	$139,095	$10,536	10.5%	$83,850	$9,750	9.75%
1984	$145,076	$11,211	11.2%	$87,310	$9,750	9.75%
1985	$192,153	$11,577	11.6%	$109,110	$9,750	9.75%
1986	$233,255	$13,451	13.5%	$119,600	$9,750	9.75%
1987	$246,947	$12,479	12.5%	$111,380	$9,750	9.75%
1988	$284,384	$15,434	15.4%	$107,420	$9,750	9.75%
1989	$340,578	$24,969	25.0%	$117,320	$9,750	9.75%
Annual Increase	13.04%	11.27%		1.61%	0.00%	

The decision worked out well for Mr. and Mrs. Greenwood, now age seventy-five. The total value of their holdings increased from $200,000 to $468,437. Total income grew from $18,050 in the first year to $36,492 in 1989.

WHY STOCKS ARE BETTER THAN BONDS

The increase in the capital value of the Top Five portfolio has helped the Greenwoods outpace inflation. They are now earning more income in real terms than in 1980. The $36,492 of 1989 income is equal to $21,473 in 1980, inflation-adjusted dollars. If the entire $200,000 had been in the Top Five portfolio, 1989 income would have been $51,484, equal to $30,295 1980 dollars. If, however, all $200,000 had been placed in Treasury bonds, the purchasing power of the Greenwood's annual income would have eroded from $19,500 in 1980 to $11,474 in 1989 real dollars.

The Treasury bond portfolio had the opposite effect of the Top Five on purchasing power: it dragged the net result down for the Greenwoods. Its static principal value and income eroded both their real net worth and their income. The $117,326 value of the Treasury bond portfolio is worth only $71,194 in 1980 dollars — even with its mild capital increase, it actually devalued in real terms. Compare this result to the progress in the capital value of the Top Five portfolio. After accounting for inflation, its 1989 real value of $206,609 is far ahead of its $100,000 starting value. Hindsight has revealed the sagacity of Mr. Widmann's recommendations, and the fallacy in Mr. Nihles' approach with regard to the battle that must be fought against inflation.

INCOME GROWTH

Dividend investing proves to be a powerful system for the income investor because of the phenomenal growth in income year after year. Given the high-dividend management strategy, income growth is logical. Every time a stock is sold, it is replaced by one with a higher yield. This process has lead to an average annual rate of income growth of 12 percent for the Top Five between 1980 and 1989.

A 12 percent rate of income growth can be put in perspective by comparison to the rate of dividend growth among the Dow Industrials. It is rare to find a Dow company with dividend growth greater than 8 percent for a ten-year period. Specifically, only G.E. (8.51), Merck (15.64) and Westinghouse (12.63) had ten-year dividend growth rates greater than 8 percent; most others averaged between 2 percent and 6 percent. Five Dow companies actually had negative dividend growth for the decade.

As noted above, an 8 percent rate of dividend growth was difficult for any Dow company to achieve. With the high-dividend strategy, however, the 8 percent figure is achieved even during the worst bear markets. Take for instance the 1966 to 1981 bear market described in Chapter III. The Dow Jones Industrial Average made practically no gain during this sixteen-year period, but this did not inhibit income performance in the high-yield groups, as income generated by the Top Five portfolio grew at an annual rate of 8.33 percent. A modest 3.93 percent annual capital growth rate also allowed the Top Five to increase principal from $100,000 to $185,277 (see Table 10.2).

Table 10.2   Performance of a Top Five Income Portfolio in a Bear Market

(All dividend income spent, not reinvested)

Year	TOP FIVE Capital Value	TOP FIVE Income	% of Original Capital
Begin	$100,000	n/a	n/a
1966	$83,470	$4,590	4.59%
1967	$104,980	$4,958	4.96%
1968	$121,284	$5,585	5.59%
1969	$101,235	$6,416	6.42%
1970	$94,524	$6,611	6.61%
1971	$93,512	$4,773	4.77%
1972	$106,155	$5,452	5.45%
1973	$91,813	$6,221	6.22%
1974	$89,316	$7,400	7.40%
1975	$140,619	$6,842	6.84%
1976	$180,826	$10,631	10.63%
1977	$168,829	$12,767	12.77%
1978	$151,676	$13,118	13.12%
1979	$163,279	$13,347	13.35%
1980	$180,456	$14,009	14.01%
1981	$179,716	$16,024	16.02%
Annual Increase	3.73%	8.13%	

Note that while the capital growth rate of the Top Five during the bear market was 70 percent slower than during the bull market of the 80's, income growth was only 30 percent slower. Since *income growth* is largely dependent upon the size of the principal source, this relationship shows that income increased faster, relative to principal, during the bear market than it did during the bull market. This relative increase in income is one factor by which dividend investing mitigates the effects of slow capital growth during bad times.

ENDOWMENT MANAGEMENT

In theory, university and artistic endowments live forever. Thus, there is no excuse for a short-term perspective on the part of a manager or fiduciary who oversees such trusts. It has been shown that a short-term focus by money managers and pressure from fiduciaries for immediate performance are obstacles to long-term growth. So it seems logical that perpetual trusts should make the greatest effort to implement investment strategies based on profitable long-term perspectives.

Situations do arise, however, when an endowment's directors must make certain sacrifices to meet short-term needs like payroll and other expenses. It is unfortunate when the income produced by an endowment is insufficient to cover the budget in a given year. Since spending principal is usually considered a last resort, significant pressure is created by the needs of whatever institution is served by an endowment to maintain the necessary income production, quarter by quarter. Even with awareness of the endowment's perpetuity, it is difficult for fiduciaries and management to avoid getting drawn into a near-term fixation. It is therefore important for these fiduciaries to understand that the capital growth offered by a high-yield investment approach will generate significantly greater income in the long run from stock dividends than will a strategy involving debt instruments with higher current yields.

In evaluating potential management strategies for an endowment, it is appropriate to examine performance over a long time period. Table 10.3 shows the performance of the Top Five over the 34-year period, 1957 to 1990, when income increased at an average compounded rate of 7.54 percent per year.

You can see how income explodes, as a percentage of original capital, in the later years. The income produced by the Top Five, as a percent of original capital, is never lower than the yield on long-term Treasury bonds, even during the earliest years. By the tenth year, the Top Five income has climbed to over 10 percent of original capital. In the thirty-fourth year, Top Five income is a phenomenal 67 percent of original capital. This level of income could never have been achieved by a money market or high-yield bond strategy. The increase in principal value over this period was also dramatic, as the original $100,000 grew to almost 1.1 million dollars.

Table 10.3.   Performance of High-Yield Income Portfolios, 1957 to 1990

(All dividend income spent, not reinvested)

Year	TOP FIVE Capital Value	TOP FIVE Income	% of Original Capital	TOP TEN Capital Value	TOP TEN Income	% of Original Capital
Begin	$100,000	n/a	n/a	$100,000	n/a	n/a
1957	$85,610	$5,670	5.67%	$87,170	$5,300	5.30%
1958	$124,023	$5,145	5.15%	$122,265	$4,812	4.81%
1959	$130,435	$8,235	8.24%	$127,400	$6,504	6.50%
1960	$109,513	$8,217	8.22%	$119,017	$6,536	6.54%
1961	$129,697	$6,209	6.21%	$141,642	$6,129	6.13%
1962	$125,378	$6,329	6.33%	$135,070	$6,360	6.36%
1963	$147,570	$6,984	6.98%	$158,923	$6,848	6.85%
1964	$178,707	$7,600	7.60%	$188,133	$7,453	7.45%
1965	$222,830	$9,454	9.45%	$217,952	$8,598	8.60%
1966	$185,996	$10,228	10.23%	$174,318	$9,503	9.50%
1967	$233,927	$11,048	11.05%	$211,309	$9,832	9.83%
1968	$270,256	$12,445	12.44%	$228,446	$10,565	10.57%
1969	$225,583	$14,297	14.30%	$188,376	$10,874	10.87%
1970	$210,626	$14,731	14.73%	$184,439	$10,493	10.49%
1971	$208,373	$10,637	10.64%	$185,546	$9,499	9.50%
1972	$236,545	$12,148	12.15%	$219,853	$9,945	9.95%
1973	$204,588	$13,862	13.86%	$216,599	$11,784	11.78%
1974	$199,023	$16,490	16.49%	$202,845	$15,963	15.96%
1975	$313,341	$15,245	15.25%	$294,004	$16,816	16.82%
1976	$402,957	$23,689	23.69%	$370,945	$20,698	20.70%
1977	$376,201	$28,449	28.45%	$343,755	$23,370	23.37%
1978	$337,979	$29,231	29.23%	$326,601	$25,403	25.40%
1979	$363,834	$29,742	29.74%	$331,239	$26,945	26.94%
1980	$402,110	$31,217	31.22%	$394,406	$28,023	28.02%
1981	$400,461	$35,707	35.71%	$373,818	$31,158	31.16%
1982	$403,504	$33,959	33.96%	$420,620	$30,504	30.50%
1983	$506,075	$38,333	38.33%	$550,634	$34,954	34.95%
1984	$527,836	$40,790	40.79%	$547,936	$37,223	37.22%
1985	$699,119	$42,121	42.12%	$679,386	$39,506	39.51%
1986	$848,661	$48,938	48.94%	$828,443	$41,986	41.99%
1987	$898,477	$45,403	45.40%	$843,190	$42,333	42.33%
1988	$1,034,687	$56,155	56.15%	$949,179	$47,640	47.64%
1989	$1,239,141	$90,845	90.85%	$1,142,621	$66,348	66.35%
1990	$1,085,859	$67,161	67.16%	$972,256	$55,988	55.99%
Annual Increase	7.27%	7.54%		6.92%	7.18%	

The long-term performance of the Top Five's sister group, the Top Ten, was also impressive. In the 1957 to 1990 period, income grew at a rate of 7.18 percent annually, while principal increased from $100,000 to almost one million dollars. Either high-yield group will do the job, although higher income will be produced by the Top Five because of the higher average yield among its issues.

Table 10.4, covering the period 1973-1990, sheds more light on the behavior of the high-yield strategy when used by an income investor. This period begins with two miserable years for the stock market. The principal value of the Top Five falls from $100,000 to $86,490 in 1973, and then to $84,137 in 1974. Income, however, rises from $5,860 in 1973 to $6,971 in 1974 — an increase of 19 percent. This episode further demonstrates how periods of poor capital performance among the high-yield shares are often offset by substantial increases in dividend income. The market rebound in 1975 brings the principal value up to $132,466, as income drops slightly to $6,445. The Top Five follows through in 1976, the fourth year of investment, bringing the market value of the portfolio to $170,351 and raising income to over 10 percent of original capital, at $10,014.

Income increased in all but three of the following thirteen years, finally ending at 28 percent of the beginning capital value. The average compound rate of income growth for the '73 to '90 period was 9.16 percent. Principal grew at the compound rate of 8.84 percent, giving the investor $459,050 to work with at the end of the eighteenth year.

The Top Ten offered similarly superb performance for the '73 to '90 period. Both income and principal grew at rates exceeding 8.5 percent. Principal increased in a more stable and linear fashion in the Top Ten, albeit more slowly than the Top Five, as the final value for this broader portfolio was $442,230. Top Ten income increased steadily, at the rate of 9.04 percent, with only two years of backtracking in 1982 and 1990. The Top Ten produced income in the eighteenth year that was 25.5 percent of original capital.

A high-dividend strategy can be used as the primary income producing investment program for any investor with a relatively long-term perspective. The method recommended in this book requires continual replacement of low-yield issues with higher-yielding stocks, thereby generating superior income growth that persists though both good times and bad. This strategy's income performance is augmented by dependable capital growth. The high rates for both income and principal are the keys

Table 10.4.   Performance of High-Yield Income Portfolios, 1973 to 1990

(All dividend income spent, not reinvested)

Year	TOP FIVE Capital Value	TOP FIVE Income	% of Original Capital	TOP TEN Capital Value	TOP TEN Income	% of Original Capital
Begin	$100,000	n/a	n/a	$100,000	n/a	n/a
1973	$86,490	$5,860	5.86%	$98,520	$5,360	5.36%
1974	$84,137	$6,971	6.97%	$92,264	$7,261	7.26%
1975	$132,466	$6,445	6.44%	$133,727	$7,649	7.65%
1976	$170,351	$10,014	10.01%	$168,724	$9,414	9.41%
1977	$159,040	$12,027	12.03%	$156,356	$10,630	10.63%
1978	$142,882	$12,357	12.36%	$148,554	$11,555	11.55%
1979	$153,812	$12,574	12.57%	$150,664	$12,256	12.26%
1980	$169,993	$13,197	13.20%	$179,395	$12,746	12.75%
1981	$169,296	$15,095	15.10%	$170,031	$14,172	14.17%
1982	$170,583	$14,356	14.36%	$191,319	$13,875	13.87%
1983	$213,945	$16,205	16.21%	$250,455	$15,899	15.90%
1984	$223,144	$17,244	17.24%	$249,228	$16,931	16.93%
1985	$295,555	$17,807	17.81%	$309,018	$17,969	17.97%
1986	$358,774	$20,689	20.69%	$376,816	$19,097	19.10%
1987	$379,834	$19,194	19.19%	$383,524	$19,255	19.26%
1988	$437,417	$23,740	23.74%	$431,733	$21,669	21.67%
1989	$523,850	$38,405	38.41%	$519,720	$30,178	30.18%
1990	$459,050	$28,393	28.39%	$442,230	$25,466	25.47%
Annual Increase	8.84%	9.16%		8.61%	9.04%	

to staying ahead of inflation in the long run. While most income investments actually cause the investor's real purchasing power to devalue over time, the Top Five or Top Ten have been shown to increase it substantially in any type of market, bull or bear.

11

Leverage

THE CYCLIC MARKET

The stock market rises and falls year after year, decade after decade. These cycles alternately anger and exhilarate investors; crashes uniformly frustrate and discourage them. Few look beyond the present in the midst of all the pressures. The stock market is, however, far more resilient than most investors think. Table 11.1 sets forth the performance of the Dow Jones Industrials in those years following a down year in the DJIA. Over the last 34 years, the DJIA has closed with a loss twelve times from January 1 of one year to January 1 of the next year. Ten out of eleven times[1] the next year has been an up year for the Dow Industrials. One hundred percent of the time, the next two years have produced a positive return.

The average recovery following a down year has been 18.21 percent in the first year and 17.98 in the second year. Returns drop off dramatically in the third, fourth and fifth years. Statistically, there is a very small chance

Table 11.1.   Dow Jones Industrials Annual Return Following a Down Year

Down Year	FIRST Year	SECOND Year	THIRD Year	FOURTH Year	FIFTH Year	AVERAGE
1957	38.92%	19.83%	-6.29%	22.16%	-7.70%	13.38%
1960	22.16%	-7.70%	20.10%	18.11%	14.45%	13.42%
1962	20.10%	18.11%	14.45%	-15.99%	19.26%	11.19%
1966	19.26%	7.60%	-11.90%	9.10%	9.90%	6.79%
1969	9.10%	9.90%	18.10%	-13.40%	-23.40%	0.06%
1973	-23.40%	44.40%	22.30%	-13.20%	2.40%	6.50%
1974	44.40%	22.30%	-13.20%	2.40%	10.20%	13.22%
1977	2.40%	10.20%	21.00%	-3.60%	26.00%	11.20%
1978	10.20%	21.00%	-3.60%	26.00%	25.50%	15.82%
1981	26.00%	25.50%	0.71%	31.14%	26.60%	21.99%
1984	31.14%	26.60%	5.80%	15.55%	31.70%	22.16%
Average	18.21%	17.98%	6.13%	7.12%	12.26%	12.34%

of loss for the individual who plunges into the market after a down year. The reward to this assiduous investor is usually substantial.

THE AGGRESSIVE INVESTOR

Since the stock market cycles around an intrinsic value, after it has fallen in a given year there is only a small probability of it falling further in the next year. In fact, pressure is actually created by a down year that drives the market upward in the subsequent years. The market discounts bad news (war, recession, inflation) into share prices. When the bad news becomes reality, there is no where to go but up. This principle can be applied by the dividend investor to greatly increase long-run return. Given

Table 11.2.   Leveraged Top Five Portfolio Annual Return Following a Down Year

Down Year	FIRST Year	SECOND Year	THIRD Year	FOURTH Year	FIFTH Year	AVERAGE
1957	91.76%	13.62%	-9.74%	38.20%	-6.90%	25.39%
1960	38.20%	-6.90%	36.54%	42.50%	29.98%	28.06%
1962	36.54%	42.50%	29.98%	-11.94%	53.42%	30.10%
1966	53.42%	31.70%	-11.24%	-10.20%	-2.04%	12.33%
1969	-10.20%	-2.04%	19.35%	-7.65%	0.68%	0.03%
1973	0.68%	120.20%	62.32%	0.42%	-14.80%	33.76%
1974	120.20%	62.32%	0.42%	-14.80%	22.90%	38.21%
1977	-14.80%	22.90%	28.20%	8.47%	8.48%	10.65%
1978	22.90%	28.20%	8.47%	8.48%	59.84%	25.58%
1981	8.48%	59.84%	12.36%	70.86%	46.78%	39.66%
1984	70.86%	46.78%	11.22%	21.41%	28.54%	35.76%
Average	38.00%	38.10%	17.08%	13.25%	20.63%	25.41%

the consistency of market recoveries, an aggressive investor might want to periodically leverage his portfolio to take advantage of the cycles.[2] The logical periods for leverage would be those two-year periods that follow down years in the DJIA, as market returns are obviously superior in those years.

In the last 34 years, an aggressive investor who leveraged during the two years following each down year in the DJIA would have seen handsome profits 90 percent of the time. Although the 10 percent rate of failure with leverage would have made things uncomfortable at times, it would not have been disabling. Table 11.2 presents the results of leveraging the five highest-yielding Dow stocks for the two years that follow a down year for the Dow average.

On average, the first and second years of the leveraged portfolio delivered returns of 38.00 percent and 38.10 percent, respectively. Consistent with the market cycle, returns diminished after the first two years. Loss years also occurred with greater frequency in years three, four and five. This pattern points to the liquidation of leverage after the second year beyond a down year. We conclude that leverage can substantially enhance the dividend investor's return without a tremendous increase in risk.

Table 11.3 displays the long-run effects of consistently leveraging a Top Five portfolio. If the Top Five dividend investor had leveraged in every two-year period that followed a down year in the DJIA, his $100,000 portfolio established in 1957 would have grown to over 39.9 million dollars by the end of 1989. A down year in 1990 left the portfolio value at $37.1 million. Compare this value to the results shown in Table 3.6 in Chapter 3 which demonstrate that the unleveraged Top Five would have turned $100,000 into $8.5 million over the same time period. We can descend even further in the comparison by reminding you that the Bottom Five would have produced only $0.65 million from $100,000 in those thirty-four years. Leverage is obviously a powerful tool that should be considered by the long-term dividend investor.

There are many timing tools and margin techniques. Some would probably enhance an individual's returns to a greater extent than those presented here. We have simply attempted to show that quantitative discipline used on a calendar year basis increases returns. Some academics will dismiss this work as rigid and retrospective. They will say that the fact that it has worked for the last thirty-four years is no guarantee that it will work next year. We agree. Unfortunately, they miss the point. One year doesn't decide the long-run performance of an investment portfolio, just as one skirmish rarely decides a war. As the above example shows, success usually follows a disciplined effort applied consistently over time.

LEVERAGE IN BEAR MARKETS

High-yield portfolios resist decline in bear markets and appreciate rapidly in bull markets. These characteristics are particularly suitable to the investor who wishes to leverage his portfolio. From 1957 to 1990, the DJIA had twelve down years while the Top Five had eight. The practice of

Table 11.3.   Thirty-Four-Year Leveraged Top Five Returns

Year	Point Change in D.J.I.A.	Top Five Portfolio Condition	Leveraged Top Five Total Return	Leveraged Top Five Portfolio Value
Begin				$100,000
1957	-56.76	Ñormal	-8.72%	$91,280
1958		Leveraged	91.76%	$175,039
1959		Leveraged	13.62%	$198,879
1960	-68.81	Normal	-9.74%	$179,508
1961		Leveraged	38.20%	$248,080
1962	-77.92	Leveraged	-6.90%	$230,963
1963		Leveraged	36.54%	$315,356
1964		Leveraged	42.50%	$449,383
1965		Normal	29.98%	$584,108
1966	-182.13	Normal	-11.94%	$514,365
1967		Leveraged	53.42%	$789,139
1968		Leveraged	31.70%	$1,039,296
1969	-138.53	Normal	-11.24%	$922,479
1970		Leveraged	-10.20%	$828,386
1971		Leveraged	-2.04%	$811,487
1972		Normal	19.35%	$968,510
1973	-176.36	Normal	-7.65%	$894,419
1974	-223.28	Leveraged	0.68%	$900,501
1975		Leveraged	120.20%	$1,982,903
1976		Leveraged	62.32%	$3,218,648
1977	-182.01	Normal	0.42%	$3,232,166
1978	-6.32	Leveraged	-14.78%	$2,754,452
1979		Leveraged	22.90%	$3,385,222
1980		Leveraged	28.20%	$4,339,854
1981	-90.26	Normal	8.47%	$4,707,440
1982		Leveraged	8.48%	$5,106,631
1983		Leveraged	59.84%	$8,162,439
1984	-53.87	Normal	12.36%	$9,171,316
1985		Leveraged	70.86%	$15,670,111
1986		Leveraged	46.78%	$23,000,589
1987		Normal	11.22%	$25,581,255
1988		Normal	21.41%	$31,058,202
1989		Normal	28.54%	$39,922,213
1990		Normal	-6.95%	$37,147,619
Average			22.64%	

Table 11.4.   The Market and the Unleveraged Top Five versus The Leveraged Top Five for Five-Year Periods

Period	Dow Industrials	Percent Change	Top Five	Percent Change	Leveraged Top Five	Percent Change
Begin	$100,000		$100,000		$100,000	
1957 to 1960*	$175,000	75.00%	$172,490	72.40%	$248,080	148.08%
1961 to 1965	$220,300	25.89%	$312,020	80.89%	$514,365	107.37%
1966 to 1970	$298,620	35.55%	$457,910	46.76%	$811,487	57.76%
1971 to 1975	$413,150	38.35%	$1,195,160	161.00%	$3,218,648	296.64%
1976 to 1980	$472,030	14.25%	$1,762,390	47.46%	$4,707,440	46.26%
1981 to 1985	$1,248,020	164.39%	$5,262,140	198.58%	$23,000,589	388.60%
1986 to 1990*	$1,927,870	54.47%	$8,498,740	61.51%	$37,147,619	61.51%
Average Annual Return	10.38%		15.37%		22.64%	

* These periods are only four years long.

leveraging the Top Five for two years following every down year in the DJIA would have caused an investor to suffer a total of ten down years over this time period. Nonetheless, the investor's average annual total return from the leveraged portfolio would have been 22.64 percent over those thirty-four years. The effect of this high rate of growth was shown in Table 11.3, in which the portfolio was leveraged in twenty out of thirty-four years.

In every five-year time period studied, the Top Five portfolio that selectively used margin dramatically beat the market itself and out-performed the unleveraged Top Five in all but one period. Table 11.4 shows the data for this comparison. One can see that the percent change in portfolio value over the five-year periods is usually remarkably higher in the leveraged portfolio than in the Dow Thirty or Top Five. In its worst period, the leveraged portfolio was still 32 percent ahead of the Dow Thirty and only 1.2 percent behind the unleveraged Top Five.

Table 11.5.   Leverage in a Bear Market

Year	Point Change in D.J.I.A.	Top Five Portfolio Condition	Leveraged Top Five Total Return	Leveraged Top Five Portfolio Value
Begin				$100,000
1966	-182.13	Normal	-11.94%	$88,060
1967		Leveraged	53.42%	$135,102
1968		Leveraged	31.70%	$177,929
1969	-138.53	Normal	-11.24%	$157,930
1970		Leveraged	-10.20%	$141,821
1971		Leveraged	-2.04%	$138,928
1972		Normal	19.35%	$165,810
1973	-176.36	Normal	-7.65%	$153,126
1974	-223.28	Leveraged	0.68%	$154,167
1975		Leveraged	120.20%	$339,476
1976		Leveraged	62.32%	$551,037
1977	-182.01	Normal	0.42%	$553,351
1978	-6.32	Leveraged	-14.78%	$471,566
1979		Leveraged	22.90%	$579,555
1980		Leveraged	28.20%	$742,989
1981	-90.26	Normal	8.47%	$805,920
Average			18.11%	

The leveraged portfolio provided the best results even through the bear markets. For the sixteen-year period 1966 to 1981, the market was locked in a trading range. The Dow Average began the period at 969 and closed at 883. If one were going to suffer from the use of margin, this period would certainly have been the litmus test. Seven of the sixteen years were down years for the DJIA. Five of those years were in severe bear markets. The leveraged Top Five portfolio suffered only six down years and provided an average annual return of 18.11 percent, while the Dow produced a measly 5.2 percent return. The effects of these rates of return on portfolio values are shown in the final table, Table 11.5. At 5.2 percent, the Dow Jones turned $100,000 into $180,007 over these difficult years. The leveraged portfolio managed four-and-a-half times that amount, turning $100,000 into $805,920 over the same period.

Endnotes

1. "Ten out of eleven" instead of "eleven out of twelve" because the 1990 down year (for which we have no data on the years that follow) was excluded.

2. In this instance, leverage means borrowing 100 percent on margin against the value of the securities in the portfolio to double all positions. A 10 percent margin expense was assumed for all years and was subtracted from the total returns shown for the leveraged portfolio.

Appendices

Appendix 1

Prudential-Bache Study of a Top Ten Portfolio

The following information is from a Prudential-Bache study conducted in 1989:

> "The following table presents numerical results from January 1972 through December 1988, assuming that total return proceeds are reinvested in a Top Ten yielding portfolio at the beginning of each calendar year. 'Total return' is defined as the 'capital return,' i.e., the gain or loss derived from changes in stock prices, plus the return from dividends received. Results do not include transaction costs."

	Portfolio of Ten Highest Yielding Dow Stocks		vs.	Dow Jones Industrial Average	
	Total Return	Capital Return		Total Return	Capital Return
1972	23.8%	18.1%		18.5%	14.6%
1973	-6.2	-11.5		-13.3	-16.6
1974	-2.9	-9.9		-23.8	-27.6
1975	58.2	49.1		45.0	38.3
1976	35.5	27.8		23.0	17.9
1977	-3.9	-10.0		-12.9	-17.3
1978	-3.1	-9.9		2.7	-3.1
1979	14.4	6.0		10.7	4.2
1980	24.8	15.6		22.2	14.9
1981	-4.5	-11.8		-3.6	-9.2
1982	25.0	15.4		27.2	19.6
1983	30.7	22.2		26.1	20.3
1984	6.0	-1.5		1.2	-3.7
1985	32.4	24.7		34.1	27.7
1986	27.9	21.3		27.4	22.6
1987	5.5	0.9		5.5	2.3
1988	24.4	18.3		16.2	11.8

Compound Annual Return:

	15.6%	8.4%		10.6%	5.4%

Source: Prudential-Bache

This Prudential-Bache study verifies the results of our research on dividend investing. Its results are consistent with ours, even though the data are not exactly the same from year to year for the Top Ten or the Dow Thirty. We think that Pru-Bache used a slightly different process for calculating the ten highest-yielding stocks than we did, and therefore purchased Top Ten portfolios that were comprised one or two different issues per year than those in our study.

Appendix 2

Similarities Between Dividend Investing and P/E Ratio Investing

A strategy directly analogous in concept to dividend investing is that of buying low price/earnings stocks. A low P/E is similar in nature to a high yield. When a stock's price is depressed, its P/E will be low relative to the P/E's of companies in similar groups. Ernest Widmann, in early work with Paul Miller, researched the S&P 400 and found that both high-yield and low P/E strategies were successful. The low P/E results were consistent with those in our research. The low P/E returns, however, were substantially lower than those of the high-yield groups. As it turns out, stocks with low P/E's are often the same stocks that have high yields. No wonder a low P/E buy and sell indicator works!

Analysis of the Dow Thirty, based on data supplied by Lord Abbett, shows how effective a low P/E strategy has been over the last fifty years. Using a process similar to the Top Ten high-yield program, the ten stocks

Table A2.1.   Comparison of P/E Strategies
June 30, 1940 to June 30, 1989

YEARS ENDING JUNE 30	DOW 30	COMPOUND VALUES	LOW 10	COMPOUND VALUES	MIDDLE 10	COMPOUND VALUES	HIGH 10	COMPOUND VALUES
		$10,000		$10,000		$10,000		$10,000
1940	-6.70%	$9,330	-6.00%	$9,400	-6.80%	$9,320	-13.00%	$8,700
1941	1.00%	$9,423	9.30%	$10,274	3.70%	$9,665	-1.60%	$8,561
1942	-16.10%	$7,906	-8.60%	$9,391	-12.30%	$8,476	-17.60%	$7,054
1943	38.80%	$10,974	52.40%	$14,311	48.60%	$12,595	32.50%	$9,347
1944	3.50%	$11,358	1.50%	$14,526	8.10%	$13,616	0.90%	$9,431
1945	11.40%	$12,653	16.50%	$16,923	12.60%	$15,331	7.30%	$10,119
1946	24.40%	$15,740	32.00%	$22,338	23.50%	$18,934	15.80%	$11,718
1947	-13.80%	$13,568	-15.50%	$18,876	-16.50%	$15,810	-14.80%	$9,984
1948	6.90%	$14,504	20.10%	$22,670	5.20%	$16,632	-2.30%	$9,754
1949	-11.60%	$12,821	-19.40%	$18,272	-10.80%	$14,836	-6.40%	$9,130
1950	24.90%	$16,014	38.40%	$25,288	19.10%	$17,669	19.80%	$10,938
1951	16.10%	$18,592	25.80%	$31,812	22.00%	$21,557	4.20%	$11,397
1952	13.00%	$21,009	18.70%	$37,761	6.00%	$22,850	7.50%	$12,252
1953	-2.20%	$20,547	-4.90%	$35,911	2.80%	$23,490	-4.30%	$11,725
1954	24.30%	$25,540	26.40%	$45,392	24.70%	$29,292	26.00%	$14,773
1955	35.30%	$34,556	61.10%	$73,126	25.80%	$36,849	23.10%	$18,186
1956	9.20%	$37,735	13.00%	$82,632	11.00%	$40,903	1.20%	$18,404
1957	2.10%	$38,527	9.10%	$90,152	0.40%	$41,066	3.90%	$19,122
1958	-5.00%	$36,601	8.10%	$97,454	-1.60%	$40,409	-12.20%	$16,789
1959	34.50%	$49,228	35.70%	$132,245	30.10%	$52,572	30.70%	$21,944
1960	-0.50%	$48,982	-1.50%	$130,261	8.90%	$57,251	-8.20%	$20,144
1961	6.80%	$52,313	16.10%	$151,233	13.70%	$65,095	-2.20%	$19,701
1962	-17.90%	$42,949	-7.30%	$140,193	-17.60%	$53,638	-24.60%	$14,855
1963	25.90%	$54,072	39.90%	$196,130	15.00%	$61,684	22.40%	$18,182
1964	17.60%	$63,589	25.20%	$245,555	15.90%	$71,492	10.80%	$20,146
1965	4.40%	$66,387	6.50%	$261,516	5.30%	$75,281	4.20%	$20,992
1966	0.20%	$66,520	-0.60%	$259,947	4.70%	$78,819	2.20%	$21,454
1967	-1.10%	$65,788	3.70%	$269,565	-4.10%	$75,587	2.40%	$21,968
1968	4.40%	$68,683	9.30%	$294,635	2.70%	$77,628	4.40%	$22,935
1969	-2.70%	$66,828	3.20%	$304,063	0.70%	$78,171	-7.70%	$21,169
1970	-21.70%	$52,327	-24.40%	$229,872	-23.50%	$59,801	-17.80%	$17,401
1971	30.40%	$68,234	26.80%	$291,478	29.50%	$77,443	35.70%	$23,613
1972	4.30%	$71,168	-3.50%	$281,276	-7.50%	$71,634	11.10%	$26,234
1973	-4.00%	$68,321	-1.20%	$277,900	-9.20%	$65,044	-9.70%	$23,689
1974	-10.00%	$61,489	5.10%	$292,073	-13.30%	$56,393	-12.00%	$20,847
1975	9.50%	$67,331	33.50%	$389,918	16.40%	$65,642	-2.40%	$20,346
1976	14.10%	$76,824	19.30%	$465,172	13.00%	$74,175	17.00%	$23,805
1977	-8.60%	$70,217	7.30%	$499,130	-1.90%	$72,766	-17.10%	$19,735
1978	-10.60%	$62,774	-8.80%	$455,206	-13.60%	$62,870	-15.00%	$16,774
1979	2.80%	$64,532	4.40%	$475,235	4.90%	$65,950	2.70%	$17,227
1980	3.10%	$66,532	11.90%	$531,788	4.20%	$68,720	-6.10%	$16,176
1981	12.60%	$74,916	24.80%	$663,672	3.70%	$71,263	1.40%	$16,403
1982	-8.30%	$68,698	-19.20%	$536,247	-9.50%	$64,493	-27.90%	$11,826
1983	50.50%	$103,390	39.20%	$746,456	34.90%	$87,001	60.20%	$18,946
1984	-7.30%	$95,842	-3.60%	$719,583	-19.70%	$69,862	-12.30%	$16,616
1985	17.90%	$112,998	27.40%	$916,749	18.60%	$82,856	11.90%	$18,593
1986	41.70%	$160,118	11.40%	$1,021,259	40.80%	$116,661	6.60%	$19,820
1987	27.80%	$204,631	18.20%	$1,207,128	19.00%	$138,827	26.10%	$24,993
1988	-11.50%	$181,099	-14.90%	$1,027,266	-9.70%	$125,360	-2.60%	$24,343
1989	13.90%	$206,272	3.70%	$1,065,274	10.80%	$138,899	20.70%	$29,382
TOTALS	7.47%	$206,272	11.31%	$1,065,274	6.57%	$138,899	3.50%	$29,382

on the Dow Jones Industrial average with the lowest P/E's were purchased on June 30, 1940. The portfolio was reviewed on June 30 of each subsequent year. Capital return statistics were monitored for this low P/E group, as well as for the middle P/E and high P/E groups. The results are shown in the following table. Note that the figures shown are only for capital appreciation, unlike the high-yield research. Dividend income was not included.

The average annual capital gain for the low P/E group was more than three times that of the high P/E group and nearly two times that of the middle group. This tremendous divergence is represented in dramatic fashion by the compound results. The low P/E stocks turned $10,000 into over $1,000,000, while the high P/E stocks yielded only $29,382, and the middle, $138,899.

The Top Five portfolio averaged about 3 percent better per year than the low P/E groups in capital gains.

Appendix 3

Complete Data Set By Year

Appendix 3 contains a complete data set for all companies in the Dow Thirty organized by year from 1957 to 1990. There are two groupings of data for each year. One segregates the data into the four research groups — the Bottom Five, Bottom Ten, Top Ten and Top Five — and offers computations of the average values of yield, appreciation, actual cash paid out in dividends and total return for each group. The other grouping contains values for all thirty companies, giving averages for the same values mentioned above.

Explanations of the columnar categories are as follows:

WSJ DIVI. The value in this column was the actual annualized dividend listed in *The Wall Street Journal* on the second trading day of the year (and hence is the value for the first trading day of the year).

WSJ YIELD   This value was calculated by dividing the *WSJ* annualized dividend by the close share price listed in *The Wall Street Journal* on the second trading day of the year.

OPENING PRICE   This value is meant to represent the year's opening price for the particular security. The close price listed in the *WSJ* on the second trading day of the year was used as the source for these figures.

CLOSING PRICE   This value is meant to represent the close price for the year for the particular security. The source for this value was the close price listed in the *WSJ* on the second trading day of the subsequent year.

STOCK DIV.   This value represents the value of any stock dividend paid to shareholders during the year. Special attention was paid to these values to ensure that the actual value of securities distributed to shareholders was represented in the total return value for the year.

SPLIT   The values in this column represent the coefficient by which the close price of the security should be multiplied to account for the effect of a stock split which occurred during the year. For instance, if the stock split three for two, the value in this column would be 1.5. If no split occurred, a value of 1 is present.

APPRECIATION   The value in this column represents the percent change in share price that occurred for a particular security over the year.

DIVIDEND   The value in this column represents the actual cash dividend paid out to shareholders over the year. The source for this data was either the S&P Dividend Record or Moody's Dividend Record.

ACT CASH YIELD   This value is calculated by dividing the value from the DIVIDEND column by the value in the OPENING PRICE column. It represents the security's annual cash yield as a percent.

TOTAL RETURN   The value in this column represents the total return for the security for the year. This value was calculated by summing the values for cash yield and appreciation, and accounting for the effect of any stock splits or stock dividends.

LIST OF 1990 DOW JONES INDUSTRIALS BY DIVIDEND-YIELD

	STOCK 1990	1990 WSJ DIVI.	1990 WSJ YIELD	1990 OPENING PRICE	1990 CLOSING PRICE	1990 STOCK DIV.	1990 SPLIT	1990 APPRECIATION	1990 DIVIDEND	ACT. CASH YIELD	TOTAL RETURN
1	General Motors	$3.00	6.74%	$44.50	$34.25		1	-23.03%	$3.00	6.74%	-16.29%
2	Sears, Roebuck	$2.00	5.16%	$38.75	$25.88		1	-33.23%	$2.00	5.16%	-28.06%
3	Allied-Signal	$1.80	5.09%	$35.38	$28.00		1	-20.85%	$1.80	5.09%	-15.76%
4	Texaco	$3.00	5.07%	$59.13	$59.63		1	.85%	$3.05	5.16%	6.00%
5	I.B.M.	$4.84	4.94%	$98.00	$112.13		1	14.41%	$4.84	4.94%	19.35%
6	Exxon	$2.40	4.80%	$50.00	$50.75		1	1.50%	$2.47	4.94%	6.44%
7	Eastman Kodak	$2.00	4.66%	$42.88	$41.13		1	-4.08%	$2.00	4.66%	.58%
8	Union Carbide	$1.00	4.10%	$24.38	$16.75		1	-31.28%	$1.00	4.10%	-27.18%
9	Chevron	$2.80	4.05%	$69.13	$72.38		1	4.70%	$2.95	4.27%	8.97%
10	Goodyear	$1.80	3.97%	$45.38	$19.00		1	-58.13%	$1.80	3.97%	-54.16%
+ 11	USX	$1.40	3.89%	$36.00	$29.75		1	-17.36%	$1.40	3.89%	-13.47%
12	Du Pont	$4.80	3.84%	$125.13	$36.13		3	-13.38%	$4.86	3.88%	-9.50%
13	Minnesota Mng. & Mfg.	$2.60	3.23%	$80.50	$84.88		1	5.43%	$2.92	3.63%	9.06%
14	Philip Morris	$1.37	3.20%	$42.75	$50.88		1	19.01%	$1.46	3.42%	22.42%
15	Westinghouse Electric	$2.40	3.18%	$75.50	$28.38		2	-24.83%	$2.70	3.58%	-21.26%
16	International Paper	$1.68	2.93%	$57.25	$52.88		1	-7.64%	$1.68	2.93%	-4.71%
17	United Technologies	$1.60	2.88%	$55.50	$47.75		1	-13.96%	$1.80	3.24%	-10.72%
18	Woolworth	$1.88	2.85%	$66.00	$30.00		2	-9.09%	$2.03	3.08%	-6.02%
19	General Electric	$1.88	2.82%	$66.75	$56.50		1	-15.36%	$1.88	2.82%	-12.54%
20	American Express	$.92	2.64%	$34.88	$20.25		1	-41.94%	$.92	2.64%	-39.30%
21	American T & T	$1.20	2.58%	$46.50	$29.75		1	-36.02%	$1.29	2.77%	-33.25%
22	Procter & Gamble	$1.80	2.55%	$70.50	$85.50		1	21.28%	$1.85	2.62%	23.90%
23	Merck	$1.80	2.29%	$78.63	$89.50		1	13.83%	$1.91	2.43%	16.26%
24	Aluminum Co of Amer	$1.60	2.12%	$75.63	$58.00		1	-23.31%	$3.05	4.03%	-19.27%
25	Boeing	$1.20	1.95%	$61.50	$44.88		1.5	9.45%	$1.43	2.32%	11.77%
26	Coca-Cola	$1.36	1.74%	$78.00	$45.25		2	16.03%	$1.60	2.05%	18.08%
+ 27	Primerica	$.32	1.09%	$29.38	$23.13		1	-21.28%	$.36	1.23%	-20.05%
28	McDonald's Corp.	$.31	.89%	$34.88	$28.50		1	-18.28%	$.33	.95%	-17.33%
29	Bethlehem Steel	$.10	.53%	$18.75	$14.00		1	-25.33%	$.40	2.13%	-23.20%
+ 30	Navistar International	$.00	.00%	$4.13	$2.25		1	-45.45%	$.00	.00%	-45.45%
	AVERAGE		3.19%					-14.50%		3.34%	-11.17%

+ Last year in the Dow 30

STOCK 1990	1990 WSJ DIVI.	1990 WSJ YIELD	1990 OPENING PRICE	1990 CLOSING PRICE	1990 STOCK DIV.	1990 SPLIT	1990 APPRECIATION	1990 DIVIDEND	ACT. CASH YIELD	TOTAL RETURN
BOTTOM FIVE:										
26 Coca-Cola	$1.36	1.74%	$78.00	$45.25		2	16.03%	$1.60	2.05%	18.08%
27 Primerica	$.32	1.09%	$29.38	$23.13		1	-21.28%	$.36	1.23%	-20.05%
28 McDonald's Corp.	$.31	.89%	$34.88	$28.50		1	-18.28%	$.33	.95%	-17.33%
29 Bethlehem Steel	$.10	.53%	$18.75	$14.00		1	-25.33%	$.40	2.13%	-23.20%
30 Navistar International	$.00	.00%	$4.13	$2.25		1	-45.45%	$.00	.00%	-45.45%
		.85%					-18.86%		1.27%	-17.59%
BOTTOM TEN:										
21 American T & T	$1.20	2.58%	$46.50	$29.75		1	-36.02%	$1.29	2.77%	-33.25%
22 Procter & Gamble	$1.80	2.55%	$70.50	$85.50		1	21.28%	$1.85	2.62%	23.90%
23 Merck	$1.80	2.29%	$78.63	$89.50		1	13.83%	$1.91	2.43%	16.26%
24 Aluminum Co of Amer	$1.60	2.12%	$75.63	$58.00		1	-23.31%	$3.05	4.03%	-19.27%
25 Boeing	$1.20	1.95%	$61.50	$44.88		1.5	9.45%	$1.43	2.32%	11.77%
26 Coca-Cola	$1.36	1.74%	$78.00	$45.25		2	16.03%	$1.60	2.05%	18.08%
27 Primerica	$.32	1.09%	$29.38	$23.13		1	-21.28%	$.36	1.23%	-20.05%
28 McDonald's Corp.	$.31	.89%	$34.88	$28.50		1	-18.28%	$.33	.95%	-17.33%
29 Bethlehem Steel	$.10	.53%	$18.75	$14.00		1	-25.33%	$.40	2.13%	-23.20%
30 Navistar International	$.00	.00%	$4.13	$2.25		1	-45.45%	$.00	.00%	-45.45%
		1.57%					-10.91%		2.05%	-8.85%
TOP TEN:										
1 General Motors	$3.00	6.74%	$44.50	$34.25		1	-23.03%	$3.00	6.74%	-16.29%
2 Sears, Roebuck	$2.00	5.16%	$38.75	$25.88		1	-33.23%	$2.00	5.16%	-28.06%
3 Allied-Signal	$1.80	5.09%	$35.38	$28.00		1	-20.85%	$1.80	5.09%	-15.76%
4 Texaco	$3.00	5.07%	$59.13	$59.63		1	.85%	$3.05	5.16%	6.00%
5 I.B.M.	$4.84	4.94%	$98.00	$112.13		1	14.41%	$4.84	4.94%	19.35%
6 Exxon	$2.40	4.80%	$50.00	$50.75		1	1.50%	$2.47	4.94%	6.44%
7 Eastman Kodak	$2.00	4.66%	$42.88	$41.13		1	-4.08%	$2.00	4.66%	.58%
8 Union Carbide	$1.00	4.10%	$24.38	$16.75		1	-31.28%	$1.00	4.10%	-27.18%
9 Chevron	$2.80	4.05%	$69.13	$72.38		1	4.70%	$2.95	4.27%	8.97%
10 Goodyear	$1.80	3.97%	$45.38	$19.00		1	-58.13%	$1.80	3.97%	-54.16%
		4.86%					-14.91%		4.90%	-10.01%
TOP FIVE:										
1 General Motors	$3.00	6.74%	$44.50	$34.25		1	-23.03%	$3.00	6.74%	-16.29%
2 Sears, Roebuck	$2.00	5.16%	$38.75	$25.88		1	-33.23%	$2.00	5.16%	-28.06%
3 Allied-Signal	$1.80	5.09%	$35.38	$28.00		1	-20.85%	$1.80	5.09%	-15.76%
4 Texaco	$3.00	5.07%	$59.13	$59.63		1	.85%	$3.05	5.16%	6.00%
5 I.B.M.	$4.84	4.94%	$98.00	$112.13		1	14.41%	$4.84	4.94%	19.35%
		5.40%					-12.37%		5.42%	-6.95%

LIST OF 1989 DOW JONES INDUSTRIALS BY DIVIDEND-YIELD

	STOCK 1989	1989 WSJ DIVI.	1989 WSJ YIELD	1989 OPENING PRICE	1989 CLOSING PRICE	1989 STOCK DIV.	1989 SPLIT	1989 APPRECIATION	1989 DIVIDEND	ACT. CASH YIELD	TOTAL RETURN
1	General Motors	$5.00	6.08%	$82.25	$44.50		2	8.21%	$6.00	7.29%	15.50%
2	Texaco	$3.00	5.88%	$51.00	$59.13	1.96%	1	17.89%	$10.10	19.80%	37.70%
3	Chevron	$2.60	5.68%	$45.75	$69.13		1	51.09%	$2.80	6.12%	57.21%
4	Allied-Signal	$1.80	5.39%	$33.38	$35.38		1	5.99%	$1.80	5.39%	11.39%
5	Exxon	$2.20	5.09%	$43.25	$50.00		1	15.61%	$2.30	5.32%	20.92%
6	Sears, Roebuck	$2.00	4.95%	$40.38	$38.75		1	-4.02%	$2.00	4.95%	.93%
7	U.S.X.	$1.40	4.79%	$29.25	$36.00		1	23.08%	$1.40	4.79%	27.86%
8	Eastman Kodak	$2.00	4.48%	$44.63	$42.88		1	-3.92%	$2.00	4.48%	.56%
9	Philip Morris	$4.50	4.46%	$100.88	$42.75		4	69.52%	$4.75	4.71%	74.23%
10	Du Pont	$3.80	4.40%	$86.38	$125.13		1	44.86%	$4.35	5.04%	49.90%
11	American T & T	$1.20	4.19%	$28.63	$46.50		1	62.45%	$1.20	4.19%	66.64%
12	United Technologies	$1.60	3.99%	$40.13	$55.50		1	38.32%	$1.60	3.99%	42.31%
13	Westinghouse Electric	$2.00	3.85%	$52.00	$75.50		1	45.19%	$2.30	4.42%	49.62%
14	General Electric	$1.64	3.73%	$44.00	$66.75		1	51.70%	$1.64	3.73%	55.43%
15	I.B.M.	$4.40	3.64%	$121.00	$98.00		1	-19.01%	$4.73	3.91%	-15.10%
16	Goodyear	$1.80	3.55%	$50.75	$45.38		1	-10.59%	$1.80	3.55%	-7.04%
17	Minnessota Mng. & Mfg.	$2.12	3.45%	$61.38	$80.50		1	31.16%	$2.60	4.24%	35.40%
18	Procter & Gamble	$2.80	3.31%	$84.50	$70.50		2	66.86%	$3.30	3.91%	70.77%
19	Woolworth	$1.64	3.23%	$50.75	$66.00		1	30.05%	$1.82	3.59%	33.64%
20	International Paper	$1.48	3.18%	$46.50	$57.25		1	23.12%	$1.48	3.18%	26.30%
21	American Express	$.84	3.15%	$26.63	$34.88		1	30.99%	$.84	3.15%	34.14%
22	Union Carbide	$.80	3.12%	$25.63	$24.38		1	-4.88%	$1.00	3.90%	-.98%
23	Coca-Cola	$1.20	2.76%	$43.50	$78.00		1	79.31%	$1.36	3.13%	82.44%
24	Boeing	$1.60	2.68%	$59.63	$61.50		1.5	54.72%	$1.75	2.94%	57.65%
25	Merck	$1.48	2.59%	$57.25	$78.63		1	37.34%	$1.64	2.86%	40.20%
26	Aluminum Co of Amer	$1.40	2.51%	$55.88	$75.63		1	35.35%	$2.72	4.87%	40.21%
27	McDonald's Corp.	$.56	1.20%	$46.75	$34.88		2	49.20%	$.61	1.30%	50.50%
28	Primerica	$.28	.96%	$29.05	$29.38		1	1.12%	$.29	1.00%	2.12%
29	Bethlehem Steel	$.00	.00%	$22.63	$18.75		1	-17.13%	$.20	.88%	-16.24%
30	Navistar	$.00	.00%	$5.50	$4.13		1	-25.00%	$.00	.00%	-25.00%
	AVERAGE		3.54%					26.29%		4.35%	30.64%

	STOCK 1989	1989 WSJ DIVI.	1989 WSJ YIELD	1989 OPENING PRICE	1989 CLOSING PRICE	1989 STOCK DIV.	1989 SPLIT	1989 APPRECIATION	1989 DIVIDEND	ACT. CASH YIELD	TOTAL RETURN
	BOTTOM FIVE:										
26	Aluminum Co of Amer	$1.40	2.51%	$55.88	$75.63		1	35.35%	$2.72	4.87%	40.21%
27	McDonald's Corp.	$.56	1.20%	$46.75	$34.88		2	49.20%	$.61	1.30%	50.50%
28	Primerica	$.28	.96%	$29.05	$29.38		1	1.12%	$.29	1.00%	2.12%
29	Bethlehem Steel	$.00	.00%	$22.63	$18.75		1	-17.13%	$.20	.88%	-16.24%
30	Navistar	$.00	.00%	$5.50	$4.13		1	-25.00%	$.00	.00%	-25.00%
			.93%					8.71%		1.61%	10.32%
	BOTTOM TEN:										
21	American Express	$.84	3.15%	$26.63	$34.88		1	30.99%	$.84	3.15%	34.14%
22	Union Carbide	$.80	3.12%	$25.63	$24.38		1	-4.88%	$1.00	3.90%	-.98%
23	Coca-Cola	$1.20	2.76%	$43.50	$78.00		1	79.31%	$1.36	3.13%	82.44%
24	Boeing	$1.60	2.68%	$59.63	$61.50		1.5	54.72%	$1.75	2.94%	57.65%
25	Merck	$1.48	2.59%	$57.25	$78.63		1	37.34%	$1.64	2.86%	40.20%
26	Aluminum Co of Amer	$1.40	2.51%	$55.88	$75.63		1	35.35%	$2.72	4.87%	40.21%
27	McDonald's Corp.	$.56	1.20%	$46.75	$34.88		2	49.20%	$.61	1.30%	50.50%
28	Primerica	$.28	.96%	$29.05	$29.38		1	1.12%	$.29	1.00%	2.12%
29	Bethlehem Steel	$.00	.00%	$22.63	$18.75		1	-17.13%	$.20	.88%	-16.24%
30	Navistar	$.00	.00%	$5.50	$4.13		1	-25.00%	$.00	.00%	-25.00%
			1.90%					24.10%		2.40%	26.50%
	TOP TEN:										
1	General Motors	$5.00	6.08%	$82.25	$44.50		2	8.21%	$6.00	7.29%	15.50%
2	Texaco	$3.00	5.88%	$51.00	$59.13	1.96%	1	17.89%	$10.10	19.80%	37.70%
3	Chevron	$2.60	5.68%	$45.75	$69.13		1	51.09%	$2.80	6.12%	57.21%
4	Allied-Signal	$1.80	5.39%	$33.38	$35.38		1	5.99%	$1.80	5.39%	11.39%
5	Exxon	$2.20	5.09%	$43.25	$50.00		1	15.61%	$2.30	5.32%	20.92%
6	Sears, Roebuck	$2.00	4.95%	$40.38	$38.75		1	-4.02%	$2.00	4.95%	.93%
7	U.S.X.	$1.40	4.79%	$29.25	$36.00		1	23.08%	$1.40	4.79%	27.86%
8	Eastman Kodak	$2.00	4.48%	$44.63	$42.88		1	-3.92%	$2.00	4.48%	.56%
9	Philip Morris	$4.50	4.46%	$100.88	$42.75		4	69.52%	$4.75	4.71%	74.23%
10	Du Pont	$3.80	4.40%	$86.38	$125.13		1	44.86%	$4.35	5.04%	49.90%
			5.20%					20.38%		6.98%	27.37%
	TOP FIVE:										
1	General Motors	$5.00	6.08%	$82.25	$44.50		2	8.21%	$6.00	7.29%	15.50%
2	Texaco	$3.00	5.88%	$51.00	$59.13	1.96%	1	17.89%	$10.10	19.80%	37.70%
3	Chevron	$2.60	5.68%	$45.75	$69.13		1	51.09%	$2.80	6.12%	57.21%
4	Allied-Signal	$1.80	5.39%	$33.38	$35.38		1	5.99%	$1.80	5.39%	11.39%
5	Exxon	$2.20	5.09%	$43.25	$50.00		1	15.61%	$2.30	5.32%	20.92%
			5.62%					19.76%		8.79%	28.54%

LIST OF 1988 DOW JONES INDUSTRIALS BY DIVIDEND-YIELD

	STOCK 1988	1988 WSJ DIVI.	1988 WSJ YIELD	1988 OPENING PRICE	1988 CLOSING PRICE	1988 STOCK DIV.	1988 SPLIT	1988 APPRECIATION	1988 DIVIDEND	ACT. CASH YIELD	TOTAL RETURN
1	General Motors	$5.00	7.91%	$63.25	$82.25		1	30.04%	$5.00	7.91%	37.94%
2	Union Carbide	$1.50	6.63%	$22.63	$25.63		1	13.26%	$1.15	5.08%	18.34%
3	Primerica	$1.60	6.31%	$25.38	$29.05		1	14.48%	$1.60	6.31%	20.79%
4	Allied-Signal	$1.80	5.83%	$30.88	$33.38		1	8.10%	$1.80	5.83%	13.93%
5	Chevron	$2.40	5.77%	$41.63	$45.75		1	9.91%	$2.55	6.13%	16.04%
6	Sears, Roebuck	$2.00	5.65%	$35.38	$40.38		1	14.13%	$2.00	5.65%	19.79%
7	Exxon	$2.00	4.94%	$40.50	$43.25		1	6.79%	$2.15	5.31%	12.10%
8	American T & T	$1.20	4.25%	$28.25	$28.63		1	1.33%	$1.20	4.25%	5.58%
9	Philip Morris	$3.60	4.11%	$87.63	$100.88		1	15.12%	$3.83	4.37%	19.49%
10	United Technologies	$1.40	4.01%	$34.88	$40.13		1	15.05%	$1.55	4.44%	19.50%
11	Du Pont	$3.40	3.82%	$89.00	$86.38		1	-2.95%	$3.70	4.16%	1.21%
12	U.S.X.	$1.20	3.81%	$31.50	$29.25		1	-7.14%	$1.25	3.97%	-3.17%
13	I.B.M.	$4.40	3.64%	$120.75	$121.00		1	.21%	$4.40	3.64%	3.85%
14	Woolworth	$1.32	3.63%	$36.38	$50.75		1	39.52%	$1.56	4.29%	43.81%
*15	Boeing	$1.40	3.61%	$38.75	$59.63		1	53.87%	$1.55	4.00%	57.87%
16	Eastman Kodak	$1.80	3.51%	$51.25	$44.63		1	-12.93%	$1.85	3.61%	-9.32%
17	Westinghouse Electric	$1.72	3.36%	$51.25	$52.00		1	1.46%	$1.93	3.77%	5.23%
18	American Express	$.76	3.17%	$24.00	$26.63		1	10.94%	$.76	3.17%	14.10%
19	Procter & Gamble	$2.70	3.10%	$87.00	$84.50		1	-2.87%	$2.80	3.22%	.34%
20	General Electric	$1.40	3.01%	$46.50	$44.00		1	-5.38%	$1.40	3.01%	-2.37%
*21	Minnessota Mng. & Mfg.	$1.86	2.81%	$66.13	$61.38		1	-7.18%	$2.12	3.21%	-3.98%
22	Coca-Cola	$1.12	2.81%	$39.88	$43.50		1	9.09%	$1.20	3.01%	12.10%
23	International Paper	$1.20	2.74%	$43.88	$46.50		1	5.98%	$1.28	2.91%	8.89%
24	Goodyear	$1.60	2.55%	$62.75	$50.75		1	-19.12%	$1.70	2.71%	-16.41%
25	Aluminum Co of Amer	$1.20	2.38%	$50.38	$55.88		1	10.92%	$1.30	2.58%	13.50%
26	Merck	$3.20	1.95%	$164.38	$57.25		3	4.49%	$3.83	2.33%	6.82%
27	McDonald's Corp.	$.50	1.10%	$45.50	$46.75		1	2.75%	$.55	1.20%	3.95%
28	Bethlehem Steel	$.00	.00%	$17.75	$22.63		1	27.46%	$.00	.00%	27.46%
29	Navistar	$.00	.00%	$4.50	$5.50		1	22.22%	$.00	.00%	22.22%
30	Texaco	$.00	.00%	$37.25	$51.00		1	36.91%	$2.25	6.04%	42.95%
	AVERAGE		3.55%					9.88%		3.87%	13.75%

* First year in the Dow 30

STOCK 1988	1988 WSJ DIVI.	1988 WSJ YIELD	1988 OPENING PRICE	1988 CLOSING PRICE	1988 STOCK DIV.	1988 SPLIT	1988 APPRECIATION	1988 DIVIDEND	ACT. CASH YIELD	TOTAL RETURN
BOTTOM FIVE:										
26 Merck	$3.20	1.95%	$164.38	$57.25		3	4.49%	$3.83	2.33%	6.82%
27 McDonald's Corp.	$.50	1.10%	$45.50	$46.75		1	2.75%	$.55	1.20%	3.95%
28 Bethlehem Steel	$.00	.00%	$17.75	$22.63			27.46%	$.00	.00%	27.46%
29 Navistar	$.00	.00%	$4.50	$5.50		1	22.22%	$.00	.00%	22.22%
30 Texaco	$.00	.00%	$37.25	$51.00		1	36.91%	$2.25	6.04%	42.95%
		.61%					18.77%		1.91%	20.68%
BOTTOM TEN:										
21 Minnessota Mng. & Mfg.	$1.86	2.81%	$66.13	$61.38		1	-7.18%	$2.12	3.21%	-3.98%
22 Coca-Cola	$1.12	2.81%	$39.88	$43.50		1	9.09%	$1.20	3.01%	12.10%
23 International Paper	$1.20	2.74%	$43.88	$46.50		1	5.98%	$1.28	2.91%	8.89%
24 Goodyear	$1.60	2.55%	$62.75	$50.75		1	-19.12%	$1.70	2.71%	-16.41%
25 Aluminum Co of Amer	$1.20	2.38%	$50.38	$55.88		1	10.92%	$1.30	2.58%	13.50%
26 Merck	$3.20	1.95%	$164.38	$57.25		3	4.49%	$3.83	2.33%	6.82%
27 McDonald's Corp.	$.50	1.10%	$45.50	$46.75		1	2.75%	$.55	1.20%	3.95%
28 Bethlehem Steel	$.00	.00%	$17.75	$22.63			27.46%	$.00	.00%	27.46%
29 Navistar	$.00	.00%	$4.50	$5.50		1	22.22%	$.00	.00%	22.22%
30 Texaco	$.00	.00%	$37.25	$51.00		1	36.91%	$2.25	6.04%	42.95%
		1.63%					9.35%		2.40%	11.75%
TOP TEN:										
1 General Motors	$5.00	7.91%	$63.25	$82.25		1	30.04%	$5.00	7.91%	37.94%
2 Union Carbide	$1.50	6.63%	$22.63	$25.63		1	13.26%	$1.15	5.08%	18.34%
3 Primerica	$1.60	6.31%	$25.38	$29.05			14.48%	$1.60	6.31%	20.79%
4 Allied-Signal	$1.80	5.83%	$30.88	$33.38		1	8.10%	$1.80	5.83%	13.93%
5 Chevron	$2.40	5.77%	$41.63	$45.75		1	9.91%	$2.55	6.13%	16.04%
6 Sears, Roebuck	$2.00	5.65%	$35.38	$40.38		1	14.13%	$2.00	5.65%	19.79%
7 Exxon	$2.00	4.94%	$40.50	$43.25		1	6.79%	$2.15	5.31%	12.10%
8 American T & T	$1.20	4.25%	$28.25	$28.63		1	1.33%	$1.20	4.25%	5.58%
9 Philip Morris	$3.60	4.11%	$87.63	$100.88		1	15.12%	$3.83	4.37%	19.49%
10 United Technologies	$1.40	4.01%	$34.88	$40.13			15.05%	$1.55	4.44%	19.50%
		5.54%					12.82%		5.53%	18.35%
TOP FIVE:										
1 General Motors	$5.00	7.91%	$63.25	$82.25		1	30.04%	$5.00	7.91%	37.94%
2 Union Carbide	$1.50	6.63%	$22.63	$25.63		1	13.26%	$1.15	5.08%	18.34%
3 Primerica	$1.60	6.31%	$25.38	$29.05			14.48%	$1.60	6.31%	20.79%
4 Allied-Signal	$1.80	5.83%	$30.88	$33.38		1	8.10%	$1.80	5.83%	13.93%
5 Chevron	$2.40	5.77%	$41.63	$45.75		1	9.91%	$2.55	6.13%	16.04%
		6.49%					15.16%		6.25%	21.41%

LIST OF 1987 DOW JONES INDUSTRIALS BY DIVIDEND-YIELD

	STOCK 1987	1987 WSJ DIVI.	1987 WSJ YIELD	1987 OPENING PRICE	1987 CLOSING PRICE	1987 STOCK DIV.	1987 SPLIT	1987 APPRECIATION	1987 DIVIDEND	ACT. CASH YIELD	TOTAL RETURN
1	Texaco	$3.00	8.16%	$36.75	$37.25		1	1.36%	$.75	2.04%	3.40%
2	General Motors	$5.00	7.48%	$66.88	$63.25			-5.42%	$5.00	7.48%	2.06%
3	Union Carbide	$1.50	6.56%	$22.88	$22.63		1	-1.09%	$1.50	6.56%	5.46%
4	U.S.X.	$1.20	5.49%	$21.88	$31.50		1	44.00%	$1.20	5.49%	49.49%
5	Chevron	$2.40	5.22%	$46.00	$41.63		1	-9.51%	$2.40	5.22%	-4.29%
6	Exxon	$3.60	5.00%	$72.00	$40.50		2	12.50%	$3.80	5.28%	17.78%
7	American T & T	$1.20	4.75%	$25.25	$28.25			11.88%	$1.20	4.75%	16.63%
8	Allied-Signal	$1.80	4.43%	$40.63	$30.88		1	-24.00%	$1.80	4.43%	-19.57%
9	Sears, Roebuck	$1.76	4.29%	$41.00	$35.38		1	-13.72%	$1.94	4.73%	-8.99%
10	Philip Morris	$3.00	4.08%	$73.50	$87.63		1	19.22%	$3.00	4.08%	23.30%
11	Goodyear	$1.60	3.73%	$42.88	$62.75		1	46.36%	$1.60	3.73%	50.09%
12	Du Pont	$3.20	3.73%	$85.88	$89.00			3.64%	$3.30	3.84%	7.48%
13	Eastman Kodak	$2.52	3.64%	$69.25	$51.25		1.5	11.01%	$2.52	3.64%	14.65%
14	I.B.M.	$4.40	3.61%	$122.00	$120.75			-1.02%	$4.40	3.61%	2.58%
15	Procter & Gamble	$2.70	3.48%	$77.63	$87.00		1	12.08%	$2.70	3.48%	15.56%
16	Aluminum Co of Amer	$1.20	3.42%	$35.13	$50.38		1	43.42%	$1.20	3.42%	46.83%
17	Primerica	$2.90	3.40%	$85.38	$25.38		2	-40.56%	$3.13	3.67%	-36.89%
18	International Paper	$2.40	3.15%	$76.13	$43.88		2	15.27%	$2.40	3.16%	18.42%
19	Minnessota Mng. & Mfg.	$3.60	3.05%	$117.88	$66.13		2	12.20%	$3.72	3.16%	15.35%
20	United Technologies	$1.40	2.99%	$46.75	$34.88		1	-25.40%	$1.40	2.99%	-22.41%
21	General Electric	$2.52	2.88%	$87.38	$46.50		2	6.44%	$2.58	2.95%	9.39%
22	Woolworth	$1.12	2.84%	$39.38	$36.38		1	-7.62%	$1.27	3.23%	-4.39%
23	American Express	$1.44	2.49%	$57.88	$24.00		2	-17.06%	$1.50	2.59%	-14.47%
24	Westinghouse Electric	$1.40	2.40%	$58.25	$51.25		1	-12.02%	$1.64	2.82%	-9.20%
+ 25	Owens-Illinois	$.95	1.80%	$52.88	$60.13		1	13.71%	$1.87	3.54%	17.25%
26	Merck	$2.20	1.75%	$126.00	$164.38		1	30.46%	$2.45	1.94%	32.40%
+ 27	INCO	$.20	1.68%	$11.88	$22.25		1	87.37%	$.20	1.68%	89.05%
28	McDonald's Corp.	$.66	1.06%	$62.00	$45.50		1.5	10.08%	$.85	1.37%	11.45%
29	Bethlehem Steel	$.00	.00%	$7.00	$17.75		1	153.57%	$.00	.00%	153.57%
30	Navistar	$.00	.00%	$4.88	$4.50		1	-7.69%	$.00	.00%	-7.69%
	AVERAGE		3.55%					12.31%		3.50%	15.81%

+ Last year in the Dow 30

#	STOCK 1987	1987 WSJ DIVI.	1987 WSJ YIELD	1987 OPENING PRICE	1987 CLOSING PRICE	1987 STOCK DIV.	1987 SPLIT	1987 APPRECIATION	1987 DIVIDEND	ACT. CASH YIELD	TOTAL RETURN
	BOTTOM FIVE:										
26	Merck	$2.20	1.75%	$126.00	$164.38		1	30.46%	$2.45	1.94%	32.40%
27	INCO	$.20	1.68%	$11.88	$22.25		1	87.37%	$.20	1.68%	89.05%
28	McDonald's Corp.	$.66	1.06%	$62.00	$45.50		1.5	10.08%	$.85	1.37%	11.45%
29	Bethlehem Steel	$.00	.00%	$7.00	$17.75		1	153.57%	$.00	.00%	153.57%
30	Navistar	$.00	.00%	$4.88	$4.50		1	-7.69%	$.00	.00%	-7.69%
			.90%					54.76%		1.00%	55.76%
	BOTTOM TEN:										
21	General Electric	$2.52	2.88%	$87.38	$46.50		2	6.44%	$2.58	2.95%	9.39%
22	Woolworth	$1.12	2.84%	$39.38	$36.38		2	-7.62%	$1.27	3.23%	-4.39%
23	American Express	$1.44	2.49%	$57.88	$24.00		2	-17.06%	$1.50	2.59%	-14.47%
24	Westinghouse Electric	$1.40	2.40%	$58.25	$51.25		1	-12.02%	$1.64	2.82%	-9.20%
25	Owens-Illinois	$.95	1.80%	$52.88	$60.13		1	13.71%	$1.87	3.54%	17.25%
26	Merck	$2.20	1.75%	$126.00	$164.38		1	30.46%	$2.45	1.94%	32.40%
27	INCO	$.20	1.68%	$11.88	$22.25		1	87.37%	$.20	1.68%	89.05%
28	McDonald's Corp.	$.66	1.06%	$62.00	$45.50		1.5	10.08%	$.85	1.37%	11.45%
29	Bethlehem Steel	$.00	.00%	$7.00	$17.75		1	153.57%	$.00	.00%	153.57%
30	Navistar	$.00	.00%	$4.88	$4.50		1	-7.69%	$.00	.00%	-7.69%
			1.69%					25.72%		2.01%	27.74%
	TOP TEN:										
1	Texaco	$3.00	8.16%	$36.75	$37.25		1	1.36%	$.75	2.04%	3.40%
2	General Motors	$5.00	7.48%	$66.88	$63.25		1	-5.42%	$5.00	7.48%	2.06%
3	Union Carbide	$1.50	6.56%	$22.88	$22.63		1	-1.09%	$1.50	6.56%	5.46%
4	USX	$1.20	5.49%	$21.88	$31.50		1	44.00%	$1.20	5.49%	49.49%
5	Chevron	$2.40	5.22%	$46.00	$41.63		1	-9.51%	$2.40	5.22%	-4.29%
6	Exxon	$3.60	5.00%	$72.00	$40.50		2	12.50%	$3.80	5.28%	17.78%
7	American T & T	$1.20	4.75%	$25.25	$28.25		1	11.88%	$1.20	4.75%	16.63%
8	Allied-Signal	$1.80	4.43%	$40.63	$30.88		1	-24.00%	$1.80	4.43%	-19.57%
9	Sears, Roebuck	$1.76	4.29%	$41.00	$35.38		1	-13.72%	$1.94	4.73%	-8.99%
10	Philip Morris	$3.00	4.08%	$73.50	$87.63		1	19.22%	$3.00	4.08%	23.30%
			5.71%					1.78%		5.11%	6.89%
	TOP FIVE:										
1	Texaco	$3.00	8.16%	$36.75	$37.25		1	1.36%	$.75	2.04%	3.40%
2	General Motors	$5.00	7.48%	$66.88	$63.25		1	-5.42%	$5.00	7.48%	2.06%
3	Union Carbide	$1.50	6.56%	$22.88	$22.63		1	-1.09%	$1.50	6.56%	5.46%
4	USX	$1.20	5.49%	$21.88	$31.50		1	44.00%	$1.20	5.49%	49.49%
5	Chevron	$2.40	5.22%	$46.00	$41.63		1	-9.51%	$2.40	5.22%	-4.29%
			6.58%					5.87%		5.36%	11.22%

LIST OF 1986 DOW JONES INDUSTRIALS BY DIVIDEND-YIELD

	STOCK 1986	1986 WSJ DIVI.	1986 WSJ YIELD	1986 OPENING PRICE	1986 CLOSING PRICE	1986 STOCK DIV.	1986 SPLIT	1986 APPRECIATION	1986 DIVIDEND	ACT. CASH YIELD	TOTAL RETURN
1	Texaco	$3.00	9.76%	$30.75	$36.75			19.51%	$3.00	9.76%	29.27%
2	General Motors	$5.00	7.05%	$70.88	$66.88		1	-5.64%	$5.00	7.05%	1.41%
3	Exxon	$3.60	6.61%	$54.50	$72.00		1	32.11%	$3.60	6.61%	38.72%
4	Chevron	$2.40	6.40%	$37.50	$46.00		1	22.67%	$2.40	6.40%	29.07%
5	Goodyear	$1.60	5.16%	$31.00	$42.88		1	38.31%	$1.60	5.16%	43.47%
6	American T & T	$1.20	4.87%	$24.63	$25.25		1	2.54%	$1.20	4.87%	7.41%
7	American Can	$2.90	4.82%	$60.13	$85.38		1	42.00%	$2.90	4.82%	46.82%
8	International Paper	$2.40	4.80%	$50.00	$76.13		1	52.25%	$2.40	4.80%	57.05%
9	Union Carbide	$3.40	4.64%	$73.25	$22.88		3	-6.31%	$4.50	6.14%	-.17%
10	Sears, Roebuck	$1.76	4.57%	$38.50	$41.00		1	6.49%	$1.76	4.57%	11.06%
11	US Steel	$1.20	4.53%	$26.50	$21.88		1	-17.45%	$1.20	4.53%	-12.92%
* 12	Philip Morris	$4.00	4.53%	$88.38	$73.50		2	66.34%	$4.45	5.04%	71.37%
13	Du Pont	$3.00	4.52%	$66.38	$85.88		1	29.38%	$3.05	4.60%	33.97%
14	Eastman Kodak	$2.20	4.33%	$50.75	$69.25		1	36.45%	$2.61	5.14%	41.60%
15	Minnessota Mng. & Mfg.	$3.50	3.95%	$88.63	$117.88		1	33.00%	$3.60	4.06%	37.07%
16	Allied Signal	$1.80	3.76%	$47.88	$40.63	11.81%	1	-3.33%	$1.80	3.76%	.43%
17	Procter & Gamble	$2.60	3.75%	$69.25	$77.63		1	12.09%	$2.68	3.86%	15.96%
18	Owens-Illinois	$1.80	3.44%	$52.38	$52.88		2	101.91%	$1.87	3.57%	105.48%
19	Woolworth	$2.00	3.38%	$59.13	$39.38		2	33.19%	$2.18	3.69%	36.88%
20	General Electric	$2.32	3.23%	$71.88	$87.38		1	21.57%	$2.32	3.23%	24.79%
21	United Technologies	$1.40	3.17%	$44.13	$46.75		1	5.95%	$1.40	3.17%	9.12%
22	Aluminum Co of Amer	$1.20	3.13%	$38.38	$35.13		1	-8.47%	$1.20	3.13%	-5.34%
23	I.B.M.	$4.40	2.89%	$152.00	$122.00		1	-19.74%	$4.40	2.89%	-16.84%
24	Westinghouse Electric	$1.20	2.73%	$44.00	$58.25		1	32.39%	$1.35	3.07%	35.45%
25	Merck	$3.60	2.61%	$138.00	$126.00		2	82.61%	$3.80	2.75%	85.36%
26	American Express	$1.36	2.57%	$52.88	$57.88		1	9.46%	$1.36	2.57%	12.03%
27	INCO	$.20	1.54%	$13.00	$11.88		1	-8.65%	$.20	1.54%	-7.12%
* 28	McDonald's Corp.	$.90	1.14%	$79.25	$62.00		1.5	17.35%	$.97	1.22%	18.57%
29	Bethlehem Steel	$.00	.00%	$15.38	$7.00		1	-54.47%	$.00	.00%	-54.47%
30	International Harvester	$.00	.00%	$8.38	$4.88		1	-41.79%	$.00	.00%	-41.79%
	AVERAGE		3.93%					17.72%		4.07%	21.79%

* First year in the Dow 30

STOCK 1986	1986 WSJ DIVI.	1986 WSJ YIELD	1986 OPENING PRICE	1986 CLOSING PRICE	1986 STOCK DIV.	1986 SPLIT	1986 APPRECIATION	1986 DIVIDEND	ACT. CASH YIELD	TOTAL RETURN
BOTTOM FIVE:										
26 American Express	$1.36	2.57%	$52.88	$57.88		1	9.46%	$1.36	2.57%	12.03%
27 INCO	$.20	1.54%	$13.00	$11.88		1	-8.65%	$.20	1.54%	-7.12%
28 McDonald's Corp.	$.90	1.14%	$79.25	$62.00		1.5	17.35%	$.97	1.22%	18.57%
29 Bethlehem Steel	$.00	.00%	$15.38	$7.00		1	-54.47%	$.00	.00%	-54.47%
30 International Harvester	$.00	.00%	$8.38	$4.88		1	-41.79%	$.00	.00%	-41.79%
		1.05%					-15.62%		1.07%	-14.56%
BOTTOM TEN:										
21 United Technologies	$1.40	3.17%	$44.13	$46.75		1	5.95%	$1.40	3.17%	9.12%
22 Aluminum Co of Amer	$1.20	3.13%	$38.38	$35.13		1	-8.47%	$1.20	3.13%	-5.34%
23 I.B.M.	$4.40	2.89%	$152.00	$122.00		1	-19.74%	$4.40	2.89%	-16.84%
24 Westinghouse Electric	$1.20	2.73%	$44.00	$58.25		1	32.39%	$1.35	3.07%	35.45%
25 Merck	$3.60	2.61%	$138.00	$126.00		2	82.61%	$3.80	2.75%	85.36%
26 American Express	$1.36	2.57%	$52.88	$57.88		1	9.46%	$1.36	2.57%	12.03%
27 INCO	$.20	1.54%	$13.00	$11.88		1	-8.65%	$.20	1.54%	-7.12%
28 McDonald's Corp.	$.90	1.14%	$79.25	$62.00		1.5	17.35%	$.97	1.22%	18.57%
29 Bethlehem Steel	$.00	.00%	$15.38	$7.00		1	-54.47%	$.00	.00%	-54.47%
30 International Harvester	$.00	.00%	$8.38	$4.88		1	-41.79%	$.00	.00%	-41.79%
		1.98%					1.46%		2.04%	3.50%
TOP TEN:										
1 Texaco	$3.00	9.76%	$30.75	$36.75		1	19.51%	$3.00	9.76%	29.27%
2 General Motors	$5.00	7.05%	$70.88	$66.88		1	-5.64%	$5.00	7.05%	1.41%
3 Exxon	$3.60	6.61%	$54.50	$72.00		1	32.11%	$3.60	6.61%	38.72%
4 Chevron	$2.40	6.40%	$37.50	$46.00		1	22.67%	$2.40	6.40%	29.07%
5 Goodyear	$1.60	5.16%	$31.00	$42.88		1	38.31%	$1.60	5.16%	43.47%
6 American T & T	$1.20	4.87%	$24.63	$25.25		1	2.54%	$1.20	4.87%	7.41%
7 American Can	$2.90	4.82%	$60.13	$85.38		1	42.00%	$2.90	4.82%	46.82%
8 International Paper	$2.40	4.80%	$50.00	$76.13		1	52.25%	$2.40	4.80%	57.05%
9 Union Carbide	$3.40	4.64%	$73.25	$22.88		3	-6.31%	$4.50	6.14%	-.17%
10 Sears, Roebuck	$1.76	4.57%	$38.50	$41.00		1	6.49%	$1.76	4.57%	11.06%
		6.01%					21.94%		6.18%	28.12%
TOP FIVE:										
1 Texaco	$3.00	9.76%	$30.75	$36.75		1	19.51%	$3.00	9.76%	29.27%
2 General Motors	$5.00	7.05%	$70.88	$66.88		1	-5.64%	$5.00	7.05%	1.41%
3 Exxon	$3.60	6.61%	$54.50	$72.00		1	32.11%	$3.60	6.61%	38.72%
4 Chevron	$2.40	6.40%	$37.50	$46.00		1	22.67%	$2.40	6.40%	29.07%
5 Goodyear	$1.60	5.16%	$31.00	$42.88		1	38.31%	$1.60	5.16%	43.47%
		7.00%					21.39%		7.00%	28.39%

LIST OF 1985 DOW JONES INDUSTRIALS BY DIVIDEND-YIELD

	STOCK 1985	1985 WSJ DIVI.	1985 WSJ YIELD	1985 OPENING PRICE	1985 CLOSING PRICE	1985 STOCK DIV.	1985 SPLIT	1985 APPRECIATION	1985 DIVIDEND	ACT. CASH YIELD	TOTAL RETURN
1	Union Carbide	$3.40	9.19%	$37.00	$73.25		1	97.97%	$3.40	9.19%	107.16%
2	Texaco	$3.00	8.82%	$34.00	$30.75		1	-9.56%	$3.00	8.82%	-.74%
3	Chevron	$2.40	7.90%	$30.38	$37.50		1	23.46%	$2.40	7.90%	31.36%
4	Exxon	$3.40	7.64%	$44.50	$54.50		1	22.47%	$3.45	7.75%	30.22%
5	American T & T	$1.20	6.23%	$19.25	$24.63		1	27.92%	$1.20	6.23%	34.16%
6	Goodyear	$1.60	6.21%	$25.75	$31.00		1	20.39%	$1.60	6.21%	26.60%
7	Du Pont	$3.00	6.15%	$48.75	$66.38		1	36.15%	$3.00	6.15%	42.31%
8	General Motors	$4.75	6.12%	$77.63	$70.88		1	-5.60%	$5.00	6.44%	.84%
+ 9	American Brands	$3.75	5.88%	$63.75	$65.50	3.09%	1	2.75%	$3.90	6.12%	8.86%
10	American Can	$2.90	5.80%	$50.00	$60.13		1	20.25%	$2.90	5.80%	26.05%
11	Sears, Roebuck	$1.76	5.54%	$31.75	$38.50		1	21.26%	$1.76	5.54%	26.80%
12	Allied Corp.	$1.80	5.29%	$34.00	$47.88		1	40.81%	$1.80	5.29%	46.10%
13	Woolworth	$1.80	4.86%	$37.00	$59.13		1	59.80%	$1.95	5.27%	65.07%
14	Procter & Gamble	$2.60	4.62%	$56.25	$69.25		1	23.11%	$2.60	4.62%	27.73%
+ 15	General Foods	$2.50	4.55%	$55.00	$120.00		1	118.18%	$2.48	4.50%	122.68%
16	Eastman Kodak	$3.20	4.51%	$70.88	$50.75		1.5	7.41%	$3.80	5.36%	12.77%
17	International Paper	$2.40	4.51%	$53.25	$50.00		1	-6.10%	$2.40	4.51%	-1.60%
18	Minnesota Mng. & Mfg.	$3.40	4.34%	$78.38	$88.63		1	13.08%	$3.50	4.47%	17.54%
19	Owens-Illinois	$1.68	4.20%	$40.00	$52.38		1	30.94%	$1.74	4.35%	35.29%
20	General Electric	$2.20	3.93%	$56.00	$71.88		1	28.35%	$2.20	3.93%	32.28%
21	US Steel	$1.00	3.88%	$25.75	$26.50		1	2.91%	$1.10	4.27%	7.18%
22	Westinghouse Electric	$1.00	3.85%	$26.00	$44.00		1	69.23%	$1.15	4.42%	73.65%
23	United Technologies	$1.40	3.82%	$36.63	$44.13		1	20.48%	$1.40	3.82%	24.30%
24	I.B.M.	$4.40	3.64%	$121.00	$152.00		1	25.62%	$4.40	3.64%	29.26%
25	Bethlehem Steel	$.60	3.48%	$17.25	$15.38		1	-10.87%	$.30	1.74%	-9.13%
26	American Express	$1.28	3.46%	$37.00	$52.88		1	42.91%	$1.30	3.51%	46.42%
27	Merck	$3.20	3.44%	$93.13	$138.00		1	48.19%	$3.20	3.44%	51.62%
28	Aluminum Co of Amer	$1.20	3.29%	$36.50	$38.38		1	5.14%	$1.20	3.29%	8.42%
29	INCO	$.20	1.63%	$12.25	$13.00		1	6.12%	$.20	1.63%	7.76%
30	International Harvester	$.00	.00%	$8.13	$8.38		1	3.08%	$.00	.00%	3.08%
	AVERAGE		4.89%					26.19%		4.94%	31.14%

+ Last year in the Dow 30

STOCK 1985	1985 WSJ DIVI.	1985 WSJ YIELD	1985 OPENING PRICE	1985 CLOSING PRICE	1985 STOCK DIV.	1985 SPLIT	1985 APPRECIATION	1985 DIVIDEND	ACT. CASH YIELD	TOTAL RETURN
BOTTOM FIVE:										
26 American Express	$1.28	3.46%	$37.00	$52.88		1	42.91%	$1.30	3.51%	46.42%
27 Merck	$3.20	3.44%	$93.13	$138.00		1	48.19%	$3.20	3.44%	51.62%
28 Aluminum Co of Amer	$1.20	3.29%	$36.50	$38.38		1	5.14%	$1.20	3.29%	8.42%
29 INCO	$.20	1.63%	$12.25	$13.00		1	6.12%	$.20	1.63%	7.76%
30 International Harvester	$.00	.00%	$8.13	$8.38		1	3.08%	$.00	.00%	3.08%
		2.36%					21.09%		2.37%	23.46%
BOTTOM TEN:										
21 US Steel	$1.00	3.88%	$25.75	$26.50		1	2.91%	$1.10	4.27%	7.18%
22 Westinghouse Electric	$1.00	3.85%	$26.00	$44.00		1	69.23%	$1.15	4.42%	73.65%
23 United Technologies	$1.40	3.82%	$36.63	$44.13		1	20.48%	$1.40	3.82%	24.30%
24 I.B.M.	$4.40	3.64%	$121.00	$152.00		1	25.62%	$4.40	3.64%	29.26%
25 Bethlehem Steel	$.60	3.48%	$17.25	$15.38		1	-10.87%	$.30	1.74%	-9.13%
26 American Express	$1.28	3.46%	$37.00	$52.88		1	42.91%	$1.30	3.51%	46.42%
27 Merck	$3.20	3.44%	$93.13	$138.00		1	48.19%	$3.20	3.44%	51.62%
28 Aluminum Co of Amer	$1.20	3.29%	$36.50	$38.38		1	5.14%	$1.20	3.29%	8.42%
29 INCO	$.20	1.63%	$12.25	$13.00		1	6.12%	$.20	1.63%	7.76%
30 International Harvester	$.00	.00%	$8.13	$8.38		1	3.08%	$.00	.00%	3.08%
		3.05%					21.28%		2.98%	24.26%
TOP TEN:										
1 Union Carbide	$3.40	9.19%	$37.00	$73.25		1	97.97%	$3.40	9.19%	107.16%
2 Texaco	$3.00	8.82%	$34.00	$30.75		1	-9.56%	$3.00	8.82%	-.74%
3 Chevron	$2.40	7.90%	$30.38	$37.50		1	23.46%	$2.40	7.90%	31.36%
4 Exxon	$3.40	7.64%	$44.50	$54.50		1	22.47%	$3.45	7.75%	30.22%
5 American T & T	$1.20	6.23%	$19.25	$24.63		1	27.92%	$1.20	6.23%	34.16%
6 Goodyear	$1.60	6.21%	$25.75	$31.00		1	20.39%	$1.60	6.21%	26.60%
7 Du Pont	$3.00	6.15%	$48.75	$66.38		1	36.15%	$3.00	6.15%	42.31%
8 General Motors	$4.75	6.12%	$77.63	$70.88	3.09%	1	-5.60%	$5.00	6.44%	.84%
9 American Brands	$3.75	5.88%	$63.75	$65.50		1	2.75%	$3.90	6.12%	8.86%
10 American Can	$2.90	5.80%	$50.00	$60.13		1	20.25%	$2.90	5.80%	26.05%
		7.13%					23.99%		7.20%	31.20%
TOP FIVE:										
1 Union Carbide	$3.40	9.19%	$37.00	$73.25		1	97.97%	$3.40	9.19%	107.16%
2 Texaco	$3.00	8.82%	$34.00	$30.75		1	-9.56%	$3.00	8.82%	-.74%
3 Chevron	$2.40	7.90%	$30.38	$37.50		1	23.46%	$2.40	7.90%	31.36%
4 Exxon	$3.40	7.64%	$44.50	$54.50		1	22.47%	$3.45	7.75%	30.22%
5 American T & T	$1.20	6.23%	$19.25	$24.63		1	27.92%	$1.20	6.23%	34.16%
		7.96%					32.45%		7.98%	40.43%

LIST OF 1984 DOW JONES INDUSTRIALS BY DIVIDEND-YIELD

	STOCK 1984	1984 WSJ DIVI.	1984 WSJ YIELD	1984 OPENING PRICE	1984 CLOSING PRICE	1984 STOCK DIV.	1984 SPLIT	1984 APPRECIATION	1984 DIVIDEND	ACT. CASH YIELD	TOTAL RETURN
1	American T & T	$5.85	9.36%	$62.50	$19.25	75.90%		6.70%	$5.85	9.36%	16.06%
2	Exxon	$3.20	8.74%	$36.63	$44.50		1	21.50%	$3.35	9.15%	30.65%
3	Texaco	$3.00	8.51%	$35.25	$34.00		1	-3.55%	$3.00	8.51%	4.96%
4	Standard Oil CA	$2.40	7.03%	$34.13	$30.38		1	-10.99%	$2.40	7.03%	-3.96%
5	American Can	$2.90	6.25%	$46.38	$50.00		1	7.82%	$2.90	6.25%	14.07%
6	American Brands	$3.60	6.06%	$59.38	$63.75		1	7.37%	$3.71	6.25%	13.62%
7	Union Carbide	$3.40	5.47%	$62.13	$37.00		1	-40.44%	$3.40	5.47%	-34.97%
8	Du Pont	$2.80	5.46%	$51.25	$48.75		1	-4.88%	$2.90	5.66%	.78%
9	Woolworth	$1.80	5.07%	$35.50	$37.00		1	4.23%	$1.80	5.07%	9.30%
10	General Foods	$2.40	4.68%	$51.25	$55.00		1	7.32%	$2.48	4.83%	12.15%
11	Goodyear	$1.40	4.55%	$30.75	$25.75		1	-16.26%	$1.50	4.88%	-11.38%
12	Owens-Illinois	$1.68	4.47%	$37.63	$40.00		1	6.31%	$1.68	4.47%	10.78%
13	Allied Corp.	$2.40	4.31%	$55.63	$34.00		1.5	-8.31%	$2.63	4.73%	-3.59%
14	Procter & Gamble	$2.40	4.21%	$57.00	$56.25		1	-1.32%	$2.50	4.39%	3.07%
15	Sears, Roebuck	$1.52	4.16%	$36.50	$31.75		1	-13.01%	$1.70	4.66%	-8.36%
16	American Express	$1.28	4.11%	$31.13	$37.00		1	18.88%	$1.28	4.11%	22.99%
17	International Paper	$2.40	4.08%	$58.88	$53.25		1	-9.55%	$2.40	4.08%	-5.48%
18	Minnesota Mng. & Mfg.	$3.30	4.01%	$82.25	$78.38		1	-4.71%	$3.40	4.13%	-.58%
19	Eastman Kodak	$3.00	3.90%	$77.00	$70.88		1	-7.95%	$3.55	4.61%	-3.34%
20	General Motors	$2.80	3.78%	$74.13	$77.63	2.71%	1	7.43%	$4.75	6.41%	13.84%
21	United Technologies	$2.60	3.61%	$72.00	$36.63		2	1.74%	$2.75	3.82%	5.56%
22	General Electric	$2.00	3.47%	$57.63	$56.00		1	-2.82%	$2.00	3.47%	.65%
23	Westinghouse Electric	$1.80	3.33%	$54.00	$26.00		2	-3.70%	$1.95	3.61%	-.09%
24	Merck	$3.00	3.32%	$90.38	$93.13		1	3.04%	$3.00	3.32%	6.36%
25	US Steel	$1.00	3.23%	$31.00	$25.75		1	-16.94%	$1.00	3.23%	-13.71%
26	I.B.M.	$3.80	3.12%	$121.75	$121.00		1	-.62%	$4.10	3.37%	2.75%
27	Aluminum Co of Amer	$1.20	2.70%	$44.50	$36.50		1	-17.98%	$1.20	2.70%	-15.28%
28	Bethlehem Steel	$.60	2.15%	$27.88	$17.25		1	-38.12%	$.60	2.15%	-35.96%
29	INCO	$.20	1.37%	$14.63	$12.25		1	-16.24%	$.20	1.37%	-14.87%
30	International Harvester	$.00	.00%	$11.63	$8.13		1	-30.11%	$.00	.00%	-30.11%
	AVERAGE		4.48%					-5.17%		4.70%	-.47%

STOCK 1984	1984 WSJ DIVI.	1984 WSJ YIELD	1984 OPENING PRICE	1984 CLOSING PRICE	1984 STOCK DIV.	1984 SPLIT	1984 APPRECIATION	1984 DIVIDEND	ACT. CASH YIELD	TOTAL RETURN
BOTTOM FIVE:										
26 I.B.M.	$3.80	3.12%	$121.75	$121.00		1	-.62%	$4.10	3.37%	2.75%
27 Aluminum Co of Amer	$1.20	2.70%	$44.50	$36.50		1	-17.98%	$1.20	2.70%	-15.28%
28 Bethlehem Steel	$.60	2.15%	$27.88	$17.25		1	-38.12%	$.60	2.15%	-35.96%
29 INCO	$.20	1.37%	$14.63	$12.25		1	-16.24%	$.20	1.37%	-14.87%
30 International Harvester	$.00	.00%	$11.63	$8.13		1	-30.11%	$.00	.00%	-30.11%
		1.87%					-20.61%		1.92%	-18.69%
BOTTOM TEN:										
21 United Technologies	$2.60	3.61%	$72.00	$36.63		2	1.74%	$2.75	3.82%	5.56%
22 General Electric	$2.00	3.47%	$57.63	$56.00		1	-2.82%	$2.00	3.47%	.65%
23 Westinghouse Electric	$1.80	3.33%	$54.00	$26.00		2	-3.70%	$1.95	3.61%	-.09%
24 Merck	$3.00	3.32%	$90.38	$93.13		1	3.04%	$3.00	3.32%	6.36%
25 US Steel	$1.00	3.23%	$31.00	$25.75		1	-16.94%	$1.00	3.23%	-13.71%
26 I.B.M.	$3.80	3.12%	$121.75	$121.00		1	-.62%	$4.10	3.37%	2.75%
27 Aluminum Co of Amer	$1.20	2.70%	$44.50	$36.50		1	-17.98%	$1.20	2.70%	-15.28%
28 Bethlehem Steel	$.60	2.15%	$27.88	$17.25		1	-38.12%	$.60	2.15%	-35.96%
29 INCO	$.20	1.37%	$14.63	$12.25		1	-16.24%	$.20	1.37%	-14.87%
30 International Harvester	$.00	.00%	$11.63	$8.13		1	-30.11%	$.00	.00%	-30.11%
		2.63%					-12.17%		2.70%	-9.47%
TOP TEN:										
1 American T & T	$5.85	9.36%	$62.50	$19.25	75.90%	1	6.70%	$5.85	9.36%	16.06%
2 Exxon	$3.20	8.74%	$36.63	$44.50		1	21.50%	$3.35	9.15%	30.65%
3 Texaco	$3.00	8.51%	$35.25	$34.00		1	-3.55%	$3.00	8.51%	4.96%
4 Standard Oil CA	$2.40	7.03%	$34.13	$30.38		1	-10.99%	$2.40	7.03%	-3.96%
5 American Can	$2.90	6.25%	$46.38	$50.00		1	7.82%	$2.90	6.25%	14.07%
6 American Brands	$3.60	6.06%	$59.38	$63.75		1	7.37%	$3.71	6.25%	13.62%
7 Union Carbide	$3.40	5.47%	$62.13	$37.00		1	-40.44%	$3.40	5.47%	-34.97%
8 Du Pont	$2.80	5.46%	$51.25	$48.75		1	-4.88%	$2.90	5.66%	-.78%
9 Woolworth	$1.80	5.07%	$35.50	$37.00		1	4.23%	$1.80	5.07%	9.30%
10 General Foods	$2.40	4.68%	$51.25	$55.00		1	7.32%	$2.48	4.83%	12.15%
		6.66%					-.49%		6.76%	6.27%
TOP FIVE:										
1 American T & T	$5.85	9.36%	$62.50	$66.69		1	6.70%	$5.85	9.36%	16.06%
2 Exxon	$3.20	8.74%	$36.63	$44.50		1	21.50%	$3.35	9.15%	30.65%
3 Texaco	$3.00	8.51%	$35.25	$34.00		1	-3.55%	$3.00	8.51%	4.96%
4 Standard Oil CA	$2.40	7.03%	$34.13	$30.38		1	-10.99%	$2.40	7.03%	-3.96%
5 American Can	$2.90	6.25%	$46.38	$50.00		1	7.82%	$2.90	6.25%	14.07%
		7.98%					4.30%		8.06%	12.36%

LIST OF 1983 DOW JONES INDUSTRIALS BY DIVIDEND-YIELD

STOCK 1983	1983 WSJ DIVI.	1983 WSJ YIELD	1983 OPENING PRICE	1983 CLOSING PRICE	1983 STOCK DIV.	1983 SPLIT	1983 APPRECIATION	1983 DIVIDEND	ACT. CASH YIELD	TOTAL RETURN
1 Exxon	$3.00	10.34%	$29.00	$36.63		1	26.29%	$3.10	10.69%	36.98%
2 Texaco	$3.00	9.80%	$30.63	$35.25		1	15.10%	$3.00	9.80%	24.90%
3 American Can	$2.90	9.43%	$30.75	$46.38		1	50.81%	$2.90	9.43%	60.24%
4 American T & T	$5.40	9.02%	$59.88	$62.50		1	4.38%	$5.85	9.77%	14.15%
5 American Brands	$3.50	7.69%	$45.50	$59.38		1	30.49%	$3.55	7.80%	38.30%
6 Standard Oil CA	$2.40	7.68%	$31.25	$34.13		1	9.20%	$2.40	7.68%	16.88%
7 Allied Corp.	$2.40	7.38%	$32.50	$55.63		1	71.15%	$2.40	7.38%	78.54%
8 Woolworth	$1.80	6.99%	$25.75	$35.50		1	37.86%	$1.80	6.99%	44.85%
9 Du Pont	$2.40	6.69%	$35.88	$51.25		1	42.86%	$2.50	6.97%	49.83%
10 Union Carbide	$3.40	6.62%	$51.38	$62.13		1	20.92%	$3.40	6.62%	27.54%
11 General Foods	$2.40	6.10%	$39.38	$51.25		1	30.16%	$2.40	6.10%	36.25%
12 Owens-Illinois	$1.68	5.79%	$29.00	$37.63		1	29.74%	$1.68	5.79%	35.53%
13 International Paper	$2.40	5.11%	$47.00	$58.88		1	25.27%	$2.40	5.11%	30.37%
14 Bethlehem Steel	$1.00	5.06%	$19.75	$27.88		1	41.14%	$.60	3.04%	44.18%
15 US Steel	$1.00	4.82%	$20.75	$31.00		1	49.40%	$1.00	4.82%	54.22%
16 Westinghouse Electric	$1.80	4.80%	$37.50	$54.00		1	44.00%	$1.80	4.80%	48.80%
17 Sears, Roebuck	$1.36	4.65%	$29.25	$36.50		1	24.79%	$1.48	5.06%	29.85%
18 United Technologies	$2.40	4.42%	$54.25	$72.00		1	32.72%	$2.55	4.70%	37.42%
19 Minnesota Mng. & Mfg.	$3.20	4.37%	$73.25	$82.25		1	12.29%	$3.30	4.51%	16.79%
20 Aluminum Co of Amer	$1.20	4.05%	$29.63	$44.50		1	60.40%	$1.20	4.05%	64.45%
21 Goodyear	$1.40	4.03%	$34.75	$30.75		1	-11.51%	$1.40	4.03%	-7.48%
22 General Motors	$2.40	3.93%	$61.00	$74.13		1	21.52%	$2.80	4.59%	26.11%
23 American Express	$2.40	3.91%	$61.38	$31.13		2	1.43%	$2.48	4.04%	5.47%
24 General Electric	$3.40	3.71%	$91.75	$57.63		2	25.61%	$3.60	3.92%	29.54%
25 I.B.M.	$3.44	3.70%	$93.00	$121.75		1	30.91%	$3.71	3.99%	34.90%
26 Procter & Gamble	$4.20	3.62%	$116.00	$57.00		2	-1.72%	$4.80	4.14%	2.41%
27 Eastman Kodak	$3.00	3.52%	$85.13	$77.00		1	-9.54%	$3.55	4.17%	-5.37%
28 Merck	$2.80	3.33%	$84.00	$90.38		1	7.59%	$2.80	3.33%	10.92%
29 INCO	$.20	1.68%	$11.88	$14.63		1	23.16%	$.20	1.68%	24.84%
30 International Harvester	$.00	.00%	$4.38	$11.63	6.78%	1	165.71%	$.00	.00%	165.71%
AVERAGE		5.41%					30.40%		5.50%	35.90%

* First year in the Dow 30

STOCK 1983	1983 WSJ DIVI.	1983 WSJ YIELD	1983 OPENING PRICE	1983 CLOSING PRICE	1983 STOCK DIV.	1983 SPLIT	1983 APPRECIATION	1983 DIVIDEND	ACT. CASH YIELD	TOTAL RETURN
BOTTOM FIVE:										
26 Procter & Gamble	$4.20	3.62%	$116.00	$57.00		2	-1.72%	$4.80	4.14%	2.41%
27 Eastman Kodak	$3.00	3.52%	$85.13	$77.00		1	-9.54%	$3.55	4.17%	-5.37%
28 Merck	$2.80	3.33%	$84.00	$90.38		1	7.59%	$2.80	3.33%	10.92%
29 INCO	$.20	1.68%	$11.88	$14.63		1	23.16%	$.20	1.68%	24.84%
30 International Harvester	$.00	.00%	$4.38	$11.63		1	165.71%	$.00	.00%	165.71%
		2.43%					37.04%		2.67%	39.70%
BOTTOM TEN:										
21 Goodyear	$1.40	4.03%	$34.75	$30.75		1	-11.51%	$1.40	4.03%	-7.48%
22 General Motors	$2.40	3.93%	$61.00	$74.13		1	21.52%	$2.80	4.59%	26.11%
23 American Express	$2.40	3.91%	$61.38	$31.13		2	1.43%	$2.48	4.04%	5.47%
24 General Electric	$3.40	3.71%	$91.75	$57.63		2	25.61%	$3.60	3.92%	29.54%
25 I.B.M.	$3.44	3.70%	$93.00	$121.75		2	30.91%	$3.71	3.99%	34.90%
26 Procter & Gamble	$4.20	3.62%	$116.00	$57.00		2	-1.72%	$4.80	4.14%	2.41%
27 Eastman Kodak	$3.00	3.52%	$85.13	$77.00		1	-9.54%	$3.55	4.17%	-5.37%
28 Merck	$2.80	3.33%	$84.00	$90.38		1	7.59%	$2.80	3.33%	10.92%
29 INCO	$.20	1.68%	$11.88	$14.63		1	23.16%	$.20	1.68%	24.84%
30 International Harvester	$.00	.00%	$4.38	$11.63		1	165.71%	$.00	.00%	165.71%
		3.14%					25.32%		3.39%	28.70%
TOP TEN:										
1 Exxon	$3.00	10.34%	$29.00	$36.63		1	26.29%	$3.10	10.69%	36.98%
2 Texaco	$3.00	9.80%	$30.63	$35.25		1	15.10%	$3.00	9.80%	24.90%
3 American Can	$2.90	9.43%	$30.75	$46.38		1	50.81%	$2.90	9.43%	60.24%
4 American T & T	$5.40	9.02%	$59.88	$62.50		1	4.38%	$5.85	9.77%	14.15%
5 American Brands	$3.50	7.69%	$45.50	$59.38		1	30.49%	$3.55	7.80%	38.30%
6 Standard Oil CA	$2.40	7.68%	$31.25	$34.13		1	9.20%	$2.40	7.68%	16.88%
7 Allied Corp.	$2.40	7.38%	$32.50	$55.63		1	71.15%	$2.40	7.38%	78.54%
8 Woolworth	$1.80	6.99%	$25.75	$35.50		1	37.86%	$1.80	6.99%	44.85%
9 Du Pont	$2.40	6.69%	$35.88	$51.25		1	42.86%	$2.50	6.97%	49.83%
10 Union Carbide	$3.40	6.62%	$51.38	$62.13		1	20.92%	$3.40	6.62%	27.54%
		8.16%					30.91%		8.31%	39.22%
TOP FIVE:										
1 Exxon	$3.00	10.34%	$29.00	$36.63		1	26.29%	$3.10	10.69%	36.98%
2 Texaco	$3.00	9.80%	$30.63	$35.25		1	15.10%	$3.00	9.80%	24.90%
3 American Can	$2.90	9.43%	$30.75	$46.38		1	50.81%	$2.90	9.43%	60.24%
4 American T & T	$5.40	9.02%	$59.88	$62.50		1	4.38%	$5.85	9.77%	14.15%
5 American Brands	$3.50	7.69%	$45.50	$59.38		1	30.49%	$3.55	7.80%	38.30%
		9.26%					25.42%		9.50%	34.92%

126

LIST OF 1982 DOW JONES INDUSTRIALS BY DIVIDEND-YIELD

STOCK 1982	1982 WSJ DIVI.	1982 WSJ YIELD	1982 OPENING PRICE	1982 CLOSING PRICE	1982 STOCK DIV.	1982 SPLIT	1982 APPRECIATION	1982 DIVIDEND	ACT. CASH YIELD	TOTAL RETURN
1 Johns-Manville	$1.92	12.91%	$14.88	$11.00			-26.05%	$.68	4.57%	-21.48%
2 Woolworth	$1.80	9.86%	$18.25	$25.75		1	41.10%	$1.80	9.86%	50.96%
3 Exxon	$3.00	9.72%	$30.88	$29.00		1	-6.07%	$3.00	9.72%	3.64%
4 American T & T	$5.40	9.23%	$58.50	$59.88		1	2.35%	$5.40	9.23%	11.58%
5 Texaco	$3.00	9.06%	$33.13	$30.63		1	-7.55%	$3.00	9.06%	1.51%
6 American Brands	$3.25	8.84%	$36.75	$45.50		1	23.81%	$3.50	9.52%	33.33%
7 American Can	$2.90	8.14%	$35.63	$30.75		1	-13.68%	$2.90	8.14%	-5.54%
8 Sears, Roebuck	$1.36	8.06%	$16.88	$29.25		1	73.33%	$1.36	8.06%	81.39%
9 General Foods	$2.20	6.93%	$31.75	$39.38		1	24.02%	$2.25	7.09%	31.10%
10 Aluminum Co of Amer	$1.80	6.92%	$26.00	$29.63		1	13.94%	$1.65	6.35%	20.29%
11 Goodyear	$1.30	6.89%	$18.88	$34.75		1	84.11%	$1.40	7.42%	91.52%
12 Bethlehem Steel	$1.60	6.81%	$23.50	$19.75		1	-15.96%	$1.30	5.53%	-10.43%
13 Westinghouse Electric	$1.80	6.79%	$26.50	$37.50		1	41.51%	$1.80	6.79%	48.30%
14 Union Carbide	$3.40	6.67%	$51.00	$51.38		1	.74%	$3.40	6.67%	7.40%
15 US Steel	$2.00	6.67%	$30.00	$20.75		1	-30.83%	$1.75	5.83%	-25.00%
16 Du Pont	$2.40	6.27%	$38.25	$35.88		1	-6.21%	$2.40	6.27%	.07%
17 International Paper	$2.40	6.11%	$39.25	$47.00		1	19.75%	$2.40	6.11%	25.86%
18 General Motors	$2.40	6.04%	$39.75	$61.00		1	53.46%	$2.40	6.04%	59.50%
19 I.B.M.	$3.44	5.91%	$58.25	$93.00		1	59.66%	$3.44	5.91%	65.56%
20 Standard Oil CA	$2.40	5.77%	$41.63	$31.25		1	-24.92%	$2.40	5.77%	-19.16%
21 United Technologies	$2.40	5.65%	$42.50	$54.25		1	27.65%	$2.40	5.65%	33.29%
22 Minnesota Mng. & Mfg.	$3.00	5.53%	$54.25	$73.25		1	35.02%	$3.20	5.90%	40.92%
23 General Electric	$3.20	5.45%	$58.75	$91.75		1	56.17%	$3.30	5.62%	61.79%
24 Owens-Illinois	$1.56	5.38%	$29.00	$29.00		1		$1.68	5.79%	5.79%
25 Allied Corp.	$2.40	5.30%	$45.25	$32.50		1	-28.18%	$2.40	5.30%	-22.87%
26 Procter & Gamble	$4.20	5.23%	$80.38	$116.00		1	44.32%	$4.20	5.23%	49.55%
27 Eastman Kodak	$3.00	4.11%	$73.00	$85.13		1	16.61%	$3.50	4.79%	21.40%
28 Merck	$2.80	3.27%	$85.50	$84.00		1	-1.75%	$2.80	3.27%	1.52%
29 INCO	$.20	1.37%	$14.63	$11.88		1	-18.80%	$.20	1.37%	-17.44%
30 International Harvester	$.00	.00%	$7.25	$4.38		1	-39.66%	$.00	.00%	-39.66%
AVERAGE		6.50%					13.26%		6.23%	19.49%

+ Last year in the Dow 30

STOCK	1982	1982 WSJ DIVI.	1982 WSJ YIELD	1982 OPENING PRICE	1982 CLOSING PRICE	1982 STOCK DIV.	1982 SPLIT	1982 APPRECIATION	1982 DIVIDEND	ACT. CASH YIELD	TOTAL RETURN
BOTTOM FIVE:											
26 Procter & Gamble	$4.20	5.23%	$80.38	$116.00		1	44.32%	$4.20	5.23%	49.55%
27 Eastman Kodak	$3.00	4.11%	$73.00	$85.13		1	16.61%	$3.50	4.79%	21.40%
28 Merck	$2.80	3.27%	$85.50	$84.00		1	-1.75%	$2.80	3.27%	1.52%
29 INCO	$.20	1.37%	$14.63	$11.88		1	-18.80%	$.20	1.37%	-17.44%
30 International Harvester	$.00	.00%	$7.25	$4.38		1	-39.66%	$.00	.00%	-39.66%
		2.80%						.14%		2.93%	3.08%
BOTTOM TEN:											
21 United Technologies	$2.40	5.65%	$42.50	$54.25		1	27.65%	$2.40	5.65%	33.29%
22 Minnesota Mng. & Mfg.	$3.00	5.53%	$54.25	$73.25		1	35.02%	$3.20	5.90%	40.92%
23 General Electric	$3.20	5.45%	$58.75	$91.75		1	56.17%	$3.30	5.62%	61.79%
24 Owens-Illinois	$1.56	5.38%	$29.00	$29.00		1		$1.68	5.79%	5.79%
25 Allied Chemical	$2.40	5.30%	$45.25	$32.50		1	-28.18%	$2.40	5.30%	-22.87%
26 Procter & Gamble	$4.20	5.23%	$80.38	$116.00		1	44.32%	$4.20	5.23%	49.55%
27 Eastman Kodak	$3.00	4.11%	$73.00	$85.13		1	16.61%	$3.50	4.79%	21.40%
28 Merck	$2.80	3.27%	$85.50	$84.00		1	-1.75%	$2.80	3.27%	1.52%
29 INCO	$.20	1.37%	$14.63	$11.88		1	-18.80%	$.20	1.37%	-17.44%
30 International Harvester	$.00	.00%	$7.25	$4.38		1	-39.66%	$.00	.00%	-39.66%
		4.13%						9.14%		4.29%	13.43%
TOP TEN:											
1 Johns-Manville	$1.92	12.91%	$14.88	$11.00		1	-26.05%	$.68	4.57%	-21.48%
2 Woolworth	$1.80	9.86%	$18.25	$25.75		1	41.10%	$1.80	9.86%	50.96%
3 Exxon	$3.00	9.72%	$30.88	$29.00		1	-6.07%	$3.00	9.72%	3.64%
4 American T & T	$5.40	9.23%	$58.50	$59.88		1	2.35%	$5.40	9.23%	11.58%
5 Texaco	$3.00	9.06%	$33.13	$30.63		1	-7.55%	$3.00	9.06%	1.51%
6 American Brands	$3.25	8.84%	$36.75	$45.50		1	23.81%	$3.50	9.52%	33.33%
7 American Can	$2.90	8.14%	$35.63	$30.75		1	-13.68%	$2.90	8.14%	-5.54%
8 Sears, Roebuck	$1.36	8.06%	$16.88	$29.25		1	73.33%	$1.36	8.06%	81.39%
9 General Foods	$2.20	6.93%	$31.75	$39.38		1	24.02%	$2.25	7.09%	31.10%
10 Aluminum Co of Amer	$1.80	6.92%	$26.00	$29.63		1	13.94%	$1.65	6.35%	20.29%
		8.97%						12.52%		8.16%	20.68%
TOP FIVE:											
1 Johns-Manville	$1.92	12.91%	$14.88	$11.00		1	-26.05%	$.68	4.57%	-21.48%
2 Woolworth	$1.80	9.86%	$18.25	$25.75		1	41.10%	$1.80	9.86%	50.96%
3 Exxon	$3.00	9.72%	$30.88	$29.00		1	-6.07%	$3.00	9.72%	3.64%
4 American T & T	$5.40	9.23%	$58.50	$59.88		1	2.35%	$5.40	9.23%	11.58%
5 Texaco	$3.00	9.06%	$33.13	$30.63		1	-7.55%	$3.00	9.06%	1.51%
		10.15%						.76%		8.49%	9.24%

LIST OF 1981 DOW JONES INDUSTRIALS BY DIVIDEND-YIELD

	STOCK 1981	1981 WSJ DIVI.	1981 WSJ YIELD	1981 OPENING PRICE	1981 CLOSING PRICE	1981 STOCK DIV.	1981 SPLIT	1981 APPRECIATION	1981 DIVIDEND	ACT. CASH YIELD	TOTAL RETURN
1	American T & T	$5.00	10.23%	$48.88	$58.50		1	19.69%	$5.00	10.23%	29.92%
2	American Can	$2.90	9.35%	$31.00	$35.63		1	14.92%	$2.90	9.35%	24.27%
3	Sears, Roebuck	$1.36	8.77%	$15.50	$16.88		1	8.87%	$1.36	8.77%	17.65%
4	American Brands	$6.20	7.99%	$77.63	$36.75		2	-5.31%	$6.43	8.28%	2.97%
5	Johns-Manville	$1.92	7.72%	$24.88	$14.88		1	-40.20%	$1.92	7.72%	-32.48%
6	Goodyear	$1.30	7.48%	$17.38	$18.88		1	8.63%	$1.30	7.48%	16.12%
7	Exxon	$6.00	7.40%	$81.13	$30.88		2	-23.88%	$6.00	7.40%	-16.49%
8	General Foods	$2.20	7.27%	$30.25	$31.75		1	4.96%	$2.20	7.27%	12.23%
9	Woolworth	$1.80	7.20%	$25.00	$18.25		1	-27.00%	$1.80	7.20%	-19.80%
10	General Motors	$2.95	6.47%	$45.63	$39.75		1	-12.88%	$2.40	5.26%	-7.62%
11	Union Carbide	$3.20	6.32%	$50.63	$51.00		1	.74%	$3.30	6.52%	7.26%
12	US Steel	$1.60	6.24%	$25.63	$30.00		1	17.07%	$2.00	7.80%	24.88%
13	Bethlehem Steel	$1.60	6.10%	$26.25	$23.50		1	-10.48%	$1.60	6.10%	-4.38%
14	International Paper	$2.40	5.63%	$42.63	$39.25		1	-7.92%	$2.40	5.63%	-2.29%
15	Procter & Gamble	$3.80	5.58%	$68.13	$80.38		1	17.98%	$3.90	5.72%	23.71%
16	Owens-Illinois	$1.40	5.54%	$25.25	$29.00		1	14.85%	$1.56	6.18%	21.03%
17	Texaco	$2.60	5.29%	$49.13	$33.13		1	-32.57%	$2.80	5.70%	-26.87%
18	Aluminum Co of Amer	$3.20	5.26%	$60.88	$26.00		2	-14.58%	$3.60	5.91%	-8.67%
19	I.B.M.	$3.44	4.98%	$69.13	$58.25		1	-15.73%	$3.44	4.98%	-10.76%
20	General Electric	$3.00	4.85%	$61.88	$58.75		1	-5.05%	$3.10	5.01%	-.04%
21	Du Pont	$2.00	4.76%	$42.00	$38.25		1	-8.93%	$2.75	6.55%	-2.38%
22	International Harvester	$1.20	4.73%	$25.38	$7.25		1	-71.43%	$.30	1.18%	-70.25%
23	Minnessota Mng. & Mfg.	$2.80	4.73%	$59.25	$54.25		1	-8.44%	$3.00	5.06%	-3.38%
24	Westinghouse Electric	$1.40	4.71%	$29.75	$26.50		1	-10.92%	$1.80	6.05%	-4.87%
25	Eastman Kodak	$3.00	4.21%	$71.25	$73.00		1	2.46%	$3.50	4.91%	7.37%
26	Allied Chemical	$2.20	4.07%	$54.00	$45.25		1	-16.20%	$2.35	4.35%	-11.85%
27	Standard Oil CA	$4.00	4.03%	$99.25	$41.63		2	-16.12%	$4.40	4.43%	-11.69%
28	United Technologies	$2.20	3.58%	$61.38	$42.50		1	-30.75%	$2.40	3.91%	-26.84%
29	INCO	$.72	3.49%	$20.63	$14.63		1	-29.09%	$.59	2.86%	-26.23%
30	Merck	$2.60	3.02%	$86.00	$85.50		1	-.58%	$2.60	3.02%	2.44%
	AVERAGE		5.90%					-9.26%		6.03%	-3.23%

STOCK	1981	1981 WSJ DIVI.	1981 WSJ YIELD	1981 OPENING PRICE	1981 CLOSING PRICE	1981 STOCK DIV.	1981 SPLIT	1981 APPRECIATION	1981 DIVIDEND	ACT. CASH YIELD	TOTAL RETURN
	BOTTOM FIVE:										
26	Allied Chemical	$2.20	4.07%	$54.00	$45.25		1	-16.20%	$2.35	4.35%	-11.85%
27	Standard Oil CA	$4.00	4.03%	$99.25	$41.63		2	-16.12%	$4.40	4.43%	-11.69%
28	United Technologies	$2.20	3.58%	$61.38	$42.50		1	-30.75%	$2.40	3.91%	-26.84%
29	INCO	$.72	3.49%	$20.63	$14.63		1	-29.09%	$.59	2.86%	-26.23%
30	Merck	$2.60	3.02%	$86.00	$85.50		1	-.58%	$2.60	3.02%	2.44%
			3.64%					-18.55%		3.72%	-14.83%
	BOTTOM TEN:										
21	Du Pont	$2.00	4.76%	$42.00	$38.25		1	-8.93%	$2.75	6.55%	-2.38%
22	International Harvester	$1.20	4.73%	$25.38	$7.25		1	-71.43%	$.30	1.18%	-70.25%
23	Minnessota Mng. & Mfg.	$2.80	4.73%	$59.25	$54.25		1	-8.44%	$3.00	5.06%	-3.38%
24	Westinghouse Electric	$1.40	4.71%	$29.75	$26.50		1	-10.92%	$1.80	6.05%	-4.87%
25	Eastman Kodak	$3.00	4.21%	$71.25	$73.00		1	2.46%	$3.50	4.91%	7.37%
26	Allied Chemical	$2.20	4.07%	$54.00	$45.25		1	-16.20%	$2.35	4.35%	-11.85%
27	Standard Oil CA	$4.00	4.03%	$99.25	$41.63		2	-16.12%	$4.40	4.43%	-11.69%
28	United Technologies	$2.20	3.58%	$61.38	$42.50		1	-30.75%	$2.40	3.91%	-26.84%
29	INCO	$.72	3.49%	$20.63	$14.63		1	-29.09%	$.59	2.86%	-26.23%
30	Merck	$2.60	3.02%	$86.00	$85.50		1	-.58%	$2.60	3.02%	2.44%
			4.13%					-19.00%		4.23%	-14.77%
	TOP TEN:										
1	American T & T	$5.00	10.23%	$48.88	$58.50		1	19.69%	$5.00	10.23%	29.92%
2	American Can	$2.90	9.35%	$31.00	$35.63		1	14.92%	$2.90	9.35%	24.27%
3	Sears, Roebuck	$1.36	8.77%	$15.50	$16.88		1	8.87%	$1.36	8.77%	17.65%
4	American Brands	$6.20	7.99%	$77.63	$36.75		2	-5.31%	$6.43	8.28%	2.97%
5	Johns-Manville	$1.92	7.72%	$24.88	$14.88		1	-40.20%	$1.92	7.72%	-32.48%
6	Goodyear	$1.30	7.48%	$17.38	$18.88		1	8.63%	$1.30	7.48%	16.12%
7	Exxon	$6.00	7.40%	$81.13	$30.88		2	-23.88%	$6.00	7.40%	-16.49%
8	General Foods	$2.20	7.27%	$30.25	$31.75		1	4.96%	$2.20	7.27%	12.23%
9	Woolworth	$1.80	7.20%	$25.00	$18.25		1	-27.00%	$1.80	7.20%	-19.80%
10	General Motors	$2.95	6.47%	$45.63	$39.75		1	-12.88%	$2.40	5.26%	-7.62%
			7.99%					-5.22%		7.90%	2.68%
	TOP FIVE:										
1	American T & T	$5.00	10.23%	$48.88	$58.50		1	19.69%	$5.00	10.23%	29.92%
2	American Can	$2.90	9.35%	$31.00	$35.63		1	14.92%	$2.90	9.35%	24.27%
3	Sears, Roebuck	$1.36	8.77%	$15.50	$16.88		1	8.87%	$1.36	8.77%	17.65%
4	American Brands	$6.20	7.99%	$77.63	$36.75		2	-5.31%	$6.43	8.28%	2.97%
5	Johns-Manville	$1.92	7.72%	$24.88	$14.88		1	-40.20%	$1.92	7.72%	-32.48%
			8.81%					-.41%		8.87%	8.47%

LIST OF 1980 DOW JONES INDUSTRIALS BY DIVIDEND-YIELD

	STOCK 1980	1980 WSJ DIVI.	1980 WSJ YIELD	1980 OPENING PRICE	1980 CLOSING PRICE	1980 STOCK DIV.	1980 SPLIT	1980 APPRECIATION	1980 DIVIDEND	ACT. CASH YIELD	TOTAL RETURN
1	General Motors	$6.00	12.15%	$49.38	$45.63		1	-7.59%	$2.95	5.97%	-1.62%
2	Goodyear	$1.30	10.10%	$12.88	$17.38		1	34.95%	$1.30	10.10%	45.05%
3	US Steel	$1.60	8.89%	$18.00	$25.63		1	42.36%	$1.60	8.89%	51.25%
4	American T & T	$4.60	8.85%	$52.00	$48.88		1	-6.01%	$5.00	9.62%	3.61%
5	American Can	$2.80	8.03%	$34.88	$31.00		1	-11.11%	$2.90	8.32%	-2.80%
6	Johns-Manville	$1.80	7.54%	$23.88	$24.88		1	4.19%	$1.92	8.04%	12.23%
7	Texaco	$2.00	7.14%	$28.00	$49.13		1	75.45%	$2.45	8.75%	84.20%
8	Union Carbide	$2.80	6.77%	$41.38	$50.63		1	22.36%	$3.10	7.49%	29.85%
9	Exxon	$3.40	6.31%	$53.88	$81.13		1	50.58%	$5.40	10.02%	60.60%
10	Sears, Roebuck	$1.12	6.18%	$18.13	$15.50		1	-14.48%	$1.34	7.39%	-7.09%
11	International Harvester	$2.30	5.95%	$38.63	$25.38		1	-34.30%	$2.50	6.47%	-27.83%
12	American Brands	$4.00	5.95%	$67.25	$77.63		1	15.43%	$5.90	8.77%	24.20%
13	Woolworth	$1.40	5.74%	$24.38	$25.00		1	2.56%	$1.75	7.18%	9.74%
14	Owens-Illinois	$1.16	5.73%	$20.25	$25.25		1	24.69%	$1.40	6.91%	31.60%
* 15	I.B.M.	$3.44	5.50%	$62.50	$69.13		1	10.60%	$3.44	5.50%	16.10%
16	International Paper	$2.00	5.46%	$36.63	$42.63		1	16.38%	$2.40	6.55%	22.94%
17	General Foods	$1.80	5.37%	$33.50	$30.25		1	-9.70%	$2.15	6.42%	-3.28%
18	General Electric	$2.60	5.33%	$48.75	$61.88		1	26.92%	$2.90	5.95%	32.87%
19	Du Pont	$2.00	5.05%	$39.63	$42.00		1	5.99%	$2.75	6.94%	12.93%
20	Westinghouse Electric	$.97	4.88%	$19.88	$29.75		1	49.69%	$1.40	7.04%	56.73%
21	Bethlehem Steel	$1.00	4.82%	$20.75	$26.25		1	26.51%	$1.60	7.71%	34.22%
22	Standard Oil CA	$2.60	4.79%	$54.25	$99.25		1	82.95%	$3.60	6.64%	89.59%
23	United Technologies	$2.00	4.73%	$42.25	$61.38		1	45.27%	$2.20	5.21%	50.47%
24	Eastman Kodak	$2.00	4.41%	$45.38	$71.25		1	57.02%	$3.05	6.72%	63.75%
25	Allied Chemical	$2.00	4.21%	$47.50	$54.00		1	13.68%	$2.15	4.53%	18.21%
26	Minnesota Mng. & Mfg.	$2.00	4.04%	$49.50	$59.25		1	19.70%	$2.80	5.66%	25.35%
27	Procter & Gamble	$3.00	4.04%	$74.25	$68.13		1	-8.25%	$3.60	4.85%	-3.40%
28	Aluminum Co of Amer	$2.00	3.62%	$55.25	$60.88		1	10.18%	$3.20	5.79%	15.97%
* 29	Merck	$2.30	3.25%	$70.75	$86.00		1	21.55%	$2.30	3.25%	24.81%
30	INCO	$.40	1.67%	$24.00	$20.63		1	-14.06%	$.69	2.88%	-11.19%
	AVERAGE		5.88%					18.45%		6.85%	25.30%

* First year in the Dow 30

STOCK 1980	1980 WSJ DIVI.	1980 WSJ YIELD	1980 OPENING PRICE	1980 CLOSING PRICE	1980 STOCK DIV.	1980 SPLIT	1980 APPRECIATION	1980 DIVIDEND	ACT. CASH YIELD	TOTAL RETURN
BOTTOM FIVE:										
26 Minnessota Mng. & Mfg.	$2.00	4.04%	$49.50	$59.25		1	19.70%	$2.80	5.66%	25.35%
27 Procter & Gamble	$3.00	4.04%	$74.25	$68.13		1	-8.25%	$3.60	4.85%	-3.40%
28 Aluminum Co of Amer	$2.00	3.62%	$55.25	$60.88		1	10.18%	$3.20	5.79%	15.97%
29 Merck	$2.30	3.25%	$70.75	$86.00		1	21.55%	$2.30	3.25%	24.81%
30 INCO	$.40	1.67%	$24.00	$20.63		1	-14.06%	$.69	2.88%	-11.19%
		3.32%					5.82%		4.48%	10.31%
BOTTOM TEN:										
21 Bethlehem Steel	$1.00	4.82%	$20.75	$26.25		1	26.51%	$1.60	7.71%	34.22%
22 Standard Oil CA	$2.60	4.79%	$54.25	$99.25		1	82.95%	$3.60	6.64%	89.59%
23 United Technologies	$2.00	4.73%	$42.25	$61.38		1	45.27%	$2.20	5.21%	50.47%
24 Eastman Kodak	$2.00	4.41%	$45.38	$71.25		1	57.02%	$3.05	6.72%	63.75%
25 Allied Chemical	$2.00	4.21%	$47.50	$54.00		1	13.68%	$2.15	4.53%	18.21%
26 Minnessota Mng. & Mfg.	$2.00	4.04%	$49.50	$59.25		1	19.70%	$2.80	5.66%	25.35%
27 Procter & Gamble	$3.00	4.04%	$74.25	$68.13		1	-8.25%	$3.60	4.85%	-3.40%
28 Aluminum Co of Amer	$2.00	3.62%	$55.25	$60.88		1	10.18%	$3.20	5.79%	15.97%
29 Merck	$2.30	3.25%	$70.75	$86.00		1	21.55%	$2.30	3.25%	24.81%
30 INCO	$.40	1.67%	$24.00	$20.63		1	-14.06%	$.69	2.88%	-11.19%
		3.96%					25.46%		5.32%	30.78%
TOP TEN:										
1 General Motors	$6.00	12.15%	$49.38	$45.63		1	-7.59%	$2.95	5.97%	-1.62%
2 Goodyear	$1.30	10.10%	$12.88	$17.38		1	34.95%	$1.30	10.10%	45.05%
3 US Steel	$1.60	8.89%	$18.00	$25.63		1	42.36%	$1.60	8.89%	51.25%
4 American T & T	$4.60	8.85%	$52.00	$48.88		1	-6.01%	$5.00	9.62%	3.61%
5 American Can	$2.80	8.03%	$34.88	$31.00		1	-11.11%	$2.90	8.32%	-2.80%
6 Johns-Manville	$1.80	7.54%	$23.88	$24.88		1	4.19%	$1.92	8.04%	12.23%
7 Texaco	$2.00	7.14%	$28.00	$49.13		1	75.45%	$2.45	8.75%	84.20%
8 Union Carbide	$2.80	6.77%	$41.38	$50.63		1	22.36%	$3.10	7.49%	29.85%
9 Exxon	$3.40	6.31%	$53.88	$81.13		1	50.58%	$5.40	10.02%	60.60%
10 Sears, Roebuck	$1.12	6.18%	$18.13	$15.50		1	-14.48%	$1.34	7.39%	-7.09%
		8.20%					19.07%		8.46%	27.53%
TOP FIVE:										
1 General Motors	$6.00	12.15%	$49.38	$45.63		1	-7.59%	$2.95	5.97%	-1.62%
2 Goodyear	$1.30	10.10%	$12.88	$17.38		1	34.95%	$1.30	10.10%	45.05%
3 US Steel	$1.60	8.89%	$18.00	$25.63		1	42.36%	$1.60	8.89%	51.25%
4 American T & T	$4.60	8.85%	$52.00	$48.88		1	-6.01%	$5.00	9.62%	3.61%
5 American Can	$2.80	8.03%	$34.88	$31.00		1	-11.11%	$2.90	8.32%	-2.80%
		9.60%					10.52%		8.58%	19.10%

LIST OF 1979 DOW JONES INDUSTRIALS BY DIVIDEND-YIELD

	STOCK 1979	1979 WSJ DIVI.	1979 WSJ YIELD	1979 OPENING PRICE	1979 CLOSING PRICE	1979 STOCK DIV.	1979 SPLIT	1979 APPRECIATION	1979 DIVIDEND	ACT. CASH YIELD	TOTAL RETURN
1	General Motors	$6.00	10.91%	$55.00	$49.38		1	-10.23%	$5.30	9.64%	-.59%
2	Texaco	$2.00	8.33%	$24.00	$28.00		1	16.67%	$2.12	8.83%	25.50%
3	Union Carbide	$2.80	8.06%	$34.75	$41.38		1	19.06%	$2.90	8.35%	27.41%
4	Goodyear	$1.30	8.00%	$16.25	$12.88		1	-20.77%	$1.30	8.00%	-12.77%
5	American Brands	$4.00	7.94%	$50.38	$67.25		1	33.50%	$4.63	9.18%	42.68%
6	American Can	$2.80	7.80%	$35.88	$34.88		1	-2.79%	$2.80	7.80%	5.02%
7	American T & T	$4.60	7.57%	$60.75	$52.00		1	-14.40%	$4.90	8.07%	-6.34%
+ 8	Esmark	$1.84	7.55%	$24.38	$27.38		1	12.31%	$1.84	7.55%	19.86%
9	Johns-Manville	$1.80	7.50%	$24.00	$23.88		1	-.52%	$1.89	7.88%	7.35%
10	US Steel	$1.60	7.23%	$22.13	$18.00		1	-18.64%	$1.60	7.23%	-11.41%
11	Woolworth	$1.40	7.23%	$19.38	$24.38		1	25.81%	$1.55	8.00%	33.81%
12	Exxon	$3.40	6.90%	$49.25	$53.88		1	9.39%	$3.90	7.92%	17.31%
13	Allied Chemical	$2.00	6.90%	$29.00	$47.50		1	63.79%	$2.00	6.90%	70.69%
14	Owens-Illinois	$1.16	6.63%	$17.50	$20.25		1	15.71%	$1.26	7.20%	22.91%
15	International Harvester	$2.30	6.24%	$36.88	$38.63		1	4.75%	$2.35	6.37%	11.12%
16	Westinghouse Electric	$.97	5.66%	$17.13	$19.88		1	16.06%	$.97	5.68%	21.73%
17	Sears, Roebuck	$1.12	5.57%	$20.13	$18.13		1	-9.94%	$1.24	6.16%	-3.78%
18	General Foods	$1.80	5.56%	$32.38	$33.50		1	3.47%	$1.90	5.87%	9.34%
19	Standard Oil CA	$2.60	5.55%	$46.88	$54.25		1	15.73%	$2.90	6.19%	21.92%
20	General Electric	$2.60	5.53%	$47.00	$48.75		1	3.72%	$2.70	5.74%	9.47%
21	International Paper	$2.00	5.42%	$36.88	$36.63		1	-.68%	$2.20	5.97%	5.29%
22	United Technologies	$2.00	5.10%	$39.25	$42.25		1	7.64%	$2.20	5.61%	13.25%
23	Bethlehem Steel	$1.00	5.03%	$19.88	$20.75		1	4.40%	$1.50	7.55%	11.95%
+ 24	Chrysler	$.40	4.27%	$9.38	$6.75		1	-28.00%	$.20	2.13%	-25.87%
25	Aluminum Co of Amer	$2.00	4.26%	$47.00	$55.25		1	17.55%	$2.60	5.53%	23.09%
26	Du Pont	$5.00	3.94%	$127.00	$39.63		3	-6.40%	$8.25	6.50%	.10%
27	Procter & Gamble	$3.00	3.40%	$88.13	$74.25		1	-15.74%	$3.30	3.74%	-12.00%
28	Eastman Kodak	$2.00	3.25%	$61.50	$45.38		1	-26.22%	$2.80	4.55%	-21.67%
29	Minnesota Mng. & Mfg.	$2.00	3.16%	$63.25	$49.50		1	-21.74%	$2.40	3.79%	-17.94%
30	INCO	$.40	2.48%	$16.13	$24.00		1	48.84%	$.50	3.10%	51.94%
	AVERAGE		6.10%					4.74%		6.57%	11.31%

+ Last year in the Dow 30

STOCK 1979	1979 WSJ DIVI.	1979 WSJ YIELD	1979 OPENING PRICE	1979 CLOSING PRICE	1979 STOCK DIV.	1979 SPLIT	1979 APPRECIATION	1979 DIVIDEND	ACT. CASH YIELD	TOTAL RETURN
BOTTOM FIVE:										
26 Du Pont	$5.00	3.94%	$127.00	$39.63		3	-6.40%	$8.25	6.50%	.10%
27 Procter & Gamble	$3.00	3.40%	$88.13	$74.25		1	-15.74%	$3.30	3.74%	-12.00%
28 Eastman Kodak	$2.00	3.25%	$61.50	$45.38		1	-26.22%	$2.80	4.55%	-21.67%
29 Minnessota Mng. & Mfg.	$2.00	3.16%	$63.25	$49.50		1	-21.74%	$2.40	3.79%	-17.94%
30 INCO	$.40	2.48%	$16.13	$24.00		1	48.84%	$.50	3.10%	51.94%
		3.25%					-4.25%		4.34%	.09%
BOTTOM TEN:										
21 International Paper	$2.00	5.42%	$36.88	$36.63		1	-.68%	$2.20	5.97%	5.29%
22 United Technologies	$2.00	5.10%	$39.25	$42.25		1	7.64%	$2.20	5.61%	13.25%
23 Bethlehem Steel	$1.00	5.03%	$19.88	$20.75		1	4.40%	$1.50	7.55%	11.95%
24 Chrysler	$.40	4.27%	$9.38	$6.75		1	-28.00%	$.20	2.13%	-25.87%
25 Aluminum Co of Amer	$2.00	4.26%	$47.00	$55.25		1	17.55%	$2.60	5.53%	23.09%
26 Du Pont	$5.00	3.94%	$127.00	$39.63		3	-6.40%	$8.25	6.50%	.10%
27 Procter & Gamble	$3.00	3.40%	$88.13	$74.25		1	-15.74%	$3.30	3.74%	-12.00%
28 Eastman Kodak	$2.00	3.25%	$61.50	$45.38		1	-26.22%	$2.80	4.55%	-21.67%
29 Minnessota Mng. & Mfg.	$2.00	3.16%	$63.25	$49.50		1	-21.74%	$2.40	3.79%	-17.94%
30 INCO	$.40	2.48%	$16.13	$24.00		1	48.84%	$.50	3.10%	51.94%
		4.03%					-2.03%		4.85%	2.81%
TOP TEN:										
1 General Motors	$6.00	10.91%	$55.00	$49.38		1	-10.23%	$5.30	9.64%	-.59%
2 Texas Corporation	$2.00	8.33%	$24.00	$28.00		1	16.67%	$2.12	8.83%	25.50%
3 Union Carbide	$2.80	8.06%	$34.75	$41.38		1	19.06%	$2.90	8.35%	27.41%
4 Goodyear	$1.30	8.00%	$16.25	$12.88		1	-20.77%	$1.30	8.00%	-12.77%
5 American Brands	$4.00	7.94%	$50.38	$67.25		1	33.50%	$4.63	9.18%	42.68%
6 American Can	$2.80	7.80%	$35.88	$34.88		1	-2.79%	$2.80	7.80%	5.02%
7 American T & T	$4.60	7.57%	$60.75	$52.00		1	-14.40%	$4.90	8.07%	-6.34%
8 Esmark	$1.84	7.55%	$24.38	$27.38		1	12.31%	$1.84	7.55%	19.86%
9 Johns-Manville	$1.80	7.50%	$24.00	$23.88		1	-.52%	$1.89	7.88%	7.35%
10 US Steel	$1.60	7.23%	$22.13	$18.00		1	-18.64%	$1.60	7.23%	-11.41%
		8.09%					1.42%		8.25%	9.67%
TOP FIVE:										
1 General Motors	$6.00	10.91%	$55.00	$49.38		1	-10.23%	$5.30	9.64%	-.59%
2 Texas Corporation	$2.00	8.33%	$24.00	$28.00		1	16.67%	$2.12	8.83%	25.50%
3 Union Carbide	$2.80	8.06%	$34.75	$41.38		1	19.06%	$2.90	8.35%	27.41%
4 Goodyear	$1.30	8.00%	$16.25	$12.88		1	-20.77%	$1.30	8.00%	-12.77%
5 American Brands	$4.00	7.94%	$50.38	$67.25		1	33.50%	$4.63	9.18%	42.68%
		8.65%					7.65%		8.80%	16.45%

LIST OF 1978 DOW JONES INDUSTRIALS BY DIVIDEND-YIELD

	STOCK 1978	1978 WSJ DIVI.	1978 WSJ YIELD	1978 OPENING PRICE	1978 CLOSING PRICE	1978 STOCK DIV.	1978 SPLIT	1978 APPRECIATION	1978 DIVIDEND	ACT. CASH YIELD	TOTAL RETURN
1	General Motors	$6.80	11.06%	$61.50	$55.00			-10.57%	$6.00	9.76%	-.81%
2	Chrysler	$1.00	7.92%	$12.63	$9.38		1	-25.74%	$.85	6.73%	-19.01%
3	Woolworth	$1.40	7.57%	$18.50	$19.38		1	4.73%	$1.40	7.57%	12.30%
4	Goodyear	$1.30	7.48%	$17.38	$16.25		1	-6.47%	$1.30	7.48%	1.01%
5	Texaco	$2.00	7.27%	$27.50	$24.00		1	-12.73%	$2.00	7.27%	-5.45%
6	American Brands	$3.04	7.15%	$42.50	$50.38		1	18.53%	$3.63	8.53%	27.06%
7	International Harvester	$2.10	7.09%	$29.63	$36.88		1	24.47%	$2.10	7.09%	31.56%
8	US Steel	$2.20	7.01%	$31.38	$22.13		1	-29.48%	$1.60	5.10%	-24.38%
9	American T & T	$4.20	7.00%	$60.00	$60.75		1	1.25%	$4.50	7.50%	8.75%
10	Union Carbide	$2.80	6.93%	$40.38	$34.75		1	-13.93%	$2.80	6.93%	-7.00%
11	Standard Oil CA	$2.40	6.32%	$38.00	$46.88		1	23.36%	$2.55	6.71%	30.07%
12	Exxon	$3.00	6.30%	$47.63	$49.25		1	3.41%	$3.30	6.93%	10.34%
13	Esmark	$1.84	6.24%	$29.50	$24.38		1	-17.37%	$1.84	6.24%	-11.14%
14	American Can	$2.40	6.17%	$38.88	$35.88		1	-7.72%	$2.65	6.82%	-.90%
15	Allied Chemical	$2.00	5.78%	$34.63	$29.00		1	-16.25%	$2.00	5.78%	-10.47%
16	Westinghouse Electric	$.97	5.39%	$18.00	$17.13		1	-4.86%	$.97	5.40%	.54%
17	General Foods	$1.64	5.27%	$31.13	$32.38		1	4.02%	$1.68	5.40%	9.41%
18	United Technologies	$1.80	5.05%	$35.63	$39.25		1	10.18%	$2.00	5.61%	15.79%
19	Johns-Manville	$1.60	5.04%	$31.75	$24.00		1	-24.41%	$1.80	5.67%	-18.74%
20	Bethlehem Steel	$1.00	4.79%	$20.88	$19.88		1	-4.79%	$1.00	4.79%	
21	INCO	$.80	4.67%	$17.13	$24.00		1	40.15%	$.70	4.09%	44.23%
22	International Paper	$2.00	4.62%	$43.25	$36.88		1	-14.74%	$2.00	4.62%	-10.12%
23	Owens-Illinois	$1.06	4.53%	$23.38	$17.50		1	-25.13%	$1.11	4.75%	-20.39%
24	General Electric	$2.20	4.51%	$48.75	$47.00		1	-3.59%	$2.40	4.92%	1.33%
25	Du Pont	$5.00	4.29%	$116.50	$127.00		1	9.01%	$7.25	6.22%	15.24%
26	Aluminum Co of Amer	$1.80	3.92%	$45.88	$47.00		1	2.45%	$1.90	4.14%	6.59%
27	Minnessota Mng. & Mfg.	$1.70	3.64%	$46.75	$63.25		1	35.29%	$2.00	4.28%	39.57%
28	Sears, Roebuck	$.96	3.51%	$27.38	$20.13		1	-26.48%	$1.23	4.49%	-21.99%
29	Eastman Kodak	$1.60	3.20%	$50.00	$61.50		1	23.00%	$2.23	4.46%	27.46%
30	Procter & Gamble	$2.60	3.06%	$84.88	$88.13		1	3.83%	$2.90	3.42%	7.25%
	AVERAGE		5.76%					-1.35%		5.96%	4.60%

STOCK 1978	1978 WSJ DIVI.	1978 WSJ YIELD	1978 OPENING PRICE	1978 CLOSING PRICE	1978 STOCK DIV.	1978 SPLIT	1978 APPRECIATION	1978 DIVIDEND	ACT. CASH YIELD	TOTAL RETURN
BOTTOM FIVE:										
26 Aluminum Co of Amer	$1.80	3.92%	$45.88	$47.00		1	2.45%	$1.90	4.14%	6.59%
27 Minnessota Mng. & Mfg.	$1.70	3.64%	$46.75	$63.25		1	35.29%	$2.00	4.28%	39.57%
28 Sears, Roebuck	$.96	3.51%	$27.38	$20.13		1	-26.48%	$1.23	4.49%	-21.99%
29 Eastman Kodak	$1.60	3.20%	$50.00	$61.50		1	23.00%	$2.23	4.46%	27.46%
30 Procter & Gamble	$2.60	3.06%	$84.88	$88.13		1	3.83%	$2.90	3.42%	7.25%
		3.47%					7.62%		4.16%	11.78%
BOTTOM TEN:										
21 INCO	$.80	4.67%	$17.13	$24.00		1	40.15%	$.70	4.09%	44.23%
22 International Paper	$2.00	4.62%	$43.25	$36.88		1	-14.74%	$2.00	4.62%	-10.12%
23 Owens-Illinois	$1.06	4.53%	$23.38	$17.50		1	-25.13%	$1.11	4.75%	-20.39%
24 General Electric	$2.20	4.51%	$48.75	$47.00		1	-3.59%	$2.40	4.92%	1.33%
25 Du Pont	$5.00	4.29%	$116.50	$127.00		1	9.01%	$7.25	6.22%	15.24%
26 Aluminum Co of Amer	$1.80	3.92%	$45.88	$47.00		1	2.45%	$1.90	4.14%	6.59%
27 Minnessota Mng. & Mfg.	$1.70	3.64%	$46.75	$63.25		1	35.29%	$2.00	4.28%	39.57%
28 Sears, Roebuck	$.96	3.51%	$27.38	$20.13		1	-26.48%	$1.23	4.49%	-21.99%
29 Eastman Kodak	$1.60	3.20%	$50.00	$61.50		1	23.00%	$2.23	4.46%	27.46%
30 Procter & Gamble	$2.60	3.06%	$84.88	$88.13		1	3.83%	$2.90	3.42%	7.25%
		4.00%					4.38%		4.54%	8.92%
TOP TEN:										
1 General Motors	$6.80	11.06%	$61.50	$55.00		1	-10.57%	$6.00	9.76%	-.81%
2 Chrysler	$1.00	7.92%	$12.63	$9.38		1	-25.74%	$.85	6.73%	-19.01%
3 Woolworth	$1.40	7.57%	$18.50	$19.38		1	4.73%	$1.40	7.57%	12.30%
4 Goodyear	$1.30	7.48%	$17.38	$16.25		1	-6.47%	$1.30	7.48%	1.01%
5 Texaco	$2.00	7.27%	$27.50	$24.00		1	-12.73%	$2.00	7.27%	-5.45%
6 American Brands	$3.04	7.15%	$42.50	$50.38		1	18.53%	$3.63	8.53%	27.06%
7 International Harvester	$2.10	7.09%	$29.63	$36.88		1	24.47%	$2.10	7.09%	31.56%
8 US Steel	$2.20	7.01%	$31.38	$22.13		1	-29.48%	$1.60	5.10%	-24.38%
9 American T & T	$4.20	7.00%	$60.00	$60.75		1	1.25%	$4.50	7.50%	8.75%
10 Union Carbide	$2.80	6.93%	$40.38	$34.75		1	-13.93%	$2.80	6.93%	-7.00%
		7.65%					-4.99%		7.40%	2.40%
TOP FIVE:										
1 General Motors	$6.80	11.06%	$61.50	$55.00		1	-10.57%	$6.00	9.76%	-.81%
2 Chrysler	$1.00	7.92%	$12.63	$9.38		1	-25.74%	$.85	6.73%	-19.01%
3 Woolworth	$1.40	7.57%	$18.50	$19.38		1	4.73%	$1.40	7.57%	12.30%
4 Goodyear	$1.30	7.48%	$17.38	$16.25		1	-6.47%	$1.30	7.48%	1.01%
5 Texaco	$2.00	7.27%	$27.50	$24.00		1	-12.73%	$2.00	7.27%	-5.45%
		8.26%					-10.16%		7.76%	-2.39%

LIST OF 1977 DOW JONES INDUSTRIALS BY DIVIDEND-YIELD

	STOCK 1977	1977 WSJ DIVI.	1977 WSJ YIELD	1977 OPENING PRICE	1977 CLOSING PRICE	1977 STOCK DIV.	1977 SPLIT	1977 APPRECIATION	1977 DIVIDEND	ACT. CASH YIELD	TOTAL RETURN
1	Texaco	$2.00	7.27%	$27.50	$27.50		1		$2.00	7.27%	7.27%
2	General Motors	$5.55	7.12%	$78.00	$61.50		1	-21.15%	$6.80	8.72%	-12.44%
3	American Brands	$2.80	6.19%	$45.25	$42.50		1	-6.08%	$2.98	6.59%	.51%
4	American Can	$2.40	6.13%	$39.13	$38.88		1	-.64%	$2.45	6.26%	5.62%
5	American T & T	$3.80	6.00%	$63.38	$60.00		1	-5.33%	$4.10	6.47%	1.14%
6	International Harvester	$1.85	5.63%	$32.88	$29.63		1	-9.89%	$1.85	5.63%	-4.26%
7	Westinghouse Electric	$.97	5.54%	$17.50	$18.00		1	2.86%	$.97	5.55%	8.41%
8	Standard Oil CA	$2.20	5.42%	$40.63	$38.00		1	-6.46%	$2.35	5.78%	-.68%
9	Exxon	$2.80	5.22%	$53.63	$47.63		1	-11.19%	$3.00	5.59%	-5.59%
10	Esmark	$1.76	5.05%	$34.88	$29.50		1	-15.41%	$1.78	5.10%	-10.31%
11	General Foods	$1.50	5.02%	$29.88	$31.13		1	4.18%	$1.64	5.49%	9.67%
12	Bethlehem Steel	$2.00	5.02%	$39.88	$20.88		1	-47.65%	$1.50	3.76%	-43.89%
13	Woolworth	$1.20	4.73%	$25.38	$18.50		1	-27.09%	$1.20	4.73%	-22.36%
14	Goodyear	$1.10	4.63%	$23.75	$17.38		1	-26.84%	$1.20	5.05%	-21.79%
15	Allied Chemical	$1.80	4.51%	$39.88	$34.63		1	-13.17%	$1.85	4.64%	-8.53%
16	US Steel	$2.20	4.46%	$49.38	$31.38		1	-36.46%	$2.20	4.46%	-32.00%
17	International Nickel	$1.40	4.24%	$33.00	$17.13		1	-48.11%	$1.25	3.79%	-44.32%
18	Johns-Manville	$1.40	4.19%	$33.38	$31.75		1	-4.87%	$1.55	4.64%	-.22%
19	Union Carbide	$2.50	4.03%	$62.00	$40.38		1	-34.88%	$2.80	4.52%	-30.36%
20	Du Pont	$5.25	3.90%	$134.75	$116.50		1	-13.54%	$5.75	4.27%	-9.28%
21	Owens-Illinois	$1.88	3.36%	$56.00	$23.38		2	-16.52%	$2.12	3.79%	-12.73%
22	General Electric	$1.80	3.25%	$55.38	$48.75		1	-11.96%	$2.00	3.61%	-8.35%
23	United Technologies	$1.20	3.10%	$38.75	$35.63		1	-8.06%	$1.65	4.26%	-3.81%
24 *	International Paper	$2.00	2.88%	$69.38	$43.25		1	-37.66%	$2.00	2.88%	-34.77%
25	Minnesota Mng. & Mfg.	$1.45	2.58%	$56.25	$46.75		1	-16.89%	$1.70	3.02%	-13.87%
26	Aluminum Co of Amer	$1.40	2.47%	$56.75	$45.88		1	-19.16%	$1.70	3.00%	-16.17%
27	Procter & Gamble	$2.20	2.37%	$93.00	$84.88		1	-8.74%	$2.60	2.80%	-5.94%
28	Sears, Roebuck	$1.60	2.35%	$68.00	$27.38		2	-19.49%	$2.08	3.06%	-16.43%
29	Eastman Kodak	$1.60	1.87%	$85.38	$50.00		1	-41.43%	$2.10	2.46%	-38.98%
30	Chrysler	$.30	1.42%	$21.13	$12.63		1	-40.24%	$.90	4.26%	-35.98%
	AVERAGE		4.33%					-18.06%		4.71%	-13.35%

* First year in the Dow 30

STOCK 1977	1977 WSJ DIVI.	1977 WSJ YIELD	1977 OPENING PRICE	1977 CLOSING PRICE	1977 STOCK DIV.	1977 SPLIT	1977 APPRECIATION	1977 DIVIDEND	ACT. CASH YIELD	TOTAL RETURN
BOTTOM FIVE:										
26 Aluminum Co of Amer	$1.40	2.47%	$56.75	$45.88		1	-19.16%	$1.70	3.00%	-16.17%
27 Procter & Gamble	$2.20	2.37%	$93.00	$84.88		1	-8.74%	$2.60	2.80%	-5.94%
28 Sears, Roebuck	$1.60	2.35%	$68.00	$27.38		2	-19.49%	$2.08	3.06%	-16.43%
29 Eastman Kodak	$1.60	1.87%	$85.38	$50.00		1	-41.43%	$2.10	2.46%	-38.98%
30 Chrysler	$.30	1.42%	$21.13	$12.63		1	-40.24%	$.90	4.26%	-35.98%
		2.10%					-25.81%		3.11%	-22.70%
BOTTOM TEN:										
21 Owens-Illinois	$1.88	3.36%	$56.00	$23.38		2	-16.52%	$2.12	3.79%	-12.73%
22 General Electric	$1.80	3.25%	$55.38	$48.75		1	-11.96%	$2.00	3.61%	-8.35%
23 United Technologies	$1.20	3.10%	$38.75	$35.63		1	-8.06%	$1.65	4.26%	-3.81%
24 International Paper	$2.00	2.88%	$69.38	$43.25		1	-37.66%	$2.00	2.88%	-34.77%
25 Minnessota Mng. & Mfg.	$1.45	2.58%	$56.25	$46.75		1	-16.89%	$1.70	3.02%	-13.87%
26 Aluminum Co of Amer	$1.40	2.47%	$56.75	$45.88		1	-19.16%	$1.70	3.00%	-16.17%
27 Procter & Gamble	$2.20	2.37%	$93.00	$84.88		1	-8.74%	$2.60	2.80%	-5.94%
28 Sears, Roebuck	$1.60	2.35%	$68.00	$27.38		2	-19.49%	$2.08	3.06%	-16.43%
29 Eastman Kodak	$1.60	1.87%	$85.38	$50.00		1	-41.43%	$2.10	2.46%	-38.98%
30 Chrysler	$.30	1.42%	$21.13	$12.63		1	-40.24%	$.90	4.26%	-35.98%
		2.56%					-22.01%		3.31%	-18.70%
TOP TEN:										
1 Texaco	$2.00	7.27%	$27.50	$27.50		1		$2.00	7.27%	7.27%
2 General Motors	$5.55	7.12%	$78.00	$61.50		1	-21.15%	$6.80	8.72%	-12.44%
3 American Brands	$2.80	6.19%	$45.25	$42.50		1	-6.08%	$2.98	6.59%	.51%
4 American Can	$2.40	6.13%	$39.13	$38.88		1	-.64%	$2.45	6.26%	5.62%
5 American T & T	$3.80	6.00%	$63.38	$60.00		1	-5.33%	$4.10	6.47%	1.14%
6 International Harvester	$1.85	5.63%	$32.88	$29.63		1	-9.89%	$1.85	5.63%	-4.26%
7 Westinghouse Electric	$.97	5.54%	$17.50	$18.00		1	2.86%	$.97	5.55%	8.41%
8 Standard Oil CA	$2.20	5.42%	$40.63	$38.00		1	-6.46%	$2.35	5.78%	-.68%
9 Exxon	$2.80	5.22%	$53.63	$47.63		1	-11.19%	$3.00	5.59%	-5.59%
10 Esmark	$1.76	5.05%	$34.88	$29.50		1	-15.41%	$1.78	5.10%	-10.31%
		5.96%					-7.33%		6.30%	-1.03%
TOP FIVE:										
1 Texaco	$2.00	7.27%	$27.50	$27.50		1		$2.00	7.27%	7.27%
2 General Motors	$5.55	7.12%	$78.00	$61.50		1	-21.15%	$6.80	8.72%	-12.44%
3 American Brands	$2.80	6.19%	$45.25	$42.50		1	-6.08%	$2.98	6.59%	.51%
4 American Can	$2.40	6.13%	$39.13	$38.88		1	-.64%	$2.45	6.26%	5.62%
5 American T & T	$3.80	6.00%	$63.38	$60.00		1	-5.33%	$4.10	6.47%	1.14%
		6.54%					-6.64%		7.06%	.42%

LIST OF 1976 DOW JONES INDUSTRIALS BY DIVIDEND-YIELD

	STOCK 1976	1976 WSJ DIVI.	1976 WSJ YIELD	1976 OPENING PRICE	1976 CLOSING PRICE	1976 STOCK DIV.	1976 SPLIT	1976 APPRECIATION	1976 DIVIDEND	ACT. CASH YIELD	TOTAL RETURN
1	Texaco	$2.00	8.38%	$23.88	$27.50		1	15.18%	$2.00	8.38%	23.56%
2	International Harvester	$1.70	7.35%	$23.13	$32.88		1	42.16%	$1.70	7.35%	49.51%
3	Westinghouse Electric	$.97	7.25%	$13.38	$17.50			30.84%	$.97	7.27%	38.11%
4	American Can	$2.20	7.10%	$31.00	$39.13		1	26.21%	$2.25	7.26%	33.47%
5	American Brands	$2.68	6.92%	$38.75	$45.25		1	16.77%	$2.80	7.23%	24.00%
6	Standard Oil CA	$2.00	6.78%	$29.50	$40.63		1	37.71%	$2.15	7.29%	45.00%
7	American T & T	$3.40	6.68%	$50.88	$63.38		1	24.57%	$3.70	7.27%	31.84%
8	Bethlehem Steel	$2.00	5.97%	$33.50	$39.88		1	19.03%	$2.00	5.97%	25.00%
9	Exxon	$5.00	5.56%	$90.00	$53.63		2	19.17%	$5.45	6.06%	25.22%
10	International Nickel	$1.40	5.52%	$25.38	$33.00		1	30.05%	$1.60	6.31%	36.35%
11	Woolworth	$1.20	5.42%	$22.13	$25.38		1	14.69%	$1.20	5.42%	20.11%
12	Allied Chemical	$1.80	5.31%	$33.88	$39.88		1	17.71%	$1.80	5.31%	23.03%
13	Johns-Manville	$1.20	5.11%	$23.50	$33.38		1	42.02%	$1.35	5.74%	47.77%
14	General Foods	$1.40	5.05%	$27.75	$29.88		1	7.66%	$1.50	5.41%	13.06%
15	Goodyear	$1.10	4.97%	$22.13	$23.75		1	7.34%	$1.10	4.97%	12.32%
16	Swift & Company	$1.52	4.71%	$32.25	$34.88		1	8.14%	$1.58	4.90%	13.04%
17	United Technologies	$2.00	4.29%	$46.63	$38.75		2	66.22%	$2.38	5.10%	71.32%
18	US Steel	$2.80	4.28%	$65.38	$49.38		1.5	13.29%	$3.18	4.86%	18.15%
19	General Motors	$2.40	4.11%	$58.38	$78.00		1	33.62%	$5.55	9.51%	43.13%
20	Union Carbide	$2.40	3.94%	$60.88	$62.00		1	1.85%	$2.50	4.11%	5.95%
+ 21	Anaconda	$.60	3.50%	$17.13	$30.00		1	75.18%	$.60	3.50%	78.69%
22	Aluminum Co of Amer	$1.34	3.44%	$39.00	$56.75		1	45.51%	$1.37	3.51%	49.03%
23	International Paper	$2.00	3.43%	$58.25	$69.38		1	19.10%	$2.00	3.43%	22.53%
24	General Electric	$1.60	3.43%	$46.63	$55.38		1	18.77%	$1.65	3.54%	22.31%
25	Du Pont	$4.25	3.37%	$126.25	$134.75		1	6.73%	$5.25	4.16%	10.89%
26	Owens-Illinois	$1.72	3.28%	$52.50	$56.00		1	6.67%	$1.88	3.58%	10.25%
27	Sears, Roebuck	$1.60	2.48%	$64.63	$68.00		1	5.22%	$1.85	2.86%	8.09%
28	Procter & Gamble	$2.00	2.24%	$89.38	$93.00		1	4.06%	$2.15	2.41%	6.46%
29	Eastman Kodak	$1.56	1.47%	$106.38	$85.38		1	-19.75%	$2.06	1.94%	-17.81%
30	Chrysler	$.00	.00%	$11.25	$21.13		1	87.78%	$.30	2.67%	90.44%
	AVERAGE		4.71%					24.12%		5.24%	29.36%

+ Last year in the Dow 30

	STOCK 1976	1976 WSJ DIVI.	1976 WSJ YIELD	1976 OPENING PRICE	1976 CLOSING PRICE	1976 STOCK DIV.	1976 SPLIT	1976 APPRECIATION	1976 DIVIDEND	ACT. CASH YIELD	TOTAL RETURN
	BOTTOM FIVE:										
26	Owens-Illinois	$1.72	3.28%	$52.50	$56.00		1	6.67%	$1.88	3.58%	10.25%
27	Sears, Roebuck	$1.60	2.48%	$64.63	$68.00		1	5.22%	$1.85	2.86%	8.09%
28	Procter & Gamble	$2.00	2.24%	$89.38	$93.00		1	4.06%	$2.15	2.41%	6.46%
29	Eastman Kodak	$1.56	1.47%	$106.38	$85.38		1	-19.75%	$2.06	1.94%	-17.81%
30	Chrysler	$.00	.00%	$11.25	$21.13		1	87.78%	$.30	2.67%	90.44%
			2.36%					-.95%		2.70%	1.75%
	BOTTOM TEN:										
21	Anaconda	$.60	3.50%	$17.13	$30.00		1	75.18%	$.60	3.50%	78.69%
22	Aluminum Co of Amer	$1.34	3.44%	$39.00	$56.75		1	45.51%	$1.37	3.51%	49.03%
23	International Paper	$2.00	3.43%	$58.25	$69.38		1	19.10%	$2.00	3.43%	22.53%
24	General Electric	$1.60	3.43%	$46.63	$55.38		1	18.77%	$1.65	3.54%	22.31%
25	Du Pont	$4.25	3.37%	$126.25	$134.75		1	6.73%	$5.25	4.16%	10.89%
26	Owens-Illinois	$1.72	3.28%	$52.50	$56.00		1	6.67%	$1.88	3.58%	10.25%
27	Sears, Roebuck	$1.60	2.48%	$64.63	$68.00		1	5.22%	$1.85	2.86%	8.09%
28	Procter & Gamble	$2.00	2.24%	$89.38	$93.00		1	4.06%	$2.15	2.41%	6.46%
29	Eastman Kodak	$1.56	1.47%	$106.38	$85.38		1	-19.75%	$2.06	1.94%	-17.81%
30	Chrysler	$.00	.00%	$11.25	$21.13		1	87.78%	$.30	2.67%	90.44%
			2.66%					24.93%		3.16%	28.09%
	TOP TEN:										
1	Texaco	$2.00	8.38%	$23.88	$27.50		1	15.18%	$2.00	8.38%	23.56%
2	International Harvester	$1.70	7.35%	$23.13	$32.88		1	42.16%	$1.70	7.35%	49.51%
3	Westinghouse Electric	$.97	7.25%	$13.38	$17.50		1	30.84%	$.97	7.27%	38.11%
4	American Can	$2.20	7.10%	$31.00	$39.13		1	26.21%	$2.25	7.26%	33.47%
5	American Brands	$2.68	6.92%	$38.75	$45.25		1	16.77%	$2.80	7.23%	24.00%
6	Standard Oil CA	$2.00	6.78%	$29.50	$40.63		1	37.71%	$2.15	7.29%	45.00%
7	American T & T	$3.40	6.68%	$50.88	$63.38		1	24.57%	$3.70	7.27%	31.84%
8	Bethlehem Steel	$2.00	5.97%	$33.50	$39.88		1	19.03%	$2.00	5.97%	25.00%
9	Exxon	$5.00	5.56%	$90.00	$53.63		2	19.17%	$5.45	6.06%	25.22%
10	International Nickel	$1.40	5.52%	$25.38	$33.00		1	30.05%	$1.60	6.31%	36.35%
			6.75%					26.17%		7.04%	33.21%
	TOP FIVE:										
1	Texaco	$2.00	8.38%	$23.88	$27.50		1	15.18%	$2.00	8.38%	23.56%
2	International Harvester	$1.70	7.35%	$23.13	$32.88		1	42.16%	$1.70	7.35%	49.51%
3	Westinghouse Electric	$.97	7.25%	$13.38	$17.50		1	30.84%	$.97	7.27%	38.11%
4	American Can	$2.20	7.10%	$31.00	$39.13		1	26.21%	$2.25	7.26%	33.47%
5	American Brands	$2.68	6.92%	$38.75	$45.25		1	16.77%	$2.80	7.23%	24.00%
			7.52%					28.60%		7.56%	36.16%

LIST OF 1975 DOW JONES INDUSTRIALS BY DIVIDEND-YIELD

STOCK 1975	1975 WSJ DIVI.	1975 WSJ YIELD	1975 OPENING PRICE	1975 CLOSING PRICE	1975 STOCK DIV.	1975 SPLIT	1975 APPRECIATION	1975 DIVIDEND	ACT. CASH YIELD	TOTAL RETURN
1 Chrysler	$1.40	17.50%	$8.00	$11.25		1	40.63%	$.00	.00%	40.63%
2 Woolworth	$1.20	12.15%	$9.88	$22.13			124.05%	$1.20	12.15%	136.20%
3 General Motors	$3.40	10.67%	$31.88	$58.38			83.14%	$2.40	7.53%	90.67%
4 Westinghouse Electric	$.97	9.58%	$10.13	$13.38		1	32.10%	$.97	9.60%	41.70%
5 Texaco	$2.00	8.99%	$22.25	$23.88		1	7.30%	$2.00	8.99%	16.29%
6 Standard Oil CA	$2.00	8.47%	$23.63	$29.50		1	24.87%	$2.00	8.47%	33.33%
7 International Harvester	$1.70	8.40%	$20.25	$23.13		1	14.20%	$1.70	8.40%	22.59%
8 Goodyear	$1.10	8.22%	$13.38	$22.13		1	65.42%	$1.10	8.22%	73.64%
9 American Brands	$2.56	8.13%	$31.50	$38.75		1	23.02%	$2.68	8.51%	31.52%
10 Bethlehem Steel	$2.00	8.04%	$24.88	$33.50		1	34.67%	$2.75	11.06%	45.73%
11 Exxon	$5.00	7.55%	$66.25	$90.00		1	35.85%	$5.00	7.55%	43.40%
12 General Foods	$1.40	7.42%	$18.88	$27.75		1	47.02%	$1.40	7.42%	54.44%
13 American Can	$2.20	7.39%	$29.75	$31.00		1	4.20%	$2.40	8.07%	12.27%
14 American T & T	$3.40	7.39%	$46.00	$50.88		1	10.60%	$3.40	7.39%	17.99%
15 Anaconda	$1.00	6.90%	$14.50	$17.13		1	18.10%	$.75	5.17%	23.28%
16 International Nickel	$1.40	6.29%	$22.25	$25.38		1	14.04%	$1.60	7.19%	21.24%
17 US Steel	$2.40	6.27%	$38.25	$65.38		1	70.92%	$2.80	7.32%	78.24%
18 United Technologies	$2.00	6.25%	$32.00	$46.63		1	45.70%	$2.00	6.25%	51.95%
19 Allied Chemical	$1.80	6.15%	$29.25	$33.88		1	15.81%	$1.80	6.15%	21.97%
20 Johns-Manville	$1.20	6.08%	$19.75	$23.50		1	18.99%	$1.20	6.08%	25.06%
21 Du Pont	$5.50	5.78%	$95.13	$126.25		1	32.72%	$4.25	4.47%	37.19%
22 International Paper	$2.00	5.46%	$36.63	$58.25		1	59.04%	$2.00	5.46%	64.51%
23 Union Carbide	$2.20	5.19%	$42.38	$60.88		1	43.66%	$2.40	5.66%	49.32%
24 Swift & Company	$1.40	4.83%	$29.00	$32.25		1.25	39.01%	$1.53	5.26%	44.27%
25 General Electric	$1.60	4.74%	$33.75	$46.63		1	38.15%	$1.60	4.74%	42.89%
26 Owens-Illinois	$1.60	4.71%	$34.00	$52.50		1	54.41%	$1.72	5.06%	59.47%
27 Aluminum Co of Amer	$1.34	4.49%	$29.88	$39.00		1	30.54%	$1.34	4.49%	35.03%
28 Sears, Roebuck	$1.60	3.18%	$50.38	$64.63		1	28.29%	$1.85	3.67%	31.96%
29 Eastman Kodak	$1.56	2.45%	$63.75	$106.38		1	66.87%	$2.06	3.23%	70.10%
30 Procter & Gamble	$1.80	2.19%	$82.25	$89.38		1	8.66%	$2.00	2.43%	11.09%
AVERAGE		7.03%					37.73%		6.53%	44.27%

STOCK 1975	1975 WSJ DIVI.	1975 WSJ YIELD	1975 OPENING PRICE	1975 CLOSING PRICE	1975 STOCK DIV.	1975 SPLIT	1975 APPRECIATION	1975 DIVIDEND	ACT. CASH YIELD	TOTAL RETURN
BOTTOM FIVE:										
26 Owens-Illinois	$1.60	4.71%	$34.00	$52.50		1	54.41%	$1.72	5.06%	59.47%
27 Aluminum Co of Amer	$1.34	4.49%	$29.88	$39.00		1	30.54%	$1.34	4.49%	35.03%
28 Sears, Roebuck	$1.60	3.18%	$50.38	$64.63		1	28.29%	$1.85	3.67%	31.96%
29 Eastman Kodak	$1.56	2.45%	$63.75	$106.38		1	66.87%	$2.06	3.23%	70.10%
30 Procter & Gamble	$1.80	2.19%	$82.25	$89.38		1	8.66%	$2.00	2.43%	11.09%
		3.40%					37.76%		3.78%	41.53%
BOTTOM TEN:										
21 Du Pont	$5.50	5.78%	$95.13	$126.25		1	32.72%	$4.25	4.47%	37.19%
22 International Paper	$2.00	5.46%	$36.63	$58.25		1	59.04%	$2.00	5.46%	64.51%
23 Union Carbide	$2.20	5.19%	$42.38	$60.88		1	43.66%	$2.40	5.66%	49.32%
24 Swift & Company	$1.40	4.83%	$29.00	$32.25		1.25	39.01%	$1.53	5.26%	44.27%
25 General Electric	$1.60	4.74%	$33.75	$46.63		1	38.15%	$1.60	4.74%	42.89%
26 Owens-Illinois	$1.60	4.71%	$34.00	$52.50		1	54.41%	$1.72	5.06%	59.47%
27 Aluminum Co of Amer	$1.34	4.49%	$29.88	$39.00		1	30.54%	$1.34	4.49%	35.03%
28 Sears, Roebuck	$1.60	3.18%	$50.38	$64.63		1	28.29%	$1.85	3.67%	31.96%
29 Eastman Kodak	$1.56	2.45%	$63.75	$106.38		1	66.87%	$2.06	3.23%	70.10%
30 Procter & Gamble	$1.80	2.19%	$82.25	$89.38		1	8.66%	$2.00	2.43%	11.09%
		4.30%					40.14%		4.45%	44.58%
TOP TEN:										
1 Chrysler	$1.40	17.50%	$8.00	$11.25		1	40.63%	$.00	.00%	40.63%
2 Woolworth	$1.20	12.15%	$9.88	$22.13		1	124.05%	$1.20	12.15%	136.20%
3 General Motors	$3.40	10.67%	$31.88	$58.38		1	83.14%	$2.40	7.53%	90.67%
4 Westinghouse Electric	$.97	9.58%	$10.13	$13.38		1	32.10%	$.97	9.60%	41.70%
5 Texaco	$2.00	8.99%	$22.25	$23.88		1	7.30%	$2.00	8.99%	16.29%
6 Standard Oil CA	$2.00	8.47%	$23.63	$29.50		1	24.87%	$2.00	8.47%	33.33%
7 International Harvester	$1.70	8.40%	$20.25	$23.13		1	14.20%	$1.70	8.40%	22.59%
8 Goodyear	$1.10	8.22%	$13.38	$22.13		1	65.42%	$1.10	8.22%	73.64%
9 American Brands	$2.56	8.13%	$31.50	$38.75		1	23.02%	$2.68	8.51%	31.52%
10 Bethlehem Steel	$2.00	8.04%	$24.88	$33.50		1	34.67%	$2.75	11.06%	45.73%
		10.01%					44.94%		8.29%	53.23%
TOP FIVE:										
1 Chrysler	$1.40	17.50%	$8.00	$11.25		1	40.63%	$.00	.00%	40.63%
2 Woolworth	$1.20	12.15%	$9.88	$22.13		1	124.05%	$1.20	12.15%	136.20%
3 General Motors	$3.40	10.67%	$31.88	$58.38		1	83.14%	$2.40	7.53%	90.67%
4 Westinghouse Electric	$.97	9.58%	$10.13	$13.38		1	32.10%	$.97	9.60%	41.70%
5 Texaco	$2.00	8.99%	$22.25	$23.88		1	7.30%	$2.00	8.99%	16.29%
		11.78%					57.44%		7.65%	65.10%

LIST OF 1974 DOW JONES INDUSTRIALS BY DIVIDEND-YIELD

	STOCK 1974	1974 WSJ DIVI.	1974 WSJ YIELD	1974 OPENING PRICE	1974 CLOSING PRICE	1974 STOCK DIV.	1974 SPLIT	1974 APPRECIATION	1974 DIVIDEND	ACT. CASH YIELD	TOTAL RETURN
1	General Motors	$5.25	11.41%	$46.00	$31.88		1	-30.71%	$3.40	7.39%	-23.32%
2	Chrysler	$1.40	9.26%	$15.13	$8.00		1	-47.11%	$1.40	9.26%	-37.85%
3	American Can	$2.20	8.19%	$26.88	$29.75		1	10.70%	$2.20	8.19%	18.88%
4	United Aircraft	$1.80	7.58%	$23.75	$32.00		1	34.74%	$1.95	8.21%	42.95%
5	Johns-Manville	$1.20	7.22%	$16.63	$19.75		1	18.80%	$1.20	7.22%	26.02%
6	American Brands	$2.38	7.10%	$33.50	$31.50		1	-5.97%	$2.56	7.64%	1.67%
7	Woolworth	$1.20	6.49%	$18.50	$9.88		1	-46.62%	$1.20	6.49%	-40.14%
8	Goodyear	$1.00	6.40%	$15.63	$13.38		1	-14.40%	$1.03	6.59%	-7.81%
9	Union Carbide	$2.10	6.20%	$33.88	$42.38		1	25.09%	$2.18	6.42%	31.51%
10	American T & T	$3.08	6.16%	$50.00	$46.00		1	-8.00%	$3.16	6.32%	-1.68%
11	Texaco	$1.76	5.97%	$29.50	$22.25		1	-24.58%	$2.10	7.12%	-17.46%
12	International Harvester	$1.50	5.61%	$26.75	$20.25		1	-24.30%	$1.60	5.98%	-18.32%
13	General Foods	$1.40	5.60%	$25.00	$18.88		1	-24.50%	$1.40	5.60%	-18.90%
14	Bethlehem Steel	$1.60	4.92%	$32.50	$24.88		1	-23.46%	$2.30	7.08%	-16.38%
15	Standard Oil CA	$1.70	4.86%	$35.00	$23.63		1	-32.50%	$1.93	5.50%	-27.00%
16	Owens-Illinois	$1.48	4.70%	$31.50	$34.00		1	7.94%	$1.57	4.98%	12.92%
17	Exxon	$4.25	4.40%	$96.50	$66.25		1	-31.35%	$5.00	5.18%	-26.17%
18	US Steel	$1.60	4.30%	$37.25	$38.50		1	3.36%	$2.20	5.91%	9.26%
19	Swift & Company	$1.00	4.00%	$25.00	$29.00		1	16.00%	$1.00	4.00%	20.00%
20	Westinghouse Electric	$.97	3.88%	$25.00	$10.13		1	-59.50%	$.97	3.89%	-55.61%
21	Du Pont	$5.75	3.58%	$160.50	$95.13		1	-40.73%	$5.50	3.43%	-37.31%
22	International Nickel	$1.20	3.44%	$34.88	$22.25		1	-36.20%	$1.60	4.59%	-31.61%
23	International Paper	$1.50	2.86%	$52.50	$36.63		1	-30.24%	$1.75	3.33%	-26.90%
24	Allied Chemical	$1.32	2.69%	$49.13	$29.25		1	-40.46%	$1.53	3.11%	-37.34%
25	Aluminum Co of Amer	$1.94	2.68%	$72.38	$29.88		1.5	-38.08%	$1.51	2.08%	-36.00%
26	General Electric	$1.60	2.55%	$62.63	$33.75		1	-46.11%	$1.60	2.55%	-43.55%
27	Sears, Roebuck	$1.60	1.99%	$80.25	$50.38		1	-37.23%	$1.85	2.31%	-34.92%
28	Procter & Gamble	$1.80	1.97%	$91.50	$82.25		1	-10.11%	$1.80	1.97%	-8.14%
29	Anaconda	$.50	1.80%	$27.75	$14.50		1	-47.75%	$1.00	3.60%	-44.14%
30	Eastman Kodak	$1.28	1.11%	$115.38	$63.75		1	-44.75%	$1.92	1.66%	-43.08%
	AVERAGE		4.96%					-20.93%		5.25%	-15.68%

STOCK 1974	1974 WSJ DIVI.	1974 WSJ YIELD	1974 OPENING PRICE	1974 CLOSING PRICE	1974 STOCK DIV.	1974 SPLIT	1974 APPRECIATION	1974 DIVIDEND	ACT. CASH YIELD	TOTAL RETURN
BOTTOM FIVE:										
26 General Electric	$1.60	2.55%	$62.63	$33.75		1	-46.11%	$1.60	2.55%	-43.55%
27 Sears, Roebuck	$1.60	1.99%	$80.25	$50.38		1	-37.23%	$1.85	2.31%	-34.92%
28 Procter & Gamble	$1.80	1.97%	$91.50	$82.25		1	-10.11%	$1.80	1.97%	-8.14%
29 Anaconda	$.50	1.80%	$27.75	$14.50		1	-47.75%	$1.00	3.60%	-44.14%
30 Eastman Kodak	$1.28	1.11%	$115.38	$63.75		1	-44.75%	$1.92	1.66%	-43.08%
		1.89%					-37.19%		2.42%	-34.77%
BOTTOM TEN:										
21 Du Pont	$5.75	3.58%	$160.50	$95.13		1	-40.73%	$5.50	3.43%	-37.31%
22 International Nickel	$1.20	3.44%	$34.88	$22.25		1	-36.20%	$1.60	4.59%	-31.61%
23 International Paper	$1.50	2.86%	$52.50	$36.63		1	-30.24%	$1.75	3.33%	-26.90%
24 Allied Chemical	$1.32	2.69%	$49.13	$29.25		1	-40.46%	$1.53	3.11%	-37.34%
25 Aluminum Co of Amer	$1.94	2.68%	$72.38	$29.88		1.5	-38.08%	$1.51	2.08%	-36.00%
26 General Electric	$1.60	2.55%	$62.63	$33.75		1	-46.11%	$1.60	2.55%	-43.55%
27 Sears, Roebuck	$1.60	1.99%	$80.25	$50.38		1	-37.23%	$1.85	2.31%	-34.92%
28 Procter & Gamble	$1.80	1.97%	$91.50	$82.25		1	-10.11%	$1.80	1.97%	-8.14%
29 Anaconda	$.50	1.80%	$27.75	$14.50		1	-47.75%	$1.00	3.60%	-44.14%
30 Eastman Kodak	$1.28	1.11%	$115.38	$63.75		1	-44.75%	$1.92	1.66%	-43.08%
		2.47%					-37.16%		2.86%	-34.30%
TOP TEN:										
1 General Motors	$5.25	11.41%	$46.00	$31.88		1	-30.71%	$3.40	7.39%	-23.32%
2 Chrysler	$1.40	9.26%	$15.13	$8.00		1	-47.11%	$1.40	9.26%	-37.85%
3 American Can	$2.20	8.19%	$26.88	$29.75		1	10.70%	$2.20	8.19%	18.88%
4 United Aircraft	$1.80	7.58%	$23.75	$32.00		1	34.74%	$1.95	8.21%	42.95%
5 Johns-Manville	$1.20	7.22%	$16.63	$19.75		1	18.80%	$1.20	7.22%	26.02%
6 American Brands	$2.38	7.10%	$33.50	$31.50		1	-5.97%	$2.56	7.64%	1.67%
7 Woolworth	$1.20	6.49%	$18.50	$9.88		1	-46.62%	$1.20	6.49%	-40.14%
8 Goodyear	$1.00	6.40%	$15.63	$13.38		1	-14.40%	$1.03	6.59%	-7.81%
9 Union Carbide	$2.10	6.20%	$33.88	$42.38		1	25.09%	$2.18	6.42%	31.51%
10 American T & T	$3.08	6.16%	$50.00	$46.00		1	-8.00%	$3.16	6.32%	-1.68%
		7.60%					-6.35%		7.37%	1.02%
TOP FIVE:										
1 General Motors	$5.25	11.41%	$46.00	$31.88		1	-30.71%	$3.40	7.39%	-23.32%
2 Chrysler	$1.40	9.26%	$15.13	$8.00		1	-47.11%	$1.40	9.26%	-37.85%
3 American Can	$2.20	8.19%	$26.88	$29.75		1	10.70%	$2.20	8.19%	18.88%
4 United Aircraft	$1.80	7.58%	$23.75	$32.00		1	34.74%	$1.95	8.21%	42.95%
5 Johns-Manville	$1.20	7.22%	$16.63	$19.75		1	18.80%	$1.20	7.22%	26.02%
		8.73%					-2.72%		8.05%	5.34%

LIST OF 1973 DOW JONES INDUSTRIALS BY DIVIDEND-YIELD

	STOCK 1973	1973 WSJ DIVI.	1973 WSJ YIELD	1973 OPENING PRICE	1973 CLOSING PRICE	1973 STOCK DIV.	1973 SPLIT	1973 APPRECIATION	1973 DIVIDEND	ACT. CASH YIELD	TOTAL RETURN
1	American Can	$2.20	6.96%	$31.63	$26.88			-15.02%	$2.20	6.96%	-8.06%
2	General Motors	$4.45	5.42%	$82.13	$46.00			-43.99%	$5.25	6.39%	-37.60%
3	American Tobacco	$2.29	5.33%	$43.00	$33.50		1	-22.09%	$2.38	5.53%	-16.56%
4	American T & T	$2.80	5.26%	$53.25	$50.00			-6.10%	$2.80	5.26%	-.85%
5	US Steel	$1.60	5.14%	$31.13	$37.25			19.68%	$1.60	5.14%	24.82%
6	General Foods	$1.40	4.79%	$29.25	$25.00			-14.53%	$1.40	4.79%	-9.74%
7	Texaco	$1.66	4.49%	$37.00	$29.50			-20.27%	$1.73	4.68%	-15.59%
8	Exxon	$3.80	4.32%	$88.00	$96.50		1	9.66%	$4.25	4.83%	14.49%
9	Allied Chemical	$1.20	4.09%	$29.38	$49.13		1	67.23%	$1.29	4.39%	71.63%
10	Bethlehem Steel	$1.20	4.09%	$29.38	$32.50		1	10.64%	$1.65	5.62%	16.26%
11	United Aircraft	$1.80	4.04%	$44.50	$23.75		1	-46.63%	$.40	.90%	-45.73%
12	Union Carbide	$2.00	3.90%	$51.25	$33.88		1	-33.90%	$2.08	4.05%	-29.85%
13	Woolworth	$1.20	3.82%	$31.38	$18.50		1	-41.04%	$1.20	3.82%	-37.21%
14	Johns-Manville	$1.20	3.66%	$32.75	$16.63		1	-49.24%	$1.20	3.66%	-45.57%
15	Standard Oil CA	$2.90	3.62%	$80.13	$35.00		2	-12.64%	$3.00	3.74%	-8.89%
16	International Paper	$1.50	3.61%	$41.50	$52.50		1	26.51%	$1.75	4.22%	30.72%
17	International Harvester	$1.40	3.61%	$38.75	$26.75		1	-30.97%	$1.50	3.87%	-27.10%
18	Owens-Illinois	$1.40	3.33%	$42.00	$31.50		1	-25.00%	$1.46	3.48%	-21.52%
19	Aluminum Co of Amer	$1.80	3.27%	$55.00	$72.38		1	31.59%	$1.91	3.46%	35.05%
20	International Nickel	$1.00	3.10%	$32.25	$34.88		1	8.14%	$1.20	3.72%	11.86%
21	Du Pont	$5.45	2.99%	$182.00	$160.50		1	-11.81%	$5.75	3.16%	-8.65%
22	Goodyear	$.88	2.83%	$31.13	$15.63		1	-49.80%	$.96	3.08%	-46.71%
23	Chrysler	$1.00	2.42%	$41.38	$15.13		1	-63.44%	$1.30	3.14%	-60.30%
24	Westinghouse Electric	$.94	2.11%	$44.50	$25.00		1	-43.82%	$.97	2.18%	-41.64%
25	Swift & Company	$.75	1.90%	$39.38	$25.00		1	-36.51%	$.75	1.90%	-34.60%
26	General Electric	$1.40	1.90%	$73.88	$62.63		1	-15.23%	$1.45	1.96%	-13.27%
27	Procter & Gamble	$1.56	1.40%	$111.25	$91.50		1	-17.75%	$1.68	1.51%	-16.24%
28	Sears, Roebuck	$1.40	1.20%	$117.00	$80.25		1	-31.41%	$1.66	1.42%	-29.99%
29	Eastman Kodak	$1.08	.72%	$149.75	$115.38		1	-22.95%	$1.60	1.07%	-21.89%
30	Anaconda	$.12	.61%	$19.75	$27.75		1	40.51%	$.50	2.53%	43.04%
	AVERAGE		3.46%					-14.67%		3.68%	-10.99%

STOCK 1973	1973 WSJ DIVI.	1973 WSJ YIELD	1973 OPENING PRICE	1973 CLOSING PRICE	1973 STOCK DIV.	1973 SPLIT	1973 APPRECIATION	1973 DIVIDEND	ACT. CASH YIELD	TOTAL RETURN
BOTTOM FIVE:										
26 General Electric	$1.40	1.90%	$73.88	$62.63		1	-15.23%	$1.45	1.96%	-13.27%
27 Procter & Gamble	$1.56	1.40%	$111.25	$91.50		1	-17.75%	$1.68	1.51%	-16.24%
28 Sears, Roebuck	$1.40	1.20%	$117.00	$80.25		1	-31.41%	$1.66	1.42%	-29.99%
29 Eastman Kodak	$1.08	.72%	$149.75	$115.38		1	-22.95%	$1.60	1.07%	-21.89%
30 Anaconda	$.12	.61%	$19.75	$27.75		1	40.51%	$.50	2.53%	43.04%
		1.16%					-9.37%		1.70%	-7.67%
BOTTOM TEN:										
21 Du Pont	$5.45	2.99%	$182.00	$160.50		1	-11.81%	$5.75	3.16%	-8.65%
22 Goodyear	$.88	2.83%	$31.13	$15.63		1	-49.80%	$.96	3.08%	-46.71%
23 Chrysler	$1.00	2.42%	$41.38	$15.13		1	-63.44%	$1.30	3.14%	-60.30%
24 Westinghouse Electric	$.94	2.11%	$44.50	$25.00		1	-43.82%	$.97	2.18%	-41.64%
25 Swift & Company	$.75	1.90%	$39.38	$25.00		1	-36.51%	$.75	1.90%	-34.60%
26 General Electric	$1.40	1.90%	$73.88	$62.63		1	-15.23%	$1.45	1.96%	-13.27%
27 Procter & Gamble	$1.56	1.40%	$111.25	$91.50		1	-17.75%	$1.68	1.51%	-16.24%
28 Sears, Roebuck	$1.40	1.20%	$117.00	$80.25		1	-31.41%	$1.66	1.42%	-29.99%
29 Eastman Kodak	$1.08	.72%	$149.75	$115.38		1	-22.95%	$1.60	1.07%	-21.89%
30 Anaconda	$.12	.61%	$19.75	$27.75		1	40.51%	$.50	2.53%	43.04%
		1.81%					-25.22%		2.20%	-23.03%
TOP TEN:										
1 American Can	$2.20	6.96%	$31.63	$26.88		1	-15.02%	$2.20	6.96%	-8.06%
2 General Motors	$4.45	5.42%	$82.13	$46.00		1	-43.99%	$5.25	6.39%	-37.60%
3 American Tobacco	$2.29	5.33%	$43.00	$33.50		1	-22.09%	$2.38	5.53%	-16.56%
4 American T & T	$2.80	5.26%	$53.25	$50.00		1	-6.10%	$2.80	5.26%	-.85%
5 US Steel	$1.60	5.14%	$31.13	$37.25		1	19.68%	$1.60	5.14%	24.82%
6 General Foods	$1.40	4.79%	$29.25	$25.00		1	-14.53%	$1.40	4.79%	-9.74%
7 Texaco	$1.66	4.49%	$37.00	$29.50		1	-20.27%	$1.73	4.68%	-15.59%
8 Exxon	$3.80	4.32%	$88.00	$96.50		1	9.66%	$4.25	4.83%	14.49%
9 Allied Chemical	$1.20	4.09%	$29.38	$49.13		1	67.23%	$1.29	4.39%	71.63%
10 Bethlehem Steel	$1.20	4.09%	$29.38	$32.50		1	10.64%	$1.65	5.62%	16.26%
		4.99%					-1.48%		5.36%	3.88%
TOP FIVE:										
1 American Can	$2.20	6.96%	$31.63	$26.88		1	-15.02%	$2.20	6.96%	-8.06%
2 General Motors	$4.45	5.42%	$82.13	$46.00		1	-43.99%	$5.25	6.39%	-37.60%
3 American Tobacco	$2.29	5.33%	$43.00	$33.50		1	-22.09%	$2.38	5.53%	-16.56%
4 American T & T	$2.80	5.26%	$53.25	$50.00		1	-6.10%	$2.80	5.26%	-.85%
5 US Steel	$1.60	5.14%	$31.13	$37.25		1	19.68%	$1.60	5.14%	24.82%
		5.62%					-13.51%		5.86%	-7.65%

146

LIST OF 1972 DOW JONES INDUSTRIALS BY DIVIDEND-YIELD

STOCK 1972	1972 WSJ DIVI.	1972 WSJ YIELD	1972 OPENING PRICE	1972 CLOSING PRICE	1972 STOCK DIV.	1972 SPLIT	1972 APPRECIATION	1972 DIVIDEND	ACT. CASH YIELD	TOTAL RETURN
1 American Can	$2.20	6.42%	$34.25	$31.63		1	-7.66%	$2.20	6.42%	-1.24%
2 United Aircraft	$1.80	6.15%	$29.25	$44.50		1	52.14%	$1.80	6.15%	58.29%
3 American T & T	$2.60	5.81%	$44.75	$53.25		1	18.99%	$2.65	5.92%	24.92%
4 US Steel	$1.60	5.25%	$30.50	$31.13		1	2.05%	$1.60	5.25%	7.30%
5 American Tobacco	$2.20	5.22%	$42.13	$43.00		1	2.08%	$2.29	5.44%	7.51%
6 Standard Oil NJ	$3.80	5.21%	$73.00	$88.00		1	20.55%	$3.80	5.21%	25.75%
7 Standard Oil CA	$2.80	4.85%	$57.75	$80.13		1	38.74%	$2.90	5.02%	43.77%
8 Union Carbide	$2.00	4.73%	$42.25	$51.25		1	21.30%	$2.00	4.73%	26.04%
9 International Harvester	$1.40	4.71%	$29.75	$38.75		1	30.25%	$1.40	4.71%	34.96%
10 Texaco	$1.60	4.60%	$34.75	$37.00		1	6.47%	$1.66	4.78%	11.25%
11 International Paper	$1.50	4.29%	$35.00	$41.50		1	18.57%	$1.50	4.29%	22.86%
12 General Motors	$3.40	4.26%	$79.75	$82.13		1	2.98%	$4.45	5.58%	8.56%
13 Allied Chemical	$1.20	4.14%	$29.00	$29.38		1	1.29%	$1.20	4.14%	5.43%
14 Aluminum Co of Amer	$1.80	4.14%	$43.50	$55.00		1	26.44%	$1.80	4.14%	30.57%
15 Bethlehem Steel	$1.20	4.10%	$29.25	$29.38		1	.43%	$1.20	4.10%	4.53%
16 General Foods	$1.40	3.93%	$35.63	$29.25		1	-17.89%	$1.40	3.93%	-13.96%
17 Du Pont	$5.00	3.46%	$144.50	$182.00		1	25.95%	$5.45	3.77%	29.72%
18 Anaconda	$.50	3.13%	$16.00	$19.75		1	23.44%	$.13	.78%	24.22%
19 International Nickel	$1.00	3.11%	$32.13	$32.25		1	.39%	$1.00	3.11%	3.50%
20 Johns-Manville	$1.20	2.93%	$41.00	$32.75		1	-20.12%	$1.20	2.93%	-17.20%
21 Owens-Illinois	$1.35	2.89%	$46.75	$42.00		1	-10.16%	$1.39	2.97%	-7.19%
22 Goodyear	$.85	2.72%	$31.25	$31.13		1	-.40%	$.88	2.83%	2.43%
23 Woolworth	$1.20	2.67%	$44.88	$31.38		1	-30.08%	$1.20	2.67%	-27.41%
24 General Electric	$1.40	2.22%	$63.00	$73.88		1	17.26%	$1.40	2.22%	19.48%
25 Chrysler	$.60	2.13%	$28.13	$41.38		1	47.11%	$.90	3.20%	50.31%
26 Westinghouse Electric	$.90	1.96%	$46.00	$44.50		1	-3.26%	$.94	2.04%	-1.22%
27 Swift & Company	$.70	1.95%	$35.88	$39.38		1	9.76%	$.70	1.95%	11.71%
28 Procter & Gamble	$1.50	1.92%	$78.00	$111.25		1	42.63%	$1.53	1.96%	44.59%
29 Sears, Roebuck	$1.40	1.37%	$102.13	$117.00		1	14.57%	$1.55	1.52%	16.08%
30 Eastman Kodak	$1.04	1.07%	$97.00	$149.75		1	54.38%	$1.37	1.41%	55.79%
AVERAGE		3.71%					12.94%		3.77%	16.71%

STOCK 1972	1972 WSJ DIVI.	1972 WSJ YIELD	1972 OPENING PRICE	1972 CLOSING PRICE	1972 STOCK DIV.	1972 SPLIT	1972 APPRECIATION	1972 DIVIDEND	ACT. CASH YIELD	TOTAL RETURN
BOTTOM FIVE:										
26 Westinghouse Electric	$.90	1.96%	$46.00	$44.50		1	-3.26%	$.94	2.04%	-1.22%
27 Swift & Company	$.70	1.95%	$35.88	$39.38		1	9.76%	$.70	1.95%	11.71%
28 Procter & Gamble	$1.50	1.92%	$78.00	$111.25		1	42.63%	$1.53	1.96%	44.59%
29 Sears, Roebuck	$1.40	1.37%	$102.13	$117.00		1	14.57%	$1.55	1.52%	16.08%
30 Eastman Kodak	$1.04	1.07%	$97.00	$149.75		1	54.38%	$1.37	1.41%	55.79%
		1.65%					23.61%		1.78%	25.39%
BOTTOM TEN:										
21 Owens-Illinois	$1.35	2.89%	$46.75	$42.00		1	-10.16%	$1.39	2.97%	-7.19%
22 Goodyear	$.85	2.72%	$31.25	$31.13		1	-.40%	$.88	2.83%	2.43%
23 Woolworth	$1.20	2.67%	$44.88	$31.38		1	-30.08%	$1.20	2.67%	-27.41%
24 General Electric	$1.40	2.22%	$63.00	$73.88		1	17.26%	$1.40	2.22%	19.48%
25 Chrysler	$.60	2.13%	$28.13	$41.38		1	47.11%	$.90	3.20%	50.31%
26 Westinghouse Electric	$.90	1.96%	$46.00	$44.50		1	-3.26%	$.94	2.04%	-1.22%
27 Swift & Company	$.70	1.95%	$35.88	$39.38		1	9.76%	$.70	1.95%	11.71%
28 Procter & Gamble	$1.50	1.92%	$78.00	$111.25		1	42.63%	$1.53	1.96%	44.59%
29 Sears, Roebuck	$1.40	1.37%	$102.13	$117.00		1	14.57%	$1.55	1.52%	16.08%
30 Eastman Kodak	$1.04	1.07%	$97.00	$149.75		1	54.38%	$1.37	1.41%	55.79%
		2.09%					14.18%		2.28%	16.46%
TOP TEN:										
1 American Can	$2.20	6.42%	$34.25	$31.63		1	-7.66%	$2.20	6.42%	-1.24%
2 United Aircraft	$1.80	6.15%	$29.25	$44.50		1	52.14%	$1.80	6.15%	58.29%
3 American T & T	$2.60	5.81%	$44.75	$53.25		1	18.99%	$2.65	5.92%	24.92%
4 US Steel	$1.60	5.25%	$30.50	$31.13		1	2.05%	$1.60	5.25%	7.30%
5 American Tobacco	$2.20	5.22%	$42.13	$43.00		1	2.08%	$2.29	5.44%	7.51%
6 Standard Oil NJ	$3.80	5.21%	$73.00	$88.00		1	20.55%	$3.80	5.21%	25.75%
7 Standard Oil CA	$2.80	4.85%	$57.75	$80.13		1	38.74%	$2.90	5.02%	43.77%
8 Union Carbide	$2.00	4.73%	$42.25	$51.25		1	21.30%	$2.00	4.73%	26.04%
9 International Harvester	$1.40	4.71%	$29.75	$38.75		1	30.25%	$1.40	4.71%	34.96%
10 Texaco	$1.60	4.60%	$34.75	$37.00		1	6.47%	$1.66	4.78%	11.25%
		5.30%					18.49%		5.36%	23.85%
TOP FIVE:										
1 American Can	$2.20	6.42%	$34.25	$31.63		1	-7.66%	$2.20	6.42%	-1.24%
2 United Aircraft	$1.80	6.15%	$29.25	$44.50		1	52.14%	$1.80	6.15%	58.29%
3 American T & T	$2.60	5.81%	$44.75	$53.25		1	18.99%	$2.65	5.92%	24.92%
4 US Steel	$1.60	5.25%	$30.50	$31.13		1	2.05%	$1.60	5.25%	7.30%
5 American Tobacco	$2.20	5.22%	$42.13	$43.00		1	2.08%	$2.29	5.44%	7.51%
		5.77%					13.52%		5.84%	19.35%

LIST OF 1971 DOW JONES INDUSTRIALS BY DIVIDEND-YIELD

	STOCK 1971	1971 WSJ DIVI.	1971 WSJ YIELD	1971 OPENING PRICE	1971 CLOSING PRICE	1971 STOCK DIV.	1971 SPLIT	1971 APPRECIATION	1971 DIVIDEND	ACT. CASH YIELD	TOTAL RETURN
1	Anaconda	$1.90	8.99%	$21.13	$16.00			-24.26%	$.50	2.37%	-21.89%
2	Bethlehem Steel	$1.80	8.00%	$22.50	$29.25		1	30.00%	$1.20	5.33%	35.33%
3	US Steel	$2.40	7.44%	$32.25	$30.50		1	-5.43%	$2.00	6.20%	.78%
4	International Harvester	$1.80	6.55%	$27.50	$29.75		1	8.18%	$1.60	5.82%	14.00%
5	American Can	$2.20	5.53%	$39.75	$34.25		1	-13.84%	$2.20	5.53%	-8.30%
6	United Aircraft	$1.80	5.35%	$33.63	$29.25		1	-13.01%	$1.80	5.35%	-7.66%
7	American T & T	$2.60	5.33%	$48.75	$44.75		1	-8.21%	$2.60	5.33%	-2.87%
8	Standard Oil CA	$2.80	5.23%	$53.50	$57.75		1	7.94%	$2.80	5.23%	13.18%
9	Standard Oil NJ	$3.75	5.16%	$72.63	$73.00		1	.52%	$3.80	5.23%	5.75%
10	Allied Chemical	$1.20	5.13%	$23.38	$29.00		1	24.06%	$1.20	5.13%	29.20%
11	Union Carbide	$2.00	5.00%	$40.00	$42.25		1	5.63%	$2.00	5.00%	10.63%
12	American Tobacco	$2.10	4.65%	$45.13	$42.13		1	-6.65%	$2.20	4.88%	-1.77%
13	Texaco	$1.60	4.60%	$34.75	$34.75		1	.00%	$1.60	4.60%	4.60%
14	International Paper	$1.50	4.43%	$33.88	$35.00		1	3.32%	$1.50	4.43%	7.75%
15	General Motors	$3.40	4.31%	$78.88	$79.75		1	1.11%	$3.40	4.31%	5.42%
16	Du Pont	$5.00	3.80%	$131.75	$144.50		1	9.68%	$5.00	3.80%	13.47%
17	International Nickel	$1.60	3.54%	$45.25	$32.13		1	-29.01%	$1.30	2.87%	-26.13%
18	Woolworth	$1.20	3.37%	$35.63	$44.88		1	25.96%	$1.20	3.37%	29.33%
19	Aluminum Co of Amer	$1.80	3.19%	$56.38	$43.50		1	-22.84%	$1.80	3.19%	-19.65%
20	Johns-Manville	$1.20	2.97%	$40.38	$41.00		1	1.55%	$1.20	2.97%	4.52%
21	General Foods	$2.60	2.97%	$87.50	$35.63		2	-18.57%	$2.80	3.20%	-15.37%
22	General Electric	$2.60	2.77%	$93.88	$63.00		2	34.22%	$2.70	2.88%	37.10%
23	Goodyear	$.85	2.72%	$31.25	$31.25		1	.00%	$.85	2.72%	2.72%
24	Westinghouse Electric	$1.80	2.68%	$67.13	$46.00		2	37.06%	$1.80	2.68%	39.74%
25	Procter & Gamble	$1.40	2.43%	$57.50	$78.00		1	35.65%	$1.45	2.52%	38.17%
26	Owens-Illinois	$1.35	2.39%	$56.50	$46.75		1	-17.26%	$1.35	2.39%	-14.87%
27	Swift & Company	$.70	2.32%	$30.13	$35.88		1	19.09%	$.70	2.32%	21.41%
28	Chrysler	$.60	2.20%	$27.25	$28.13		1	3.21%	$.60	2.20%	5.41%
29	Sears, Roebuck	$1.20	1.59%	$75.50	$102.13		1	35.26%	$1.45	1.92%	37.19%
30	Eastman Kodak	$1.00	1.37%	$73.00	$97.00		1	32.88%	$1.32	1.81%	34.68%
	AVERAGE		4.20%					5.21%		3.85%	9.06%

STOCK 1971	1971 WSJ DIVI.	1971 WSJ YIELD	1971 OPENING PRICE	1971 CLOSING PRICE	1971 STOCK DIV.	1971 SPLIT	1971 APPRECIATION	1971 DIVIDEND	ACT. CASH YIELD	TOTAL RETURN
BOTTOM FIVE:										
26 Owens-Illinois	$1.35	2.39%	$56.50	$46.75		1	-17.26%	$1.35	2.39%	-14.87%
27 Swift & Company	$.70	2.32%	$30.13	$35.88		1	19.09%	$.70	2.32%	21.41%
28 Chrysler	$.60	2.20%	$27.25	$28.13		1	3.21%	$.60	2.20%	5.41%
29 Sears, Roebuck	$1.20	1.59%	$75.50	$102.13		1	35.26%	$1.45	1.92%	37.19%
30 Eastman Kodak	$1.00	1.37%	$73.00	$97.00		1	32.88%	$1.32	1.81%	34.68%
		1.97%					14.64%		2.13%	16.77%
BOTTOM TEN:										
21 General Foods	$2.60	2.97%	$87.50	$35.63		2	-18.57%	$2.80	3.20%	-15.37%
22 General Electric	$2.60	2.77%	$93.88	$63.00		2	34.22%	$2.70	2.88%	37.10%
23 Goodyear	$.85	2.72%	$31.25	$31.25		1	.00%	$.85	2.72%	2.72%
24 Westinghouse Electric	$1.80	2.68%	$67.13	$46.00		2	37.06%	$1.80	2.68%	39.74%
25 Procter & Gamble	$1.40	2.43%	$57.50	$78.00		1	35.65%	$1.45	2.52%	38.17%
26 Owens-Illinois	$1.35	2.39%	$56.50	$46.75		1	-17.26%	$1.35	2.39%	-14.87%
27 Swift & Company	$.70	2.32%	$30.13	$35.88		1	19.09%	$.70	2.32%	21.41%
28 Chrysler	$.60	2.20%	$27.25	$28.13		1	3.21%	$.60	2.20%	5.41%
29 Sears, Roebuck	$1.20	1.59%	$75.50	$102.13		1	35.26%	$1.45	1.92%	37.19%
30 Eastman Kodak	$1.00	1.37%	$73.00	$97.00		1	32.88%	$1.32	1.81%	34.68%
		2.35%					16.15%		2.46%	18.62%
TOP TEN:										
1 Anaconda	$1.90	8.99%	$21.13	$16.00		1	-24.26%	$.50	2.37%	-21.89%
2 Bethlehem Steel	$1.80	8.00%	$22.50	$29.25		1	30.00%	$1.20	5.33%	35.33%
3 US Steel	$2.40	7.44%	$32.25	$30.50		1	-5.43%	$2.00	6.20%	-.78%
4 International Harvester	$1.80	6.55%	$27.50	$29.75		1	8.18%	$1.60	5.82%	14.00%
5 American Can	$2.20	5.53%	$39.75	$34.25		1	-13.84%	$2.20	5.53%	-8.30%
6 United Aircraft	$1.80	5.35%	$33.63	$29.25		1	-13.01%	$1.80	5.35%	-7.66%
7 American T & T	$2.60	5.33%	$48.75	$44.75		1	-8.21%	$2.60	5.33%	-2.87%
8 Standard Oil CA	$2.80	5.23%	$53.50	$57.75		1	7.94%	$2.80	5.23%	13.18%
9 Standard Oil NJ	$3.75	5.16%	$72.63	$73.00		1	.52%	$3.80	5.23%	5.75%
10 Allied Chemical	$1.20	5.13%	$23.38	$29.00		1	24.06%	$1.20	5.13%	29.20%
		6.27%					.60%		5.15%	5.75%
TOP FIVE:										
1 Anaconda	$1.90	8.99%	$21.13	$16.00		1	-24.26%	$.50	2.37%	-21.89%
2 Bethlehem Steel	$1.80	8.00%	$22.50	$29.25		1	30.00%	$1.20	5.33%	35.33%
3 US Steel	$2.40	7.44%	$32.25	$30.50		1	-5.43%	$2.00	6.20%	-.78%
4 International Harvester	$1.80	6.55%	$27.50	$29.75		1	8.18%	$1.60	5.82%	14.00%
5 American Can	$2.20	5.53%	$39.75	$34.25		1	-13.84%	$2.20	5.53%	-8.30%
		7.30%					-1.07%		5.05%	3.98%

LIST OF 1970 DOW JONES INDUSTRIALS BY DIVIDEND-YIELD

	STOCK 1970	1970 WSJ DIVI.	1970 WSJ YIELD	1970 OPENING PRICE	1970 CLOSING PRICE	1970 STOCK DIV.	1970 SPLIT	1970 APPRECIATION	1970 DIVIDEND	ACT. CASH YIELD	TOTAL RETURN
1	US Steel	$2.40	6.91%	$34.75	$32.25		1	-7.19%	$2.40	6.91%	-.29%
2	International Harvester	$1.80	6.89%	$26.13	$27.50		1	5.26%	$1.80	6.89%	12.15%
3	Bethlehem Steel	$1.80	6.64%	$27.13	$22.50		1	-17.05%	$1.80	6.64%	-10.41%
4	Anaconda	$1.90	6.18%	$30.75	$21.13		1	-31.30%	$1.90	6.18%	-25.12%
5	Standard Oil NJ	$3.75	6.05%	$62.00	$72.63		1	17.14%	$3.75	6.05%	23.19%
6	General Motors	$4.30	6.04%	$71.25	$78.88		1	10.70%	$3.40	4.77%	15.47%
7	Chrysler	$2.00	5.67%	$35.25	$27.25		1	-22.70%	$.60	1.70%	-20.99%
8	American Tobacco	$2.00	5.61%	$35.63	$45.13		1	26.67%	$2.10	5.89%	32.56%
9	Standard Oil CA	$2.80	5.36%	$52.25	$53.50		1	2.39%	$2.80	5.36%	7.75%
10	American Can	$2.20	5.27%	$41.75	$39.75		1	-4.79%	$2.20	5.27%	.48%
11	American T & T	$2.60	5.27%	$49.38	$48.75		1	-1.27%	$2.60	5.27%	4.00%
12	Union Carbide	$2.00	5.26%	$38.00	$40.00		1	5.26%	$2.00	5.26%	10.53%
13	Texaco	$1.60	5.20%	$30.75	$34.75		1	13.01%	$1.60	5.20%	18.21%
14	Du Pont	$5.25	4.90%	$107.13	$131.75		1	22.99%	$5.00	4.67%	27.65%
15	Allied Chemical	$1.20	4.78%	$25.13	$23.38		1	-6.97%	$1.20	4.78%	-2.19%
16	United Aircraft	$1.80	4.47%	$40.25	$33.63		1	-16.46%	$1.80	4.47%	-11.99%
17	Johns-Manville	$1.20	4.02%	$29.88	$40.38		1	35.15%	$1.20	4.02%	39.16%
18	International Paper	$1.50	3.92%	$38.25	$33.88		1	-11.44%	$1.50	3.92%	-7.52%
19	General Electric	$2.60	3.39%	$76.63	$93.88		1	22.51%	$2.60	3.39%	25.91%
20	Woolworth	$1.20	3.14%	$38.25	$35.63		1	-6.86%	$1.20	3.14%	-3.73%
21	General Foods	$2.60	3.13%	$83.00	$87.50		1	5.42%	$2.60	3.13%	8.55%
22	Westinghouse Electric	$1.80	3.02%	$59.63	$67.13		1	12.58%	$1.80	3.02%	15.60%
23	International Nickel	$1.20	2.70%	$44.38	$45.25		1	1.97%	$1.40	3.15%	5.13%
24	Goodyear	$.85	2.70%	$31.25	$31.25		1	-.79%	$.85	2.70%	1.90%
25	Aluminum Co of Amer	$1.80	2.52%	$71.50	$56.38		1	-21.15%	$1.80	2.52%	-18.64%
26	Procter & Gamble	$2.60	2.36%	$110.00	$57.50		2	4.55%	$2.75	2.50%	7.05%
27	Owens-Illinois	$1.35	2.18%	$62.00	$56.50		1	-8.87%	$1.35	2.18%	-6.69%
28	Swift & Company	$.60	1.91%	$31.38	$30.13		1	-3.98%	$.60	1.91%	-2.07%
29	Sears, Roebuck	$1.20	1.79%	$67.00	$75.50		1	12.69%	$1.35	2.01%	14.70%
30	Eastman Kodak	$1.00	1.22%	$81.75	$73.00		1	-10.70%	$1.28	1.57%	-9.14%
	AVERAGE		4.28%					.89%		4.15%	5.04%

STOCK 1970	1970 WSJ DIVI.	1970 WSJ YIELD	1970 OPENING PRICE	1970 CLOSING PRICE	1970 STOCK DIV.	1970 SPLIT	1970 APPRECIATION	1970 DIVIDEND	ACT. CASH YIELD	TOTAL RETURN
BOTTOM FIVE:										
26 Procter & Gamble	$2.60	2.36%	$110.00	$57.50		2	4.55%	$2.75	2.50%	7.05%
27 Owens-Illinois	$1.35	2.18%	$62.00	$56.50		1	-8.87%	$1.35	2.18%	-6.69%
28 Swift & Company	$.60	1.91%	$31.38	$30.13		1	-3.98%	$.60	1.91%	-2.07%
29 Sears, Roebuck	$1.20	1.79%	$67.00	$75.50		1	12.69%	$1.35	2.01%	14.70%
30 Eastman Kodak	$1.00	1.22%	$81.75	$73.00		1	-10.70%	$1.28	1.57%	-9.14%
		1.89%					-1.27%		2.03%	.77%
BOTTOM TEN:										
21 General Foods	$2.60	3.13%	$83.00	$87.50		1	5.42%	$2.60	3.13%	8.55%
22 Westinghouse Electric	$1.80	3.02%	$59.63	$67.13		1	12.58%	$1.80	3.02%	15.60%
23 International Nickel	$1.20	2.70%	$44.38	$45.25		1	1.97%	$1.40	3.15%	5.13%
24 Goodyear	$.85	2.70%	$31.50	$31.25		1	-.79%	$.85	2.70%	1.90%
25 Aluminum Co of Amer	$1.80	2.52%	$71.50	$56.38		1	-21.15%	$1.80	2.52%	-18.64%
26 Procter & Gamble	$2.60	2.36%	$110.00	$57.50		2	4.55%	$2.75	2.50%	7.05%
27 Owens-Illinois	$1.35	2.18%	$62.00	$56.50		1	-8.87%	$1.35	2.18%	-6.69%
28 Swift & Company	$.60	1.91%	$31.38	$30.13		1	-3.98%	$.60	1.91%	-2.07%
29 Sears, Roebuck	$1.20	1.79%	$67.00	$75.50		1	12.69%	$1.35	2.01%	14.70%
30 Eastman Kodak	$1.00	1.22%	$81.75	$73.00		1	-10.70%	$1.28	1.57%	-9.14%
		2.35%					-.83%		2.47%	1.64%
TOP TEN:										
1 US Steel	$2.40	6.91%	$34.75	$32.25			-7.19%	$2.40	6.91%	-.29%
2 International Harvester	$1.80	6.89%	$26.13	$27.50		1	5.26%	$1.80	6.89%	12.15%
3 Bethlehem Steel	$1.80	6.64%	$27.13	$22.50		1	-17.05%	$1.80	6.64%	-10.41%
4 Anaconda	$1.90	6.18%	$30.75	$21.13		1	-31.30%	$1.90	6.18%	-25.12%
5 Standard Oil NJ	$3.75	6.05%	$62.00	$72.63		1	17.14%	$3.75	6.05%	23.19%
6 General Motors	$4.30	6.04%	$71.25	$78.88		1	10.70%	$3.40	4.77%	15.47%
7 Chrysler	$2.00	5.67%	$35.25	$27.25			-22.70%	$.60	1.70%	-20.99%
8 American Tobacco	$2.00	5.61%	$35.63	$45.13		1	26.67%	$2.10	5.89%	32.56%
9 Standard Oil CA	$2.80	5.36%	$52.25	$53.50		1	2.39%	$2.80	5.36%	7.75%
10 American Can	$2.20	5.27%	$41.75	$39.75			-4.79%	$2.20	5.27%	.48%
		6.06%					-2.09%		5.57%	3.48%
TOP FIVE:										
1 US Steel	$2.40	6.91%	$34.75	$32.25			-7.19%	$2.40	6.91%	-.29%
2 International Harvester	$1.80	6.89%	$26.13	$27.50		1	5.26%	$1.80	6.89%	12.15%
3 Bethlehem Steel	$1.80	6.64%	$27.13	$22.50		1	-17.05%	$1.80	6.64%	-10.41%
4 Anaconda	$1.90	6.18%	$30.75	$21.13		1	-31.30%	$1.90	6.18%	-25.12%
5 Standard Oil NJ	$3.75	6.05%	$62.00	$72.63		1	17.14%	$3.75	6.05%	23.19%
		6.53%					-6.63%		6.53%	-.10%

LIST OF 1969 DOW JONES INDUSTRIALS BY DIVIDEND-YIELD

STOCK 1969	1969 WSJ DIVI.	1969 WSJ YIELD	1969 OPENING PRICE	1969 CLOSING PRICE	1969 STOCK DIV.	1969 SPLIT	1969 APPRECIATION	1969 DIVIDEND	ACT. CASH YIELD	TOTAL RETURN
1 US Steel	$2.40	5.52%	$43.50	$34.75		1	-20.11%	$2.40	5.52%	-14.60%
2 General Motors	$4.30	5.37%	$80.13	$71.25		1	-11.08%	$4.30	5.37%	-5.71%
3 Bethlehem Steel	$1.60	5.12%	$31.25	$27.13		1	-13.20%	$1.75	5.60%	-7.60%
4 American Tobacco	$1.90	4.87%	$39.00	$35.63		1	-8.65%	$2.00	5.13%	-3.53%
5 International Harvester	$1.80	4.85%	$37.13	$26.13		1	-29.63%	$1.80	4.85%	-24.78%
6 Standard Oil NJ	$3.65	4.63%	$78.75	$62.00		1	-21.27%	$3.75	4.76%	-16.51%
7 American T & T	$2.40	4.49%	$53.50	$49.38		1	-7.71%	$2.40	4.49%	-3.22%
8 Union Carbide	$2.00	4.37%	$45.75	$38.00		1	-16.94%	$2.00	4.37%	-12.57%
9 International Paper	$1.50	4.12%	$36.38	$38.25		1	5.15%	$1.50	4.12%	9.28%
10 Anaconda	$2.50	3.91%	$64.00	$30.75		1	-51.95%	$2.20	3.44%	-48.52%
11 American Can	$2.20	3.80%	$57.88	$41.75		1	-27.86%	$2.20	3.80%	-24.06%
12 Standard Oil CA	$2.70	3.74%	$72.25	$52.25		1	-27.68%	$2.80	3.88%	-23.81%
13 Chrysler	$2.00	3.49%	$57.25	$35.25		1	-38.43%	$2.00	3.49%	-34.93%
14 Du Pont	$5.50	3.37%	$163.25	$107.13		1	-34.38%	$5.25	3.22%	-31.16%
15 Texaco	$2.80	3.35%	$83.50	$30.75		2	-26.35%	$3.10	3.71%	-22.63%
16 Allied Chemical	$1.20	3.24%	$37.00	$25.13		1	-32.09%	$1.20	3.24%	-28.85%
17 International Nickel	$1.20	3.06%	$39.25	$44.38		1	13.06%	$1.20	3.06%	16.11%
18 Woolworth	$1.00	3.04%	$32.88	$38.25		1	16.35%	$1.15	3.50%	19.85%
19 General Foods	$2.40	2.93%	$82.00	$83.00		1	1.22%	$2.60	3.17%	4.39%
20 Procter & Gamble	$2.40	2.79%	$86.00	$110.00		1	27.91%	$2.60	3.02%	30.93%
21 Johns-Manville	$2.40	2.75%	$87.13	$29.88		2	-31.42%	$2.40	2.75%	-28.67%
22 General Electric	$2.60	2.74%	$94.88	$76.63		1	-19.24%	$2.60	2.74%	-16.50%
23 Goodyear	$1.50	2.69%	$55.75	$31.50		2	13.00%	$1.65	2.96%	15.96%
24 United Aircraft	$1.80	2.65%	$68.00	$40.25		1	-40.81%	$1.80	2.65%	-38.16%
25 Westinghouse Electric	$1.80	2.59%	$69.50	$59.63		1	-14.21%	$1.80	2.59%	-11.62%
26 Aluminum Co of Amer	$1.80	2.47%	$72.75	$71.50		1	-1.72%	$1.80	2.47%	.76%
27 Swift & Company	$.60	1.98%	$30.25	$31.38		1	3.72%	$.60	1.98%	5.70%
28 Sears, Roebuck	$1.20	1.98%	$60.75	$67.00		1	10.29%	$1.35	2.22%	12.51%
29 Owens-Illinois	$1.35	1.87%	$72.25	$62.00		1	-14.19%	$1.35	1.87%	-12.32%
30 Eastman Kodak	$.88	1.19%	$74.00	$81.75		1	10.47%	$1.22	1.65%	12.12%
AVERAGE		3.43%					-12.92%		3.52%	-9.40%

STOCK 1969	1969 WSJ DIVI.	1969 WSJ YIELD	1969 OPENING PRICE	1969 CLOSING PRICE	1969 STOCK DIV.	1969 SPLIT	1969 APPRECIATION	1969 DIVIDEND	ACT. CASH YIELD	TOTAL RETURN
BOTTOM FIVE:										
26 Aluminum Co of Amer	$1.80	2.47%	$72.75	$71.50		1	-1.72%	$1.80	2.47%	.76%
27 Swift & Company	$.60	1.98%	$30.25	$31.38		1	3.72%	$.60	1.98%	5.70%
28 Sears, Roebuck	$1.20	1.98%	$60.75	$67.00		1	10.29%	$1.35	2.22%	12.51%
29 Owens-Illinois	$1.35	1.87%	$72.25	$62.00		1	-14.19%	$1.35	1.87%	-12.32%
30 Eastman Kodak	$.88	1.19%	$74.00	$81.75		1	10.47%	$1.22	1.65%	12.12%
		1.90%					1.71%		2.04%	3.75%
BOTTOM TEN:										
21 Johns-Manville	$2.40	2.75%	$87.13	$29.88		2	-31.42%	$2.40	2.75%	-28.67%
22 General Electric	$2.60	2.74%	$94.88	$76.63		1	-19.24%	$2.60	2.74%	-16.50%
23 Goodyear	$1.50	2.69%	$55.75	$31.50		2	13.00%	$1.65	2.96%	15.96%
24 United Aircraft	$1.80	2.65%	$68.00	$40.25		1	-40.81%	$1.80	2.65%	-38.16%
25 Westinghouse Electric	$1.80	2.59%	$69.50	$59.63		1	-14.21%	$1.80	2.59%	-11.62%
26 Aluminum Co of Amer	$1.80	2.47%	$72.75	$71.50		1	-1.72%	$1.80	2.47%	.76%
27 Swift & Company	$.60	1.98%	$30.25	$31.38		1	3.72%	$.60	1.98%	5.70%
28 Sears, Roebuck	$1.20	1.98%	$60.75	$67.00		1	10.29%	$1.35	2.22%	12.51%
29 Owens-Illinois	$1.35	1.87%	$72.25	$62.00		1	-14.19%	$1.35	1.87%	-12.32%
30 Eastman Kodak	$.88	1.19%	$74.00	$81.75		1	10.47%	$1.22	1.65%	12.12%
		2.29%					-8.41%		2.39%	-6.02%
TOP TEN:										
1 US Steel	$2.40	5.52%	$43.50	$34.75		1	-20.11%	$2.40	5.52%	-14.60%
2 General Motors	$4.30	5.37%	$80.13	$71.25		1	-11.08%	$4.30	5.37%	-5.71%
3 Bethlehem Steel	$1.60	5.12%	$31.25	$27.13		1	-13.20%	$1.75	5.60%	-7.60%
4 American Tobacco	$1.90	4.87%	$39.00	$35.63		1	-8.65%	$2.00	5.13%	-3.53%
5 International Harvester	$1.80	4.85%	$37.13	$26.13		1	-29.63%	$1.80	4.85%	-24.78%
6 Standard Oil NJ	$3.65	4.63%	$78.75	$62.00		1	-21.27%	$3.75	4.76%	-16.51%
7 American T & T	$2.40	4.49%	$53.50	$49.38		1	-7.71%	$2.40	4.49%	-3.22%
8 Union Carbide	$2.00	4.37%	$45.75	$38.00		1	-16.94%	$2.00	4.37%	-12.57%
9 International Paper	$1.50	4.12%	$36.38	$38.25		1	5.15%	$1.50	4.12%	9.28%
10 Anaconda	$2.50	3.91%	$64.00	$30.75		1	-51.95%	$2.20	3.44%	-48.52%
		4.72%					-17.54%		4.76%	-12.78%
TOP FIVE:										
1 US Steel	$2.40	5.52%	$43.50	$34.75		1	-20.11%	$2.40	5.52%	-14.60%
2 General Motors	$4.30	5.37%	$80.13	$71.25		1	-11.08%	$4.30	5.37%	-5.71%
3 Bethlehem Steel	$1.60	5.12%	$31.25	$27.13		1	-13.20%	$1.75	5.60%	-7.60%
4 American Tobacco	$1.90	4.87%	$39.00	$35.63		1	-8.65%	$2.00	5.13%	-3.53%
5 International Harvester	$1.80	4.85%	$37.13	$26.13		1	-29.63%	$1.80	4.85%	-24.78%
		5.14%					-16.53%		5.29%	-11.24%

LIST OF 1968 DOW JONES INDUSTRIALS BY DIVIDEND-YIELD

STOCK 1968	1968 WSJ DIVI.	1968 WSJ YIELD	1968 OPENING PRICE	1968 CLOSING PRICE	1968 STOCK DIV.	1968 SPLIT	1968 APPRECIATION	1968 DIVIDEND	ACT. CASH YIELD	TOTAL RETURN
1 US Steel	$2.40	5.70%	$42.13	$43.50		1	3.26%	$2.40	5.70%	8.96%
2 American Tobacco	$1.80	5.58%	$32.25	$39.00		1	20.93%	$1.88	5.81%	26.74%
3 Anaconda	$2.50	5.28%	$47.38	$64.00		1	35.09%	$2.25	4.75%	39.84%
4 International Harvester	$1.80	5.05%	$35.63	$37.13		1	4.21%	$1.80	5.05%	9.26%
5 Standard Oil NJ	$3.45	5.00%	$69.00	$78.75		1	14.13%	$3.65	5.29%	19.42%
6 Allied Chemical	$1.90	4.72%	$40.25	$37.00		1	-8.07%	$1.73	4.29%	-3.79%
7 American T & T	$2.40	4.65%	$51.63	$53.50		1	3.63%	$2.40	4.65%	8.28%
8 General Motors	$3.80	4.59%	$82.75	$80.13		1	-3.17%	$4.30	5.20%	2.02%
9 Bethlehem Steel	$1.50	4.48%	$33.50	$31.25		1	-6.72%	$1.60	4.78%	-1.94%
10 International Paper	$1.35	4.37%	$30.88	$36.38		1	17.81%	$1.39	4.50%	22.32%
11 American Can	$2.20	4.26%	$51.63	$57.88		1	12.11%	$2.20	4.26%	16.37%
12 Union Carbide	$2.00	4.07%	$49.13	$45.75		1	-6.87%	$2.00	4.07%	-2.80%
13 Johns-Manville	$2.20	4.04%	$54.50	$87.13		1	59.86%	$2.20	4.04%	63.90%
14 Standard Oil CA	$2.50	3.97%	$63.00	$72.25		1	14.68%	$2.70	4.29%	18.97%
15 Woolworth	$1.00	3.92%	$25.50	$32.88		1	28.92%	$1.00	3.92%	32.84%
16 Swift & Company	$1.20	3.74%	$32.13	$30.25		1	-5.84%	$.90	2.80%	-3.04%
17 Chrysler	$2.00	3.56%	$56.25	$57.25		1	1.78%	$2.00	3.56%	5.33%
18 General Foods	$2.40	3.41%	$70.38	$82.00		1	16.52%	$2.40	3.41%	19.93%
19 Texaco	$2.60	3.20%	$81.38	$83.50		1	2.61%	$2.90	3.56%	6.18%
20 Du Pont	$5.00	3.17%	$157.75	$163.25		1	3.49%	$5.50	3.49%	6.97%
21 General Electric	$2.60	2.72%	$95.63	$94.88		1	-.78%	$2.60	2.72%	1.93%
22 Goodyear	$1.35	2.41%	$56.00	$55.75		1	-.45%	$1.43	2.54%	2.10%
23 International Nickel	$2.80	2.40%	$116.50	$39.25		2.5	-15.77%	$3.08	2.64%	-13.13%
24 Owens-Illinois	$1.35	2.39%	$56.38	$72.25		1	28.16%	$1.35	2.39%	30.55%
25 Procter & Gamble	$2.20	2.37%	$93.00	$86.00		1	-7.53%	$2.40	2.58%	-4.95%
26 Westinghouse Electric	$1.60	2.25%	$71.25	$69.50		1	-2.46%	$1.80	2.53%	.07%
27 Aluminum Co of Amer	$1.80	2.22%	$81.00	$72.75		1	-10.19%	$1.80	2.22%	-7.96%
28 United Aircraft	$1.60	1.94%	$82.38	$68.00		1	-17.45%	$1.70	2.06%	-15.39%
29 Sears, Roebuck	$1.00	1.78%	$56.13	$60.75		1	8.24%	$1.30	2.32%	10.56%
30 Eastman Kodak	$1.60	1.09%	$146.25	$74.00		2	1.20%	$2.18	1.49%	2.69%
AVERAGE		3.61%					6.38%		3.70%	10.07%

STOCK	1968	1968 WSJ DIVI.	1968 WSJ YIELD	1968 OPENING PRICE	1968 CLOSING PRICE	1968 STOCK DIV.	1968 SPLIT	1968 APPRECIATION	1968 DIVIDEND	ACT. CASH YIELD	TOTAL RETURN
BOTTOM FIVE:											
26	Westinghouse Electric	$1.60	2.25%	$71.25	$69.50		1	-2.46%	$1.80	2.53%	.07%
27	Aluminum Co of Amer	$1.80	2.22%	$81.00	$72.75		1	-10.19%	$1.80	2.22%	-7.96%
28	United Aircraft	$1.60	1.94%	$82.38	$68.00		1	-17.45%	$1.70	2.06%	-15.39%
29	Sears, Roebuck	$1.00	1.78%	$56.13	$60.75		1	8.24%	$1.30	2.32%	10.56%
30	Eastman Kodak	$1.60	1.09%	$146.25	$74.00		2	1.20%	$2.18	1.49%	2.69%
			1.86%					-4.13%		2.12%	-2.01%
BOTTOM TEN:											
21	General Electric	$2.60	2.72%	$95.63	$94.88		1	-.78%	$2.60	2.72%	1.93%
22	Goodyear	$1.35	2.41%	$56.00	$55.75		1	-.45%	$1.43	2.54%	2.10%
23	International Nickel	$2.80	2.40%	$116.50	$39.25		2.5	-15.77%	$3.08	2.64%	-13.13%
24	Owens-Illinois	$1.35	2.39%	$56.38	$72.25		1	28.16%	$1.35	2.39%	30.55%
25	Procter & Gamble	$2.20	2.37%	$93.00	$86.00			-7.53%	$2.40	2.58%	-4.95%
26	Westinghouse Electric	$1.60	2.25%	$71.25	$69.50		1	-2.46%	$1.80	2.53%	.07%
27	Aluminum Co of Amer	$1.80	2.22%	$81.00	$72.75		1	-10.19%	$1.80	2.22%	-7.96%
28	United Aircraft	$1.60	1.94%	$82.38	$68.00		1	-17.45%	$1.70	2.06%	-15.39%
29	Sears, Roebuck	$1.00	1.78%	$56.13	$60.75		1	8.24%	$1.30	2.32%	10.56%
30	Eastman Kodak	$1.60	1.09%	$146.25	$74.00		2	1.20%	$2.18	1.49%	2.69%
			2.16%					-1.70%		2.35%	.65%
TOP TEN:											
1	US Steel	$2.40	5.70%	$42.13	$43.50		1	3.26%	$2.40	5.70%	8.96%
2	American Tobacco	$1.80	5.58%	$32.25	$39.00		1	20.93%	$1.88	5.81%	26.74%
3	Anaconda	$2.50	5.28%	$47.38	$64.00		1	35.09%	$2.25	4.75%	39.84%
4	International Harvester	$1.80	5.05%	$35.63	$37.13		1	4.21%	$1.80	5.05%	9.26%
5	Standard Oil NJ	$3.45	5.00%	$69.00	$78.75		1	14.13%	$3.65	5.29%	19.42%
6	Allied Chemical	$1.90	4.72%	$40.25	$37.00		1	-8.07%	$1.73	4.29%	-3.79%
7	American T & T	$2.40	4.65%	$51.63	$53.50		1	3.63%	$2.40	4.65%	8.28%
8	General Motors	$3.80	4.59%	$82.75	$80.13		1	-3.17%	$4.30	5.20%	2.02%
9	Bethlehem Steel	$1.50	4.48%	$33.50	$31.25		1	-6.72%	$1.60	4.78%	-1.94%
10	International Paper	$1.35	4.37%	$30.88	$36.38		1	17.81%	$1.39	4.50%	22.32%
			4.94%					8.11%		5.00%	13.11%
TOP FIVE:											
1	US Steel	$2.40	5.70%	$42.13	$43.50		1	3.26%	$2.40	5.70%	8.96%
2	American Tobacco	$1.80	5.58%	$32.25	$39.00		1	20.93%	$1.88	5.81%	26.74%
3	Anaconda	$2.50	5.28%	$47.38	$64.00		1	35.09%	$2.25	4.75%	39.84%
4	International Harvester	$1.80	5.05%	$35.63	$37.13		1	4.21%	$1.80	5.05%	9.26%
5	Standard Oil NJ	$3.45	5.00%	$69.00	$78.75		1	14.13%	$3.65	5.29%	19.42%
			5.32%					15.53%		5.32%	20.85%

LIST OF 1967 DOW JONES INDUSTRIALS BY DIVIDEND-YIELD

STOCK 1967	1967 WSJ DIVI.	1967 WSJ YIELD	1967 OPENING PRICE	1967 CLOSING PRICE	1967 STOCK DIV.	1967 SPLIT	1967 APPRECIATION	1967 DIVIDEND	ACT. CASH YIELD	TOTAL RETURN
1 General Motors	$4.55	6.61%	$68.88	$82.75		1	20.15%	$3.80	5.52%	25.66%
2 Chrysler	$2.00	6.40%	$31.25	$56.25		1	80.00%	$2.00	6.40%	86.40%
3 US Steel	$2.40	6.23%	$38.50	$42.13		1	9.42%	$2.40	6.23%	15.65%
4 Anaconda	$5.00	6.21%	$80.50	$47.38		2	17.70%	$4.75	5.90%	23.60%
5 American Tobacco	$1.80	5.67%	$31.75	$32.25			1.57%	$1.80	5.67%	7.24%
6 Allied Chemical	$1.90	5.59%	$34.00	$40.25	2.00%	1	20.75%	$1.90	5.59%	26.34%
7 International Paper	$1.35	5.32%	$25.38	$30.88		1	21.67%	$1.35	5.32%	27.00%
8 Standard Oil NJ	$3.30	5.21%	$63.38	$69.00		1	8.88%	$3.45	5.44%	14.32%
9 International Harvester	$1.80	5.16%	$34.88	$35.63		1	2.15%	$1.80	5.16%	7.31%
10 Woolworth	$1.00	5.10%	$19.63	$25.50		1	29.94%	$1.00	5.10%	35.03%
11 Bethlehem Steel	$1.50	4.94%	$30.38	$33.50		1	10.29%	$1.50	4.94%	15.23%
12 American Can	$2.20	4.64%	$47.38	$51.63		1	8.97%	$2.20	4.64%	13.61%
13 Johns-Manville	$2.20	4.57%	$48.13	$54.50		1	13.25%	$2.20	4.57%	17.82%
14 Swift & Company	$2.00	4.38%	$45.63	$32.13		2	40.82%	$2.20	4.82%	45.64%
15 Standard Oil CA	$2.50	4.17%	$60.00	$63.00	5.00%	1	10.25%	$2.50	4.17%	14.42%
16 Union Carbide	$2.00	4.11%	$48.63	$49.13		1	1.03%	$2.00	4.11%	5.14%
17 American T & T	$2.20	4.05%	$54.38	$51.63		1	-5.06%	$2.20	4.05%	-1.01%
18 Du Pont	$5.75	3.92%	$146.50	$157.75		1	7.68%	$5.00	3.41%	11.09%
19 Texaco	$2.60	3.75%	$69.25	$81.38		1	17.51%	$2.70	3.90%	21.41%
20 Goodyear	$1.35	3.31%	$40.75	$56.00		1	37.42%	$1.35	3.31%	40.74%
21 International Nickel	$2.80	3.21%	$87.13	$116.50		1	33.72%	$3.00	3.44%	37.16%
22 General Foods	$2.20	3.13%	$70.25	$70.38		1	.18%	$2.35	3.35%	3.52%
23 Westinghouse Electric	$1.40	2.98%	$47.00	$71.25		1	51.60%	$1.60	3.40%	55.00%
24 General Electric	$2.60	2.92%	$89.00	$95.63		1	7.44%	$2.60	2.92%	10.37%
25 Procter & Gamble	$2.00	2.81%	$71.25	$93.00		1	30.53%	$2.20	3.09%	33.61%
26 Owens-Illinois	$1.35	2.55%	$53.00	$56.38		1	6.37%	$1.35	2.55%	8.92%
27 Sears, Roebuck	$1.00	2.23%	$44.75	$56.13		1	25.42%	$1.20	2.68%	28.10%
28 Aluminum Co of Amer	$1.60	2.09%	$76.63	$81.00		1	5.71%	$1.75	2.28%	7.99%
29 United Aircraft	$1.60	1.97%	$81.13	$82.38		1	1.54%	$1.60	1.97%	3.51%
30 Eastman Kodak	$1.60	1.27%	$126.25	$146.25		1	15.84%	$2.15	1.70%	17.54%
AVERAGE		4.15%					17.76%		4.19%	21.95%

STOCK 1967	1967 WSJ DIVI.	1967 WSJ YIELD	1967 OPENING PRICE	1967 CLOSING PRICE	1967 STOCK DIV.	1967 SPLIT	1967 APPRECIATION	1967 DIVIDEND	ACT. CASH YIELD	TOTAL RETURN
BOTTOM FIVE:										
26 Owens-Illinois	$1.35	2.55%	$53.00	$56.38		1	6.37%	$1.35	2.55%	8.92%
27 Sears, Roebuck	$1.00	2.23%	$44.75	$56.13		1	25.42%	$1.20	2.68%	28.10%
28 Aluminum Co of Amer	$1.60	2.09%	$76.63	$81.00		1	5.71%	$1.75	2.28%	7.99%
29 United Aircraft	$1.60	1.97%	$81.13	$82.38		1	1.54%	$1.60	1.97%	3.51%
30 Eastman Kodak	$1.60	1.27%	$126.25	$146.25		1	15.84%	$2.15	1.70%	17.54%
		2.02%					10.98%		2.24%	13.21%
BOTTOM TEN:										
21 International Nickel	$2.80	3.21%	$87.13	$116.50		1	33.72%	$3.00	3.44%	37.16%
22 General Foods	$2.20	3.13%	$70.25	$70.38		1	.18%	$2.35	3.35%	3.52%
23 Westinghouse Electric	$1.40	2.98%	$47.00	$71.25		1	51.60%	$1.60	3.40%	55.00%
24 General Electric	$2.60	2.92%	$89.00	$95.63		1	7.44%	$2.60	2.92%	10.37%
25 Procter & Gamble	$2.00	2.81%	$71.25	$93.00		1	30.53%	$2.20	3.09%	33.61%
26 Owens-Illinois	$1.35	2.55%	$53.00	$56.38		1	6.37%	$1.35	2.55%	8.92%
27 Sears, Roebuck	$1.00	2.23%	$44.75	$56.13		1	25.42%	$1.20	2.68%	28.10%
28 Aluminum Co of Amer	$1.60	2.09%	$76.63	$81.00		1	5.71%	$1.75	2.28%	7.99%
29 United Aircraft	$1.60	1.97%	$81.13	$82.38		1	1.54%	$1.60	1.97%	3.51%
30 Eastman Kodak	$1.60	1.27%	$126.25	$146.25		1	15.84%	$2.15	1.70%	17.54%
		2.52%					17.83%		2.74%	20.57%
TOP TEN:										
1 General Motors	$4.55	6.61%	$68.88	$82.75		1	20.15%	$3.80	5.52%	25.66%
2 Chrysler	$2.00	6.40%	$31.25	$56.25		1	80.00%	$2.00	6.40%	86.40%
3 US Steel	$2.40	6.23%	$38.50	$42.13		1	9.42%	$2.40	6.23%	15.65%
4 Anaconda	$5.00	6.21%	$80.50	$47.38		2	17.70%	$4.75	5.90%	23.60%
5 American Tobacco	$1.80	5.67%	$31.75	$32.25	2.00%	1	1.57%	$1.80	5.67%	7.24%
6 Allied Chemical	$1.90	5.59%	$34.00	$40.25		1	20.75%	$1.90	5.59%	26.34%
7 International Paper	$1.35	5.32%	$25.38	$30.88		1	21.67%	$1.35	5.32%	27.00%
8 Standard Oil NJ	$3.30	5.21%	$63.38	$69.00		1	8.88%	$3.45	5.44%	14.32%
9 International Harvester	$1.80	5.16%	$34.88	$35.63		1	2.15%	$1.80	5.16%	7.31%
10 Woolworth	$1.00	5.10%	$19.63	$25.50		1	29.94%	$1.00	5.10%	35.03%
		5.75%					21.22%		5.63%	26.86%
TOP FIVE:										
1 General Motors	$4.55	6.61%	$68.88	$82.75		1	20.15%	$3.80	5.52%	25.66%
2 Chrysler	$2.00	6.40%	$31.25	$56.25		1	80.00%	$2.00	6.40%	86.40%
3 US Steel	$2.40	6.23%	$38.50	$42.13		1	9.42%	$2.40	6.23%	15.65%
4 Anaconda	$5.00	6.21%	$80.50	$47.38		2	17.70%	$4.75	5.90%	23.60%
5 American Tobacco	$1.80	5.67%	$31.75	$32.25		1	1.57%	$1.80	5.67%	7.24%
		6.22%					25.77%		5.94%	31.71%

LIST OF 1966 DOW JONES INDUSTRIALS BY DIVIDEND-YIELD

	STOCK 1966	1966 WSJ DIVI.	1966 WSJ YIELD	1966 OPENING PRICE	1966 CLOSING PRICE	1966 STOCK DIV.	1966 SPLIT	1966 APPRECIATION	1966 DIVIDEND	ACT. CASH YIELD	TOTAL RETURN
1	General Motors	$5.20	5.07%	$102.63	$68.88		1	-32.89%	$4.55	4.43%	-28.45%
2	Anaconda	$3.75	4.46%	$84.13	$80.50			-4.31%	$5.00	5.94%	1.63%
3	American Tobacco	$1.70	4.42%	$38.50	$31.75		1	-17.53%	$1.80	4.68%	-12.86%
4	American Can	$2.20	3.97%	$55.38	$47.38		1	-14.45%	$2.20	3.97%	-10.47%
5	Johns-Manville	$2.20	3.96%	$55.63	$48.13		1	-13.48%	$2.20	3.96%	-9.53%
6	International Paper	$1.20	3.93%	$30.50	$25.38		1	-16.80%	$1.24	4.07%	-12.74%
7	Standard Oil NJ	$3.15	3.90%	$80.75	$63.38		1	-21.52%	$3.30	4.09%	-17.43%
8	Allied Chemical	$1.90	3.86%	$49.25	$34.00	2.00%	1	-29.58%	$1.90	3.86%	-25.73%
9	US Steel	$2.00	3.86%	$51.88	$38.50		1	-25.78%	$2.10	4.05%	-21.73%
10	Bethlehem Steel	$1.50	3.76%	$39.88	$30.38		1	-23.82%	$1.80	4.51%	-19.31%
11	Swift & Company	$2.00	3.74%	$53.50	$45.63		1	-14.72%	$2.00	3.74%	-10.98%
12	Chrysler	$2.00	3.71%	$53.88	$31.25		1	-42.00%	$2.00	3.71%	-38.28%
13	American T & T	$2.20	3.58%	$61.50	$54.38		1	-11.59%	$2.20	3.58%	-8.01%
14	International Harvester	$1.50	3.28%	$45.75	$34.88		1	-23.77%	$1.73	3.78%	-19.99%
15	Woolworth	$1.00	3.21%	$31.13	$19.63		1	-36.95%	$1.00	3.21%	-33.73%
16	Standard Oil CA	$2.50	3.14%	$79.50	$60.00		1	-24.53%	$2.50	3.14%	-21.38%
17	International Nickel	$2.80	3.12%	$89.63	$87.13		1	-2.79%	$2.80	3.12%	.33%
18	Texaco	$2.40	3.00%	$80.13	$69.25		1	-13.57%	$2.50	3.12%	-10.45%
19	Union Carbide	$2.00	2.91%	$68.75	$48.63		1	-29.27%	$2.00	2.91%	-26.36%
20	Procter & Gamble	$1.85	2.68%	$69.00	$71.25		1	3.26%	$2.00	2.90%	6.16%
21	General Foods	$2.20	2.68%	$82.13	$70.25		1	-14.46%	$2.20	2.68%	-11.78%
22	Goodyear	$1.25	2.61%	$47.88	$40.75		1	-14.88%	$1.30	2.72%	-12.17%
23	Du Pont	$6.00	2.53%	$237.50	$146.50		1	-38.32%	$5.75	2.42%	-35.89%
24	Westinghouse Electric	$1.40	2.25%	$62.13	$47.00		1	-24.35%	$1.40	2.25%	-22.09%
25	General Electric	$2.60	2.22%	$116.88	$89.00		1	-23.85%	$2.60	2.22%	-21.63%
26	Owens-Illinois	$1.35	2.13%	$63.50	$53.00		1	-16.54%	$1.35	2.13%	-14.41%
27	United Aircraft	$1.60	1.90%	$84.00	$81.13		1	-3.42%	$1.60	1.90%	-1.52%
28	Aluminum Co of Amer	$1.40	1.85%	$75.88	$76.63		1	.99%	$1.40	2.04%	3.03%
29	Sears, Roebuck	$1.00	1.56%	$64.25	$44.75		1	-30.35%	$1.15	1.79%	-28.56%
30	Eastman Kodak	$1.40	1.18%	$119.00	$126.25		1	6.09%	$1.90	1.60%	7.69%
	AVERAGE		3.15%					-18.51%		3.28%	-15.22%

STOCK 1966	1966 WSJ DIVI.	1966 WSJ YIELD	1966 OPENING PRICE	1966 CLOSING PRICE	1966 STOCK DIV.	1966 SPLIT	1966 APPRECIATION	1966 DIVIDEND	ACT. CASH YIELD	TOTAL RETURN
BOTTOM FIVE:										
26 Owens-Illinois	$1.35	2.13%	$63.50	$53.00		1	-16.54%	$1.35	2.13%	-14.41%
27 United Aircraft	$1.60	1.90%	$84.00	$81.13		1	-3.42%	$1.60	1.90%	-1.52%
28 Aluminum Co of Amer	$1.40	1.85%	$75.88	$76.63		1	.99%	$1.55	2.04%	3.03%
29 Sears, Roebuck	$1.00	1.56%	$64.25	$44.75		1	-30.35%	$1.15	1.79%	-28.56%
30 Eastman Kodak	$1.40	1.18%	$119.00	$126.25		1	6.09%	$1.90	1.60%	7.69%
		1.72%					-8.65%		1.89%	-6.75%
BOTTOM TEN:										
21 General Foods	$2.20	2.68%	$82.13	$70.25		1	-14.46%	$2.20	2.68%	-11.78%
22 Goodyear	$1.25	2.61%	$47.88	$40.75		1	-14.88%	$1.30	2.72%	-12.17%
23 Du Pont	$6.00	2.53%	$237.50	$146.50		1	-38.32%	$5.75	2.42%	-35.89%
24 Westinghouse Electric	$1.40	2.25%	$62.13	$47.00		1	-24.35%	$1.40	2.25%	-22.09%
25 General Electric	$2.60	2.22%	$116.88	$89.00		1	-23.85%	$2.60	2.22%	-21.63%
26 Owens-Illinois	$1.35	2.13%	$63.50	$53.00		1	-16.54%	$1.35	2.13%	-14.41%
27 United Aircraft	$1.60	1.90%	$84.00	$81.13		1	-3.42%	$1.60	1.90%	-1.52%
28 Aluminum Co of Amer	$1.40	1.85%	$75.88	$76.63		1	.99%	$1.55	2.04%	3.03%
29 Sears, Roebuck	$1.00	1.56%	$64.25	$44.75		1	-30.35%	$1.15	1.79%	-28.56%
30 Eastman Kodak	$1.40	1.18%	$119.00	$126.25		1	6.09%	$1.90	1.60%	7.69%
		2.09%					-15.91%		2.18%	-13.73%
TOP TEN:										
1 General Motors	$5.20	5.07%	$102.63	$68.88		1	-32.89%	$4.55	4.43%	-28.45%
2 Anaconda	$3.75	4.46%	$84.13	$80.50		1	-4.31%	$5.00	5.94%	1.63%
3 American Tobacco	$1.70	4.42%	$38.50	$31.75		1	-17.53%	$1.80	4.68%	-12.86%
4 American Can	$2.20	3.97%	$55.38	$47.38		1	-14.45%	$2.20	3.97%	-10.47%
5 Johns-Manville	$2.20	3.96%	$55.63	$48.13		1	-13.48%	$2.20	3.96%	-9.53%
6 International Paper	$1.20	3.93%	$30.50	$25.38	2.00%		-16.80%	$1.24	4.07%	-12.74%
7 Standard Oil NJ	$3.15	3.90%	$80.75	$63.38		1	-21.52%	$3.30	4.09%	-17.43%
8 Allied Chemical	$1.90	3.86%	$49.25	$34.00		1	-29.58%	$1.90	3.86%	-25.73%
9 US Steel	$2.00	3.86%	$51.88	$38.50		1	-25.78%	$2.10	4.05%	-21.73%
10 Bethlehem Steel	$1.50	3.76%	$39.88	$30.38		1	-23.82%	$1.80	4.51%	-19.31%
		4.12%					-20.02%		4.36%	-15.66%
TOP FIVE:										
1 General Motors	$5.20	5.07%	$102.63	$68.88		1	-32.89%	$4.55	4.43%	-28.45%
2 Anaconda	$3.75	4.46%	$84.13	$80.50		1	-4.31%	$5.00	5.94%	1.63%
3 American Tobacco	$1.70	4.42%	$38.50	$31.75		1	-17.53%	$1.80	4.68%	-12.86%
4 American Can	$2.20	3.97%	$55.38	$47.38		1	-14.45%	$2.20	3.97%	-10.47%
5 Johns-Manville	$2.20	3.96%	$55.63	$48.13		1	-13.48%	$2.20	3.96%	-9.53%
		4.37%					-16.53%		4.60%	-11.94%

160

STOCK 1965	1965 WSJ DIVI.	1965 WSJ YIELD	1965 OPENING PRICE	1965 CLOSING PRICE	1965 STOCK DIV.	1965 SPLIT	1965 APPRECIATION	1965 DIVIDEND	ACT. CASH YIELD	TOTAL RETURN
1 Anaconda	$2.50	4.77%	$52.38	$84.13			60.62%	$3.75	7.16%	67.78%
2 American Tobacco	$1.60	4.72%	$33.88	$38.50		1	13.65%	$1.65	4.87%	18.52%
3 General Motors	$4.45	4.67%	$95.38	$102.63			7.60%	$5.25	5.50%	13.11%
4 American Can	$2.00	4.61%	$43.38	$55.38		1	27.67%	$2.00	4.61%	32.28%
5 Bethlehem Steel	$1.50	4.29%	$35.00	$39.88		1	13.93%	$1.50	4.29%	18.21%
6 International Paper	$1.40	4.26%	$32.88	$30.50		1	-7.22%	$1.25	3.80%	-3.42%
7 US Steel	$2.00	3.94%	$50.75	$51.88		1	2.22%	$2.00	3.94%	6.16%
8 International Harvester	$2.80	3.78%	$74.13	$45.75		2	23.44%	$2.95	3.98%	27.42%
9 Johns-Manville	$2.00	3.74%	$53.50	$55.63		1	3.97%	$2.05	3.83%	7.80%
10 Woolworth	$1.00	3.62%	$27.63	$31.13		1	12.67%	$1.00	3.62%	16.29%
11 Allied Chemical	$1.80	3.53%	$51.00	$49.25	2.00%	1	-1.50%	$1.90	3.73%	2.23%
12 Swift & Company	$2.00	3.44%	$58.13	$53.50		1	-7.96%	$2.00	3.44%	-4.52%
13 Standard Oil NJ	$3.00	3.39%	$88.50	$80.75		1	-8.76%	$3.15	3.56%	-5.20%
14 United Aircraft	$2.00	3.11%	$64.25	$84.00		1.5	96.11%	$2.10	3.27%	99.38%
15 Standard Oil CA	$2.20	3.02%	$72.75	$79.50		1	9.28%	$2.28	3.13%	12.41%
16 Du Pont	$7.25	3.00%	$241.75	$237.50		1	-1.76%	$6.00	2.48%	.72%
17 International Nickel	$2.50	2.98%	$83.88	$89.63		1	6.86%	$3.05	3.64%	10.49%
18 American T & T	$2.00	2.88%	$69.50	$61.50		1	-11.51%	$2.00	2.88%	-8.63%
19 Union Carbide	$3.60	2.84%	$126.75	$68.75		2	8.48%	$4.00	3.16%	11.64%
20 Westinghouse Electric	$1.20	2.82%	$42.50	$62.13		1	46.18%	$1.25	2.94%	49.12%
21 Texaco	$2.20	2.55%	$86.25	$80.13		1	-7.10%	$2.45	2.84%	-4.26%
22 Goodyear	$1.15	2.54%	$45.25	$47.88		1	5.80%	$1.20	2.65%	8.45%
23 General Foods	$2.00	2.47%	$81.00	$82.13		1	1.39%	$2.05	2.53%	3.92%
24 General Electric	$2.20	2.41%	$91.13	$116.88		1	28.26%	$2.30	2.52%	30.78%
25 Owens-Illinois Glass	$2.50	2.39%	$104.50	$63.50		2	21.53%	$2.70	2.58%	24.11%
26 Aluminum Co of Amer	$1.40	2.31%	$60.63	$75.88		1	25.15%	$1.40	2.31%	27.46%
27 Procter & Gamble	$1.75	2.15%	$81.25	$69.00		1	-15.08%	$1.85	2.28%	-12.80%
28 Eastman Kodak	$2.40	1.73%	$138.75	$119.00		2	71.53%	$3.35	2.41%	73.95%
29 Chrysler	$1.00	1.66%	$60.25	$53.88		2	-10.58%	$1.25	2.07%	-8.51%
30 Sears, Roebuck	$1.80	1.41%	$127.63	$64.25		2	.69%	$2.25	1.76%	2.45%
AVERAGE		3.17%					13.85%		3.39%	17.24%

STOCK 1965	1965 WSJ DIVI.	1965 WSJ YIELD	1965 OPENING PRICE	1965 CLOSING PRICE	1965 STOCK DIV.	1965 SPLIT	1965 APPRECIATION	1965 DIVIDEND	ACT. CASH YIELD	TOTAL RETURN
BOTTOM FIVE:										
26 Aluminum Co of Amer	$1.40	2.31%	$60.63	$75.88		1	25.15%	$1.40	2.31%	27.46%
27 Procter & Gamble	$1.75	2.15%	$81.25	$69.00		1	-15.08%	$1.85	2.28%	-12.80%
28 Eastman Kodak	$2.40	1.73%	$138.75	$119.00		2	71.53%	$3.35	2.41%	73.95%
29 Chrysler	$1.00	1.66%	$60.25	$53.88		1	-10.58%	$1.25	2.07%	-8.51%
30 Sears, Roebuck	$1.80	1.41%	$127.63	$64.25		2	.69%	$2.25	1.76%	2.45%
		1.85%					14.34%		2.17%	16.51%
BOTTOM TEN:										
21 Texaco	$2.20	2.55%	$86.25	$80.13		1	-7.10%	$2.45	2.84%	-4.26%
22 Goodyear	$1.15	2.54%	$45.25	$47.88		1	5.80%	$1.20	2.65%	8.45%
23 General Foods	$2.00	2.47%	$81.00	$82.13		1	1.39%	$2.05	2.53%	3.92%
24 General Electric	$2.20	2.41%	$91.13	$116.88		2	28.26%	$2.30	2.52%	30.78%
25 Owens-Illinois Glass	$2.50	2.39%	$104.50	$63.50		1	21.53%	$2.70	2.58%	24.11%
26 Aluminum Co of Amer	$1.40	2.31%	$60.63	$75.88		1	25.15%	$1.40	2.31%	27.46%
27 Procter & Gamble	$1.75	2.15%	$81.25	$69.00		1	-15.08%	$1.85	2.28%	-12.80%
28 Eastman Kodak	$2.40	1.73%	$138.75	$119.00		2	71.53%	$3.35	2.41%	73.95%
29 Chrysler	$1.00	1.66%	$60.25	$53.88		1	-10.58%	$1.25	2.07%	-8.51%
30 Sears, Roebuck	$1.80	1.41%	$127.63	$64.25		2	.69%	$2.25	1.76%	2.45%
		2.16%					12.16%		2.40%	14.56%
TOP TEN:										
1 Anaconda	$2.50	4.77%	$52.38	$84.13		1	60.62%	$3.75	7.16%	67.78%
2 American Tobacco	$1.60	4.72%	$33.88	$38.50		1	13.65%	$1.65	4.87%	18.52%
3 General Motors	$4.45	4.67%	$95.38	$102.63		1	7.60%	$5.25	5.50%	13.11%
4 American Can	$2.00	4.61%	$43.38	$55.38		1	27.67%	$2.00	4.61%	32.28%
5 Bethlehem Steel	$1.50	4.29%	$35.00	$39.88		1	13.93%	$1.50	4.29%	18.21%
6 International Paper	$1.40	4.26%	$32.88	$30.50		1	-7.22%	$1.25	3.80%	-3.42%
7 US Steel	$2.00	3.94%	$50.75	$51.88		1	2.22%	$2.00	3.94%	6.16%
8 International Harvester	$2.80	3.78%	$74.13	$45.75		2	23.44%	$2.95	3.98%	27.42%
9 Johns-Manville	$2.00	3.74%	$53.50	$55.63		1	3.97%	$2.05	3.83%	7.80%
10 Woolworth	$1.00	3.62%	$27.63	$31.13		1	12.67%	$1.00	3.62%	16.29%
		4.24%					15.85%		4.56%	20.42%
TOP FIVE:										
1 Anaconda	$2.50	4.77%	$52.38	$84.13		1	60.62%	$3.75	7.16%	67.78%
2 American Tobacco	$1.60	4.72%	$33.88	$38.50		1	13.65%	$1.65	4.87%	18.52%
3 General Motors	$4.45	4.67%	$95.38	$102.63		1	7.60%	$5.25	5.50%	13.11%
4 American Can	$2.00	4.61%	$43.38	$55.38		1	27.67%	$2.00	4.61%	32.28%
5 Bethlehem Steel	$1.50	4.29%	$35.00	$39.88		1	13.93%	$1.50	4.29%	18.21%
		4.61%					24.69%		5.29%	29.98%

LIST OF 1964 DOW JONES INDUSTRIALS BY DIVIDEND-YIELD

	STOCK 1964	1964 WSJ DIVI.	1964 WSJ YIELD	1964 OPENING PRICE	1964 CLOSING PRICE	1964 STOCK DIV.	1964 SPLIT	1964 APPRECIATION	1964 DIVIDEND	ACT. CASH YIELD	TOTAL RETURN
1	American Tobacco	$1.50	5.33%	$28.13	$33.88		1	20.44%	$1.60	5.69%	26.13%
2	Anaconda	$2.50	5.21%	$48.00	$52.38		1	9.11%	$2.50	5.21%	14.32%
3	General Motors	$4.00	4.98%	$80.25	$95.38		1	18.85%	$4.45	5.55%	24.39%
4	United Aircraft	$2.00	4.65%	$43.00	$64.25		1	49.42%	$2.00	4.65%	54.07%
5	Bethlehem Steel	$1.50	4.62%	$32.50	$35.00		1	7.69%	$1.50	4.62%	12.31%
6	American Can	$2.00	4.57%	$43.75	$43.38		1	-.86%	$2.00	4.57%	3.71%
7	International Harvester	$2.40	4.09%	$58.63	$74.13		1	26.44%	$2.70	4.61%	31.04%
8	Johns-Manville	$2.00	4.06%	$49.25	$53.50		1	8.63%	$2.00	4.06%	12.69%
9	Woolworth	$2.80	3.76%	$74.50	$27.63		3	11.24%	$2.90	3.89%	15.13%
10	Swift & Company	$1.60	3.66%	$43.75	$58.13		1	32.86%	$1.75	4.00%	36.86%
11	US Steel	$2.00	3.64%	$54.88	$50.75		1	-7.52%	$2.00	3.64%	-3.87%
12	Standard Oil NJ	$2.75	3.62%	$75.88	$88.50		1	16.64%	$3.00	3.95%	20.59%
13	Westinghouse Electric	$1.20	3.53%	$34.00	$42.50		1	25.00%	$1.20	3.53%	28.53%
14	Standard Oil CA	$2.00	3.33%	$60.13	$72.75	5.00%	1	27.05%	$2.05	3.41%	30.46%
15	Allied Chemical	$1.80	3.26%	$55.25	$51.00		1	-7.69%	$1.80	3.26%	-4.43%
16	International Paper	$1.05	3.24%	$32.38	$32.88		1	1.54%	$1.16	3.58%	5.13%
17	Du Pont	$7.75	3.22%	$240.50	$241.75	19.83%	1	20.35%	$7.25	3.01%	23.36%
18	International Nickel	$2.20	3.20%	$68.75	$83.88		1	22.00%	$2.75	4.00%	26.00%
19	Union Carbide	$3.60	2.94%	$122.25	$126.75		1	3.68%	$3.60	2.94%	6.63%
20	Owens-Illinois Glass	$2.50	2.91%	$85.88	$104.50		1	21.69%	$2.50	2.91%	24.60%
21	Texaco	$2.00	2.87%	$69.75	$86.25	5.00%	1	29.84%	$2.30	3.30%	33.14%
22	American T & T	$3.60	2.58%	$139.50	$69.50		2	-.36%	$3.90	2.80%	2.44%
23	General Electric	$2.20	2.54%	$86.75	$91.13		1	5.04%	$2.20	2.54%	7.58%
24	Goodyear	$1.00	2.40%	$41.63	$45.25		1	8.71%	$1.11	2.67%	11.38%
25	General Foods	$2.00	2.23%	$89.88	$81.00		1	-9.87%	$2.00	2.23%	-7.65%
26	Procter & Gamble	$1.60	2.03%	$78.88	$81.25		1	3.01%	$1.75	2.22%	5.23%
27	Eastman Kodak	$2.20	1.90%	$115.50	$138.75	5.00%	1	26.14%	$2.60	2.25%	28.39%
28	Aluminum Co of Amer	$1.20	1.76%	$68.25	$60.63		1	-11.17%	$1.20	1.76%	-9.41%
29	Sears, Roebuck	$1.60	1.64%	$97.75	$127.63		1	30.56%	$1.90	1.94%	32.51%
30	Chrysler	$1.00	1.19%	$83.75	$60.25	4.00%	2	49.64%	$2.00	2.39%	52.02%
	AVERAGE		3.30%					14.60%		3.51%	18.11%

STOCK 1964	1964 WSJ DIVI.	1964 WSJ YIELD	1964 OPENING PRICE	1964 CLOSING PRICE	1964 STOCK DIV.	1964 SPLIT	1964 APPRECIATION	1964 DIVIDEND	ACT. CASH YIELD	TOTAL RETURN
BOTTOM FIVE:										
26 Procter & Gamble	$1.60	2.03%	$78.88	$81.25		1	3.01%	$1.75	2.22%	5.23%
27 Eastman Kodak	$2.20	1.90%	$115.50	$138.75	5.00%	1	26.14%	$2.60	2.25%	28.39%
28 Aluminum Co of Amer	$1.20	1.76%	$68.25	$60.63		1	-11.17%	$1.20	1.76%	-9.41%
29 Sears, Roebuck	$1.60	1.64%	$97.75	$127.63		1	30.56%	$1.90	1.94%	32.51%
30 Chrysler	$1.00	1.19%	$83.75	$60.25	4.00%	2	49.64%	$2.00	2.39%	52.02%
		1.70%					19.63%		2.11%	21.75%
BOTTOM TEN:										
21 Texaco	$2.00	2.87%	$69.75	$86.25	5.00%	1	29.84%	$2.30	3.30%	33.14%
22 American T & T	$3.60	2.58%	$139.50	$69.50		2	-.36%	$3.90	2.80%	2.44%
23 General Electric	$2.20	2.54%	$86.75	$91.13		1	5.04%	$2.20	2.54%	7.58%
24 Goodyear	$1.00	2.40%	$41.63	$45.25		1	8.71%	$1.11	2.67%	11.38%
25 General Foods	$2.00	2.23%	$89.88	$81.00		1	-9.87%	$2.00	2.23%	-7.65%
26 Procter & Gamble	$1.60	2.03%	$78.88	$81.25		1	3.01%	$1.75	2.22%	5.23%
27 Eastman Kodak	$2.20	1.90%	$115.50	$138.75	5.00%	1	26.14%	$2.60	2.25%	28.39%
28 Aluminum Co of Amer	$1.20	1.76%	$68.25	$60.63		1	-11.17%	$1.20	1.76%	-9.41%
29 Sears, Roebuck	$1.60	1.64%	$97.75	$127.63		1	30.56%	$1.90	1.94%	32.51%
30 Chrysler	$1.00	1.19%	$83.75	$60.25	4.00%	2	49.64%	$2.00	2.39%	52.02%
		2.11%					13.15%		2.41%	15.56%
TOP TEN:										
1 American Tobacco	$1.50	5.33%	$28.13	$33.88		1	20.44%	$1.60	5.69%	26.13%
2 Anaconda	$2.50	5.21%	$48.00	$52.38		1	9.11%	$2.50	5.21%	14.32%
3 General Motors	$4.00	4.98%	$80.25	$95.38		1	18.85%	$4.45	5.55%	24.39%
4 United Aircraft	$2.00	4.65%	$43.00	$64.25		1	49.42%	$2.00	4.65%	54.07%
5 Bethlehem Steel	$1.50	4.62%	$32.50	$35.00		1	7.69%	$1.50	4.62%	12.31%
6 American Can	$2.00	4.57%	$43.75	$43.38		1	-.86%	$2.00	4.57%	3.71%
7 International Harvester	$2.40	4.09%	$58.63	$74.13		1	26.44%	$2.70	4.61%	31.04%
8 Johns-Manville	$2.00	4.06%	$49.25	$53.50		1	8.63%	$2.00	4.06%	12.69%
9 Woolworth	$2.80	3.76%	$74.50	$27.63		3	11.24%	$2.90	3.89%	15.13%
10 Swift & Company	$1.60	3.66%	$43.75	$58.13		1	32.86%	$1.75	4.00%	36.86%
		4.49%					18.38%		4.68%	23.07%
TOP FIVE:										
1 American Tobacco	$1.50	5.33%	$28.13	$33.88		1	20.44%	$1.60	5.69%	26.13%
2 Anaconda	$2.50	5.21%	$48.00	$52.38		1	9.11%	$2.50	5.21%	14.32%
3 General Motors	$4.00	4.98%	$80.25	$95.38		1	18.85%	$4.45	5.55%	24.39%
4 United Aircraft	$2.00	4.65%	$43.00	$64.25		1	49.42%	$2.00	4.65%	54.07%
5 Bethlehem Steel	$1.50	4.62%	$32.50	$35.00		1	7.69%	$1.50	4.62%	12.31%
		4.96%					21.10%		5.14%	26.25%

LIST OF 1963 DOW JONES INDUSTRIALS BY DIVIDEND-YIELD

	STOCK 1963	1963 WSJ DIVI.	1963 WSJ YIELD	1963 OPENING PRICE	1963 CLOSING PRICE	1963 STOCK DIV.	1963 SPLIT	1963 APPRECIATION	1963 DIVIDEND	ACT. CASH YIELD	TOTAL RETURN
1	US Steel	$2.75	6.29%	$43.75	$54.88			25.43%	$2.00	4.57%	30.00%
2	Anaconda	$2.50	6.10%	$41.00	$48.00		1	17.07%	$2.50	6.10%	23.17%
3	Bethlehem Steel	$1.50	5.17%	$29.00	$32.50			12.07%	$1.50	5.17%	17.24%
4	General Motors	$3.00	5.15%	$58.25	$80.25		1	37.77%	$4.00	6.87%	44.64%
5	American Tobacco	$1.50	5.13%	$29.25	$28.13		1	-3.85%	$1.50	5.13%	1.28%
6	International Harvester	$2.40	4.81%	$49.88	$58.63		1	17.54%	$2.40	4.81%	22.36%
7	Johns-Manville	$2.00	4.76%	$42.00	$49.25		1	17.26%	$2.00	4.76%	22.02%
8	American Can	$2.00	4.40%	$45.50	$43.75		1	-3.85%	$2.00	4.40%	.55%
9	Standard Oil (NJ)	$2.50	4.26%	$58.63	$75.88		1	29.42%	$2.75	4.69%	34.12%
10	Allied Chemical	$1.80	4.16%	$43.25	$55.25		1	27.75%	$1.80	4.16%	31.91%
11	Swift & Company	$1.60	3.99%	$40.13	$43.75		1	9.03%	$1.60	3.99%	13.02%
12	International Paper	$1.05	3.94%	$26.63	$32.38	2.00%	1	24.03%	$1.05	3.94%	27.97%
13	United Aircraft	$2.00	3.90%	$51.25	$43.00		1	-16.10%	$2.00	3.90%	-12.20%
14	Woolworth	$2.50	3.90%	$64.13	$74.50		1	16.18%	$2.73	4.26%	20.44%
15	Westinghouse Electric	$1.20	3.75%	$32.00	$34.00		1	6.25%	$1.20	3.75%	10.00%
16	Union Carbide	$3.60	3.53%	$101.88	$122.25		1	20.00%	$3.60	3.53%	23.53%
17	Owens-Illinois Glass	$2.50	3.39%	$73.75	$85.88		1	16.44%	$2.50	3.39%	19.83%
18	Standard Oil of Calif.	$2.00	3.21%	$62.38	$60.13	5.00%	1	1.21%	$2.00	3.21%	4.42%
19	International Nickel	$2.00	3.20%	$62.50	$68.75		1	10.00%	$2.25	3.60%	13.60%
20	Du Pont	$7.50	3.30%	$234.50	$240.50	12.32%	1	14.88%	$7.75	3.30%	18.18%
21	American T & T	$3.60	3.13%	$115.00	$139.50		1	21.30%	$3.60	3.13%	24.43%
22	Goodyear	$1.00	3.02%	$33.13	$41.63		1	25.66%	$1.00	3.02%	28.68%
23	Texaco	$1.80	2.97%	$60.63	$69.75		1	15.05%	$2.10	3.46%	18.52%
24	General Electric	$2.00	2.62%	$76.38	$86.75		1	13.58%	$2.00	2.62%	16.20%
25	General Foods	$1.80	2.31%	$78.00	$89.88		1	15.22%	$1.95	2.50%	17.72%
26	Aluminum Co of Amer	$1.20	2.23%	$53.88	$68.25		1	26.68%	$1.20	2.23%	28.91%
27	Procter & Gamble	$1.50	2.12%	$70.88	$78.88		1	11.29%	$1.60	2.26%	13.54%
28	Eastman Kodak	$2.20	2.05%	$107.38	$115.50		1	7.57%	$2.55	2.37%	9.94%
29	Sears, Roebuck	$1.40	1.85%	$75.50	$97.75		1	29.47%	$1.65	2.19%	31.66%
30	Chrysler	$1.00	1.38%	$72.25	$83.75		2	131.83%	$1.75	2.42%	134.26%
	AVERAGE		3.66%					19.21%		3.79%	23.00%

STOCK 1963	1963 WSJ DIVI.	1963 WSJ YIELD	1963 OPENING PRICE	1963 CLOSING PRICE	1963 STOCK DIV.	1963 SPLIT	1963 APPRECIATION	1963 DIVIDEND	ACT. CASH YIELD	TOTAL RETURN
BOTTOM FIVE:										
26 Aluminum Co of Amer	$1.20	2.23%	$53.88	$68.25		1	26.68%	$1.20	2.23%	28.91%
27 Procter & Gamble	$1.50	2.12%	$70.88	$78.88		1	11.29%	$1.60	2.26%	13.54%
28 Eastman Kodak	$2.20	2.05%	$107.38	$115.50		1	7.57%	$2.55	2.37%	9.94%
29 Sears, Roebuck	$1.40	1.85%	$75.50	$97.75		1	29.47%	$1.65	2.19%	31.66%
30 Chrysler	$1.00	1.38%	$72.25	$83.75		2	131.83%	$1.75	2.42%	134.26%
		1.93%					41.37%		2.29%	43.66%
BOTTOM TEN:										
21 American T & T	$3.60	3.13%	$115.00	$139.50		1	21.30%	$3.60	3.13%	24.43%
22 Goodyear	$1.00	3.02%	$33.13	$41.63		1	25.66%	$1.00	3.02%	28.68%
23 Texaco	$1.80	2.97%	$60.63	$69.75		1	15.05%	$2.10	3.46%	18.52%
24 General Electric	$2.00	2.62%	$76.38	$86.75		1	13.58%	$2.00	2.62%	16.20%
25 General Foods	$1.80	2.31%	$78.00	$89.88		1	15.22%	$1.95	2.50%	17.72%
26 Aluminum Co of Amer	$1.20	2.23%	$53.88	$68.25		1	26.68%	$1.20	2.23%	28.91%
27 Procter & Gamble	$1.50	2.12%	$70.88	$78.88		1	11.29%	$1.60	2.26%	13.54%
28 Eastman Kodak	$2.20	2.05%	$107.38	$115.50		1	7.57%	$2.55	2.37%	9.94%
29 Sears, Roebuck	$1.40	1.85%	$75.50	$97.75		1	29.47%	$1.65	2.19%	31.66%
30 Chrysler	$1.00	1.38%	$72.25	$83.75		2	131.83%	$1.75	2.42%	134.26%
		2.37%					29.77%		2.62%	32.39%
TOP TEN:										
1 US Steel	$2.75	6.29%	$43.75	$54.88		1	25.43%	$2.00	4.57%	30.00%
2 Anaconda	$2.50	6.10%	$41.00	$48.00		1	17.07%	$2.50	6.10%	23.17%
3 Bethlehem Steel	$1.50	5.17%	$29.00	$32.50		1	12.07%	$1.50	5.17%	17.24%
4 General Motors	$3.00	5.15%	$58.25	$80.25		1	37.77%	$4.00	6.87%	44.64%
5 American Tobacco	$1.50	5.13%	$29.25	$28.13		1	-3.85%	$1.50	5.13%	1.28%
6 International Harvester	$2.40	4.81%	$49.88	$58.63		1	17.54%	$2.40	4.81%	22.36%
7 Johns-Manville	$2.00	4.76%	$42.00	$49.25		1	17.26%	$2.00	4.76%	22.02%
8 American Can	$2.00	4.40%	$45.50	$43.75		1	-3.85%	$2.00	4.40%	.55%
9 Standard Oil (NJ)	$2.50	4.26%	$58.63	$75.88		1	29.42%	$2.75	4.69%	34.12%
10 Allied Chemical	$1.80	4.16%	$43.25	$55.25		1	27.75%	$1.80	4.16%	31.91%
		5.02%					17.66%		5.07%	22.73%
TOP FIVE:										
1 US Steel	$2.75	6.29%	$43.75	$54.88		1	25.43%	$2.00	4.57%	30.00%
2 Anaconda	$2.50	6.10%	$41.00	$48.00		1	17.07%	$2.50	6.10%	23.17%
3 Bethlehem Steel	$1.50	5.17%	$29.00	$32.50		1	12.07%	$1.50	5.17%	17.24%
4 General Motors	$3.00	5.15%	$58.25	$80.25		1	37.77%	$4.00	6.87%	44.64%
5 American Tobacco	$1.50	5.13%	$29.25	$28.13		1	-3.85%	$1.50	5.13%	1.28%
		5.57%					17.70%		5.57%	23.27%

LIST OF 1962 DOW JONES INDUSTRIALS BY DIVIDEND-YIELD

STOCK 1962	1962 WSJ DIVI.	1962 WSJ YIELD	1962 OPENING PRICE	1962 CLOSING PRICE	1962 STOCK DIV.	1962 SPLIT	1962 APPRECIATION	1962 DIVIDEND	ACT. CASH YIELD	TOTAL RETURN
1 Bethlehem Steel	$2.40	5.58%	$43.00	$29.00		1	-32.56%	$2.18	5.07%	-27.49%
2 Anaconda	$2.50	5.05%	$49.50	$41.00		1	-17.17%	$2.50	5.05%	-12.12%
3 United Aircraft	$2.00	4.73%	$42.25	$51.25		1	21.30%	$2.00	4.73%	26.04%
4 International Harvester	$2.40	4.60%	$52.13	$49.88		1	-4.32%	$2.40	4.60%	.29%
5 Standard Oil NJ	$2.30	4.55%	$50.50	$58.63		1	16.09%	$2.50	4.95%	21.04%
6 American Can	$2.00	4.32%	$46.25	$45.50		1	-1.62%	$2.00	4.32%	2.70%
7 US Steel	$3.00	3.89%	$77.13	$43.75		1	-43.27%	$2.70	3.50%	-39.77%
8 Swift & Company	$1.60	3.73%	$42.88	$40.13		1	-6.41%	$1.60	3.73%	-2.68%
9 Standard Oil CA	$2.00	3.61%	$55.38	$62.38	5.00%	1	18.27%	$2.00	3.61%	21.88%
10 General Motors	$2.00	3.55%	$56.38	$58.25		1	3.33%	$3.00	5.32%	8.65%
11 Johns-Manville	$2.00	3.54%	$56.50	$42.00		1	-25.66%	$2.00	3.54%	-22.12%
12 Allied Chemical	$1.80	3.24%	$55.50	$43.25		1	-22.07%	$1.80	3.24%	-18.83%
13 Westinghouse Electric	$1.20	3.16%	$38.00	$32.00		1	-15.79%	$1.20	3.16%	-12.63%
14 Du Pont	$7.50	3.11%	$241.50	$234.50	12.06%	1	9.16%	$7.50	3.11%	12.27%
15 Union Carbide	$3.60	3.01%	$119.75	$101.88		1	-14.93%	$3.60	3.01%	-11.92%
16 International Paper	$1.05	2.87%	$36.63	$26.63	2.00%	1	-25.85%	$1.05	2.87%	-22.98%
17 Texaco	$1.60	2.83%	$56.50	$60.63		1	7.30%	$1.85	3.27%	10.58%
18 American Tobacco	$2.80	2.79%	$100.25	$29.25		2	-41.65%	$3.00	2.99%	-38.65%
19 Woolworth	$2.50	2.75%	$91.00	$64.13		1	-29.53%	$2.50	2.75%	-26.79%
20 American T & T	$3.60	2.69%	$133.63	$115.00		1	-13.94%	$3.60	2.69%	-11.24%
21 General Electric	$2.00	2.68%	$74.75	$76.38		1	2.17%	$2.00	2.68%	4.85%
22 Owens-Illinois Glass	$2.50	2.64%	$94.75	$73.75		1	-22.16%	$2.50	2.64%	-19.53%
23 Goodyear	$.90	2.02%	$44.50	$33.13		1	-25.56%	$.95	2.13%	-23.43%
24 Chrysler	$1.00	2.00%	$50.00	$72.25		1	44.50%	$1.00	2.00%	46.50%
25 International Nickel	$1.60	1.89%	$84.88	$62.50		1	-26.36%	$1.90	2.24%	-24.12%
26 Aluminum Co of Amer	$1.20	1.84%	$65.38	$53.88		1	-17.59%	$1.20	1.84%	-15.76%
27 Eastman Kodak	$2.00	1.81%	$110.75	$107.38		1	-3.05%	$2.30	2.08%	-.97%
28 General Foods	$1.60	1.72%	$93.25	$78.00		1	-16.35%	$1.75	1.88%	-14.48%
29 Sears, Roebuck	$1.40	1.65%	$85.00	$75.50		1	-11.18%	$1.65	1.94%	-9.24%
30 Procter & Gamble	$1.40	1.53%	$91.50	$70.88		1	-22.54%	$1.50	1.64%	-20.90%
AVERAGE		3.11%					-10.58%		3.22%	-7.36%

STOCK 1962	1962 WSJ DIVI.	1962 WSJ YIELD	1962 OPENING PRICE	1962 CLOSING PRICE	1962 STOCK DIV.	1962 SPLIT	1962 APPRECIATION	1962 DIVIDEND	ACT. CASH YIELD	TOTAL RETURN
BOTTOM FIVE:										
26 Aluminum Co of Amer	$1.20	1.84%	$65.38	$53.88		1	-17.59%	$1.20	1.84%	-15.76%
27 Eastman Kodak	$2.00	1.81%	$110.75	$107.38		1	-3.05%	$2.30	2.08%	-.97%
28 General Foods	$1.60	1.72%	$93.25	$78.00		1	-16.35%	$1.75	1.88%	-14.48%
29 Sears, Roebuck	$1.40	1.65%	$85.00	$75.50		1	-11.18%	$1.65	1.94%	-9.24%
30 Procter & Gamble	$1.40	1.53%	$91.50	$70.88		1	-22.54%	$1.50	1.64%	-20.90%
		1.71%					-14.14%		1.87%	-12.27%
BOTTOM TEN:										
21 General Electric	$2.00	2.68%	$74.75	$76.38		1	2.17%	$2.00	2.68%	4.85%
22 Owens-Illinois Glass	$2.50	2.64%	$94.75	$73.75		1	-22.16%	$2.50	2.64%	-19.53%
23 Goodyear	$.90	2.02%	$44.50	$33.13		1	-25.56%	$.95	2.13%	-23.43%
24 Chrysler	$1.00	2.00%	$50.00	$72.25		1	44.50%	$1.00	2.00%	46.50%
25 International Nickel	$1.60	1.89%	$84.88	$62.50		1	-26.36%	$1.90	2.24%	-24.12%
26 Aluminum Co of Amer	$1.20	1.84%	$65.38	$53.88		1	-17.59%	$1.20	1.84%	-15.76%
27 Eastman Kodak	$2.00	1.81%	$110.75	$107.38		1	-3.05%	$2.30	2.08%	-.97%
28 General Foods	$1.60	1.72%	$93.25	$78.00		1	-16.35%	$1.75	1.88%	-14.48%
29 Sears, Roebuck	$1.40	1.65%	$85.00	$75.50		1	-11.18%	$1.65	1.94%	-9.24%
30 Procter & Gamble	$1.40	1.53%	$91.50	$70.88		1	-22.54%	$1.50	1.64%	-20.90%
		1.98%					-9.81%		2.11%	-7.71%
TOP TEN:										
1 Bethlehem Steel	$2.40	5.58%	$43.00	$29.00		1	-32.56%	$2.18	5.07%	-27.49%
2 Anaconda	$2.50	5.05%	$49.50	$41.00		1	-17.17%	$2.50	5.05%	-12.12%
3 United Aircraft	$2.00	4.73%	$42.25	$51.25		1	21.30%	$2.00	4.73%	26.04%
4 International Harvester	$2.40	4.60%	$52.13	$49.88		1	-4.32%	$2.40	4.60%	.29%
5 Standard Oil NJ	$2.30	4.55%	$50.50	$58.63		1	16.09%	$2.50	4.95%	21.04%
6 American Can	$2.00	4.32%	$46.25	$45.50		1	-1.62%	$2.00	4.32%	2.70%
7 US Steel	$3.00	3.89%	$77.13	$43.75		1	-43.27%	$2.70	3.50%	-39.77%
8 Swift & Company	$1.60	3.73%	$42.88	$40.13		1	-6.41%	$1.60	3.73%	-2.68%
9 Standard Oil CA	$2.00	3.61%	$55.38	$62.38	5.00%	1	18.27%	$2.00	3.61%	21.88%
10 General Motors	$2.00	3.55%	$56.38	$58.25		1	3.33%	$3.00	5.32%	8.65%
		4.36%					-4.64%		4.49%	-.15%
TOP FIVE:										
1 Bethlehem Steel	$2.40	5.58%	$43.00	$29.00		1	-32.56%	$2.18	5.07%	-27.49%
2 Anaconda	$2.50	5.05%	$49.50	$41.00		1	-17.17%	$2.50	5.05%	-12.12%
3 United Aircraft	$2.00	4.73%	$42.25	$51.25		1	21.30%	$2.00	4.73%	26.04%
4 International Harvester	$2.40	4.60%	$52.13	$49.88		1	-4.32%	$2.40	4.60%	.29%
5 Standard Oil NJ	$2.30	4.55%	$50.50	$58.63		1	16.09%	$2.50	4.95%	21.04%
		4.90%					-3.33%		4.88%	1.55%

LIST OF 1961 DOW JONES INDUSTRIALS BY DIVIDEND-YIELD

	STOCK 1961	1961 WSJ DIVI.	1961 WSJ YIELD	1961 OPENING PRICE	1961 CLOSING PRICE	1961 STOCK DIV.	1961 SPLIT	1961 APPRECIATION	1961 DIVIDEND	ACT. CASH YIELD	TOTAL RETURN
1	Bethlehem Steel	$2.40	5.85%	$41.00	$43.00		1	4.88%	$2.40	5.85%	10.73%
2	American Can	$2.00	5.71%	$35.00	$46.25		1	32.14%	$2.00	5.71%	37.86%
3	Anaconda	$2.50	5.67%	$44.13	$49.50		1	12.18%	$2.50	5.67%	17.85%
4	International Harvester	$2.40	5.55%	$43.25	$52.13		1	20.52%	$2.40	5.55%	26.07%
5	Standard Oil NJ	$2.25	5.45%	$41.25	$50.50		1	22.42%	$2.30	5.58%	28.00%
6	United Aircraft	$2.00	5.30%	$37.75	$42.25		1	11.92%	$2.00	5.30%	17.22%
7	General Motors	$2.00	4.82%	$41.50	$56.38		1	35.84%	$2.50	6.02%	41.87%
8	Standard Oil CA	$2.00	4.20%	$47.63	$55.38		1	16.27%	$2.00	4.20%	20.47%
9	US Steel	$3.00	3.94%	$76.13	$77.13		1	1.31%	$3.00	3.94%	5.25%
10	Woolworth	$2.50	3.64%	$68.63	$91.00		1	32.60%	$2.50	3.64%	36.25%
11	Du Pont	$6.70	3.59%	$186.50	$241.50		1	29.49%	$7.50	4.02%	33.51%
12	American Tobacco	$2.30	3.52%	$65.25	$100.25		1	53.64%	$2.80	4.29%	57.93%
13	Swift & Company	$1.60	3.51%	$45.63	$42.88		1	-6.03%	$1.85	4.05%	-1.97%
14	Allied Chemical	$1.80	3.48%	$51.75	$55.50		1	7.25%	$1.80	3.48%	10.72%
15	Johns-Manville	$2.00	3.47%	$57.63	$56.50		1	-1.95%	$2.00	3.47%	1.52%
16	International Paper	$1.01	3.24%	$31.13	$36.63	2.00%	1	20.02%	$1.05	3.37%	23.40%
17	American T & T	$3.30	3.19%	$103.50	$133.63		1	29.11%	$3.45	3.33%	32.44%
18	Union Carbide	$3.60	3.09%	$116.50	$119.75		1	2.79%	$3.60	3.09%	5.88%
19	Texaco	$2.60	3.09%	$84.25	$56.50		2	34.12%	$3.10	3.68%	37.80%
20	General Electric	$2.00	2.77%	$72.25	$74.75		1	3.46%	$2.00	2.77%	6.23%
21	International Nickel	$1.60	2.74%	$58.38	$84.88		1	45.40%	$1.60	2.74%	48.14%
22	Owens-Illinois Glass	$2.50	2.72%	$91.75	$94.75		1	3.27%	$2.50	2.72%	5.99%
23	Goodyear	$.90	2.64%	$34.13	$44.50	2.00%	1	33.01%	$.90	2.64%	35.65%
24	Chrysler	$1.00	2.58%	$38.75	$50.00		1	29.03%	$1.00	2.58%	31.61%
25	Westinghouse Electric	$1.20	2.53%	$47.50	$38.00		1	-20.00%	$1.20	2.53%	-17.47%
26	Sears, Roebuck	$1.20	2.15%	$55.75	$85.00		1	52.47%	$1.40	2.51%	54.98%
27	General Foods	$1.40	1.99%	$70.50	$93.25		1	32.27%	$1.55	2.20%	34.47%
28	Procter & Gamble	$2.60	1.91%	$136.00	$91.50		2	34.56%	$2.75	2.02%	36.58%
29	Eastman Kodak	$2.00	1.84%	$108.75	$110.75		1	1.84%	$2.25	2.07%	3.91%
30	Aluminum Co of Amer	$1.20	1.73%	$69.50	$65.38		1	-5.94%	$1.20	1.73%	-4.21%
	AVERAGE		3.53%					18.93%		3.69%	22.62%

STOCK 1961	1961 WSJ DIVI.	1961 WSJ YIELD	1961 OPENING PRICE	1961 CLOSING PRICE	1961 STOCK DIV.	1961 SPLIT	1961 APPRECIATION	1961 DIVIDEND	ACT. CASH YIELD	TOTAL RETURN
BOTTOM FIVE:										
26 Sears, Roebuck	$1.20	2.15%	$55.75	$85.00		1	52.47%	$1.40	2.51%	54.98%
27 General Foods	$1.40	1.99%	$70.50	$93.25		1	32.27%	$1.55	2.20%	34.47%
28 Procter & Gamble	$2.60	1.91%	$136.00	$91.50		2	34.56%	$2.75	2.02%	36.58%
29 Eastman Kodak	$2.00	1.84%	$108.75	$110.75		1	1.84%	$2.25	2.07%	3.91%
30 Aluminum Co of Amer	$1.20	1.73%	$69.50	$65.38		1	-5.94%	$1.20	1.73%	-4.21%
		1.92%					23.04%		2.11%	25.15%
BOTTOM TEN:										
21 International Nickel	$1.60	2.74%	$58.38	$84.88		1	45.40%	$1.60	2.74%	48.14%
22 Owens-Illinois Glass	$2.50	2.72%	$91.75	$94.75		1	3.27%	$2.50	2.72%	5.99%
23 Goodyear	$.90	2.64%	$34.13	$44.50	2.00%	1	33.01%	$.90	2.64%	35.65%
24 Chrysler	$1.00	2.58%	$38.75	$50.00		1	29.03%	$1.00	2.58%	31.61%
25 Westinghouse Electric	$1.20	2.53%	$47.50	$38.00		1	-20.00%	$1.20	2.53%	-17.47%
26 Sears, Roebuck	$1.20	2.15%	$55.75	$85.00		1	52.47%	$1.40	2.51%	54.98%
27 General Foods	$1.40	1.99%	$70.50	$93.25		1	32.27%	$1.55	2.20%	34.47%
28 Procter & Gamble	$2.60	1.91%	$136.00	$91.50		2	34.56%	$2.75	2.02%	36.58%
29 Eastman Kodak	$2.00	1.84%	$108.75	$110.75		1	1.84%	$2.25	2.07%	3.91%
30 Aluminum Co of Amer	$1.20	1.73%	$69.50	$65.38		1	-5.94%	$1.20	1.73%	-4.21%
		2.28%					20.59%		2.37%	22.96%
TOP TEN:										
1 Bethlehem Steel	$2.40	5.85%	$41.00	$43.00		1	4.88%	$2.40	5.85%	10.73%
2 American Can	$2.00	5.71%	$35.00	$46.25		1	32.14%	$2.00	5.71%	37.86%
3 Anaconda	$2.50	5.67%	$44.13	$49.50		1	12.18%	$2.50	5.67%	17.85%
4 International Harvester	$2.40	5.55%	$43.25	$52.13		1	20.52%	$2.40	5.55%	26.07%
5 Standard Oil NJ	$2.25	5.45%	$41.25	$50.50		1	22.42%	$2.30	5.58%	28.00%
6 United Aircraft	$2.00	5.30%	$37.75	$42.25		1	11.92%	$2.00	5.30%	17.22%
7 General Motors	$2.00	4.82%	$41.50	$56.38		1	35.84%	$2.50	6.02%	41.87%
8 Standard Oil CA	$2.00	4.20%	$47.63	$55.38		1	16.27%	$2.00	4.20%	20.47%
9 US Steel	$3.00	3.94%	$76.13	$77.13		1	1.31%	$3.00	3.94%	5.25%
10 Woolworth	$2.50	3.64%	$68.63	$91.00		1	32.60%	$2.50	3.64%	36.25%
		5.01%					19.01%		5.15%	24.16%
TOP FIVE:										
1 Bethlehem Steel	$2.40	5.85%	$41.00	$43.00		1	4.88%	$2.40	5.85%	10.73%
2 American Can	$2.00	5.71%	$35.00	$46.25		1	32.14%	$2.00	5.71%	37.86%
3 Anaconda	$2.50	5.67%	$44.13	$49.50		1	12.18%	$2.50	5.67%	17.85%
4 International Harvester	$2.40	5.55%	$43.25	$52.13		1	20.52%	$2.40	5.55%	26.07%
5 Standard Oil NJ	$2.25	5.45%	$41.25	$50.50		1	22.42%	$2.30	5.58%	28.00%
		5.65%					18.43%		5.67%	24.10%

LIST OF 1960 DOW JONES INDUSTRIALS BY DIVIDEND-YIELD

	STOCK 1960	1960 WSJ DIVI.	1960 WSJ YIELD	1960 OPENING PRICE	1960 CLOSING PRICE	1960 STOCK DIV.	1960 SPLIT	1960 APPRECIATION	1960 DIVIDEND	ACT. CASH YIELD	TOTAL RETURN
1	United Aircraft	$2.00	5.03%	$39.75	$37.75		1	-5.03%	$2.00	5.03%	.00%
2	International Harvester	$2.40	4.90%	$49.00	$43.25		1	-11.73%	$2.40	4.90%	-6.84%
3	American Can	$2.00	4.62%	$43.25	$35.00		1	-19.08%	$2.00	4.62%	-14.45%
4	Standard Oil NJ	$2.25	4.52%	$49.75	$41.25		1	-17.09%	$2.25	4.52%	-12.56%
5	Bethlehem Steel	$2.40	4.26%	$56.38	$41.00		1	-27.27%	$7.00	12.42%	-14.86%
6	American T & T	$3.30	4.11%	$80.38	$103.50		1	28.77%	$3.30	4.11%	32.88%
7	Johns-Manville	$2.00	4.08%	$49.00	$57.63		1	17.60%	$2.00	4.08%	21.68%
8	Standard Oil CA	$2.00	4.04%	$49.50	$47.63		1	-3.79%	$2.00	4.04%	.25%
* 9	Anaconda	$2.50	3.85%	$64.88	$44.13		1	-31.98%	$2.50	3.85%	-28.13%
10	Woolworth	$2.50	3.78%	$66.13	$68.63		1	3.78%	$2.50	3.78%	7.56%
11	American Tobacco	$4.00	3.74%	$107.00	$65.25		2	21.96%	$5.45	5.09%	27.06%
12	General Motors	$2.00	3.67%	$54.50	$41.50		1	-23.85%	$2.00	3.67%	-20.18%
* 13	Swift & Company	$1.60	3.37%	$47.50	$45.63		1	-3.95%	$1.85	3.89%	-.05%
14	Allied Chemical	$3.60	3.17%	$113.50	$51.75		2	-8.81%	$3.60	3.17%	-5.64%
15	US Steel	$3.00	2.96%	$101.38	$76.13		1	-24.91%	$3.00	2.96%	-21.95%
16	Texaco	$2.40	2.78%	$86.38	$84.25	2.00%	1	-.51%	$2.85	3.30%	2.79%
17	Du Pont	$7.00	2.66%	$262.75	$186.50		1	-29.02%	$6.75	2.57%	-26.45%
18	General Foods	$2.60	2.51%	$103.75	$70.50		2	35.90%	$2.70	2.60%	38.51%
19	Union Carbide	$3.60	2.45%	$147.00	$116.50		1	-20.75%	$3.60	2.45%	-18.30%
* 20	Procter & Gamble	$2.20	2.45%	$89.88	$136.00		1	51.32%	$2.60	2.89%	54.21%
21	Owens-Illinois Glass	$2.50	2.38%	$104.88	$91.75		1	-12.51%	$2.50	2.38%	-10.13%
22	Sears, Roebuck	$1.20	2.38%	$50.50	$55.75		1	10.40%	$1.45	2.87%	13.27%
23	International Nickel	$2.60	2.37%	$109.63	$58.38		2	6.50%	$3.05	2.78%	9.28%
24	International Paper	$3.00	2.22%	$134.88	$31.13	2.00%	3	-29.38%	$3.04	2.25%	-27.13%
25	Westinghouse Electric	$2.40	2.19%	$109.50	$47.50		2	-13.24%	$2.40	2.19%	-11.05%
26	General Electric	$2.00	2.07%	$96.63	$72.25	2.00%	1	-25.23%	$2.00	2.07%	-23.16%
27	Goodyear	$.90	1.93%	$46.63	$34.13		1	-25.35%	$.90	1.93%	-23.42%
28	Eastman Kodak	$1.80	1.68%	$107.00	$108.75		1	1.64%	$3.60	3.36%	5.00%
29	Chrysler	$1.00	1.45%	$69.00	$38.75		1	-43.84%	$1.50	2.17%	-41.67%
* 30	Aluminum Co of Amer	$1.20	1.13%	$106.50	$69.50		1	-34.74%	$1.20	1.13%	-33.62%
	AVERAGE		3.09%					-7.81%		3.57%	-4.24%

* First year in the Dow 30

STOCK	1960	1960 WSJ DIVI.	1960 WSJ YIELD	1960 OPENING PRICE	1960 CLOSING PRICE	1960 STOCK DIV.	1960 SPLIT	1960 APPRECIATION	1960 DIVIDEND	ACT. CASH YIELD	TOTAL RETURN
	BOTTOM FIVE:										
26	General Electric	$2.00	2.07%	$96.63	$72.25		1	-25.23%	$2.00	2.07%	-23.16%
27	Goodyear	$.90	1.93%	$46.63	$34.13	2.00%	1	-25.35%	$.90	1.93%	-23.42%
28	Eastman Kodak	$1.80	1.68%	$107.00	$108.75		1	1.64%	$3.60	3.36%	5.00%
29	Chrysler	$1.00	1.45%	$69.00	$38.75		1	-43.84%	$1.50	2.17%	-41.67%
30	Aluminum Co of Amer	$1.20	1.13%	$106.50	$69.50		1	-34.74%	$1.20	1.13%	-33.62%
			1.65%					-25.50%		2.13%	-23.37%
	BOTTOM TEN:										
21	Owens-Illinois Glass	$2.50	2.38%	$104.88	$91.75		1	-12.51%	$2.50	2.38%	-10.13%
22	Sears, Roebuck	$1.20	2.38%	$50.50	$55.75		1	10.40%	$1.45	2.87%	13.27%
23	International Nickel	$2.60	2.37%	$109.63	$58.38		2	6.50%	$3.05	2.78%	9.28%
24	International Paper	$3.00	2.22%	$134.88	$31.13		3	-29.38%	$3.04	2.25%	-27.13%
25	Westinghouse Electric	$2.40	2.19%	$109.50	$47.50	2.00%	2	-13.24%	$2.40	2.19%	-11.05%
26	General Electric	$2.00	2.07%	$96.63	$72.25		1	-25.23%	$2.00	2.07%	-23.16%
27	Goodyear	$.90	1.93%	$46.63	$34.13	2.00%	1	-25.35%	$.90	1.93%	-23.42%
28	Eastman Kodak	$1.80	1.68%	$107.00	$108.75		1	1.64%	$3.60	3.36%	5.00%
29	Chrysler	$1.00	1.45%	$69.00	$38.75		1	-43.84%	$1.50	2.17%	-41.67%
30	Aluminum Co of Amer	$1.20	1.13%	$106.50	$69.50		1	-34.74%	$1.20	1.13%	-33.62%
			1.98%					-16.58%		2.31%	-14.26%
	TOP TEN:										
1	United Aircraft	$2.00	5.03%	$39.75	$37.75		1	-5.03%	$2.00	5.03%	.00%
2	International Harvester	$2.40	4.90%	$49.00	$43.25		1	-11.73%	$2.40	4.90%	-6.84%
3	American Can	$2.00	4.62%	$43.25	$35.00		1	-19.08%	$2.00	4.62%	-14.45%
4	Standard Oil NJ	$2.25	4.52%	$49.75	$41.25		1	-17.09%	$2.25	4.52%	-12.56%
5	Bethlehem Steel	$2.40	4.26%	$56.38	$41.00		1	-27.27%	$7.00	12.42%	-14.86%
6	American T & T	$3.30	4.11%	$80.38	$103.50		1	28.77%	$3.30	4.11%	32.88%
7	Johns-Manville	$2.00	4.08%	$49.00	$57.63		1	17.60%	$2.00	4.08%	21.68%
8	Standard Oil CA	$2.00	4.04%	$49.50	$47.63		1	-3.79%	$2.00	4.04%	.25%
9	Anaconda	$2.50	3.85%	$64.88	$44.13		1	-31.98%	$2.50	3.85%	-28.13%
10	Woolworth	$2.50	3.78%	$66.13	$68.63		1	3.78%	$2.50	3.78%	7.56%
			4.32%					-6.58%		5.14%	-1.45%
	TOP FIVE:										
1	United Aircraft	$2.00	5.03%	$39.75	$37.75		1	-5.03%	$2.00	5.03%	.00%
2	International Harvester	$2.40	4.90%	$49.00	$43.25		1	-11.73%	$2.40	4.90%	-6.84%
3	American Can	$2.00	4.62%	$43.25	$35.00		1	-19.08%	$2.00	4.62%	-14.45%
4	Standard Oil NJ	$2.25	4.52%	$49.75	$41.25		1	-17.09%	$2.25	4.52%	-12.56%
5	Bethlehem Steel	$2.40	4.26%	$56.38	$41.00		1	-27.27%	$7.00	12.42%	-14.86%
			4.67%					-16.04%		6.30%	-9.74%

LIST OF 1959 DOW JONES INDUSTRIALS BY DIVIDEND-YIELD

	STOCK 1959	1959 WSJ DIVI.	1959 WSJ YIELD	1959 OPENING PRICE	1959 CLOSING PRICE	1959 STOCK DIV.	1959 SPLIT	1959 APPRECIATION	1959 DIVIDEND	ACT. CASH YIELD	TOTAL RETURN
1	United Aircraft	$3.00	5.00%	$60.00	$39.75		1	-33.75%	$2.50	4.17%	-29.58%
2	International Harvester	$2.00	4.83%	$41.38	$49.00		1	18.43%	$2.00	4.83%	23.26%
3	Woolworth	$2.50	4.64%	$53.88	$66.13		1	22.74%	$2.50	4.64%	27.38%
4	Bethlehem Steel	$2.40	4.56%	$52.63	$56.38		1	7.13%	$7.00	13.30%	20.43%
5	American Tobacco	$4.00	4.16%	$96.13	$107.00		1	11.31%	$6.00	6.24%	17.56%
6	American Can	$2.00	4.00%	$50.00	$43.25		1	-13.50%	$2.00	4.00%	-9.50%
7	American T & T	$9.00	3.99%	$225.50	$80.38		3	6.93%	$9.45	4.19%	11.12%
8	General Motors	$2.00	3.99%	$50.13	$54.50		1	8.73%	$2.00	3.99%	12.72%
9	National Steel	$3.00	3.96%	$75.75	$97.00		1	28.05%	$3.00	3.96%	32.01%
+ 10	Standard Oil NJ	$2.25	3.89%	$57.88	$49.75		1	-14.04%	$2.25	3.89%	-10.15%
11	Johns-Manville	$2.00	3.74%	$53.50	$49.00		1	-8.41%	$2.00	3.74%	-4.67%
+ 12	Corn Products Refining	$2.00	3.67%	$54.50	$56.50		1	3.67%	$2.00	3.67%	7.34%
13	Standard Oil CA	$2.00	3.32%	$60.25	$49.50		1	-17.84%	$2.00	3.32%	-14.52%
14	Allied Chemical	$3.00	3.25%	$92.25	$113.50		1	23.04%	$3.15	3.41%	26.45%
+ 15	National Distillers	$1.00	3.20%	$31.25	$33.75		1	8.00%	$1.10	3.52%	11.52%
+ 16	American Smelting	$1.50	3.08%	$48.63	$53.13		1	9.25%	$1.00	2.06%	11.31%
17	US Steel	$3.00	3.05%	$98.25	$101.38		1	3.18%	$3.00	3.05%	6.23%
18	General Foods	$2.20	2.93%	$75.00	$103.75		1	38.33%	$2.55	3.40%	41.73%
19	International Nickel	$2.60	2.92%	$89.00	$109.63		1	23.17%	$3.00	3.37%	26.54%
20	Union Carbide	$3.60	2.85%	$126.13	$147.00		1	16.55%	$3.60	2.85%	19.41%
21	Chrysler	$1.50	2.78%	$53.88	$69.00		1	28.07%	$1.00	1.86%	29.93%
22	Du Pont	$6.00	2.78%	$215.50	$262.75		1	21.93%	$7.00	3.25%	25.17%
23	Westinghouse Electric	$2.00	2.76%	$72.50	$109.50		1	51.03%	$2.10	2.90%	53.93%
24	Procter & Gamble	$2.00	2.70%	$74.00	$89.88		1	21.45%	$2.20	2.97%	24.43%
25	International Paper	$3.00	2.56%	$117.25	$134.88	2.00%	1	17.33%	$3.00	2.56%	19.89%
26	General Electric	$2.00	2.54%	$78.75	$96.63		1	22.70%	$2.00	2.54%	25.24%
27	Sears, Roebuck	$1.00	2.53%	$39.50	$50.50		1	27.85%	$1.30	3.29%	31.14%
28	Texas Corporation	$2.00	2.32%	$86.25	$86.38	2.00%	1	2.15%	$2.60	3.01%	5.16%
29	Goodyear	$2.40	1.97%	$122.00	$46.63	2.00%	3	16.94%	$2.48	2.03%	18.98%
30	Eastman Kodak	$2.60	1.74%	$149.75	$107.00		2	42.90%	$3.12	2.08%	44.99%
	AVERAGE		3.32%					13.11%		3.74%	16.85%

+ Last year in the Dow 30

STOCK 1959	1959 WSJ DIVI.	1959 WSJ YIELD	1959 OPENING PRICE	1959 CLOSING PRICE	1959 STOCK DIV.	1959 SPLIT	1959 APPRECIATION	1959 DIVIDEND	ACT. CASH YIELD	TOTAL RETURN
BOTTOM FIVE:										
26 General Electric	$2.00	2.54%	$78.75	$96.63		1	22.70%	$2.00	2.54%	25.24%
27 Sears, Roebuck	$1.00	2.53%	$39.50	$50.50		1	27.85%	$1.30	3.29%	31.14%
28 Texas Corporation	$2.00	2.32%	$86.25	$86.38	2.00%	1	2.15%	$2.60	3.01%	5.16%
29 Goodyear	$2.40	1.97%	$122.00	$46.63	2.00%	3	16.94%	$2.48	2.03%	18.98%
30 Eastman Kodak	$2.60	1.74%	$149.75	$107.00		2	42.90%	$3.12	2.08%	44.99%
		2.22%					22.51%		2.59%	25.10%
BOTTOM TEN:										
21 Chrysler	$1.50	2.78%	$53.88	$69.00		1	28.07%	$1.00	1.86%	29.93%
22 Du Pont	$6.00	2.78%	$215.50	$262.75			21.93%	$7.00	3.25%	25.17%
23 Westinghouse Electric	$2.00	2.76%	$72.50	$109.50		1	51.03%	$2.10	2.90%	53.93%
24 Procter & Gamble	$2.00	2.70%	$74.00	$89.88		1	21.45%	$2.20	2.97%	24.43%
25 International Paper	$3.00	2.56%	$117.25	$134.88	2.00%	1	17.33%	$3.00	2.56%	19.89%
26 General Electric	$2.00	2.54%	$78.75	$96.63		1	22.70%	$2.00	2.54%	25.24%
27 Sears, Roebuck	$1.00	2.53%	$39.50	$50.50		1	27.85%	$1.30	3.29%	31.14%
28 Texas Corporation	$2.00	2.32%	$86.25	$86.38	2.00%	1	2.15%	$2.60	3.01%	5.16%
29 Goodyear	$2.40	1.97%	$122.00	$46.63	2.00%	3	16.94%	$2.48	2.03%	18.98%
30 Eastman Kodak	$2.60	1.74%	$149.75	$107.00		2	42.90%	$3.12	2.08%	44.99%
		2.47%					25.24%		2.65%	27.89%
TOP TEN:										
1 United Aircraft	$3.00	5.00%	$60.00	$39.75		1	-33.75%	$2.50	4.17%	-29.58%
2 International Harvester	$2.00	4.83%	$41.38	$49.00		1	18.43%	$2.00	4.83%	23.26%
3 Woolworth	$2.50	4.64%	$53.88	$66.13		1	22.74%	$2.50	4.64%	27.38%
4 Bethlehem Steel	$2.40	4.56%	$52.63	$56.38		1	7.13%	$7.00	13.30%	20.43%
5 American Tobacco	$4.00	4.16%	$96.13	$107.00		1	11.31%	$6.00	6.24%	17.56%
6 American Can	$2.00	4.00%	$50.00	$43.25			-13.50%	$2.00	4.10%	-9.50%
7 American T & T	$9.00	3.99%	$225.50	$80.38		3	6.93%	$9.45	4.19%	11.12%
8 General Motors	$3.00	3.99%	$50.13	$54.50		1	8.73%	$2.00	3.99%	12.72%
9 National Steel	$3.00	3.96%	$75.75	$97.00		1	28.05%	$3.00	3.96%	32.01%
10 Standard Oil NJ	$2.25	3.89%	$57.88	$49.75		1	-14.04%	$2.25	3.89%	-10.15%
		4.30%					4.20%		5.32%	9.52%
TOP FIVE:										
1 United Aircraft	$3.00	5.00%	$60.00	$39.75		1	-33.75%	$2.50	4.17%	-29.58%
2 International Harvester	$2.00	4.83%	$41.38	$49.00		1	18.43%	$2.00	4.83%	23.26%
3 Woolworth	$2.50	4.64%	$53.88	$66.13		1	22.74%	$2.50	4.64%	27.38%
4 Bethlehem Steel	$2.40	4.56%	$52.63	$56.38		1	7.13%	$7.00	13.30%	20.43%
5 American Tobacco	$4.00	4.16%	$96.13	$107.00		1	11.31%	$6.00	6.24%	17.56%
		4.64%					5.17%		6.64%	11.81%

LIST OF 1958 DOW JONES INDUSTRIALS BY DIVIDEND-YIELD

	STOCK	1958 WSJ DIVI.	1958 WSJ YIELD	1958 OPENING PRICE	1958 CLOSING PRICE	1958 STOCK DIV.	1958 SPLIT	1958 APPRECIATION	1958 DIVIDEND	ACT. CASH YIELD	TOTAL RETURN
1	American Smelting	$3.00	8.16%	$36.75	$54.50		1	48.30%	$1.50	4.08%	52.38%
2	National Steel	$4.00	7.48%	$53.50	$75.75		1	41.59%	$3.00	5.61%	47.20%
3	International Harvester	$2.00	7.11%	$28.13	$41.38		1	47.11%	$2.00	7.11%	54.22%
4	Woolworth	$2.50	6.76%	$37.00	$53.88		1	45.61%	$2.50	6.76%	52.36%
5	Bethlehem Steel	$2.40	6.46%	$37.13	$52.63		1	41.75%	$2.40	6.46%	48.22%
6	General Motors	$2.00	5.82%	$34.38	$50.13		1	45.82%	$2.00	5.82%	51.64%
7	US Steel	$3.00	5.71%	$52.50	$98.25		1	87.14%	$3.00	5.71%	92.86%
8	Chrysler	$3.00	5.61%	$53.50	$53.88		1	.70%	$1.50	2.80%	3.50%
9	United Aircraft	$3.00	5.59%	$53.63	$60.00		1	11.89%	$3.00	5.59%	17.48%
10	American T & T	$9.00	5.29%	$170.00	$225.50		1	32.65%	$9.00	5.29%	37.94%
11	Johns-Manville	$2.00	5.28%	$37.88	$53.50		1	41.25%	$2.00	5.28%	46.53%
12	American Tobacco	$4.00	5.16%	$77.50	$96.13		1	24.03%	$5.00	6.45%	30.48%
13	National Distillers	$1.00	4.82%	$20.75	$31.25		1	50.60%	$1.00	4.82%	55.42%
14	American Can	$2.00	4.76%	$42.00	$50.00		1	19.05%	$2.00	4.76%	23.81%
15	Corn Products Refining	$1.60	4.67%	$34.25	$54.50		1	59.12%	$1.75	5.11%	64.23%
16	Standard Oil NJ	$2.25	4.51%	$49.88	$57.88		1	16.04%	$2.25	4.51%	20.55%
17	Standard Oil CA	$1.90	4.11%	$46.25	$60.25		1	30.27%	$2.00	4.32%	34.59%
18	Allied Chemical	$3.00	4.05%	$74.00	$92.25		1	24.66%	$3.00	4.05%	28.72%
19	Sears, Roebuck	$1.00	3.94%	$25.38	$39.50		1	55.67%	$1.10	4.33%	60.00%
20	General Foods	$1.95	3.92%	$49.75	$75.00		1	50.75%	$2.20	4.42%	55.18%
21	Union Carbide	$3.60	3.80%	$94.75	$126.13		1	33.11%	$3.60	3.80%	36.91%
22	Du Pont	$6.50	3.69%	$176.25	$215.50		1	22.27%	$6.00	3.40%	25.67%
23	International Nickel	$2.60	3.60%	$72.25	$89.00		1	23.18%	$2.60	3.60%	26.78%
24	Procter & Gamble	$2.00	3.52%	$56.88	$74.00		1	30.11%	$2.00	3.52%	33.63%
25	International Paper	$3.00	3.48%	$86.25	$117.25	2.00%	1	38.66%	$3.00	3.48%	42.14%
26	General Electric	$2.00	3.29%	$60.88	$78.75		1	29.36%	$2.00	3.29%	32.65%
27	Westinghouse Electric	$2.00	3.17%	$63.00	$72.50		1	15.08%	$2.00	3.17%	18.25%
28	Texas Corporation	$2.00	3.17%	$63.13	$86.25		1	36.63%	$2.35	3.72%	40.36%
29	Goodyear	$2.40	2.87%	$83.50	$122.00	2.00%	1	49.03%	$2.40	2.87%	51.90%
30	Eastman Kodak	$.90	.91%	$99.00	$149.75		1	51.26%	$2.85	2.88%	54.14%
	AVERAGE		4.69%					36.76%		4.57%	41.33%

STOCK	1958 WSJ DIVI.	1958 WSJ YIELD	1958 OPENING PRICE	1958 CLOSING PRICE	1958 STOCK DIV.	1958 SPLIT	1958 APPRECIATION	1958 DIVIDEND	ACT. CASH YIELD	TOTAL RETURN
BOTTOM FIVE:										
26 General Electric	$2.00	3.29%	$60.88	$78.75			29.36%	$2.00	3.29%	32.65%
27 Westinghouse Electric	$2.00	3.17%	$63.00	$72.50			15.08%	$2.00	3.17%	18.25%
28 Texas Corporation	$2.00	3.17%	$63.13	$86.25		1	36.63%	$2.35	3.72%	40.36%
29 Goodyear	$2.40	2.87%	$83.50	$122.00	2.00%	1	49.03%	$2.40	2.87%	51.90%
30 Eastman Kodak	$.90	.91%	$99.00	$149.75		1	51.26%	$2.85	2.83%	54.14%
		2.68%					36.27%		3.19%	39.46%
BOTTOM TEN:										
21 Union Carbide	$3.60	3.80%	$94.75	$126.13		1	33.11%	$3.60	3.80%	36.91%
22 Du Pont	$6.50	3.69%	$176.25	$215.50		1	22.27%	$6.00	3.40%	25.67%
23 International Nickel	$2.60	3.60%	$72.25	$89.00		1	23.18%	$2.60	3.60%	26.78%
24 Procter & Gamble	$2.00	3.52%	$56.88	$74.00		1	30.11%	$2.00	3.52%	33.63%
25 International Paper	$3.00	3.48%	$86.25	$117.25	2.00%	1	38.66%	$3.00	3.48%	42.14%
26 General Electric	$2.00	3.29%	$60.88	$78.75			29.36%	$2.00	3.29%	32.65%
27 Westinghouse Electric	$2.00	3.17%	$63.00	$72.50			15.08%	$2.00	3.17%	18.25%
28 Texas Corporation	$2.00	3.17%	$63.13	$86.25		1	36.63%	$2.35	3.72%	40.36%
29 Goodyear	$2.40	2.87%	$83.50	$122.00	2.00%	1	49.03%	$2.40	2.87%	51.90%
30 Eastman Kodak	$.90	.91%	$99.00	$149.75		1	51.26%	$2.85	2.83%	54.14%
		3.15%					32.87%		3.37%	36.24%
TOP TEN:										
1 American Smelting	$3.00	8.16%	$36.75	$54.50		1	48.30%	$1.50	4.08%	52.38%
2 National Steel	$4.00	7.48%	$53.50	$75.75		1	41.59%	$3.00	5.61%	47.20%
3 International Harvester	$2.00	7.11%	$28.13	$41.38		1	47.11%	$2.00	7.11%	54.22%
4 Woolworth	$2.50	6.76%	$37.13	$53.88		1	45.61%	$2.50	6.76%	52.36%
5 Bethlehem Steel	$2.40	6.46%	$37.13	$52.63		1	41.75%	$2.40	6.46%	48.22%
6 General Motors	$2.00	5.82%	$34.38	$50.13		1	45.82%	$2.00	5.82%	51.64%
7 US Steel	$3.00	5.71%	$52.50	$98.25		1	87.14%	$3.00	5.71%	92.86%
8 Chrysler	$3.00	5.61%	$53.50	$53.88		1	.70%	$1.50	2.80%	3.50%
9 United Aircraft	$3.00	5.59%	$53.63	$60.00		1	11.89%	$3.00	5.59%	17.48%
10 American T & T	$9.00	5.29%	$170.00	$225.50		1	32.65%	$9.00	5.29%	37.94%
		6.40%					40.26%		5.52%	45.78%
TOP FIVE:										
1 American Smelting	$3.00	8.16%	$36.75	$54.50		1	48.30%	$1.50	4.08%	52.38%
2 National Steel	$4.00	7.48%	$53.50	$75.75		1	41.59%	$3.00	5.61%	47.20%
3 International Harvester	$2.00	7.11%	$28.13	$41.38		1	47.11%	$2.00	7.11%	54.22%
4 Woolworth	$2.50	6.76%	$37.13	$53.88		1	45.61%	$2.50	6.76%	52.36%
5 Bethlehem Steel	$2.40	6.46%	$37.13	$52.63		1	41.75%	$2.40	6.46%	48.22%
		7.19%					44.87%		6.00%	50.88%

LIST OF 1957 DOW JONES INDUSTRIALS BY DIVIDEND-YIELD

	STOCK 1957	1957 WSJ DIVI.	1957 WSJ YIELD	1957 OPENING PRICE	1957 CLOSING PRICE	1957 STOCK DIV.	1957 SPLIT	1957 APPRECIATION	1957 DIVIDEND	ACT. CASH YIELD	TOTAL RETURN
1	American Smelting	$3.50	6.15%	$56.88	$36.75		1	-35.39%	$3.00	5.27%	-30.11%
2	Woolworth	$2.50	5.70%	$43.88	$37.00		1	-15.67%	$2.50	5.70%	-9.97%
3	American Tobacco	$4.00	5.47%	$73.13	$77.50		1	5.98%	$5.00	6.84%	12.82%
4	International Harvester	$2.00	5.26%	$38.00	$28.13		1	-25.99%	$2.00	5.26%	-20.72%
5	American T & T	$9.00	5.25%	$171.50	$170.00		1	-.87%	$9.00	5.25%	4.37%
6	National Steel	$4.00	5.16%	$77.50	$53.50		1	-30.97%	$4.00	5.16%	-25.81%
7	Corn Products Refining	$1.50	5.13%	$29.25	$34.25		1	17.09%	$1.50	5.13%	22.22%
8	American Can	$2.00	4.85%	$41.25	$42.00		1	1.82%	$2.00	4.85%	6.67%
9	General Motors	$2.00	4.64%	$43.13	$34.38		1	-20.29%	$2.00	4.64%	-15.65%
10	Bethlehem Steel	$8.50	4.35%	$195.38	$37.13		4	-23.99%	$9.60	4.91%	-19.08%
11	Chrysler	$3.00	4.34%	$69.13	$53.50		1	-22.60%	$4.00	5.79%	-16.82%
12	General Foods	$1.80	4.19%	$43.00	$49.75		1	15.70%	$1.95	4.53%	20.23%
13	Johns-Manville	$2.00	4.12%	$48.50	$37.88		1	-21.91%	$2.00	4.12%	-17.78%
14	National Distillers	$1.00	3.76%	$26.63	$20.75	2.00%	1	-20.51%	$1.00	3.76%	-16.75%
15	Standard Oil CA	$1.80	3.72%	$48.38	$46.25		1	-4.39%	$1.90	3.93%	-.47%
16	US Steel	$2.60	3.64%	$71.50	$52.50		1	-26.57%	$3.00	4.20%	-22.38%
17	Standard Oil NJ	$2.10	3.62%	$58.00	$49.88		1	-14.01%	$2.25	3.88%	-10.13%
18	Procter & Gamble	$1.80	3.58%	$50.25	$56.88		1	13.18%	$1.95	3.88%	17.06%
19	Westinghouse Electric	$2.00	3.50%	$57.13	$63.00		1	10.28%	$2.00	3.50%	13.79%
20	Sears, Roebuck	$1.00	3.49%	$28.63	$25.38		1	-11.35%	$1.00	3.49%	-7.86%
21	Du Pont	$6.50	3.41%	$190.50	$176.25		1	-7.48%	$6.50	3.41%	-4.07%
22	United Aircraft	$3.00	3.39%	$88.50	$53.63	20.00%	1	-27.29%	$3.00	3.39%	-23.90%
23	Texas Corporation	$2.00	3.38%	$59.25	$63.13	2.00%	1	8.67%	$2.35	3.97%	12.64%
24	General Electric	$2.00	3.35%	$59.63	$60.88		1	2.10%	$2.00	3.35%	5.45%
25	Allied Chemical	$3.00	3.17%	$94.75	$74.00		1	-21.90%	$3.00	3.17%	-18.73%
26	Goodyear	$2.40	2.90%	$82.63	$83.50	2.00%	1	3.08%	$2.40	2.90%	5.98%
27	International Paper	$3.00	2.80%	$107.00	$86.25	2.00%	1	-17.78%	$3.00	2.80%	-14.98%
28	Union Carbide	$3.15	2.75%	$114.38	$94.75		1	-17.16%	$3.60	3.15%	-14.01%
29	Eastman Kodak	$2.40	2.74%	$87.50	$99.00	5.00%	1	18.80%	$2.65	3.03%	21.83%
30	International Nickel	$2.60	2.37%	$109.63	$72.25		1	-34.09%	$3.75	3.42%	-30.67%
	AVERAGE		4.01%					-10.12%		4.22%	-5.89%

STOCK	1957	1957 WSJ DIVI.	1957 WSJ YIELD	1957 OPENING PRICE	1957 CLOSING PRICE	1957 STOCK DIV.	1957 SPLIT	1957 APPRECIATION	1957 DIVIDEND	ACT. CASH YIELD	TOTAL RETURN
BOTTOM FIVE:											
26	Goodyear	$2.40	2.90%	$82.63	$83.50	2.00%	1	3.08%	$2.40	2.90%	5.98%
27	International Paper	$3.00	2.80%	$107.00	$86.25	2.00%	1	-17.78%	$3.00	2.80%	-14.98%
28	Union Carbide	$3.15	2.75%	$114.38	$94.75		1	-17.16%	$3.60	3.15%	-14.01%
29	Eastman Kodak	$2.40	2.74%	$87.50	$99.00	5.00%	1	18.80%	$2.65	3.03%	21.83%
30	International Nickel	$2.60	2.37%	$109.63	$72.25		1	-34.09%	$3.75	3.42%	-30.67%
			2.72%					-9.43%		3.06%	-6.37%
BOTTOM TEN:											
21	Du Pont	$6.50	3.41%	$190.50	$176.25		1	-7.48%	$6.50	3.41%	-4.07%
22	United Aircraft	$3.00	3.39%	$88.50	$53.63	20.00%	1	-27.29%	$3.00	3.39%	-23.90%
23	Texas Corporation	$2.00	3.38%	$59.25	$63.13	2.00%	1	8.67%	$2.35	3.97%	12.64%
24	General Electric	$2.00	3.35%	$59.63	$60.88		1	2.10%	$2.00	3.35%	5.45%
25	Allied Chemical	$3.00	3.17%	$94.75	$74.00		1	-21.90%	$3.00	3.17%	-18.73%
26	Goodyear	$2.40	2.90%	$82.63	$83.50	2.00%	1	3.08%	$2.40	2.90%	5.98%
27	International Paper	$3.00	2.80%	$107.00	$86.25	2.00%	1	-17.78%	$3.00	2.80%	-14.98%
28	Union Carbide	$3.15	2.75%	$114.38	$94.75		1	-17.16%	$3.60	3.15%	-14.01%
29	Eastman Kodak	$2.40	2.74%	$87.50	$99.00	5.00%	1	18.80%	$2.65	3.03%	21.83%
30	International Nickel	$2.60	2.37%	$109.63	$72.25		1	-34.09%	$3.75	3.42%	-30.67%
			3.03%					-9.31%		3.26%	-6.05%
TOP TEN:											
1	American Smelting	$3.50	6.15%	$56.88	$36.75		1	-35.39%	$3.00	5.27%	-30.11%
2	Woolworth	$2.50	5.70%	$43.88	$37.00		1	-15.67%	$2.50	5.70%	-9.97%
3	American Tobacco	$4.00	5.47%	$73.13	$77.50		1	5.98%	$5.00	6.84%	12.82%
4	International Harvester	$2.00	5.26%	$38.00	$28.13		1	-25.99%	$2.00	5.26%	-20.72%
5	American T & T	$9.00	5.25%	$171.50	$170.00		1	-.87%	$9.00	5.25%	4.37%
6	National Steel	$4.00	5.16%	$77.50	$53.50		1	-30.97%	$4.00	5.16%	-25.81%
7	Corn Products Refining	$1.50	5.13%	$29.25	$34.25		1	17.09%	$1.50	5.13%	22.22%
8	American Can	$2.00	4.85%	$41.25	$42.00		1	1.82%	$2.00	4.85%	6.67%
9	General Motors	$2.00	4.64%	$43.13	$34.38		1	-20.29%	$2.00	4.64%	-15.65%
10	Bethlehem Steel	$8.50	4.35%	$195.38	$37.13		4	-23.99%	$9.60	4.91%	-19.08%
			5.20%					-12.83%		5.30%	-7.53%
TOP FIVE:											
1	American Smelting	$3.50	6.15%	$56.88	$36.75		1	-35.39%	$3.00	5.27%	-30.11%
2	Woolworth	$2.50	5.70%	$43.88	$37.00		1	-15.67%	$2.50	5.70%	-9.97%
3	American Tobacco	$4.00	5.47%	$73.13	$77.50		1	5.98%	$5.00	6.84%	12.82%
4	International Harvester	$2.00	5.26%	$38.00	$28.13		1	-25.99%	$2.00	5.26%	-20.72%
5	American T & T	$9.00	5.25%	$171.50	$170.00		1	-.87%	$9.00	5.25%	4.37%
			5.57%					-14.39%		5.66%	-8.72%

Appendix 4

Complete Data Set By Company

Appendix 4 contains a complete data set organized by company. It lists all available data for each company for all the years the company was listed in the Dow Jones Industrials between 1957 and 1990. If a company left the Dow list during a year, it was assumed that the stock was still held in the investment portfolio until year-end. Data for such a year was therefore for the complete year and did not end on the day the company left the list.

Explanations of the columnar categories are identical to those for Appendix 3 with the exception of the RANK category, is simply the company's yield rank in the Dow Thirty at the beginning of the year in question.

179

ALCOA/ALUMINUM COMPANY OF AMERICA

YEAR	RANK	STOCK	WSJ DIVI.	WSJ YIELD	OPENING PRICE	CLOSING PRICE	STOCK DIV.	SPLIT	APPRECIATION	ACTUAL DIVIDEND	TOTAL RETURN
1957											
1958											
1959											
1960	30	Aluminum Co of Amer	$1.20	1.13%	$106.50	$69.50		1	-34.74%	$1.20	-33.62%
1961	30	Aluminum Co of Amer	$1.20	1.73%	$69.50	$65.38		1	-5.94%	$1.20	-4.21%
1962	26	Aluminum Co of Amer	$1.20	1.84%	$65.38	$53.88		1	-17.59%	$1.20	-15.76%
1963	26	Aluminum Co of Amer	$1.20	2.23%	$53.88	$68.25		1	26.68%	$1.20	28.91%
1964	28	Aluminum Co of Amer	$1.20	1.76%	$68.25	$60.63		1	-11.17%	$1.20	-9.41%
1965	26	Aluminum Co of Amer	$1.40	2.31%	$60.63	$75.88		1	25.15%	$1.40	27.46%
1966	28	Aluminum Co of Amer	$1.40	1.85%	$75.88	$76.63		1	.99%	$1.55	3.03%
1967	28	Aluminum Co of Amer	$1.60	2.09%	$76.63	$81.00		1	5.71%	$1.75	7.99%
1968	27	Aluminum Co of Amer	$1.80	2.22%	$81.00	$72.75		1	-10.19%	$1.75	-7.96%
1969	26	Aluminum Co of Amer	$1.80	2.47%	$72.75	$71.50		1	-1.72%	$1.80	.76%
1970	25	Aluminum Co of Amer	$1.80	2.52%	$71.50	$56.38		1	-21.15%	$1.80	-18.64%
1971	19	Aluminum Co of Amer	$1.80	3.19%	$56.38	$43.50		1	-22.84%	$1.80	-19.65%
1972	14	Aluminum Co of Amer	$1.80	4.14%	$43.50	$55.00		1	26.44%	$1.80	30.57%
1973	19	Aluminum Co of Amer	$1.80	3.27%	$55.00	$72.38		1	31.59%	$1.91	35.05%
1974	25	Aluminum Co of Amer	$1.94	2.68%	$72.38	$29.88		1	-38.08%	$1.51	-36.00%
1975	27	Aluminum Co of Amer	$1.34	4.49%	$29.88	$39.00		1.5	30.54%	$1.34	35.03%
1976	22	Aluminum Co of Amer	$1.34	3.44%	$39.00	$56.75		1	45.51%	$1.37	49.03%
1977	26	Aluminum Co of Amer	$1.40	2.47%	$56.75	$45.88		1	-19.16%	$1.70	-16.17%
1978	26	Aluminum Co of Amer	$1.80	3.92%	$45.88	$47.00		1	2.45%	$1.90	6.59%
1979	25	Aluminum Co of Amer	$2.00	4.26%	$47.00	$55.25		1	17.55%	$2.60	23.09%
1980	28	Aluminum Co of Amer	$2.00	3.62%	$55.25	$60.88		1	10.18%	$3.20	15.97%
1981	18	Aluminum Co of Amer	$3.20	5.26%	$60.88	$26.00		2	-14.58%	$3.60	-8.67%
1982	10	Aluminum Co of Amer	$1.80	6.92%	$26.00	$29.63		1	13.94%	$1.65	20.29%
1983	20	Aluminum Co of Amer	$1.20	4.05%	$29.63	$44.50		1	50.21%	$1.20	54.26%
1984	27	Aluminum Co of Amer	$1.20	2.70%	$44.50	$36.50		1	-17.98%	$1.20	-15.28%
1985	28	Aluminum Co of Amer	$1.20	3.29%	$36.50	$38.38		1	5.14%	$1.20	8.42%
1986	22	Aluminum Co of Amer	$1.20	3.13%	$38.38	$35.13		1	-8.47%	$1.20	-5.34%
1987	16	Aluminum Co of Amer	$1.20	3.42%	$35.13	$50.38		1	43.42%	$1.20	46.83%
1988	25	Aluminum Co of Amer	$1.20	2.38%	$50.38	$55.88		1	10.92%	$1.30	13.50%
1989	26	Aluminum Co of Amer	$1.40	2.51%	$55.88	$75.63		1	35.35%	$2.72	40.21%
1990	24	Aluminum Co of Amer	$1.60	2.12%	$75.63	$58.00		1	-23.31%	$3.05	-19.27%
AVG.	24.1								4.35%		7.65%

ALLIED CHEMICAL/ALLIED CORP./ALLIED SIGNAL

YEAR	RANK	STOCK	WSJ DIVI.	WSJ YIELD	OPENING PRICE	CLOSING PRICE	STOCK DIV.	SPLIT	APPRECIATION	ACTUAL DIVIDEND	TOTAL RETURN
1957	25	Allied Chemical	$3.00	3.17%	$94.75	$74.00		1	-21.90%	$3.00	-18.73%
1958	18	Allied Chemical	$3.00	4.05%	$74.00	$92.25		1	24.66%	$3.00	28.72%
1959	14	Allied Chemical	$3.00	3.25%	$92.25	$113.50		1	23.04%	$3.15	26.45%
1960	14	Allied Chemical	$3.60	3.17%	$113.50	$51.75		2	-8.81%	$3.60	-5.64%
1961	14	Allied Chemical	$1.80	3.48%	$51.75	$55.50		1	7.25%	$1.80	10.72%
1962	12	Allied Chemical	$1.80	3.24%	$55.50	$43.25		1	-22.07%	$1.80	-18.83%
1963	10	Allied Chemical	$1.80	4.16%	$43.25	$55.25		1	27.75%	$1.80	31.91%
1964	15	Allied Chemical	$1.80	3.26%	$55.25	$51.00		1	-7.69%	$1.80	-4.43%
1965	11	Allied Chemical	$1.80	3.53%	$51.00	$49.25	2.00%	1	-1.50%	$1.90	2.23%
1966	8	Allied Chemical	$1.90	3.86%	$49.25	$34.00	2.00%	1	-29.58%	$1.90	-25.73%
1967	6	Allied Chemical	$1.90	5.59%	$34.00	$40.25	2.00%	1	20.75%	$1.90	26.34%
1968	6	Allied Chemical	$1.90	5.59%	$34.00	$40.25	2.00%	1	20.75%	$1.90	26.34%
1969	16	Allied Chemical	$1.20	3.24%	$37.00	$25.13		1	-32.09%	$1.20	-28.85%
1970	15	Allied Chemical	$1.20	4.78%	$25.13	$23.38		1	-6.97%	$1.20	-2.19%
1971	10	Allied Chemical	$1.20	5.13%	$23.38	$29.00		1	24.06%	$1.20	29.20%
1972	13	Allied Chemical	$1.20	4.14%	$29.00	$29.38		1	1.29%	$1.20	5.43%
1973	9	Allied Chemical	$1.20	4.09%	$29.38	$49.13		1	67.23%	$1.29	71.63%
1974	24	Allied Chemical	$1.32	2.69%	$49.13	$29.25		1	-40.46%	$1.53	-37.34%
1975	19	Allied Chemical!	$1.80	6.15%	$29.25	$33.88		1	15.81%	$1.80	21.97%
1976	12	Allied Chemical	$1.80	5.31%	$33.88	$39.88		1	17.71%	$1.80	23.03%
1977	15	Allied Chemical	$1.80	4.51%	$39.88	$34.63		1	-13.17%	$1.85	-8.53%
1978	15	Allied Chemical	$2.00	5.78%	$34.63	$29.00		1	-16.25%	$2.00	-10.47%
1979	13	Allied Chemical	$2.00	6.90%	$29.00	$47.50		1	63.79%	$2.00	70.69%
1980	25	Allied Chemical	$2.00	4.21%	$47.50	$54.00		1	13.68%	$2.15	18.21%
1981	26	Allied Chemical	$2.20	4.07%	$54.00	$45.25		1	-16.20%	$2.35	-11.85%
1982	25	Allied Corp.	$2.40	5.30%	$45.25	$32.50		1	-28.18%	$2.40	-22.87%
1983	7	Allied Corp.	$2.40	7.38%	$32.50	$55.63		1	71.15%	$2.40	78.54%
1984	13	Allied Corp.	$2.40	4.31%	$55.63	$34.00		1.5	-8.31%	$2.63	-3.59%
1985	12	Allied Corp.	$1.80	5.29%	$34.00	$47.88		1	40.81%	$1.80	46.10%
1986	16	Allied Signal	$1.80	3.76%	$47.88	$40.63	11.81%	1	-3.33%	$1.80	.43%
1987	8	Allied-Signal	$1.80	4.43%	$40.63	$30.88		1	-24.00%	$1.80	-19.57%
1988	4	Allied-Signal	$1.80	5.83%	$30.88	$33.38		1	8.10%	$1.80	13.93%
1989	4	Allied-Signal	$1.80	5.39%	$33.38	$35.38		1	5.99%	$1.80	11.39%
1990	3	Allied-Signal	$1.80	5.09%	$35.38	$28.00		1	-20.85%	$1.80	-15.76%
AVG.	13.4								4.48%		9.08%

AMERICAN CAN/PRIMERICA

YEAR	RANK	STOCK	WSJ DIVI.	WSJ YIELD	OPENING PRICE	CLOSING PRICE	STOCK DIV.	SPLIT	APPRECIATION	ACTUAL DIVIDEND	TOTAL RETURN
1957	8	American Can	$2.00	4.85%	$41.25	$42.00		1	1.82%	$2.00	6.67%
1958	14	American Can	$2.00	4.76%	$42.00	$50.00		1	19.05%	$2.00	23.81%
1959	6	American Can	$2.00	4.00%	$50.00	$43.25		1	-13.50%	$2.00	-9.50%
1960	3	American Can	$2.00	4.62%	$43.25	$35.00		1	-19.08%	$2.00	-14.45%
1961	2	American Can	$2.00	5.71%	$35.00	$46.25		1	32.14%	$2.00	37.86%
1962	6	American Can	$2.00	4.32%	$46.25	$45.50		1	-1.62%	$2.00	2.70%
1963	8	American Can	$2.00	4.40%	$45.50	$43.75		1	-3.85%	$2.00	.55%
1964	6	American Can	$2.00	4.57%	$43.75	$43.38		1	-.86%	$2.00	3.71%
1965	4	American Can	$2.00	4.61%	$43.38	$55.38		1	27.67%	$2.00	32.28%
1966	4	American Can	$2.20	3.97%	$55.38	$47.38		1	-14.45%	$2.20	-10.47%
1967	12	American Can	$2.20	4.64%	$47.38	$51.63		1	8.97%	$2.20	13.61%
1968	11	American Can	$2.20	4.26%	$51.63	$57.88		1	12.11%	$2.20	16.37%
1969	11	American Can	$2.20	3.80%	$57.88	$41.75		1	-27.86%	$2.20	-24.06%
1970	10	American Can	$2.20	5.27%	$41.75	$39.75		1	-4.79%	$2.20	.48%
1971	5	American Can	$2.20	5.53%	$39.75	$34.25		1	-13.84%	$2.20	-8.30%
1972	1	American Can	$2.20	6.42%	$34.25	$31.63		1	-7.66%	$2.20	-1.24%
1973	1	American Can	$2.20	6.96%	$31.63	$26.88		1	-15.02%	$2.20	-8.06%
1974	3	American Can	$2.20	8.19%	$26.88	$29.75		1	10.70%	$2.20	18.88%
1975	13	American Can	$2.20	7.39%	$29.75	$31.00		1	4.20%	$2.40	12.27%
1976	4	American Can	$2.40	7.10%	$31.00	$39.13		1	26.21%	$2.25	33.47%
1977	4	American Can	$2.40	6.13%	$39.13	$38.88		1	-.64%	$2.45	5.62%
1978	14	American Can	$2.40	6.17%	$38.88	$35.88		1	-7.72%	$2.65	-.90%
1979	6	American Can	$2.80	7.80%	$35.88	$34.88		1	-2.79%	$2.80	5.02%
1980	6	American Can	$2.80	8.03%	$34.88	$31.00		1	-11.11%	$2.90	-2.80%
1981	2	American Can	$2.90	9.35%	$31.00	$35.63		1	14.92%	$2.90	24.27%
1982	7	American Can	$2.90	8.14%	$35.63	$30.75		1	-13.68%	$2.90	-5.54%
1983	3	American Can	$2.90	9.43%	$30.75	$46.38		1	50.81%	$2.90	60.24%
1984	5	American Can	$2.90	6.25%	$46.38	$50.00		1	7.82%	$2.90	14.07%
1985	10	American Can	$2.90	5.80%	$50.00	$60.13		1	20.25%	$2.90	26.05%
1986	7	American Can	$2.90	4.82%	$60.13	$85.38		1	42.00%	$2.90	46.82%
1987	17	Primerica	$2.90	3.40%	$85.38	$25.38		2	-40.56%	$3.13	-36.89%
1988	3	Primerica	$1.60	6.31%	$25.38	$29.05		1	14.48%	$1.60	20.79%
1989	28	Primerica	$.28	.96%	$29.05	$29.38		1	1.12%	$.29	2.12%
1990	27	Primerica	$.32	1.09%	$29.38	$23.13		1	-21.28%	$.36	-20.05%

AVG: 7.97   2.18%   7.81%

183

AMERICAN EXPRESS

YEAR	RANK	STOCK	WSJ DIVI.	WSJ YIELD	OPENING PRICE	CLOSING PRICE	STOCK DIV.	SPLIT	APPRECIATION	ACTUAL DIVIDEND	TOTAL RETURN
1957											
1958											
1959											
1960											
1961											
1962											
1963											
1964											
1965											
1966											
1967											
1968											
1969											
1970											
1971											
1972											
1973											
1974											
1975											
1976											
1977											
1978											
1979											
1980											
1981											
1982											
1983	23	American Express	$2.40	3.91%	$61.38	$31.13		2	1.43%	$2.48	5.47%
1984	16	American Express	$1.28	4.11%	$31.13	$37.00		1	18.88%	$1.28	22.99%
1985	26	American Express	$1.28	3.46%	$37.00	$52.88		1	42.91%	$1.30	46.42%
1986	26	American Express	$1.36	2.57%	$52.88	$57.88		1	9.46%	$1.36	12.03%
1987	23	American Express	$1.44	2.49%	$57.88	$24.00		2	-17.06%	$1.50	-14.47%
1988	18	American Express	$.76	3.17%	$24.00	$26.63		1	10.94%	$.76	14.10%
1989	21	American Express	$.84	3.15%	$26.63	$34.88		1	30.99%	$.84	34.14%
1990	20	American Express	$.92	2.64%	$34.88	$20.25		1	-41.94%	$.92	-39.30%
AVG:	21.6								6.95%		10.17%

AMERICAN TELEPHONE & TELEGRAPH (AT & T)

YEAR	RANK	STOCK	WSJ DIVI.	WSJ YIELD	OPENING PRICE	CLOSING PRICE	STOCK DIV.	SPLIT	APPRECIATION	ACTUAL DIVIDEND	TOTAL RETURN
1957	5	American T & T	$9.00	5.25%	$171.50	$170.00		1	-.87%	$9.00	4.37%
1958	10	American T & T	$9.00	5.29%	$170.00	$225.50		1	32.65%	$9.00	37.94%
1959	7	American T & T	$9.00	3.99%	$225.50	$80.38		3	6.93%	$9.45	11.12%
1960	6	American T & T	$3.30	4.11%	$80.38	$103.50		1	28.77%	$3.30	32.88%
1961	17	American T & T	$3.30	3.19%	$103.50	$133.63		1	29.11%	$3.45	32.44%
1962	20	American T & T	$3.60	2.69%	$133.63	$115.00		1	-13.94%	$3.60	-11.24%
1963	21	American T & T	$3.60	3.13%	$115.00	$139.50		1	21.30%	$3.60	24.43%
1964	22	American T & T	$3.60	2.58%	$139.50	$69.50		2	-.36%	$3.90	2.44%
1965	18	American T & T	$2.00	2.88%	$69.50	$61.50		1	-11.51%	$2.00	-8.63%
1966	13	American T & T	$2.20	3.58%	$61.50	$54.38		1	-11.59%	$2.20	-8.01%
1967	17	American T & T	$2.20	4.05%	$54.38	$51.63		1	-5.06%	$2.20	-1.01%
1968	7	American T & T	$2.40	4.65%	$51.63	$53.50		1	3.63%	$2.40	8.28%
1969	11	American T & T	$2.40	4.49%	$53.50	$49.38		1	-7.71%	$2.40	-3.22%
1970	11	American T & T	$2.60	5.27%	$49.38	$48.75		1	-1.27%	$2.60	4.00%
1971	7	American T & T	$2.60	5.33%	$48.75	$44.75		1	-8.21%	$2.60	-2.87%
1972	3	American T & T	$2.60	5.81%	$44.75	$53.25		1	18.99%	$2.65	24.92%
1973	4	American T & T	$2.80	5.26%	$53.25	$50.00		1	-6.10%	$2.80	-.85%
1974	10	American T & T	$3.08	6.16%	$50.00	$46.00		1	-8.00%	$3.16	-1.68%
1975	14	American T & T	$3.40	7.39%	$46.00	$50.88		1	10.60%	$3.40	17.99%
1976	7	American T & T	$3.40	6.68%	$50.88	$63.38		1	24.57%	$3.70	31.84%
1977	5	American T & T	$3.80	6.00%	$63.38	$60.00		1	-5.33%	$4.10	1.14%
1978	9	American T & T	$4.20	7.00%	$60.00	$60.75		1	1.25%	$4.50	8.75%
1979	7	American T & T	$4.60	7.57%	$60.75	$52.00		1	-14.40%	$4.90	-6.34%
1980	5	American T & T	$4.60	8.85%	$52.00	$48.88		1	-6.01%	$5.00	3.61%
1981	1	American T & T	$5.00	10.23%	$48.88	$58.50		1	19.69%	$5.00	29.92%
1982	4	American T & T	$5.40	9.23%	$58.50	$59.88		1	2.35%	$5.40	11.58%
1983	4	American T & T	$5.40	9.02%	$59.88	$62.50		1	4.38%	$5.85	14.15%
1984	1	American T & T	$5.85	9.36%	$62.50	$19.25	75.90%	1	6.70%	$5.85	16.06%
1985	5	American T & T	$1.20	6.23%	$19.25	$24.63		1	27.92%	$1.20	34.16%
1986	6	American T & T	$1.20	4.87%	$24.63	$25.25		1	2.54%	$1.20	7.41%
1987	7	American T & T	$1.20	4.75%	$25.25	$28.25		1	11.88%	$1.20	16.63%
1988	8	American T & T	$1.20	4.25%	$28.25	$28.63		1	1.33%	$1.20	5.58%
1989	11	American T & T	$1.20	4.19%	$28.63	$46.50		1	62.45%	$1.20	66.64%
1990	21	American T & T	$1.20	2.58%	$46.50	$29.75		1	-36.02%	$1.29	-33.25%

AVG: 9.41 5.31% 10.92%

AMERICAN TOBACCO/AMERICAN BRANDS

YEAR	RANK	STOCK	WSJ DIVI.	WSJ YIELD	OPENING PRICE	CLOSING PRICE	STOCK DIV.	SPLIT	APPRECIATION	ACTUAL DIVIDEND	TOTAL RETURN
1957	3	American Tobacco	$4.00	5.47%	$73.13	$77.50		1	5.98%	$5.00	12.82%
1958	12	American Tobacco	$4.00	5.16%	$77.50	$96.13		1	24.03%	$5.00	30.48%
1959	5	American Tobacco	$4.00	4.16%	$96.13	$107.00		1	11.31%	$6.00	17.56%
1960	11	American Tobacco	$4.00	3.74%	$107.00	$65.25		2	21.96%	$5.45	27.06%
1961	12	American Tobacco	$2.30	3.52%	$65.25	$100.25		1	53.64%	$2.80	57.93%
1962	18	American Tobacco	$2.80	2.79%	$100.25	$29.25		2	-41.65%	$3.00	-38.65%
1963	5	American Tobacco	$1.50	5.13%	$29.25	$28.13		1	-3.85%	$1.50	1.28%
1964	1	American Tobacco	$1.50	5.33%	$28.13	$33.88		1	20.44%	$1.60	26.13%
1965	2	American Tobacco	$1.60	4.72%	$33.88	$38.50		1	13.65%	$1.65	18.52%
1966	3	American Tobacco	$1.70	4.42%	$38.50	$31.75		1	-17.53%	$1.80	-12.86%
1967	5	American Tobacco	$1.80	5.67%	$31.75	$32.25		1	1.57%	$1.80	7.24%
1968	2	American Tobacco	$1.80	5.58%	$32.25	$39.00		1	20.93%	$1.88	26.74%
1969	4	American Tobacco	$1.90	4.87%	$39.00	$35.63		1	-8.65%	$2.00	-3.53%
1970	8	American Tobacco	$2.00	5.61%	$35.63	$45.13		1	26.67%	$2.10	32.56%
1971	12	American Tobacco	$2.10	4.65%	$45.13	$42.13		1	-6.65%	$2.20	-1.77%
1972	5	American Tobacco	$2.20	5.22%	$42.13	$43.00		1	2.08%	$2.29	7.51%
1973	3	American Tobacco	$2.29	5.33%	$43.00	$33.50		1	-22.09%	$2.38	-16.56%
1974	6	American Brands	$2.38	7.10%	$33.50	$31.50		1	-5.97%	$2.56	1.67%
1975	9	American Brands	$2.56	8.13%	$31.50	$38.75		1	23.02%	$2.68	31.52%
1976	5	American Brands	$2.68	6.92%	$38.75	$45.25		1	16.77%	$2.80	24.00%
1977	3	American Brands	$2.80	6.19%	$45.25	$42.50		1	-6.08%	$2.98	.51%
1978	6	American Brands	$3.04	7.15%	$42.50	$50.38		1	18.53%	$3.63	27.06%
1979	5	American Brands	$4.00	7.94%	$50.38	$67.25		1	33.50%	$4.63	42.68%
1980	13	American Brands	$4.00	5.95%	$67.25	$77.63		1	15.43%	$5.90	24.20%
1981	4	American Brands	$6.20	7.99%	$77.63	$36.75		2	-5.31%	$6.43	2.97%
1982	6	American Brands	$3.25	8.84%	$36.75	$45.50		1	23.81%	$3.50	33.33%
1983	5	American Brands	$3.50	7.69%	$45.50	$59.38		1	30.49%	$3.55	38.30%
1984	6	American Brands	$3.60	6.06%	$59.38	$63.75		1	7.37%	$3.71	13.62%
1985	9	American Brands	$3.75	5.88%	$63.75	$65.50		1	2.75%	$3.90	8.86%

AVG: 6.48   8.83%   15.21%

ANACONDA

YEAR	RANK	STOCK	WSJ DIVI.	WSJ YIELD	OPENING PRICE	CLOSING PRICE	STOCK DIV.	SPLIT	APPRECIATION	ACTUAL DIVIDEND	TOTAL RETURN
1957											
1958											
1959											
1960	9	Anaconda	$2.50	3.85%	$64.88	$44.13		1	-31.98%	$2.50	-28.13%
1961	3	Anaconda	$2.50	5.67%	$44.13	$49.50		1	12.18%	$2.50	17.85%
1962	2	Anaconda	$2.50	5.05%	$49.50	$41.00		1	-17.17%	$2.50	-12.12%
1963	2	Anaconda	$2.50	6.10%	$41.00	$48.00		1	17.07%	$2.50	23.17%
1964	2	Anaconda	$2.50	5.21%	$48.00	$52.38		1	9.11%	$2.50	14.32%
1965	1	Anaconda	$3.75	4.77%	$52.38	$84.13		1	60.62%	$3.75	67.78%
1966	2	Anaconda	$5.00	4.46%	$84.13	$80.50		1	-4.31%	$5.00	1.63%
1967	4	Anaconda	$5.00	6.21%	$80.50	$47.38		2	17.70%	$4.75	23.60%
1968	3	Anaconda	$2.50	5.28%	$47.38	$64.00		1	35.09%	$2.25	39.84%
1969	10	Anaconda	$2.50	3.91%	$64.00	$30.75		1	-51.95%	$2.20	-48.52%
1970	4	Anaconda	$1.90	6.18%	$30.75	$21.13		1	-31.30%	$1.90	-25.12%
1971	1	Anaconda	$1.90	8.99%	$21.13	$16.00		1	-24.26%	$.50	-21.89%
1972	18	Anaconda	$.50	3.13%	$16.00	$19.75		1	23.44%	$.13	24.22%
1973	30	Anaconda	$.12	.61%	$19.75	$27.75		1	40.51%	$.50	43.04%
1974	29	Anaconda	$.50	1.80%	$27.75	$14.50		1	-47.75%	$1.00	-44.14%
1975	15	Anaconda	$1.00	6.90%	$14.50	$17.13		1	18.10%	$.75	23.28%
1976	21	Anaconda	$.60	3.50%	$17.13	$50.00		1	75.18%	$.60	78.69%
AVG:	9.18								5.90%		10.44%

BETHLEHEM STEEL

YEAR	RANK	STOCK	WSJ DIVI.	WSJ YIELD	OPENING PRICE	CLOSING PRICE	STOCK DIV.	SPLIT	APPRECIATION	ACTUAL DIVIDEND	TOTAL RETURN
1957	10	Bethlehem Steel	$8.50	4.35%	$195.38	$37.13	.00%	4	-23.99%	$9.60	-19.08%
1958	5	Bethlehem Steel	$2.40	6.46%	$37.13	$52.63		1	41.75%	$2.40	48.22%
1959	4	Bethlehem Steel	$2.40	4.56%	$52.63	$56.38		1	7.13%	$7.00	20.43%
1960	5	Bethlehem Steel	$2.40	4.26%	$56.38	$41.00		1	-27.27%	$7.00	-14.86%
1961	1	Bethlehem Steel	$2.40	5.85%	$41.00	$43.00		1	4.88%	$2.40	10.73%
1962	1	Bethlehem Steel	$2.40	5.58%	$43.00	$29.00		1	-32.56%	$2.18	-27.49%
1963	3	Bethlehem Steel	$1.50	5.17%	$29.00	$32.50		1	12.07%	$1.50	17.24%
1964	5	Bethlehem Steel	$1.50	4.62%	$32.50	$35.00		1	7.69%	$1.50	12.31%
1965	5	Bethlehem Steel	$1.50	4.29%	$35.00	$39.88		1	13.93%	$1.50	18.21%
1966	10	Bethlehem Steel	$1.50	3.76%	$39.88	$30.38		1	-23.82%	$1.80	-19.31%
1967	11	Bethlehem Steel	$1.50	4.94%	$30.38	$33.50		1	10.29%	$1.50	15.23%
1968	9	Bethlehem Steel	$1.50	4.48%	$33.50	$31.25		1	-6.72%	$1.60	-1.94%
1969	3	Bethlehem Steel	$1.60	5.12%	$31.25	$27.13		1	-13.20%	$1.75	-7.60%
1970	3	Bethlehem Steel	$1.80	6.64%	$27.13	$22.50		1	-17.05%	$1.80	-10.41%
1971	2	Bethlehem Steel	$1.80	8.00%	$22.50	$29.25		1	30.00%	$1.20	35.33%
1972	15	Bethlehem Steel	$1.20	4.10%	$29.25	$29.38		1	.43%	$1.20	4.53%
1973	10	Bethlehem Steel	$1.20	4.09%	$29.38	$32.50		1	10.64%	$1.65	16.26%
1974	14	Bethlehem Steel	$1.60	4.92%	$32.50	$24.88		1	-23.46%	$2.30	-16.38%
1975	10	Bethlehem Steel	$2.00	8.04%	$24.88	$33.50		1	34.67%	$2.75	45.73%
1976	8	Bethlehem Steel	$2.00	5.97%	$33.50	$39.88		1	19.03%	$2.00	25.00%
1977	12	Bethlehem Steel	$2.00	5.02%	$39.88	$20.88		1	-47.65%	$1.50	-43.89%
1978	20	Bethlehem Steel	$1.00	4.79%	$20.88	$19.88		1	-4.79%	$1.00	.00%
1979	23	Bethlehem Steel	$1.00	5.03%	$19.88	$20.75		1	4.40%	$1.50	11.95%
1980	21	Bethlehem Steel	$1.00	4.82%	$20.75	$26.25		1	26.51%	$1.50	34.22%
1981	13	Bethlehem Steel	$1.60	6.10%	$26.25	$23.50		1	-10.48%	$1.60	-4.38%
1982	12	Bethlehem Steel	$1.60	6.81%	$23.50	$19.75		1	-15.96%	$1.30	-10.43%
1983	14	Bethlehem Steel	$1.00	5.06%	$19.75	$27.88		1	41.14%	$.60	44.18%
1984	28	Bethlehem Steel	$.60	2.15%	$27.88	$17.25		1	-38.12%	$.60	-35.96%
1985	25	Bethlehem Steel	$.60	3.48%	$17.25	$15.38		1	-10.87%	$.30	-9.13%
1986	29	Bethlehem Steel	$.00	.00%	$15.38	$7.00		1	-54.47%	$.00	-54.47%
1987	29	Bethlehem Steel	$.00	.00%	$7.00	$17.75		1	153.57%	$.00	153.57%
1988	28	Bethlehem Steel	$.00	.00%	$17.75	$22.63		1	27.46%	$.00	27.46%
1989	29	Bethlehem Steel	$.00	.00%	$22.63	$18.75		1	-17.13%	$.20	-16.24%
1990	29	Bethlehem Steel	$.10	.53%	$18.75	$14.00		1	-25.33%	$.40	-23.20%

AVG: 13.1   1.55%   6.64%

BOEING

YEAR	RANK	STOCK	WSJ DIVI.	WSJ YIELD	OPENING PRICE	CLOSING PRICE	STOCK DIV.	SPLIT	APPRECIATION	ACTUAL DIVIDEND	TOTAL RETURN
1957											
1958											
1959											
1960											
1961											
1962											
1963											
1964											
1965											
1966											
1967											
1968											
1969											
1970											
1971											
1972											
1973											
1974											
1975											
1976											
1977											
1978											
1979											
1980											
1981											
1982											
1983											
1984											
1985											
1986											
1987											
1988	15	Boeing	$1.40	3.61%	$38.75	$59.63		1	53.87%	$1.55	57.87%
1989	24	Boeing	$1.60	2.68%	$59.63	$61.50		1.5	54.72%	$1.75	57.65%
1990	25	Boeing	$1.20	1.95%	$61.50	$44.88		1.5	9.45%	$1.43	11.77%
AVG:	21.3								39.35%		42.43%

AMERICAN SMELTING

YEAR	RANK	STOCK	WSJ DIVI.	WSJ YIELD	OPENING PRICE	CLOSING PRICE	STOCK DIV.	SPLIT	APPRECIATION	ACTUAL DIVIDEND	TOTAL RETURN
1957	1	American Smelting	$3.50	6.15%	$56.88	$36.75		1	-35.39%	$3.00	-30.11%
1958	1	American Smelting	$3.00	8.16%	$36.75	$54.50		1	48.30%	$1.50	52.38%
1959	16	American Smelting	$1.50	3.08%	$48.63	$53.13		1	9.25%	$1.00	11.31%
AVG:	6								7.39%		11.19%

CHRYSLER

YEAR	RANK	STOCK	WSJ DIVI.	WSJ YIELD	OPENING PRICE	CLOSING PRICE	STOCK DIV.	SPLIT	APPRECIATION	ACTUAL DIVIDEND	TOTAL RETURN
1957	11	Chrysler	$3.00	4.34%	$69.13	$53.50		1	-22.60%	$4.00	-16.82%
1958	8	Chrysler	$3.00	5.61%	$53.50	$53.88			.70%	$1.50	3.50%
1959	21	Chrysler	$1.50	2.78%	$53.88	$69.00		1	28.07%	$1.00	29.93%
1960	29	Chrysler	$1.00	1.45%	$69.00	$38.75		1	-43.84%	$1.50	-41.67%
1961	24	Chrysler	$1.00	2.58%	$38.75	$50.00		1	29.03%	$1.00	31.61%
1962	24	Chrysler	$1.00	2.00%	$50.00	$72.25		1	44.50%	$1.00	46.50%
1963	30	Chrysler	$1.00	1.38%	$72.25	$83.75		2	131.83%	$1.75	134.26%
1964	30	Chrysler	$1.00	1.19%	$83.75	$60.25	4.00%	2	49.64%	$2.00	52.02%
1965	29	Chrysler	$1.00	1.66%	$60.25	$53.88		1	-10.58%	$1.25	-8.51%
1966	12	Chrysler	$2.00	3.71%	$53.88	$31.25		1	-42.00%	$2.00	-38.28%
1967	2	Chrysler	$2.00	6.40%	$31.25	$56.25		1	80.00%	$2.00	86.40%
1968	17	Chrysler	$2.00	3.56%	$56.25	$57.25		1	1.78%	$2.00	5.33%
1969	13	Chrysler	$2.00	3.49%	$57.25	$35.25		1	-38.43%	$2.00	-34.93%
1970	7	Chrysler	$2.00	5.67%	$35.25	$27.25		1	-22.70%	$.60	-20.99%
1971	28	Chrysler	$.60	2.20%	$27.25	$28.13		1	3.21%	$.60	5.41%
1972	25	Chrysler	$.60	2.13%	$28.13	$41.38		1	47.11%	$.90	50.31%
1973	23	Chrysler	$1.00	2.42%	$41.38	$15.13		1	-63.44%	$1.30	-60.30%
1974	2	Chrysler	$1.40	9.26%	$15.13	$8.00		1	-47.11%	$1.40	-37.85%
1975	1	Chrysler	$1.40	17.50%	$8.00	$11.25		1	40.63%	$.00	40.63%
1976	30	Chrysler	$.00		$11.25	$21.13		1	87.78%	$.30	90.44%
1977	30	Chrysler	$.30	1.42%	$21.13	$12.63		1	-40.24%	$.90	-35.98%
1978	2	Chrysler	$1.00	7.92%	$12.63	$9.38		1	-25.74%	$.85	-19.01%
1979	24	Chrysler	$.40	4.27%	$9.38	$6.75		1	-28.00%	$.20	-25.87%
AVG:	18.3								6.94%		10.27%

COCA-COLA

YEAR	RANK	STOCK	WSJ DIVI.	WSJ YIELD	OPENING PRICE	CLOSING PRICE	STOCK DIV.	SPLIT	APPRECIATION	ACTUAL DIVIDEND	TOTAL RETURN
1957											
1958											
1959											
1960											
1961											
1962											
1963											
1964											
1965											
1966											
1967											
1968											
1969											
1970											
1971											
1972											
1973											
1974											
1975											
1976											
1977											
1978											
1979											
1980											
1981											
1982											
1983											
1984											
1985											
1986											
1987											
1988	22	Coca-Cola	$1.12	2.81%	$39.88	$43.50		1	9.09%	$1.20	12.10%
1989	23	Coca-Cola	$1.20	2.76%	$43.50	$78.00		1	79.31%	$1.36	82.44%
1990	26	Coca-Cola	$1.36	1.74%	$78.00	$45.25		2	16.03%	$1.60	18.08%
AVG:	23.7								34.81%		37.54%

CORN PRODUCTS REFINING

YEAR	RANK	STOCK	WSJ DIVI.	WSJ YIELD	OPENING PRICE	CLOSING PRICE	STOCK DIV.	SPLIT	APPRECIATION	ACTUAL DIVIDEND	TOTAL RETURN
1957	7	Corn Products Refini	$1.50	5.13%	$29.25	$34.25		1	17.09%	$1.50	22.22%
1958	15	Corn Products Refini	$1.60	4.67%	$34.25	$54.50		1	59.12%	$1.75	64.23%
1959	12	Corn Products Refini	$2.00	3.67%	$54.50	$56.50		1	3.67%	$2.00	7.34%
AVG:	11.3								26.63%		31.27%

DU PONT

YEAR	RANK	STOCK	WSJ DIVI.	WSJ YIELD	OPENING PRICE	CLOSING PRICE	STOCK DIV.	SPLIT	APPRECIATION	ACTUAL DIVIDEND	TOTAL RETURN
1957	21	Du Pont	$6.50	3.41%	$190.50	$176.25		1	-7.48%	$6.50	-4.07%
1958	22	Du Pont	$6.50	3.69%	$215.25	$215.50			22.27%	$6.00	25.67%
1959	22	Du Pont	$6.00	2.78%	$215.50	$262.75			21.93%	$7.00	25.17%
1960	17	Du Pont	$7.00	2.66%	$262.75	$186.50		1	-29.02%	$6.75	-26.45%
1961	11	Du Pont	$6.70	3.59%	$186.50	$241.50			29.49%	$7.50	33.51%
1962	14	Du Pont	$7.50	3.11%	$241.50	$234.50	12.06%		9.16%	$7.50	12.27%
1963	20	Du Pont	$7.50	3.20%	$234.50	$240.50	12.32%		14.88%	$7.75	18.18%
1964	17	Du Pont	$7.75	3.22%	$240.50	$241.75	19.83%		20.35%	$7.25	23.36%
1965	16	Du Pont	$7.25	3.00%	$241.75	$237.50			-1.76%	$6.00	.72%
1966	23	Du Pont	$6.00	2.53%	$237.50	$146.50		1	-38.32%	$5.75	-35.89%
1967	18	Du Pont	$5.75	3.92%	$146.50	$157.75			7.68%	$5.00	11.09%
1968	20	Du Pont	$5.00	3.17%	$157.75	$163.25			3.49%	$5.50	6.97%
1969	14	Du Pont	$5.50	3.37%	$163.25	$107.13		1	-34.38%	$5.25	-31.16%
1970	14	Du Pont	$5.25	4.90%	$107.13	$131.75			22.99%	$5.00	27.65%
1971	16	Du Pont	$5.00	3.80%	$131.75	$144.50			9.68%	$5.00	13.47%
1972	17	Du Pont	$5.00	3.46%	$144.50	$182.00			25.95%	$5.45	29.72%
1973	21	Du Pont	$5.45	2.99%	$182.00	$160.50			-11.81%	$5.75	-8.65%
1974	21	Du Pont	$5.75	3.58%	$160.50	$95.13		1	-40.73%	$5.50	-37.31%
1975	21	Du Pont	$5.50	5.78%	$95.13	$126.25			32.72%	$4.25	37.19%
1976	25	Du Pont	$4.25	3.37%	$126.25	$134.75			6.73%	$5.25	10.89%
1977	20	Du Pont	$5.25	3.90%	$134.75	$116.50		1	-13.54%	$5.75	-9.28%
1978	25	Du Pont	$5.00	4.29%	$116.50	$127.00			9.01%	$7.25	15.24%
1979	26	Du Pont	$2.00	3.94%	$127.00	$39.63		3	-6.40%	$8.25	.10%
1980	19	Du Pont	$2.00	5.05%	$39.63	$42.00		1	5.99%	$2.75	12.93%
1981	21	Du Pont	$2.00	4.76%	$42.00	$38.25			-8.93%	$2.75	-2.38%
1982	16	Du Pont	$2.40	6.27%	$38.25	$35.88		1	-6.21%	$2.40	.07%
1983	9	Du Pont	$2.40	6.69%	$35.88	$51.25			42.86%	$2.50	49.83%
1984	8	Du Pont	$2.80	5.46%	$51.25	$48.75			-4.88%	$2.90	.78%
1985	7	Du Pont	$3.00	6.15%	$48.75	$66.38			36.15%	$3.00	42.31%
1986	13	Du Pont	$3.00	4.52%	$66.38	$85.88		1	29.38%	$3.05	33.97%
1987	12	Du Pont	$3.20	3.73%	$85.88	$89.00			3.64%	$3.30	7.48%
1988	11	Du Pont	$3.40	3.82%	$89.00	$86.38			-2.95%	$3.70	1.21%
1989	10	Du Pont	$3.80	4.40%	$86.38	$125.13		1	44.86%	$4.35	49.90%
1990	12	Du Pont	$4.80	3.84%	$125.13	$36.13		3	-13.38%	$4.86	-9.50%

| AVG: | 17.0 | | | | | | | | 3.58% | | 7.78% |

EASTMAN KODAK

YEAR	RANK	STOCK	WSJ DIVI.	WSJ YIELD	OPENING PRICE	CLOSING PRICE	STOCK DIV.	SPLIT	APPRECIATION	ACTUAL DIVIDEND	TOTAL RETURN
1957	29	Eastman Kodak	$2.40	2.74%	$87.50	$99.00	5.00%	1	18.80%	$2.65	21.83%
1958	30	Eastman Kodak	$.90	.91%	$99.00	$149.75		1	51.26%	$2.85	54.14%
1959	30	Eastman Kodak	$2.60	1.74%	$149.75	$107.00		2	42.90%	$3.12	44.99%
1960	28	Eastman Kodak	$1.80	1.68%	$107.00	$108.75		1	1.64%	$3.60	5.00%
1961	29	Eastman Kodak	$2.00	1.84%	$108.75	$110.75		1	1.84%	$2.25	3.91%
1962	27	Eastman Kodak	$2.00	1.81%	$110.75	$107.38		1	-3.05%	$2.30	-.97%
1963	28	Eastman Kodak	$2.20	2.05%	$107.38	$115.50		1	7.57%	$2.55	9.94%
1964	27	Eastman Kodak	$2.20	1.90%	$115.50	$138.75	5.00%	1	26.14%	$2.60	28.39%
1965	28	Eastman Kodak	$2.40	1.73%	$138.75	$119.00		2	71.53%	$3.35	73.95%
1966	30	Eastman Kodak	$1.40	1.18%	$119.00	$126.25		1	6.09%	$1.90	7.69%
1967	30	Eastman Kodak	$1.60	1.27%	$126.25	$146.25		1	15.84%	$2.15	17.54%
1968	30	Eastman Kodak	$1.60	1.09%	$146.25	$74.00		2	1.20%	$2.18	2.69%
1969	30	Eastman Kodak	$.88	1.19%	$74.00	$81.75		1	10.47%	$1.22	12.12%
1970	30	Eastman Kodak	$1.00	1.22%	$81.75	$73.00		1	-10.70%	$1.28	-9.14%
1971	30	Eastman Kodak	$1.00	1.37%	$73.00	$97.00		1	32.88%	$1.32	34.68%
1972	30	Eastman Kodak	$1.04	1.07%	$97.00	$149.75		1	54.38%	$1.37	55.79%
1973	29	Eastman Kodak	$1.08	.72%	$149.75	$115.38		1	-22.95%	$1.60	-21.89%
1974	30	Eastman Kodak	$1.28	1.11%	$115.38	$63.75		1	-44.75%	$1.92	-43.08%
1975	29	Eastman Kodak	$1.56	2.45%	$63.75	$106.38		1	66.87%	$2.06	70.10%
1976	29	Eastman Kodak	$1.56	1.47%	$106.38	$85.38		1	-19.75%	$2.06	-17.81%
1977	29	Eastman Kodak	$1.60	1.87%	$85.38	$50.00		1	-41.43%	$2.10	-38.98%
1978	29	Eastman Kodak	$1.60	3.20%	$50.00	$61.50		1	23.00%	$2.23	27.46%
1979	28	Eastman Kodak	$2.00	3.25%	$61.50	$45.38		1	-26.22%	$2.80	-21.67%
1980	24	Eastman Kodak	$2.00	4.41%	$45.38	$71.25		1	57.02%	$3.05	63.75%
1981	25	Eastman Kodak	$3.00	4.21%	$71.25	$73.00		1	2.46%	$3.50	7.37%
1982	27	Eastman Kodak	$3.00	4.11%	$73.00	$85.13		1	16.61%	$3.50	21.40%
1983	27	Eastman Kodak	$3.00	3.52%	$85.13	$77.00		1	-9.54%	$3.55	-5.37%
1984	19	Eastman Kodak	$3.00	3.90%	$77.00	$70.88		1	-7.95%	$3.55	-3.34%
1985	16	Eastman Kodak	$3.20	4.51%	$70.88	$50.75		1.5	7.41%	$3.80	12.77%
1986	14	Eastman Kodak	$2.20	4.33%	$50.75	$69.25		1	36.45%	$2.61	41.60%
1987	13	Eastman Kodak	$2.52	3.64%	$69.25	$51.25		1.5	11.01%	$2.52	14.65%
1988	16	Eastman Kodak	$1.80	3.51%	$51.25	$44.63		1	-12.93%	$1.85	-9.32%
1989	8	Eastman Kodak	$2.00	4.48%	$44.63	$42.88		1	-3.92%	$2.00	-.56%
1990	7	Eastman Kodak	$2.00	4.66%	$42.88	$41.13		1	-4.08%	$2.00	.58%
AVG:	25.4								10.47%		13.57%

194

GENERAL ELECTRIC/G.E.

YEAR	RANK	STOCK	WSJ DIVI.	WSJ YIELD	OPENING PRICE	CLOSING PRICE	STOCK DIV.	SPLIT	APPRECIATION	ACTUAL DIVIDEND	TOTAL RETURN
1957	24	General Electric	$2.00	3.35%	$59.63	$60.88		1	2.10%	$2.00	5.45%
1958	26	General Electric	$2.00	3.29%	$60.88	$78.75		1	29.36%	$2.00	32.65%
1959	26	General Electric	$2.00	2.54%	$78.75	$96.63		1	22.70%	$2.00	25.24%
1960	26	General Electric	$2.00	2.07%	$96.63	$72.25		1	-25.23%	$2.00	-23.16%
1961	20	General Electric	$2.00	2.77%	$72.25	$74.75		1	3.46%	$2.00	6.23%
1962	21	General Electric	$2.00	2.68%	$74.75	$76.38		1	2.17%	$2.00	4.85%
1963	24	General Electric	$2.00	2.62%	$76.38	$86.75		1	13.58%	$2.00	16.20%
1964	23	General Electric	$2.20	2.54%	$86.75	$91.13		1	5.04%	$2.20	7.58%
1965	24	General Electric	$2.20	2.41%	$91.13	$116.88		1	28.26%	$2.30	30.78%
1966	25	General Electric	$2.60	2.22%	$116.88	$89.00		1	-23.85%	$2.60	-21.63%
1967	24	General Electric	$2.60	2.92%	$89.00	$95.63		1	7.44%	$2.60	10.37%
1968	21	General Electric	$2.60	2.72%	$95.63	$94.88		1	-.78%	$2.60	1.93%
1969	22	General Electric	$2.60	2.74%	$94.88	$76.63		1	-19.24%	$2.60	-16.50%
1970	19	General Electric	$2.60	3.39%	$76.63	$93.88		1	22.51%	$2.60	25.91%
1971	22	General Electric	$2.60	2.77%	$93.88	$63.00		2	34.22%	$2.70	37.10%
1972	24	General Electric	$1.40	2.22%	$63.00	$73.88		1	17.26%	$1.40	19.48%
1973	26	General Electric	$1.40	1.90%	$73.88	$62.63		1	-15.23%	$1.45	-13.27%
1974	26	General Electric	$1.60	2.55%	$62.63	$33.75		1	-46.11%	$1.60	-43.55%
1975	25	General Electric	$1.60	4.74%	$33.75	$46.63		1	38.15%	$1.60	42.89%
1976	24	General Electric	$1.60	3.43%	$46.63	$55.38		1	18.77%	$1.65	22.31%
1977	22	General Electric	$1.80	3.25%	$55.38	$48.75		1	-11.96%	$2.00	-8.35%
1978	24	General Electric	$2.20	4.51%	$48.75	$47.00		1	-3.59%	$2.40	1.33%
1979	20	General Electric	$2.60	5.53%	$47.00	$48.75		1	3.72%	$2.70	9.47%
1980	19	General Electric	$2.60	5.33%	$48.75	$61.88		1	26.92%	$2.90	32.87%
1981	20	General Electric	$3.00	4.85%	$61.88	$58.75		1	-5.05%	$3.10	-.04%
1982	23	General Electric	$3.20	5.45%	$58.75	$91.75		1	56.17%	$3.30	61.79%
1983	24	General Electric	$3.40	3.71%	$91.75	$57.63		2	25.61%	$3.60	29.54%
1984	22	General Electric	$2.00	3.47%	$57.63	$56.00		1	-2.82%	$2.00	.65%
1985	20	General Electric	$2.20	3.93%	$56.00	$71.88		1	28.35%	$2.20	32.28%
1986	20	General Electric	$2.32	3.23%	$71.88	$87.38		1	21.57%	$2.32	24.79%
1987	21	General Electric	$2.52	2.88%	$87.38	$46.50		2	6.44%	$2.58	9.39%
1988	20	General Electric	$1.40	3.01%	$46.50	$44.00		1	-5.38%	$1.40	-2.37%
1989	14	General Electric	$1.64	3.73%	$44.00	$66.75		1	51.70%	$1.64	55.43%
1990	19	General Electric	$1.88	2.82%	$66.75	$56.50		1	-15.36%	$1.88	-12.54%

| AVG: | 22.4 | | | | | | | | 8.56% | | 11.91% |

GENERAL FOODS

YEAR	RANK	STOCK	WSJ DIVI.	WSJ YIELD	OPENING PRICE	CLOSING PRICE	STOCK DIV.	SPLIT	APPRECIATION	ACTUAL DIVIDEND	TOTAL RETURN
1957	12	General Foods	$1.80	4.19%	$43.00	$49.75		1	15.70%	$1.95	20.23%
1958	20	General Foods	$1.95	3.92%	$49.75	$75.00		1	50.75%	$2.20	55.18%
1959	18	General Foods	$2.20	2.93%	$75.00	$103.75		1	38.33%	$2.55	41.73%
1960	18	General Foods	$2.60	2.51%	$103.75	$70.50	2.00%	2	35.90%	$2.70	38.51%
1961	27	General Foods	$1.40	1.99%	$70.50	$93.25		1	34.91%	$1.55	37.11%
1962	28	General Foods	$1.60	1.72%	$93.25	$78.00		1	-16.35%	$1.75	-14.48%
1963	25	General Foods	$1.80	2.31%	$78.00	$89.88		1	15.22%	$1.95	17.72%
1964	25	General Foods	$2.00	2.23%	$89.88	$81.00		1	-9.87%	$2.00	-7.65%
1965	23	General Foods	$2.00	2.47%	$81.00	$82.13		1	1.39%	$2.05	3.92%
1966	21	General Foods	$2.20	2.68%	$82.13	$70.25		1	-14.46%	$2.20	-11.78%
1967	22	General Foods	$2.20	3.13%	$70.25	$70.38		1	.18%	$2.35	3.52%
1968	18	General Foods	$2.40	3.41%	$70.38	$82.00		1	16.52%	$2.40	19.93%
1969	19	General Foods	$2.40	2.93%	$82.00	$83.00		1	1.22%	$2.60	4.39%
1970	21	General Foods	$2.60	3.13%	$83.00	$87.50		1	5.42%	$2.60	8.55%
1971	21	General Foods	$2.60	2.97%	$87.50	$35.63		2	-18.57%	$2.80	-15.37%
1972	16	General Foods	$1.40	3.93%	$35.63	$29.25		1	-17.89%	$1.40	-13.96%
1973	6	General Foods	$1.40	4.79%	$29.25	$25.00		1	-14.53%	$1.40	-9.74%
1974	13	General Foods	$1.40	5.60%	$25.00	$18.88		1	-24.50%	$1.40	-18.90%
1975	12	General Foods	$1.40	7.42%	$18.88	$27.75		1	47.02%	$1.40	54.44%
1976	14	General Foods	$1.40	5.05%	$27.75	$29.88		1	7.66%	$1.50	13.06%
1977	11	General Foods	$1.50	5.02%	$29.88	$31.13		1	4.18%	$1.64	9.67%
1978	17	General Foods	$1.64	5.27%	$31.13	$32.38		1	4.02%	$1.68	9.41%
1979	18	General Foods	$1.80	5.56%	$32.38	$33.50		1	3.47%	$1.90	9.34%
1980	18	General Foods	$1.80	5.37%	$33.50	$30.25		1	-9.70%	$2.15	-3.28%
1981	8	General Foods	$2.20	7.27%	$30.25	$31.75		1	4.96%	$2.20	12.23%
1982	9	General Foods	$2.20	6.93%	$31.75	$39.38		1	24.02%	$2.25	31.10%
1983	11	General Foods	$2.40	6.10%	$39.38	$51.25		1	30.16%	$2.40	36.25%
1984	10	General Foods	$2.40	4.68%	$51.25	$55.00		1	7.32%	$2.48	12.15%
1985	15	General Foods	$2.50	4.55%	$55.00	$120.00		1	118.18%	$2.48	122.68%
AVG:	17.1								11.75%		16.07%

GENERAL MOTORS

YEAR	RANK	STOCK	WSJ DIVI.	WSJ YIELD	OPENING PRICE	CLOSING PRICE	STOCK DIV.	SPLIT	APPRECIATION	ACTUAL DIVIDEND	TOTAL RETURN
1957	9	General Motors	$2.00	4.64%	$43.13	$34.38			-20.29%	$2.00	-15.65%
1958	6	General Motors	$2.00	5.82%	$34.38	$50.13		1	45.82%	$2.00	51.64%
1959	8	General Motors	$2.00	3.99%	$50.13	$54.50		1	8.73%	$2.00	12.72%
1960	12	General Motors	$2.00	3.67%	$54.50	$41.50		1	-23.85%	$2.00	-20.18%
1961	7	General Motors	$2.00	4.82%	$41.50	$56.38		1	35.84%	$2.50	41.87%
1962	10	General Motors	$2.00	3.55%	$56.38	$58.25		1	3.33%	$3.00	8.65%
1963	4	General Motors	$3.00	5.15%	$58.25	$80.25		1	37.77%	$4.00	44.64%
1964	3	General Motors	$4.00	4.98%	$80.25	$95.38		1	18.85%	$4.45	24.39%
1965	3	General Motors	$4.45	4.67%	$95.38	$102.63		1	7.60%	$5.25	13.11%
1966	1	General Motors	$5.20	5.07%	$102.63	$68.88	2.00%	1	-31.54%	$4.55	-27.11%
1967	8	General Motors	$3.80	4.59%	$82.75	$80.13		1	-3.17%	$4.30	2.02%
1968	2	General Motors	$4.30	5.37%	$80.13	$71.25		1	-11.08%	$4.30	-5.71%
1969	2	General Motors	$4.30	5.37%	$80.13	$71.25		1	-11.08%	$4.30	-5.71%
1970	6	General Motors	$4.30	6.04%	$71.25	$78.88		1	10.70%	$3.40	15.47%
1971	15	General Motors	$3.40	4.31%	$78.88	$79.75		1	1.11%	$3.40	5.42%
1972	12	General Motors	$3.40	4.26%	$79.75	$82.13		1	2.98%	$4.45	8.56%
1973	2	General Motors	$4.45	5.42%	$82.13	$46.00		1	-43.99%	$5.25	-37.60%
1974	1	General Motors	$5.25	11.41%	$46.00	$31.88		1	-30.71%	$3.40	-23.32%
1975	3	General Motors	$3.40	10.67%	$31.88	$58.38		1	83.14%	$2.40	90.67%
1976	19	General Motors	$2.40	4.11%	$58.38	$78.00		1	33.62%	$5.55	43.13%
1977	2	General Motors	$5.55	7.12%	$78.00	$61.50		1	-21.15%	$6.80	-12.44%
1978	1	General Motors	$6.80	11.06%	$61.50	$55.00		1	-10.57%	$6.00	-.81%
1979	1	General Motors	$6.00	10.91%	$55.00	$49.38		1	-10.23%	$5.30	-.59%
1980	2	General Motors	$6.00	12.15%	$49.38	$45.63		1	-7.59%	$2.95	-1.62%
1981	10	General Motors	$2.95	6.47%	$45.63	$39.75		1	-12.88%	$2.40	-7.62%
1982	18	General Motors	$2.40	6.04%	$39.75	$61.00		1	53.46%	$2.40	59.50%
1983	22	General Motors	$2.40	3.93%	$61.00	$74.13	2.71%	1	21.52%	$2.80	26.11%
1984	20	General Motors	$2.80	3.78%	$74.13	$77.63	3.09%	1	7.43%	$4.75	13.84%
1985	8	General Motors	$4.75	6.12%	$77.63	$70.88		1	-5.60%	$5.00	.84%
1986	2	General Motors	$5.00	7.05%	$70.88	$66.88		1	-5.64%	$5.00	1.41%
1987	2	General Motors	$5.00	7.48%	$66.88	$63.25		1	-5.42%	$5.00	2.06%
1988	1	General Motors	$5.00	7.91%	$63.25	$82.25		1	30.04%	$5.00	37.94%
1989	1	General Motors	$5.00	6.08%	$82.25	$44.50		2	8.21%	$6.00	15.50%
1990	1	General Motors	$3.00	6.74%	$44.50	$34.25		1	-23.03%	$3.00	-16.29%

AVG: 6.59

3.89%

10.14%

GOODYEAR TIRE & RUBBER

YEAR	RANK	STOCK	WSJ DIVI.	WSJ YIELD	OPENING PRICE	CLOSING PRICE	STOCK DIV.	SPLIT	APPRECIATION	ACTUAL DIVIDEND	TOTAL RETURN
1957	26	Goodyear	$2.40	2.90%	$82.63	$83.50	2.00%	1	3.08%	$2.40	5.98%
1958	29	Goodyear	$2.40	2.87%	$83.50	$122.00	2.00%	1	49.03%	$2.40	51.90%
1959	29	Goodyear	$2.40	1.97%	$122.00	$46.63	2.00%	3	16.94%	$2.48	18.98%
1960	27	Goodyear	$.90	1.93%	$46.63	$34.13	2.00%	1	-25.35%	$.90	-23.42%
1961	23	Goodyear	$.90	2.64%	$34.13	$44.50	2.00%	1	33.01%	$.90	35.65%
1962	22	Goodyear	$.90	2.02%	$44.50	$33.13		1	-25.56%	$.95	-23.43%
1963	22	Goodyear	$1.00	3.02%	$33.13	$41.63		1	25.66%	$1.00	28.68%
1964	24	Goodyear	$1.00	2.40%	$41.63	$45.25		1	8.71%	$1.11	11.38%
1965	22	Goodyear	$1.15	2.54%	$45.25	$47.88		1	5.80%	$1.20	8.45%
1966	22	Goodyear	$1.25	2.61%	$47.88	$40.75		1	-14.88%	$1.30	-12.17%
1967	20	Goodyear	$1.35	3.31%	$40.75	$56.00		1	37.42%	$1.35	40.74%
1968	22	Goodyear	$1.35	2.41%	$56.00	$55.75		1	-.45%	$1.43	2.10%
1969	23	Goodyear	$1.50	2.69%	$55.75	$31.50		2	13.00%	$1.65	15.96%
1970	24	Goodyear	$.85	2.70%	$31.50	$31.25		1	-.79%	$.85	1.90%
1971	23	Goodyear	$.85	2.72%	$31.25	$31.25		1		$.85	2.72%
1972	22	Goodyear	$.85	2.72%	$31.25	$31.13		1	-.40%	$.88	2.43%
1973	22	Goodyear	$.88	2.83%	$31.13	$15.63		1	-49.80%	$.96	-46.71%
1974	8	Goodyear	$1.00	6.40%	$15.63	$13.38		1	-14.40%	$1.03	-7.81%
1975	8	Goodyear	$1.10	8.22%	$13.38	$22.13		1	65.42%	$1.10	73.64%
1976	15	Goodyear	$1.10	4.97%	$22.13	$23.75		1	7.34%	$1.10	12.32%
1977	14	Goodyear	$1.10	4.63%	$23.75	$17.38		1	-26.84%	$1.20	-21.79%
1978	4	Goodyear	$1.30	7.48%	$17.38	$16.25		1	-6.47%	$1.30	1.01%
1979	4	Goodyear	$1.30	8.00%	$16.25	$12.88		1	-20.77%	$1.30	-12.77%
1980	3	Goodyear	$1.30	10.10%	$12.88	$17.38		1	34.95%	$1.30	45.05%
1981	6	Goodyear	$1.30	7.48%	$17.38	$18.88		1	8.63%	$1.30	16.12%
1982	11	Goodyear	$1.30	6.89%	$18.88	$34.75		1	84.11%	$1.40	91.52%
1983	21	Goodyear	$1.40	4.03%	$34.75	$30.75		1	-11.51%	$1.40	-7.48%
1984	11	Goodyear	$1.40	4.55%	$30.75	$25.75		1	-16.26%	$1.50	-11.38%
1985	6	Goodyear	$1.60	6.21%	$25.75	$31.00		1	20.39%	$1.60	26.60%
1986	5	Goodyear	$1.60	5.16%	$31.00	$42.88		1	38.31%	$1.60	43.47%
1987	11	Goodyear	$1.60	3.73%	$42.88	$62.75		1	46.36%	$1.60	50.09%
1988	24	Goodyear	$1.60	2.55%	$62.75	$50.75		1	-19.12%	$1.70	-16.41%
1989	16	Goodyear	$1.80	3.55%	$50.75	$45.38		1	-10.59%	$1.80	-7.04%
1990	10	Goodyear	$1.80	3.97%	$45.38	$19.00		1	-58.13%	$1.80	-54.16%

AVG: 17.1   5.79%   10.06%

INTERNATIONAL BUSINESS MACHINES (I.B.M.)

YEAR	RANK	STOCK	WSJ DIVI.	WSJ YIELD	OPENING PRICE	CLOSING PRICE	STOCK DIV.	SPLIT	APPRECIATION	ACTUAL DIVIDEND	TOTAL RETURN
1957											
1958											
1959											
1960											
1961											
1962											
1963											
1964											
1965											
1966											
1967											
1968											
1969											
1970											
1971											
1972											
1973											
1974											
1975											
1976											
1977											
1978											
1979											
1980	16	I.B.M.	$3.44	5.50%	$62.50	$69.13		1	10.60%	$3.44	16.10%
1981	19	I.B.M.	$3.44	4.98%	$69.13	$58.25		1	-15.73%	$3.44	-10.76%
1982	19	I.B.M.	$3.44	5.91%	$58.25	$93.00		1	59.66%	$3.44	65.56%
1983	25	I.B.M.	$3.44	3.70%	$93.00	$121.75		1	30.91%	$3.71	34.90%
1984	26	I.B.M.	$3.80	3.12%	$121.75	$121.00		1	-.62%	$4.10	2.75%
1985	24	I.B.M.	$4.40	3.64%	$121.00	$152.00		1	25.62%	$4.40	29.26%
1986	23	I.B.M.	$4.40	2.89%	$152.00	$122.00		1	-19.74%	$4.40	-16.84%
1987	14	I.B.M.	$4.40	3.61%	$122.00	$120.75		1	-1.02%	$4.40	2.58%
1988	13	I.B.M.	$4.40	3.64%	$120.75	$121.00		1	.21%	$4.40	3.85%
1989	15	I.B.M.	$4.40	3.64%	$121.00	$98.00		1	-19.01%	$4.73	-15.10%
1990	5	I.B.M.	$4.84	4.94%	$98.00	$112.13		1	14.42%	$4.84	19.36%

AVG: 18.1   7.75%   11.97%

INTERNATIONAL NICKEL CO./INCO

YEAR	RANK	STOCK	WSJ DIVI.	WSJ YIELD	OPENING PRICE	CLOSING PRICE	STOCK DIV.	SPLIT	APPRECIATION	ACTUAL DIVIDEND	TOTAL RETURN
1957	30	INCO	$2.60	2.37%	$109.63	$72.25		1	-34.09%	$3.75	-30.67%
1958	23	INCO	$2.60	3.60%	$72.25	$89.00		1	23.18%	$2.60	26.78%
1959	19	INCO	$2.60	2.92%	$89.00	$109.63		1	23.17%	$3.00	26.54%
1960	23	INCO	$2.60	2.37%	$109.63	$58.38		2	6.50%	$3.05	9.28%
1961	21	INCO	$1.60	2.74%	$58.38	$84.88		1	45.40%	$1.60	48.14%
1962	25	INCO	$1.60	1.89%	$84.88	$62.50		1	-26.36%	$1.90	-24.12%
1963	19	INCO	$2.00	3.20%	$62.50	$68.75		1	10.00%	$1.20	13.60%
1964	18	INCO	$2.20	3.20%	$68.75	$83.88		1	22.00%	$2.25	26.00%
1965	17	INCO	$2.50	2.98%	$83.88	$89.63		1	6.86%	$2.75	10.49%
1966	17	INCO	$2.80	3.12%	$89.63	$87.13		1	-2.79%	$3.05	.33%
1967	21	INCO	$2.80	3.21%	$87.13	$116.50		1	33.72%	$2.80	37.16%
1968	23	INCO	$2.80	2.40%	$116.50	$39.25		2.5	-15.77%	$3.00	-13.13%
1969	17	INCO	$1.20	3.06%	$39.25	$44.38		1	13.06%	$3.08	16.11%
1970	23	INCO	$1.20	2.70%	$44.38	$45.25		1	1.97%	$1.20	5.13%
1971	17	INCO	$1.60	3.54%	$45.25	$32.13		1	-29.01%	$1.40	-26.13%
1972	19	INCO	$1.00	3.11%	$32.13	$32.25		1	.39%	$1.30	3.50%
1973	20	INCO	$1.00	3.10%	$32.25	$34.88		1	8.14%	$1.00	11.86%
1974	22	INCO	$1.20	3.44%	$34.88	$22.25		1	-36.20%	$1.20	-31.61%
1975	16	INCO	$1.40	6.29%	$22.25	$25.38		1	14.04%	$1.60	21.24%
1976	10	INCO	$1.40	5.52%	$25.38	$33.00		1	30.05%	$1.60	36.35%
1977	17	INCO	$1.40	4.24%	$33.00	$17.13		1	-48.11%	$1.25	-44.32%
1978	21	INCO	$.80	4.67%	$17.13	$24.00		1	40.15%	$.70	44.23%
1979	30	INCO	$.40	2.48%	$16.13	$24.00		1	48.84%	$.50	51.94%
1980	30	INCO	$.40	1.67%	$24.00	$20.63		1	-14.06%	$.69	-11.19%
1981	29	INCO	$.72	3.49%	$20.63	$14.63		1	-29.09%	$.59	-26.23%
1982	29	INCO	$.20	1.37%	$14.63	$11.88		1	-18.80%	$.20	-17.44%
1983	29	INCO	$.20	1.68%	$11.88	$14.63		1	23.16%	$.20	24.84%
1984	29	INCO	$.20	1.37%	$14.63	$12.25		1	-16.24%	$.20	-14.87%
1985	29	INCO	$.20	1.63%	$12.25	$13.00		1	6.12%	$.20	7.76%
1986	27	INCO	$.20	1.54%	$13.00	$11.88		1	-8.65%	$.20	-7.12%
1987	27	INCO	$.20	1.68%	$11.88	$22.25		1	87.37%	$.20	89.05%

AVG: 22.5

APPRECIATION 5.32%   TOTAL RETURN 8.50%

INTERNATIONAL PAPER

YEAR	RANK	STOCK	WSJ DIVI.	WSJ YIELD	OPENING PRICE	CLOSING PRICE	STOCK DIV.	SPLIT	APPRECIATION	ACTUAL DIVIDEND	TOTAL RETURN
1957	27	International Paper	$3.00	2.80%	$107.00	$86.25	2.00%	1	-17.78%	$3.00	-14.98%
1958	25	International Paper	$3.00	3.48%	$86.25	$117.25	2.00%	1	38.66%	$3.00	42.14%
1959	25	International Paper	$3.00	2.56%	$117.25	$134.88	2.00%	1	17.33%	$3.00	19.89%
1960	24	International Paper	$3.00	2.22%	$134.88	$31.13	2.00%	3	-29.38%	$3.04	-27.13%
1961	16	International Paper	$1.01	3.24%	$31.13	$36.63	2.00%	1	20.02%	$1.05	23.40%
1962	16	International Paper	$1.05	2.87%	$36.63	$26.63	2.00%	1	-25.85%	$1.05	-22.98%
1963	12	International Paper	$1.05	3.94%	$26.63	$32.38	2.00%	1	24.03%	$1.05	27.97%
1964	16	International Paper	$1.05	3.24%	$32.38	$32.88	2.00%	1	1.54%	$1.16	5.13%
1965	6	International Paper	$1.40	4.26%	$32.88	$30.50		1	-7.22%	$1.25	-3.42%
1966	6	International Paper	$1.20	3.93%	$30.50	$25.38		1	-16.80%	$1.24	-12.74%
1967	7	International Paper	$1.35	5.32%	$25.38	$30.88		1	21.67%	$1.35	27.00%
1968	10	International Paper	$1.35	4.37%	$30.88	$36.38		1	17.81%	$1.39	22.32%
1969	9	International Paper	$1.50	4.12%	$36.38	$38.25		1	5.15%	$1.50	9.28%
1970	18	International Paper	$1.50	3.92%	$38.25	$33.88		1	-11.44%	$1.50	-7.52%
1971	14	International Paper	$1.50	4.43%	$33.88	$35.00		1	3.32%	$1.50	7.75%
1972	11	International Paper	$1.50	4.29%	$35.00	$41.50		1	18.57%	$1.50	22.86%
1973	16	International Paper	$1.50	3.61%	$41.50	$52.50		1	26.51%	$1.75	30.72%
1974	23	International Paper	$1.50	2.86%	$52.50	$36.63		1	-30.24%	$1.75	-26.90%
1975	22	International Paper	$2.00	5.46%	$36.63	$58.25		1	59.04%	$2.00	64.51%
1976	23	International Paper	$2.00	3.43%	$58.25	$69.38		1	19.10%	$2.00	22.53%
1977	24	International Paper	$2.00	2.88%	$69.38	$43.25		1	-37.66%	$2.00	-34.77%
1978	22	International Paper	$2.00	4.62%	$43.25	$36.88		1	-14.74%	$2.00	-10.12%
1979	21	International Paper	$2.00	5.42%	$36.88	$36.63		1	-.68%	$2.20	5.29%
1980	17	International Paper	$2.00	5.46%	$36.63	$42.63		1	16.38%	$2.40	22.94%
1981	14	International Paper	$2.40	5.63%	$42.63	$39.25		1	-7.92%	$2.40	-2.29%
1982	17	International Paper	$2.40	6.11%	$39.25	$47.00		1	19.75%	$2.40	25.86%
1983	13	International Paper	$2.40	5.11%	$47.00	$58.88		1	25.27%	$2.40	30.37%
1984	17	International Paper	$2.40	4.08%	$58.88	$53.25		1	-9.55%	$2.40	-5.48%
1985	17	International Paper	$2.40	4.51%	$53.25	$50.00		1	-6.10%	$2.40	-1.60%
1986	8	International Paper	$2.40	4.80%	$50.00	$76.13		1	52.25%	$2.40	57.05%
1987	18	International Paper	$2.40	3.15%	$76.13	$43.88		2	15.27%	$2.40	18.42%
1988	23	International Paper	$1.20	2.74%	$43.88	$46.50		1	5.98%	$1.28	8.89%
1989	20	International Paper	$1.48	3.18%	$46.50	$57.25		1	23.12%	$1.48	26.30%
1990	16	International Paper	$1.68	2.93%	$57.25	$52.88		1	-7.64%	$1.68	-4.71%
AVG:	16.9								6.11%		10.18%

INTERNATIONAL HARVESTER/NAVISTAR

YEAR	RANK	STOCK	WSJ DIVI.	WSJ YIELD	OPENING PRICE	CLOSING PRICE	STOCK DIV.	SPLIT	APPRECIATION	ACTUAL DIVIDEND	TOTAL RETURN
1957	4	Int'l Harvester	$2.00	5.26%	$38.00	$28.13	.00%	1	-25.99%	$2.00	-20.72%
1958	2	Int'l Harvester	$2.00	7.11%	$28.13	$41.38		1	47.11%	$2.00	54.22%
1959	3	Int'l Harvester	$2.00	4.83%	$41.38	$49.00		1	18.43%	$2.00	23.26%
1960	2	Int'l Harvester	$2.40	4.90%	$49.00	$43.25		1	-11.73%	$2.40	-6.84%
1961	4	Int'l Harvester	$2.40	5.55%	$43.25	$52.13		1	20.52%	$2.40	26.07%
1962	4	Int'l Harvester	$2.40	4.60%	$52.13	$49.88		1	-4.32%	$2.40	.29%
1963	6	Int'l Harvester	$2.40	4.81%	$49.88	$58.63		1	17.54%	$2.40	22.36%
1964	7	Int'l Harvester	$2.40	4.09%	$58.63	$74.13	.00%	1	26.44%	$2.70	31.04%
1965	8	Int'l Harvester	$2.80	3.78%	$74.13	$45.75		2	23.44%	$2.95	27.42%
1966	14	Int'l Harvester	$1.50	3.28%	$45.75	$34.88		1	-23.77%	$1.73	-19.99%
1967	9	Int'l Harvester	$1.80	5.16%	$34.88	$35.63		1	2.15%	$1.80	7.31%
1968	4	Int'l Harvester	$1.80	5.05%	$35.63	$37.13		1	4.21%	$1.80	9.26%
1969	5	Int'l Harvester	$1.80	4.85%	$37.13	$26.13		1	-29.63%	$1.80	-24.78%
1970	2	Int'l Harvester	$1.80	6.89%	$26.13	$27.50		1	5.26%	$1.80	12.15%
1971	4	Int'l Harvester	$1.80	6.55%	$27.50	$29.75		1	8.18%	$1.60	14.00%
1972	9	Int'l Harvester	$1.40	4.71%	$29.75	$38.75		1	30.25%	$1.40	34.96%
1973	17	Int'l Harvester	$1.40	3.61%	$38.75	$26.75		1	-30.97%	$1.50	-27.10%
1974	12	Int'l Harvester	$1.50	5.61%	$26.75	$20.25		1	-24.30%	$1.60	-18.32%
1975	7	Int'l Harvester	$1.70	8.40%	$20.25	$23.13		1	14.20%	$1.70	22.59%
1976	6	Int'l Harvester	$1.70	7.35%	$23.13	$32.88	.00%	1	42.16%	$1.85	49.51%
1977	6	Int'l Harvester	$1.85	5.63%	$32.88	$29.63		1	-9.89%	$2.10	-4.26%
1978	7	Int'l Harvester	$2.10	7.09%	$29.63	$36.88		1	24.47%	$2.35	31.56%
1979	15	Int'l Harvester	$2.30	6.24%	$36.88	$38.63		1	4.75%	$2.50	11.12%
1980	12	Int'l Harvester	$2.30	5.95%	$38.63	$25.38		1	-34.30%	$2.50	-27.83%
1981	22	Int'l Harvester	$1.20	4.73%	$25.38	$7.25		1	-71.43%	$.30	-70.25%
1982	30	Int'l Harvester	$.00	.00%	$7.25	$4.38		1	-39.66%	$.00	-39.66%
1983	30	Int'l Harvester	$.00	.00%	$4.38	$11.63		1	165.71%	$.00	165.71%
1984	30	Int'l Harvester	$.00	.00%	$11.63	$8.13		1	-30.11%	$.00	-30.11%
1985	30	Int'l Harvester	$.00	.00%	$8.13	$8.38		1	3.08%	$.00	3.08%
1986	30	Int'l Harvester	$.00	.00%	$8.38	$4.88		1	-41.79%	$.00	-41.79%
1987	30	Navistar	$.00	.00%	$4.88	$4.50		1	-7.69%	$.00	-7.69%
1988	29	Navistar	$.00	.00%	$4.50	$5.50		1	22.22%	$.00	22.22%
1989	30	Navistar	$.00	.00%	$5.50	$4.13		1	-25.00%	$.00	-25.00%
1990	30	Navistar	$.00	.00%	$4.13	$2.25		1	-45.45%	$.00	-45.45%
AVG:	13.4								.71%		4.66%

JOHNS-MANVILLE/MANVILLE CORP.

YEAR	RANK	STOCK	WSJ DIVI.	WSJ YIELD	OPENING PRICE	CLOSING PRICE	STOCK DIV.	SPLIT	APPRECIATION	ACTUAL DIVIDEND	TOTAL RETURN
1957	13	Johns-Manville	$2.00	4.12%	$48.50	$37.88			-21.91%	$2.00	-17.78%
1958	11	Johns-Manville	$2.00	5.28%	$37.88	$53.50		1	41.25%	$2.00	46.53%
1959	11	Johns-Manville	$2.00	3.74%	$53.50	$49.00		1	-8.41%	$2.00	-4.67%
1960	7	Johns-Manville	$2.00	4.08%	$49.00	$57.63		1	17.60%	$2.00	21.68%
1961	15	Johns-Manville	$2.00	3.47%	$57.63	$56.50		1	-1.95%	$2.00	1.52%
1962	11	Johns-Manville	$2.00	3.54%	$56.50	$42.00		1	-25.66%	$2.00	-22.12%
1963	7	Johns-Manville	$2.00	4.76%	$42.00	$49.25		1	17.26%	$2.00	22.02%
1964	8	Johns-Manville	$2.00	4.06%	$49.25	$53.50		1	8.63%	$2.00	12.69%
1965	9	Johns-Manville	$2.00	3.74%	$53.50	$55.63		1	3.97%	$2.05	7.80%
1966	5	Johns-Manville	$2.20	3.96%	$55.63	$48.13		1	-13.48%	$2.20	-9.53%
1967	13	Johns-Manville	$2.20	4.57%	$48.13	$54.50		1	13.25%	$2.20	17.82%
1968	13	Johns-Manville	$2.20	4.04%	$54.50	$87.13		1	59.86%	$2.20	63.90%
1969	21	Johns-Manville	$2.40	2.75%	$87.13	$29.88		2	-31.42%	$2.40	-28.67%
1970	17	Johns-Manville	$1.20	4.02%	$29.88	$40.38		1	35.15%	$1.20	39.16%
1971	20	Johns-Manville	$1.20	2.97%	$40.38	$41.00		1	1.55%	$1.20	4.52%
1972	20	Johns-Manville	$1.20	2.93%	$41.00	$32.75		1	-20.12%	$1.20	-17.20%
1973	14	Johns-Manville	$1.20	3.66%	$32.75	$16.63		1	-49.24%	$1.20	-45.57%
1974	5	Johns-Manville	$1.20	7.22%	$16.63	$19.75		1	18.80%	$1.20	26.02%
1975	20	Johns-Manville	$1.20	6.08%	$19.75	$23.50		1	18.99%	$1.20	25.06%
1976	13	Johns-Manville	$1.40	5.11%	$23.50	$33.38		1	42.02%	$1.35	47.77%
1977	18	Johns-Manville	$1.40	4.19%	$33.38	$31.75		1	-4.87%	$1.55	-.22%
1978	19	Johns-Manville	$1.60	5.04%	$31.75	$24.00		1	-24.41%	$1.80	-18.74%
1979	9	Johns-Manville	$1.80	7.50%	$24.00	$23.88		1	-.52%	$1.89	7.35%
1980	7	Johns-Manville	$1.80	7.54%	$23.88	$24.88		1	4.19%	$1.92	12.23%
1981	5	Johns-Manville	$1.92	7.72%	$24.88	$14.88		1	-40.20%	$1.92	-32.48%
1982	1	Johns-Manville	$1.92	12.91%	$14.88	$11.00		1	-26.05%	$.68	-21.48%

AVG: 12   .55%   5.29%

McDONALD'S CORP.

YEAR	RANK	STOCK	WSJ DIVI.	WSJ YIELD	OPENING PRICE	CLOSING PRICE	STOCK DIV.	SPLIT	APPRECIATION	ACTUAL DIVIDEND	TOTAL RETURN
1957											
1958											
1959											
1960											
1961											
1962											
1963											
1964											
1965											
1966											
1967											
1968											
1969											
1970											
1971											
1972											
1973											
1974											
1975											
1976											
1977											
1978											
1979											
1980											
1981											
1982											
1983											
1984											
1985											
1986	28	McDonald's Corp.	$.90	1.14%	$79.25	$62.00		1.5	17.35%	$.97	18.57%
1987	28	McDonald's Corp.	$.66	1.06%	$62.00	$45.50		1.5	10.08%	$.85	11.45%
1988	27	McDonald's Corp.	$.50	1.10%	$45.50	$46.75		1	2.75%	$.55	3.95%
1989	27	McDonald's Corp.	$.56	1.20%	$46.75	$34.88		2	49.20%	$.61	50.50%
1990	28	McDonald's Corp.	$.31	.89%	$34.88	$28.50		1	-18.28%	$.33	-17.33%
AVG:	27.6								12.22%		13.43%

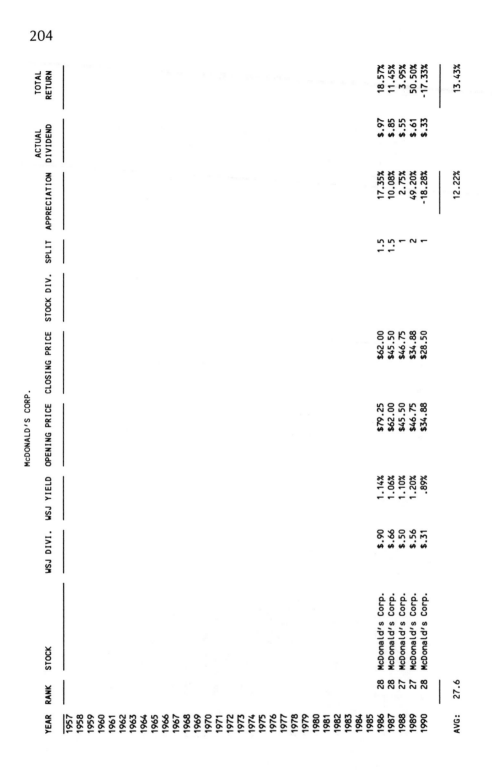

MERCK

YEAR	RANK	STOCK	WSJ DIVI.	WSJ YIELD	OPENING PRICE	CLOSING PRICE	STOCK DIV.	SPLIT	APPRECIATION	ACTUAL DIVIDEND	TOTAL RETURN
1957											
1958											
1959											
1960											
1961											
1962											
1963											
1964											
1965											
1966											
1967											
1968											
1969											
1970											
1971											
1972											
1973											
1974											
1975											
1976											
1977											
1978											
1979											
1980	29	Merck	$2.30	3.25%	$70.75	$86.00		1	21.55%	$2.30	24.81%
1981	30	Merck	$2.60	3.02%	$86.00	$85.50		1	-.58%	$2.60	2.44%
1982	28	Merck	$2.80	3.27%	$85.50	$84.00		1	-1.75%	$2.80	1.52%
1983	28	Merck	$2.80	3.33%	$84.00	$90.38		1	7.59%	$2.80	10.92%
1984	24	Merck	$3.00	3.32%	$90.38	$93.13		1	3.04%	$3.00	6.36%
1985	27	Merck	$3.20	3.44%	$93.13	$138.00		1	48.19%	$3.20	51.62%
1986	25	Merck	$3.60	2.61%	$138.00	$126.00		2	82.61%	$3.80	85.36%
1987	26	Merck	$2.20	1.75%	$126.00	$164.38		1	30.46%	$2.45	32.40%
1988	26	Merck	$3.20	1.95%	$164.38	$57.25		3	4.49%	$3.83	6.82%
1989	25	Merck	$1.48	2.59%	$57.25	$78.63		1	37.34%	$1.64	40.20%
1990	23	Merck	$1.80	2.29%	$78.63	$89.50		1	13.83%	$1.91	16.26%
AVG:	26.5								22.43%		25.34%

MINNESSOTA MINING & MANUFACTURING

YEAR	RANK	STOCK	WSJ DIVI.	WSJ YIELD	OPENING PRICE	CLOSING PRICE	STOCK DIV.	SPLIT	APPRECIATION	ACTUAL DIVIDEND	TOTAL RETURN
1957											
1958											
1959											
1960											
1961											
1962											
1963											
1964											
1965											
1966											
1967											
1968											
1969											
1970											
1971											
1972											
1973											
1974											
1975											
1976											
1977	25	Minnessota Mng. & Mf	$1.45	2.58%	$56.25	$46.75		1	-16.89%	$1.70	-13.87%
1978	27	Minnessota Mng. & Mf	$1.70	3.64%	$46.75	$63.25		1	35.29%	$2.00	39.57%
1979	29	Minnessota Mng. & Mf	$2.00	3.16%	$63.25	$49.50		1	-21.74%	$2.40	-17.94%
1980	26	Minnessota Mng. & Mf	$2.00	4.04%	$49.50	$59.25		1	19.70%	$2.80	25.35%
1981	23	Minnessota Mng. & Mf	$2.80	4.73%	$59.25	$54.25		1	-8.44%	$3.00	-3.38%
1982	22	Minnessota Mng. & Mf	$3.00	5.53%	$54.25	$73.25		1	35.02%	$3.20	40.92%
1983	19	Minnessota Mng. & Mf	$3.20	4.37%	$73.25	$82.25		1	12.29%	$3.30	16.79%
1984	18	Minnessota Mng. & Mf	$3.30	4.01%	$82.25	$78.38		1	-4.71%	$3.40	-.58%
1985	18	Minnessota Mng. & Mf	$3.40	4.34%	$78.38	$88.63		1	13.08%	$3.50	17.54%
1986	15	Minnessota Mng. & Mf	$3.50	3.95%	$88.63	$117.88		2	33.00%	$3.60	37.07%
1987	19	Minnessota Mng. & Mf	$3.60	3.05%	$117.88	$66.13		1	12.20%	$3.72	15.35%
1988	21	Minnessota Mng. & Mf	$1.86	2.81%	$66.13	$61.38		1	-7.18%	$2.12	-3.98%
1989	17	Minnessota Mng. & Mf	$2.12	3.45%	$61.38	$80.50		1	31.16%	$2.60	35.40%
1990	13	Minnessota Mng. & Mf	$2.60	3.23%	$80.50	$84.88		1	5.43%	$2.92	9.06%

| AVG: | 20.9 | | | | | | | | 9.87% | | 14.09% |

NATIONAL DISTILLERS

YEAR	RANK	STOCK	WSJ DIVI.	WSJ YIELD	OPENING PRICE	CLOSING PRICE	STOCK DIV.	SPLIT	APPRECIATION	ACTUAL DIVIDEND	TOTAL RETURN
1957	14	National Distillers	$1.00	3.76%	$26.63	$20.75	2.00%	1	-20.51%	$1.00	-16.75%
1958	13	National Distillers	$1.00	4.82%	$20.75	$31.25		1	50.60%	$1.00	55.42%
1959	15	National Distillers	$1.00	3.20%	$31.25	$33.75		1	8.00%	$1.10	11.52%
AVG:	14								12.70%		16.73%

NATIONAL STEEL

YEAR	RANK	STOCK	WSJ DIVI.	WSJ YIELD	OPENING PRICE	CLOSING PRICE	STOCK DIV.	SPLIT	APPRECIATION	ACTUAL DIVIDEND	TOTAL RETURN
1957	6	National Steel	$4.00	5.16%	$77.50	$53.50		1	-30.97%	$4.00	-25.81%
1958	3	National Steel	$4.00	7.48%	$53.50	$75.75		1	41.59%	$3.00	47.20%
1959	9	National Steel	$3.00	3.96%	$75.75	$97.00		1	28.05%	$3.00	32.01%
AVG:	6								12.89%		17.80%

OWENS-ILLINOIS GLASS

YEAR	RANK	STOCK	WSJ DIVI.	WSJ YIELD	OPENING PRICE	CLOSING PRICE	STOCK DIV.	SPLIT	APPRECIATION	ACTUAL DIVIDEND	TOTAL RETURN
1957											
1958											
1959											
1960	21	Owens-Illinois Glass	$2.50	2.38%	$104.88	$91.75		1	-12.51%	$2.50	-10.13%
1961	22	Owens-Illinois Glass	$2.50	2.72%	$91.75	$94.75		1	3.27%	$2.50	5.99%
1962	22	Owens-Illinois Glass	$2.50	2.64%	$94.75	$73.75		1	-22.16%	$2.50	-19.53%
1963	17	Owens-Illinois Glass	$2.50	3.39%	$73.75	$85.88		1	16.44%	$2.50	19.83%
1964	20	Owens-Illinois Glass	$2.50	2.91%	$85.88	$104.50		1	21.69%	$2.50	24.60%
1965	25	Owens-Illinois Glass	$2.50	2.39%	$104.50	$63.50		2	21.53%	$2.70	24.11%
1966	26	Owens-Illinois	$1.35	2.13%	$63.50	$53.00		1	-16.54%	$1.35	-14.41%
1967	26	Owens-Illinois	$1.35	2.55%	$53.00	$56.38		1	6.37%	$1.35	8.92%
1968	24	Owens-Illinois	$1.35	2.39%	$56.38	$72.25		1	28.16%	$1.35	30.55%
1969	29	Owens-Illinois	$1.35	1.87%	$72.25	$62.00		1	-14.19%	$1.35	-12.32%
1970	27	Owens-Illinois	$1.35	2.18%	$62.00	$56.50		1	-8.87%	$1.35	-6.69%
1971	26	Owens-Illinois	$1.35	2.39%	$56.50	$46.75		1	-17.26%	$1.35	-14.87%
1972	21	Owens-Illinois	$1.35	2.89%	$46.75	$42.00		1	-10.16%	$1.39	-7.19%
1973	18	Owens-Illinois	$1.40	3.33%	$42.00	$31.50		1	-25.00%	$1.46	-21.52%
1974	16	Owens-Illinois	$1.48	4.70%	$31.50	$34.00		1	7.94%	$1.57	12.92%
1975	26	Owens-Illinois	$1.60	4.71%	$34.00	$52.50		1	54.41%	$1.72	59.47%
1976	26	Owens-Illinois	$1.72	3.28%	$52.50	$56.00		1	6.67%	$1.88	10.25%
1977	21	Owens-Illinois	$1.88	3.36%	$56.00	$23.38		2	-16.52%	$2.12	-12.73%
1978	23	Owens-Illinois	$1.06	4.53%	$23.38	$17.50		1	-25.13%	$1.11	-20.39%
1979	14	Owens-Illinois	$1.16	6.63%	$17.50	$20.25		1	15.71%	$1.26	22.91%
1980	15	Owens-Illinois	$1.16	5.73%	$20.25	$25.25		1	24.69%	$1.40	31.60%
1981	16	Owens-Illinois	$1.40	5.54%	$25.25	$29.00		1	14.85%	$1.56	21.03%
1982	24	Owens-Illinois	$1.56	5.38%	$29.00	$29.00		1		$1.68	5.79%
1983	12	Owens-Illinois	$1.68	5.79%	$29.00	$37.63		1	29.74%	$1.68	35.53%
1984	12	Owens-Illinois	$1.68	4.47%	$37.63	$40.00		1	6.31%	$1.68	10.78%
1985	19	Owens-Illinois	$1.68	4.20%	$40.00	$52.38		1	30.94%	$1.74	35.29%
1986	18	Owens-Illinois	$1.80	3.44%	$52.38	$52.88		2	101.91%	$1.87	105.48%
1987	25	Owens-Illinois	$.95	1.80%	$52.88	$60.13		1	13.71%	$1.87	17.25%
AVG:	21.1								8.43%		12.23%

PHILIP MORRIS

YEAR	RANK	STOCK	WSJ DIVI.	WSJ YIELD	OPENING PRICE	CLOSING PRICE	STOCK DIV.	SPLIT	APPRECIATION	ACTUAL DIVIDEND	TOTAL RETURN
1957											
1958											
1959											
1960											
1961											
1962											
1963											
1964											
1965											
1966											
1967											
1968											
1969											
1970											
1971											
1972											
1973											
1974											
1975											
1976											
1977											
1978											
1979											
1980											
1981											
1982											
1983											
1984											
1985											
1986	12	Philip Morris	$4.00	4.53%	$88.38	$73.50		2	66.34%	$4.45	71.37%
1987	10	Philip Morris	$3.00	4.08%	$73.50	$87.63		1	19.22%	$3.00	23.30%
1988	9	Philip Morris	$3.60	4.11%	$87.63	$100.88		1	15.12%	$3.83	19.49%
1989	9	Philip Morris	$4.50	4.46%	$100.88	$42.75		4	69.52%	$4.75	74.23%
1990	14	Philip Morris	$1.37	3.20%	$42.75	$50.88		1	19.01%	$1.46	22.42%
AVG:	10.8								37.84%		42.16%

PROCTER & GAMBLE

YEAR	RANK	STOCK	WSJ DIVI.	WSJ YIELD	OPENING PRICE	CLOSING PRICE	STOCK DIV.	SPLIT	APPRECIATION	ACTUAL DIVIDEND	TOTAL RETURN
1957	18	Procter & Gamble	$1.80	3.58%	$50.25	$56.88		1	13.18%	$1.95	17.06%
1958	24	Procter & Gamble	$2.00	3.52%	$56.88	$74.00			30.11%	$2.00	33.63%
1959	24	Procter & Gamble	$2.00	2.70%	$74.00	$89.88		1	21.45%	$2.20	24.43%
1960	20	Procter & Gamble	$2.20	2.45%	$89.88	$136.00		1	51.32%	$2.60	54.21%
1961	28	Procter & Gamble	$2.60	1.91%	$136.00	$91.50		2	34.56%	$2.75	36.58%
1962	30	Procter & Gamble	$1.40	1.53%	$91.50	$70.88		1	-22.54%	$1.50	-20.90%
1963	27	Procter & Gamble	$1.50	2.12%	$70.88	$78.88		1	11.29%	$1.60	13.54%
1964	26	Procter & Gamble	$1.60	2.03%	$78.88	$81.25		1	3.01%	$1.75	5.23%
1965	27	Procter & Gamble	$1.75	2.15%	$81.25	$69.00		1	-15.08%	$1.85	-12.80%
1966	20	Procter & Gamble	$1.85	2.68%	$69.00	$71.25		1	3.26%	$2.00	6.16%
1967	25	Procter & Gamble	$2.00	2.81%	$71.25	$93.00		1	30.53%	$2.20	33.61%
1968	25	Procter & Gamble	$2.20	2.37%	$93.00	$86.00		1	-7.53%	$2.40	-4.95%
1969	20	Procter & Gamble	$2.40	2.79%	$86.00	$110.00		1	27.91%	$2.60	30.93%
1970	26	Procter & Gamble	$2.60	2.36%	$110.00	$57.50		2	4.55%	$2.75	7.05%
1971	25	Procter & Gamble	$1.40	2.43%	$57.50	$78.00		1	35.65%	$1.45	38.17%
1972	28	Procter & Gamble	$1.50	1.92%	$78.00	$111.25		1	42.63%	$1.53	44.59%
1973	27	Procter & Gamble	$1.56	1.40%	$111.25	$91.50		1	-17.75%	$1.68	-16.24%
1974	28	Procter & Gamble	$1.80	1.97%	$91.50	$82.25		1	-10.11%	$1.80	-8.14%
1975	30	Procter & Gamble	$1.80	2.19%	$82.25	$89.38		1	8.66%	$2.00	11.09%
1976	28	Procter & Gamble	$2.00	2.24%	$89.38	$93.00		1	4.06%	$2.15	6.46%
1977	27	Procter & Gamble	$2.20	2.37%	$93.00	$84.88		1	-8.74%	$2.60	-5.94%
1978	30	Procter & Gamble	$2.60	3.06%	$84.88	$88.13		1	3.83%	$2.90	7.25%
1979	27	Procter & Gamble	$3.00	3.40%	$88.13	$74.25		1	-15.74%	$3.30	-12.00%
1980	27	Procter & Gamble	$3.00	4.04%	$74.25	$68.13		1	-8.25%	$3.60	-3.40%
1981	15	Procter & Gamble	$3.80	5.58%	$68.13	$80.38		1	17.98%	$3.90	23.71%
1982	26	Procter & Gamble	$4.20	5.23%	$80.38	$116.00		1	44.32%	$4.20	49.55%
1983	26	Procter & Gamble	$4.20	3.62%	$116.00	$57.00		2	-1.72%	$4.80	2.41%
1984	14	Procter & Gamble	$2.40	4.21%	$57.00	$56.25		1	-1.32%	$2.50	3.07%
1985	14	Procter & Gamble	$2.60	4.62%	$56.25	$69.25		1	23.11%	$2.60	27.73%
1986	17	Procter & Gamble	$2.60	3.75%	$69.25	$77.63		1	12.09%	$2.68	15.96%
1987	15	Procter & Gamble	$2.70	3.48%	$77.63	$87.00		1	12.08%	$2.70	15.56%
1988	19	Procter & Gamble	$2.70	3.10%	$87.00	$84.50		1	-2.87%	$2.80	.34%
1989	18	Procter & Gamble	$2.80	3.31%	$84.50	$70.50		2	66.86%	$3.30	70.77%
1990	22	Procter & Gamble	$1.80	2.55%	$70.50	$85.50		1	21.28%	$1.85	23.90%

AVG: 23.6   12.12%   15.25%

SEARS, ROEBUCK

YEAR	RANK	STOCK	WSJ DIVI.	WSJ YIELD	OPENING PRICE	CLOSING PRICE	STOCK DIV.	SPLIT	APPRECIATION	ACTUAL DIVIDEND	TOTAL RETURN
1957	20	Sears, Roebuck	$1.00	3.49%	$28.63	$25.38			-11.35%	$1.00	-7.86%
1958	19	Sears, Roebuck	$1.00	3.94%	$25.38	$39.50		1	55.67%	$1.10	60.00%
1959	27	Sears, Roebuck	$1.00	2.53%	$39.50	$50.50		1	27.85%	$1.30	31.14%
1960	22	Sears, Roebuck	$1.20	2.38%	$50.50	$55.75		1	10.40%	$1.45	13.27%
1961	26	Sears, Roebuck	$1.20	2.15%	$55.75	$85.00		1	52.47%	$1.40	54.98%
1962	29	Sears, Roebuck	$1.40	1.65%	$85.00	$75.50		1	-11.18%	$1.65	-9.24%
1963	29	Sears, Roebuck	$1.40	1.85%	$75.50	$97.75		1	29.47%	$1.65	31.66%
1964	29	Sears, Roebuck	$1.60	1.64%	$97.75	$127.63		1	30.56%	$1.90	32.51%
1965	30	Sears, Roebuck	$1.80	1.41%	$127.63	$64.25		2	.69%	$2.25	2.45%
1966	29	Sears, Roebuck	$1.00	1.56%	$64.25	$44.75		1	-30.35%	$1.15	-28.56%
1967	27	Sears, Roebuck	$1.00	2.23%	$44.75	$56.13		1	25.42%	$1.20	28.10%
1968	29	Sears, Roebuck	$1.00	1.78%	$56.13	$60.75		1	8.24%	$1.30	10.56%
1969	28	Sears, Roebuck	$1.20	1.98%	$60.75	$67.00		1	10.29%	$1.35	12.51%
1970	29	Sears, Roebuck	$1.20	1.79%	$67.00	$75.50		1	12.69%	$1.35	14.70%
1971	29	Sears, Roebuck	$1.20	1.59%	$75.50	$102.13		1	35.26%	$1.45	37.19%
1972	29	Sears, Roebuck	$1.40	1.37%	$102.13	$117.00		1	14.57%	$1.55	16.08%
1973	28	Sears, Roebuck	$1.40	1.20%	$117.00	$80.25		1	-31.41%	$1.66	-29.99%
1974	27	Sears, Roebuck	$1.60	1.99%	$80.25	$50.38		1	-37.23%	$1.85	-34.92%
1975	28	Sears, Roebuck	$1.60	3.18%	$50.38	$64.63		1	28.29%	$1.85	31.96%
1976	27	Sears, Roebuck	$1.60	2.48%	$64.63	$68.00		1	5.22%	$1.85	8.09%
1977	28	Sears, Roebuck	$1.60	2.35%	$68.00	$27.38		2	-19.49%	$2.08	-16.43%
1978	28	Sears, Roebuck	$.96	3.51%	$27.38	$20.13		1	-26.48%	$1.23	-21.99%
1979	17	Sears, Roebuck	$1.12	5.57%	$20.13	$18.13		1	-9.94%	$1.24	-3.78%
1980	10	Sears, Roebuck	$1.12	6.18%	$18.13	$15.50		1	-14.48%	$1.34	-7.09%
1981	3	Sears, Roebuck	$1.36	8.77%	$15.50	$16.88		1	8.87%	$1.36	17.65%
1982	8	Sears, Roebuck	$1.36	8.06%	$16.88	$29.25		1	73.33%	$1.36	81.39%
1983	17	Sears, Roebuck	$1.36	4.65%	$29.25	$36.50		1	24.79%	$1.48	29.85%
1984	15	Sears, Roebuck	$1.52	4.16%	$36.50	$31.75		1	-13.01%	$1.70	-8.36%
1985	11	Sears, Roebuck	$1.76	5.54%	$31.75	$38.50		1	21.26%	$1.76	26.80%
1986	10	Sears, Roebuck	$1.76	4.57%	$38.50	$41.00		1	6.49%	$1.76	11.06%
1987	9	Sears, Roebuck	$1.76	4.29%	$41.00	$35.38		1	-13.72%	$1.94	-8.99%
1988	6	Sears, Roebuck	$2.00	5.65%	$35.38	$40.38		1	14.13%	$2.00	19.79%
1989	6	Sears, Roebuck	$2.00	4.95%	$40.38	$38.75		1	-4.02%	$2.00	.93%
1990	2	Sears, Roebuck	$2.00	5.16%	$38.75	$25.88		1	-33.23%	$2.00	-28.06%

AVG: 20.9   7.06%   10.81%

STANDARD OIL OF CALIFORNIA/CHEVRON

YEAR	RANK	STOCK		WSJ DIVI.	WSJ YIELD	OPENING PRICE	CLOSING PRICE	STOCK DIV.	SPLIT	APPRECIATION	ACTUAL DIVIDEND	TOTAL RETURN
1957	15	Standard Oil	CA	$1.80	3.72%	$48.38	$46.25		1	-4.39%	$1.90	-.47%
1958	17	Standard Oil	CA	$1.90	4.11%	$46.25	$60.25		1	30.27%	$2.00	34.59%
1959	13	Standard Oil	CA	$2.00	3.32%	$60.25	$49.50		1	-17.84%	$2.00	-14.52%
1960	8	Standard Oil	CA	$2.00	4.04%	$49.50	$47.63		1	-3.79%	$2.00	.25%
1961	8	Standard Oil	CA	$2.00	4.20%	$47.63	$55.38		1	16.27%	$2.00	20.47%
1962	9	Standard Oil	CA	$2.00	3.61%	$55.38	$62.38		1	18.27%	$2.00	21.88%
1963	18	Standard Oil	CA	$2.00	3.21%	$62.38	$60.13	5.00%	1	1.21%	$2.00	4.42%
1964	14	Standard Oil	CA	$2.00	3.33%	$60.13	$72.75	5.00%	1	27.05%	$2.05	30.46%
1965	15	Standard Oil	CA	$2.20	3.02%	$72.75	$79.50	5.00%	1	9.28%	$2.28	12.41%
1966	16	Standard Oil	CA	$2.50	3.14%	$79.50	$60.00		1	-24.53%	$2.50	-21.38%
1967	15	Standard Oil	CA	$2.50	4.17%	$60.00	$63.00	5.00%	1	10.25%	$2.50	14.42%
1968	14	Standard Oil	CA	$2.50	3.97%	$63.00	$72.25		1	14.68%	$2.70	18.97%
1969	12	Standard Oil	CA	$2.70	3.74%	$72.25	$52.25		1	-27.68%	$2.80	-23.81%
1970	9	Standard Oil	CA	$2.80	5.36%	$52.25	$53.50		1	2.39%	$2.80	7.75%
1971	8	Standard Oil	CA	$2.80	5.23%	$53.50	$57.75		1	7.94%	$2.80	13.18%
1972	7	Standard Oil	CA	$2.80	4.85%	$57.75	$80.13		1	38.74%	$2.90	43.77%
1973	15	Standard Oil	CA	$2.90	3.62%	$80.13	$35.00		2	-12.64%	$3.00	-8.89%
1974	15	Standard Oil	CA	$1.70	4.86%	$35.00	$23.63		1	-32.50%	$1.93	-27.00%
1975	6	Standard Oil	CA	$2.00	8.47%	$23.63	$29.50		1	24.87%	$2.00	33.33%
1976	6	Standard Oil	CA	$2.00	6.78%	$29.50	$40.63		1	37.71%	$2.15	45.00%
1977	8	Standard Oil	CA	$2.20	5.42%	$40.63	$38.00		1	-6.46%	$2.35	-.68%
1978	11	Standard Oil	CA	$2.40	6.32%	$38.00	$46.88		1	23.36%	$2.55	30.07%
1979	19	Standard Oil	CA	$2.60	5.55%	$46.88	$54.25		1	15.73%	$2.90	21.92%
1980	22	Standard Oil	CA	$2.60	4.79%	$54.25	$99.25		1	82.95%	$3.60	89.59%
1981	27	Standard Oil	CA	$4.00	4.03%	$99.25	$41.63		2	-16.12%	$4.40	-11.69%
1982	20	Standard Oil	CA	$2.40	5.77%	$41.63	$31.25		1	-24.92%	$2.40	-19.16%
1983	6	Standard Oil	CA	$2.40	7.68%	$31.25	$34.13		1	9.20%	$2.40	16.88%
1984	4	Standard Oil	CA	$2.40	7.03%	$34.13	$30.38		1	-10.99%	$2.40	-3.96%
1985	3	Chevron		$2.40	7.90%	$30.38	$37.50		1	23.46%	$2.40	31.36%
1986	4	Chevron		$2.40	6.40%	$37.50	$46.00		1	22.67%	$2.40	29.07%
1987	5	Chevron		$2.40	5.22%	$46.00	$41.63		1	-9.51%	$2.40	-4.29%
1988	5	Chevron		$2.40	5.77%	$41.63	$45.75		1	9.91%	$2.55	16.04%
1989	3	Chevron		$2.60	5.68%	$45.75	$69.13		1	51.09%	$2.80	57.21%
1990	9	Chevron		$2.80	4.05%	$69.13	$72.38		1	4.70%	$2.95	8.97%

AVG: 11.4   8.55%   13.71%

STANDARD OIL NEW JERSEY/EXXON

YEAR	RANK	STOCK	WSJ DIVI.	WSJ YIELD	OPENING PRICE	CLOSING PRICE	STOCK DIV.	SPLIT	APPRECIATION	ACTUAL DIVIDEND	TOTAL RETURN
1957	17	Standard Oil NJ	$2.10	3.62%	$58.00	$49.88		1	-14.01%	$2.25	-10.13%
1958	16	Standard Oil NJ	$2.25	4.51%	$49.88	$57.88		1	16.04%	$2.25	20.55%
1959	10	Standard Oil NJ	$2.25	3.89%	$57.88	$49.75		1	-14.04%	$2.25	-10.15%
1960	4	Standard Oil NJ	$2.25	4.52%	$49.75	$41.25		1	-17.09%	$2.25	-12.56%
1961	5	Standard Oil NJ	$2.25	5.45%	$41.25	$50.50		1	22.42%	$2.30	28.00%
1962	5	Standard Oil NJ	$2.30	4.55%	$50.50	$58.63		1	16.09%	$2.50	21.04%
1963	9	Standard Oil NJ	$2.50	4.26%	$58.63	$75.88		1	29.42%	$2.75	34.12%
1964	12	Standard Oil NJ	$2.75	3.62%	$75.88	$88.50		1	16.64%	$3.00	20.59%
1965	13	Standard Oil NJ	$3.00	3.39%	$88.50	$80.75		1	-8.76%	$3.15	-5.20%
1966	7	Standard Oil NJ	$3.15	3.90%	$80.75	$63.38		1	-21.52%	$3.30	-17.43%
1967	8	Standard Oil NJ	$3.30	5.21%	$63.38	$69.00		1	8.88%	$3.45	14.32%
1968	5	Standard Oil NJ	$3.45	5.00%	$69.00	$78.75		1	14.13%	$3.65	19.42%
1969	6	Standard Oil NJ	$3.65	4.63%	$78.75	$62.00		1	-21.27%	$3.75	-16.51%
1970	5	Standard Oil NJ	$3.75	6.05%	$62.00	$72.63		1	17.14%	$3.75	23.19%
1971	9	Standard Oil NJ	$3.75	5.16%	$72.63	$73.00		1	.52%	$3.80	5.75%
1972	6	Standard Oil NJ	$3.80	5.21%	$73.00	$88.00		1	20.55%	$3.80	25.75%
1973	8	Exxon	$3.80	4.32%	$88.00	$96.50		1	9.66%	$4.25	14.49%
1974	17	Exxon	$4.25	4.40%	$96.50	$66.25		1	-31.35%	$5.00	-26.17%
1975	11	Exxon	$5.00	7.55%	$66.25	$90.00		1	35.85%	$5.00	43.40%
1976	9	Exxon	$5.00	5.56%	$90.00	$53.63		2	19.17%	$5.45	25.22%
1977	9	Exxon	$2.80	5.22%	$53.63	$47.63		1	-11.19%	$3.00	-5.59%
1978	12	Exxon	$3.00	6.30%	$47.63	$49.25		1	3.41%	$3.30	10.34%
1979	12	Exxon	$3.40	6.90%	$49.25	$53.88		1	9.39%	$3.90	17.31%
1980	10	Exxon	$3.40	6.31%	$53.88	$81.13		1	50.58%	$5.40	60.60%
1981	7	Exxon	$6.00	7.40%	$81.13	$30.88		2	-23.88%	$6.00	-16.49%
1982	3	Exxon	$3.00	9.72%	$30.88	$29.00		1	-6.07%	$3.00	3.64%
1983	1	Exxon	$3.00	10.34%	$29.00	$36.63		1	26.29%	$3.10	36.98%
1984	2	Exxon	$3.20	8.74%	$36.63	$44.50		1	21.50%	$3.35	30.65%
1985	4	Exxon	$3.40	7.64%	$44.50	$54.50		1	22.47%	$3.45	30.22%
1986	3	Exxon	$3.60	6.61%	$54.50	$72.00		1	32.11%	$3.60	38.72%
1987	6	Exxon	$3.60	5.00%	$72.00	$40.50		2	12.50%	$3.80	17.78%
1988	7	Exxon	$2.00	4.94%	$40.50	$43.25		1	6.79%	$2.15	12.10%
1989	5	Exxon	$2.20	5.09%	$43.25	$50.00		1	15.61%	$2.30	20.92%
1990	6	Exxon	$2.40	4.80%	$50.00	$50.75		1	1.50%	$2.47	6.44%

AVG: 7.91 | | | | | | | | | 7.63% | | 13.57%

SWIFT & COMPANY/ESMARK

YEAR	RANK	STOCK	WSJ DIVI.	WSJ YIELD	OPENING PRICE	CLOSING PRICE	STOCK DIV.	SPLIT	APPRECIATION	ACTUAL DIVIDEND	TOTAL RETURN
1957											
1958											
1959											
1960	13	Swift & Company	$1.60	3.37%	$47.50	$45.63		1	-3.95%	$1.85	-.05%
1961	13	Swift & Company	$1.60	3.51%	$45.63	$42.88		1	-6.03%	$1.85	-1.97%
1962	8	Swift & Company	$1.60	3.73%	$42.88	$40.13		1	-6.41%	$1.60	-2.68%
1963	11	Swift & Company	$1.60	3.99%	$40.13	$43.75		1	9.03%	$1.60	13.02%
1964	10	Swift & Company	$1.60	3.66%	$43.75	$58.13		1	32.86%	$1.75	36.86%
1965	12	Swift & Company	$2.00	3.44%	$58.13	$53.50		1	-7.96%	$2.00	-4.52%
1966	11	Swift & Company	$2.00	3.74%	$53.50	$45.63		1	-14.72%	$2.00	-10.98%
1967	14	Swift & Company	$2.00	4.38%	$45.63	$32.13		2	40.82%	$2.20	45.64%
1968	16	Swift & Company	$1.20	3.74%	$32.13	$30.25		1	-5.84%	$.90	-3.04%
1969	27	Swift & Company	$.60	1.98%	$30.25	$31.38		1	3.72%	$.60	5.70%
1970	28	Swift & Company	$.60	1.91%	$31.38	$30.13		1	-3.98%	$.60	-2.07%
1971	27	Swift & Company	$.70	2.32%	$30.13	$35.88		1	19.09%	$.70	21.41%
1972	27	Swift & Company	$.70	1.95%	$35.88	$39.38		1	9.76%	$.70	11.71%
1973	25	Swift & Company	$.75	1.90%	$39.38	$25.00		1	-36.51%	$.75	-34.60%
1974	19	Swift & Company	$1.00	4.00%	$25.00	$29.00		1	16.00%	$1.00	20.00%
1975	24	Swift & Company	$1.40	4.83%	$29.00	$32.25		1.25	39.01%	$1.53	44.27%
1976	16	Swift & Company	$1.52	4.71%	$32.25	$34.88		1	8.14%	$1.58	13.04%
1977	10	Esmark	$1.76	5.05%	$34.88	$29.50		1	-15.41%	$1.78	-10.31%
1978	13	Esmark	$1.84	6.24%	$29.50	$24.38		1	-17.37%	$1.84	-11.14%
1979	8	Esmark	$1.84	7.55%	$24.38	$27.38		1	12.31%	$1.84	19.86%

AVG: 16.6   3.63%   8.79%

TEXAS CORPORATION/TEXACO

YEAR	RANK	STOCK	WSJ DIVI.	WSJ YIELD	OPENING PRICE	CLOSING PRICE	STOCK DIV.	SPLIT	APPRECIATION	ACTUAL DIVIDEND	TOTAL RETURN
1957	23	Texas Corporation	$2.00	3.38%	$59.25	$63.13	2.00%	1	8.67%	$2.35	12.64%
1958	28	Texas Corporation	$2.00	3.17%	$63.13	$86.25		1	36.63%	$2.35	40.36%
1959	28	Texas Corporation	$2.00	2.32%	$86.25	$86.38	2.00%	1	2.15%	$2.60	5.16%
1960	16	Texas Corporation	$2.40	2.78%	$86.38	$84.25	2.00%	1	-.51%	$2.85	2.79%
1961	19	Texas Corporation	$2.60	3.09%	$84.25	$56.50		2	34.12%	$3.10	37.80%
1962	17	Texas Corporation	$1.60	2.83%	$56.50	$60.63		1	7.30%	$1.85	10.58%
1963	23	Texas Corporation	$1.80	2.97%	$60.63	$69.75		1	15.05%	$2.10	18.52%
1964	21	Texas Corporation	$2.00	2.87%	$69.75	$86.25	5.00%	1	29.84%	$2.30	33.14%
1965	21	Texas Corporation	$2.20	2.55%	$86.25	$80.13		1	-7.10%	$2.45	-4.26%
1966	18	Texas Corporation	$2.40	3.00%	$80.13	$69.25		1	-13.57%	$2.50	-10.45%
1967	19	Texas Corporation	$2.60	3.75%	$69.25	$81.38		1	17.51%	$2.70	21.41%
1968	19	Texas Corporation	$2.60	3.20%	$81.38	$83.50		1	2.61%	$2.90	6.18%
1969	15	Texas Corporation	$2.80	3.35%	$83.50	$30.75		2	-26.35%	$3.10	-22.63%
1970	13	Texas Corporation	$1.60	5.20%	$30.75	$34.75		1	13.01%	$1.60	18.21%
1971	13	Texas Corporation	$1.60	4.60%	$34.75	$34.75		1	.00%	$1.60	4.60%
1972	10	Texas Corporation	$1.60	4.60%	$34.75	$37.00		1	6.47%	$1.66	11.25%
1973	7	Texas Corporation	$1.66	4.49%	$37.00	$29.50		1	-20.27%	$1.73	-15.59%
1974	11	Texas Corporation	$1.76	5.97%	$29.50	$22.25		1	-24.58%	$2.10	-17.46%
1975	5	Texas Corporation	$2.00	8.99%	$22.25	$23.88		1	7.30%	$2.00	16.29%
1976	1	Texas Corporation	$2.00	8.38%	$23.88	$27.50		1	15.18%	$2.00	23.56%
1977	1	Texas Corporation	$2.00	7.27%	$27.50	$27.50		1	.00%	$2.00	7.27%
1978	5	Texas Corporation	$2.00	7.27%	$27.50	$24.00		1	-12.73%	$2.00	-5.45%
1979	2	Texas Corporation	$2.00	8.33%	$24.00	$28.00		1	16.67%	$2.12	25.50%
1980	8	Texas Corporation	$2.00	7.14%	$28.00	$49.13		1	75.45%	$2.45	84.20%
1981	17	Texas Corporation	$2.60	5.29%	$49.13	$33.13		1	-32.57%	$2.80	-26.87%
1982	5	Texas Corporation	$3.00	9.06%	$33.13	$30.63		1	-7.55%	$3.00	1.51%
1983	2	Texas Corporation	$3.00	9.80%	$30.63	$35.25		1	15.10%	$3.00	24.90%
1984	3	Texas Corporation	$3.00	8.51%	$35.25	$34.00		1	-3.55%	$3.00	4.96%
1985	2	Texaco	$3.00	8.82%	$34.00	$30.75		1	-9.56%	$3.00	-.74%
1986	1	Texaco	$3.00	9.76%	$30.75	$36.75		1	19.51%	$3.00	29.27%
1987	1	Texaco	$3.00	8.16%	$36.75	$37.25		1	1.36%	$.75	3.40%
1988	30	Texaco	$.00	.00%	$37.25	$51.00	1.96%	1	36.91%	$2.25	42.95%
1989	2	Texaco	$3.00	5.88%	$51.00	$59.13		1	17.89%	$10.10	37.70%
1990	4	Texaco	$3.00	5.07%	$59.13	$59.63		1	.85%	$3.05	6.00%

AVG: 12.1   6.51%   12.55%

UNION CARBIDE

YEAR	RANK	STOCK	WSJ DIVI.	WSJ YIELD	OPENING PRICE	CLOSING PRICE	STOCK DIV.	SPLIT	APPRECIATION	ACTUAL DIVIDEND	TOTAL RETURN
1957	28	Union Carbide	$3.15	2.75%	$114.38	$94.75		1	-17.16%	$3.60	-14.01%
1958	21	Union Carbide	$3.60	3.80%	$94.75	$126.13		1	33.11%	$3.60	36.91%
1959	20	Union Carbide	$3.60	2.85%	$126.13	$147.00		1	16.55%	$3.60	19.41%
1960	19	Union Carbide	$3.60	2.45%	$147.00	$116.50		1	-20.75%	$3.60	-18.30%
1961	18	Union Carbide	$3.60	3.09%	$116.50	$119.75		1	2.79%	$3.60	5.88%
1962	15	Union Carbide	$3.60	3.01%	$119.75	$101.88		1	-14.93%	$3.60	-11.92%
1963	16	Union Carbide	$3.60	3.53%	$101.88	$122.25		1	20.00%	$3.60	23.53%
1964	19	Union Carbide	$3.60	2.94%	$122.25	$126.75		1	3.68%	$3.60	6.63%
1965	19	Union Carbide	$3.60	2.84%	$126.75	$68.75		2	8.48%	$4.00	11.64%
1966	19	Union Carbide	$2.00	2.91%	$68.75	$48.63		1	-29.27%	$2.00	-26.36%
1967	16	Union Carbide	$2.00	4.11%	$48.63	$49.13		1	1.03%	$2.00	5.14%
1968	12	Union Carbide	$2.00	4.07%	$49.13	$45.75		1	-6.87%	$2.00	-2.80%
1969	8	Union Carbide	$2.00	4.37%	$45.75	$38.00		1	-16.94%	$2.00	-12.57%
1970	12	Union Carbide	$2.00	5.26%	$38.00	$40.00		1	5.26%	$2.00	10.53%
1971	11	Union Carbide	$2.00	5.00%	$40.00	$42.25		1	5.63%	$2.00	10.63%
1972	8	Union Carbide	$2.00	4.73%	$42.25	$51.25		1	21.30%	$2.00	26.04%
1973	12	Union Carbide	$2.00	3.90%	$51.25	$33.88		1	-33.90%	$2.08	-29.85%
1974	9	Union Carbide	$2.10	6.20%	$33.88	$42.38		1	25.09%	$2.18	31.51%
1975	23	Union Carbide	$2.20	5.19%	$42.38	$60.88		1	43.66%	$2.40	49.32%
1976	20	Union Carbide	$2.40	3.94%	$60.88	$62.00		1	1.85%	$2.50	5.95%
1977	19	Union Carbide	$2.50	4.03%	$62.00	$40.38		1	-34.88%	$2.80	-30.36%
1978	10	Union Carbide	$2.80	6.93%	$40.38	$34.75		1	-13.93%	$2.80	-7.00%
1979	3	Union Carbide	$2.80	8.06%	$34.75	$41.38		1	19.06%	$2.90	27.41%
1980	9	Union Carbide	$2.80	6.77%	$41.38	$50.63		1	22.36%	$3.10	29.85%
1981	11	Union Carbide	$3.20	6.32%	$50.63	$51.00		1	.74%	$3.30	7.26%
1982	14	Union Carbide	$3.40	6.67%	$51.00	$51.38		1	.74%	$3.40	7.40%
1983	10	Union Carbide	$3.40	6.62%	$51.38	$62.13		1	20.92%	$3.40	27.54%
1984	7	Union Carbide	$3.40	5.47%	$62.13	$37.00		1	-40.44%	$3.40	-34.97%
1985	1	Union Carbide	$3.40	9.19%	$37.00	$73.25		3	97.97%	$3.40	107.16%
1986	9	Union Carbide	$3.40	4.64%	$73.25	$22.88		1	-6.31%	$4.50	-.17%
1987	3	Union Carbide	$1.50	6.56%	$22.88	$22.63		1	-1.09%	$1.50	5.46%
1988	2	Union Carbide	$1.50	6.63%	$22.63	$25.63		1	13.26%	$1.15	18.34%
1989	22	Union Carbide	$.80	3.12%	$25.63	$24.38		1	-4.88%	$1.00	-.98%
1990	8	Union Carbide	$1.00	4.10%	$24.38	$16.75		1	-31.28%	$1.00	-27.18%

AVG: 13.3   2.67%   7.56%

UNITED AIRCRAFT/UNITED TECHNOLOGIES

YEAR	RANK	STOCK	WSJ DIVI.	WSJ YIELD	OPENING PRICE	CLOSING PRICE	STOCK DIV.	SPLIT	APPRECIATION	ACTUAL DIVIDEND	TOTAL RETURN
1957	22	United Technologies	$3.00	3.39%	$88.50	$53.63	20.00%	1	-27.29%	$3.00	-23.90%
1958	9	United Technologies	$3.00	5.59%	$53.63	$60.00		1	11.89%	$3.00	17.48%
1959	1	United Technologies	$3.00	5.00%	$60.00	$39.75		1	-33.75%	$2.50	-29.58%
1960	1	United Technologies	$2.00	5.03%	$39.75	$37.75		1	-5.03%	$2.00	0.00%
1961	6	United Technologies	$2.00	5.30%	$37.75	$42.25		1	11.92%	$2.00	17.22%
1962	3	United Technologies	$2.00	4.73%	$42.25	$51.25		1	21.30%	$2.00	26.04%
1963	13	United Technologies	$2.00	3.90%	$51.25	$43.00		1	-16.10%	$2.00	-12.20%
1964	14	United Technologies	$2.00	4.65%	$43.00	$64.25		1	49.42%	$2.00	54.07%
1965	27	United Technologies	$2.00	3.11%	$64.25	$84.25		1.5	96.11%	$2.10	99.38%
1966	29	United Technologies	$1.60	1.90%	$84.00	$81.13		1	-3.42%	$1.60	-1.52%
1967	28	United Technologies	$1.60	1.97%	$81.13	$82.38		1	1.54%	$1.60	3.51%
1968	24	United Technologies	$1.60	1.94%	$82.38	$68.00		1	-17.45%	$1.70	-15.39%
1969	16	United Technologies	$1.80	2.65%	$68.00	$40.25		1	-40.81%	$1.80	-38.16%
1970	6	United Technologies	$1.80	4.47%	$40.25	$33.63		1	-16.46%	$1.80	-11.99%
1971	2	United Technologies	$1.80	5.35%	$33.63	$29.25		1	-13.01%	$1.80	-7.66%
1972	11	United Technologies	$1.80	6.15%	$29.25	$44.50		1	52.14%	$1.80	58.29%
1973	4	United Technologies	$1.80	4.04%	$44.50	$23.75		1	-46.63%	$.40	-45.73%
1974	18	United Technologies	$1.80	7.58%	$23.75	$32.00		1	34.74%	$1.95	42.95%
1975	17	United Technologies	$2.00	6.25%	$32.00	$46.63		1	45.70%	$2.00	51.95%
1976	23	United Technologies	$2.00	4.29%	$46.63	$38.75		2	66.22%	$2.38	71.32%
1977	18	United Technologies	$1.20	3.10%	$38.75	$35.63		1	-8.06%	$1.65	-3.81%
1978	22	United Technologies	$1.80	5.05%	$35.63	$39.25		1	10.18%	$2.00	15.79%
1979	23	United Technologies	$2.00	5.10%	$39.25	$42.25		1	7.64%	$2.20	13.25%
1980	28	United Technologies	$2.00	4.73%	$42.25	$61.38		1	45.27%	$2.20	50.47%
1981	21	United Technologies	$2.20	3.58%	$61.38	$42.50		1	-30.75%	$2.40	-26.84%
1982	18	United Technologies	$2.40	5.65%	$42.50	$54.25		1	27.65%	$2.40	33.29%
1983	21	United Technologies	$2.40	4.42%	$54.25	$72.00		1	32.72%	$2.55	37.42%
1984	23	United Technologies	$2.60	3.61%	$72.00	$36.63		2	1.74%	$2.75	5.56%
1985	21	United Technologies	$1.40	3.82%	$36.63	$44.13		1	20.48%	$1.40	24.30%
1986	20	United Technologies	$1.40	3.17%	$44.13	$46.75		1	5.95%	$1.40	9.12%
1987	10	United Technologies	$1.40	2.99%	$46.75	$34.88		1	-25.40%	$1.40	-22.41%
1988	12	United Technologies	$1.40	4.01%	$34.88	$40.13		1	15.05%	$1.40	19.50%
1989	17	United Technologies	$1.60	3.99%	$40.13	$55.50		1	38.32%	$1.55	42.31%
1990	17	United Technologies	$1.60	2.88%	$55.50	$47.75		1	-13.96%	$1.60	-10.72%

AVG: 15.6   8.76%   13.04%

U.S. STEEL/USX

YEAR	RANK	STOCK	WSJ DIVI.	WSJ YIELD	OPENING PRICE	CLOSING PRICE	STOCK DIV.	SPLIT	APPRECIATION	ACTUAL DIVIDEND	TOTAL RETURN
1957	16	US Steel	$2.60	3.64%	$71.50	$52.50		1	-26.57%	$3.00	-22.38%
1958	7	US Steel	$3.00	5.71%	$52.50	$98.25		1	87.14%	$3.00	92.86%
1959	17	US Steel	$3.00	3.05%	$98.25	$101.38		1	3.18%	$3.00	6.23%
1960	15	US Steel	$3.00	2.96%	$101.38	$76.13		1	-24.91%	$3.00	-21.95%
1961	9	US Steel	$3.00	3.94%	$76.13	$77.13		1	1.31%	$3.00	5.25%
1962	7	US Steel	$3.00	3.89%	$77.13	$43.75		1	-43.27%	$2.70	-39.77%
1963	1	US Steel	$2.75	6.29%	$43.75	$54.88		1	25.43%	$2.00	30.00%
1964	11	US Steel	$2.00	3.64%	$54.88	$50.75		1	-7.52%	$2.00	-3.87%
1965	7	US Steel	$2.00	3.94%	$50.75	$51.88		1	2.22%	$2.00	6.16%
1966	9	US Steel	$2.00	3.86%	$51.88	$38.50		1	-25.78%	$2.10	-21.73%
1967	3	US Steel	$2.40	6.23%	$38.50	$42.13		1	9.42%	$2.40	15.65%
1968	1	US Steel	$2.40	5.70%	$42.13	$43.50		1	3.26%	$2.40	8.96%
1969	1	US Steel	$2.40	5.52%	$43.50	$34.75		1	-20.11%	$2.40	-14.60%
1970	1	US Steel	$2.40	6.91%	$34.75	$32.25		1	-7.19%	$2.40	-.29%
1971	3	US Steel	$2.40	7.44%	$32.25	$30.50		1	-5.43%	$2.00	.78%
1972	4	US Steel	$1.60	5.25%	$30.50	$31.13		1	2.05%	$1.60	7.30%
1973	5	US Steel	$1.60	5.14%	$31.13	$37.25		1	19.68%	$1.60	24.82%
1974	18	US Steel	$1.60	4.30%	$37.25	$38.50		1	3.36%	$2.20	9.26%
1975	17	US Steel	$2.40	6.27%	$38.25	$65.38		1	70.92%	$2.80	78.24%
1976	18	US Steel	$2.80	4.28%	$65.38	$49.38		1.5	13.29%	$3.18	18.15%
1977	16	US Steel	$2.20	4.46%	$49.38	$31.38		1	-36.46%	$2.20	-32.00%
1978	8	US Steel	$2.20	7.01%	$31.38	$22.13		1	-29.48%	$1.60	-24.38%
1979	10	US Steel	$1.60	7.23%	$22.13	$18.00		1	-18.64%	$1.60	-11.41%
1980	4	US Steel	$1.60	8.89%	$18.00	$25.63		1	42.36%	$1.60	51.25%
1981	12	US Steel	$1.60	6.24%	$25.63	$30.00		1	17.07%	$2.00	24.88%
1982	15	US Steel	$2.00	6.67%	$30.00	$20.75		1	-30.83%	$1.75	-25.00%
1983	15	US Steel	$1.00	4.82%	$20.75	$31.00		1	49.40%	$1.00	54.22%
1984	25	US Steel	$1.00	3.23%	$31.00	$25.75		1	-16.94%	$1.00	-13.71%
1985	21	US Steel	$1.00	3.88%	$25.75	$26.50		1	2.91%	$1.10	7.18%
1986	11	US Steel	$1.20	4.53%	$26.50	$21.88		1	-17.45%	$1.20	-12.92%
1987	4	U.S.X.	$1.20	5.49%	$21.88	$31.50		1	44.00%	$1.20	49.49%
1988	12	U.S.X.	$1.20	3.81%	$31.50	$29.25		1	-7.14%	$1.25	-3.17%
1989	7	U.S.X.	$1.40	4.79%	$29.25	$36.00		1	23.08%	$1.40	27.86%
1990	11	U.S.X.	$1.40	3.89%	$36.00	$29.75		1	-17.36%	$1.40	-13.47%

| AVG: | 10.0 | | | | | | | | 2.50% | | 7.58% |

WESTINGHOUSE ELECTRIC

YEAR	RANK	STOCK	WSJ DIVI.	WSJ YIELD	OPENING PRICE	CLOSING PRICE	STOCK DIV.	SPLIT	APPRECIATION	ACTUAL DIVIDEND	TOTAL RETURN
1957	19	Westinghouse Elec.	$2.00	3.50%	$57.13	$63.00			10.28%	$2.00	13.79%
1958	27	Westinghouse Elec.	$2.00	3.17%	$63.00	$72.50			15.08%	$2.00	18.25%
1959	23	Westinghouse Elec.	$2.00	2.76%	$72.50	$109.50		1	51.03%	$2.10	53.93%
1960	25	Westinghouse Elec.	$2.40	2.19%	$109.50	$47.50		2	-13.24%	$2.40	-11.05%
1961	25	Westinghouse Elec.	$1.20	2.53%	$47.50	$38.00		1	-20.00%	$1.20	-17.47%
1962	13	Westinghouse Elec.	$1.20	3.16%	$38.00	$32.00		1	-15.79%	$1.20	-12.63%
1963	15	Westinghouse Elec.	$1.20	3.75%	$32.00	$34.00		1	6.25%	$1.20	10.00%
1964	13	Westinghouse Elec.	$1.20	3.53%	$34.00	$42.50		1	25.00%	$1.20	28.53%
1965	20	Westinghouse Elec.	$1.20	2.82%	$42.50	$62.13		1	46.18%	$1.25	49.12%
1966	24	Westinghouse Elec.	$1.40	2.25%	$62.13	$47.00		1	-24.35%	$1.40	-22.09%
1967	23	Westinghouse Elec.	$1.40	2.98%	$47.00	$71.25		1	51.60%	$1.60	55.00%
1968	26	Westinghouse Elec.	$1.60	2.25%	$71.25	$69.50		1	-2.46%	$1.80	.07%
1969	25	Westinghouse Elec.	$1.80	2.59%	$69.50	$59.63		1	-14.21%	$1.80	-11.62%
1970	22	Westinghouse Elec.	$1.80	3.02%	$59.63	$67.13		1	12.58%	$1.80	15.60%
1971	24	Westinghouse Elec.	$1.80	2.68%	$67.13	$46.00		2	37.06%	$1.80	39.74%
1972	26	Westinghouse Elec.	$.90	1.96%	$46.00	$44.50		1	-3.26%	$.94	-1.22%
1973	24	Westinghouse Elec.	$.94	2.11%	$44.50	$25.00		1	-43.82%	$.97	-41.64%
1974	20	Westinghouse Elec.	$.97	3.88%	$25.00	$10.13		1	-59.50%	$.97	-55.61%
1975	4	Westinghouse Elec.	$.97	9.58%	$10.13	$13.38		1	32.10%	$.97	41.70%
1976	3	Westinghouse Elec.	$.97	7.25%	$13.38	$17.50		1	30.84%	$.97	38.11%
1977	7	Westinghouse Elec.	$.97	5.54%	$17.50	$18.00		1	2.86%	$.97	8.41%
1978	16	Westinghouse Elec.	$.97	5.39%	$18.00	$17.13		1	-4.86%	$.97	.54%
1979	16	Westinghouse Elec.	$.97	5.66%	$17.13	$19.88		1	16.06%	$.97	21.73%
1980	20	Westinghouse Elec.	$.97	4.88%	$19.88	$29.75		1	49.69%	$1.40	56.73%
1981	24	Westinghouse Elec.	$1.40	4.71%	$29.75	$26.50		1	-10.92%	$1.80	-4.87%
1982	13	Westinghouse Elec.	$1.80	6.79%	$26.50	$37.50		1	41.51%	$1.80	48.30%
1983	16	Westinghouse Elec.	$1.80	4.80%	$37.50	$54.00		1	44.00%	$1.80	48.80%
1984	23	Westinghouse Elec.	$1.80	3.33%	$54.00	$26.00		2	-3.70%	$1.95	-.09%
1985	22	Westinghouse Elec.	$1.00	3.85%	$26.00	$44.00		1	69.23%	$1.15	73.65%
1986	24	Westinghouse Elec.	$1.20	2.73%	$44.00	$58.25		1	32.39%	$1.35	35.45%
1987	24	Westinghouse Elec.	$1.40	2.40%	$58.25	$51.25		1	-12.02%	$1.64	-9.20%
1988	17	Westinghouse Elec.	$1.72	3.36%	$51.25	$52.00		1	1.46%	$1.93	5.23%
1989	13	Westinghouse Elec.	$2.00	3.85%	$52.00	$75.50		1	45.19%	$2.30	49.62%
1990	15	Westinghouse Elec.	$2.40	3.18%	$75.50	$28.38		2	-24.83%	$2.70	-21.26%

AVG: 19.1   10.81%   14.81%

WOOLWORTH, F.W.

YEAR	RANK	STOCK	WSJ DIVI.	WSJ YIELD	OPENING PRICE	CLOSING PRICE	STOCK DIV.	SPLIT	APPRECIATION	ACTUAL DIVIDEND	TOTAL RETURN
1957	2	Woolworth	$2.50	5.70%	$43.88	$37.00		1	-15.67%	$2.50	-9.97%
1958	4	Woolworth	$2.50	6.76%	$37.00	$53.88		1	45.61%	$2.50	52.36%
1959	2	Woolworth	$2.50	4.64%	$53.88	$66.13		1	22.74%	$2.50	27.38%
1960	10	Woolworth	$2.50	3.78%	$66.13	$68.63		1	3.78%	$2.50	7.56%
1961	10	Woolworth	$2.50	3.64%	$68.63	$91.00		1	32.60%	$2.50	36.25%
1962	19	Woolworth	$2.50	2.75%	$91.00	$64.13		1	-29.53%	$2.50	-26.79%
1963	14	Woolworth	$2.50	3.90%	$64.13	$74.50		1	16.18%	$2.73	20.44%
1964	9	Woolworth	$2.80	3.76%	$74.50	$27.63		3	11.24%	$2.90	15.13%
1965	10	Woolworth	$1.00	3.62%	$27.63	$31.13		1	12.67%	$1.00	16.29%
1966	15	Woolworth	$1.00	3.21%	$31.13	$19.63		1	-36.95%	$1.00	-33.73%
1967	10	Woolworth	$1.00	5.10%	$19.63	$25.50		1	29.94%	$1.00	35.03%
1968	15	Woolworth	$1.00	3.92%	$25.50	$32.88		1	28.92%	$1.00	32.84%
1969	18	Woolworth	$1.00	3.04%	$32.88	$38.25		1	16.35%	$1.15	19.85%
1970	20	Woolworth	$1.20	3.14%	$38.25	$35.63		1	-6.86%	$1.20	-3.73%
1971	18	Woolworth	$1.20	3.37%	$35.63	$44.88		1	25.96%	$1.20	29.33%
1972	23	Woolworth	$1.20	2.67%	$44.88	$31.38		1	-30.08%	$1.20	-27.41%
1973	13	Woolworth	$1.20	3.82%	$31.38	$18.50		1	-41.04%	$1.20	-37.21%
1974	7	Woolworth	$1.20	6.49%	$18.50	$9.88		1	-46.62%	$1.20	-40.14%
1975	2	Woolworth	$1.20	12.15%	$9.88	$22.13		1	124.05%	$1.20	136.20%
1976	11	Woolworth	$1.20	5.42%	$22.13	$25.38		1	14.69%	$1.20	20.11%
1977	13	Woolworth	$1.20	4.73%	$25.38	$18.50		1	-27.09%	$1.20	-22.36%
1978	3	Woolworth	$1.40	7.57%	$18.50	$19.38		1	4.73%	$1.40	12.30%
1979	11	Woolworth	$1.40	7.23%	$19.38	$24.38		1	25.81%	$1.55	33.81%
1980	14	Woolworth	$1.40	5.74%	$24.38	$25.00		1	2.56%	$1.75	9.74%
1981	9	Woolworth	$1.80	7.20%	$25.00	$18.25		1	-27.00%	$1.80	-19.80%
1982	2	Woolworth	$1.80	9.86%	$18.25	$25.75		1	41.10%	$1.80	50.96%
1983	8	Woolworth	$1.80	6.99%	$25.75	$35.50		1	37.86%	$1.80	44.85%
1984	9	Woolworth	$1.80	5.07%	$35.50	$37.00		1	4.23%	$1.80	9.30%
1985	13	Woolworth	$1.80	4.86%	$37.00	$59.13		1	59.80%	$1.95	65.07%
1986	19	Woolworth	$2.00	3.38%	$59.13	$39.38		2	33.19%	$2.18	36.88%
1987	22	Woolworth	$1.12	2.84%	$39.38	$36.38		1	-7.62%	$1.27	-4.39%
1988	14	Woolworth	$1.32	3.63%	$36.38	$50.75		1	39.52%	$1.56	43.81%
1989	19	Woolworth	$1.64	3.23%	$50.75	$66.00		1	30.05%	$1.82	33.64%
1990	18	Woolworth	$1.88	2.85%	$66.00	$30.00		2	-9.09%	$2.03	-6.02%

AVG: 11.9 | | | | | | | | | 11.35% | | 16.40%

Appendix 5

Annual Rates of Turnover in the Top Five and Top Ten

The annual rate of turnover for a portfolio is the key for estimating transaction costs and the rate and timing by which capital gains taxes will have to be paid. Average rates of turnover for the high-yield portfolios are relatively low at 40 percent for the Top Five and 29 percent for the Top Ten. These low rates help to hold down transaction costs for the dividend investor and also reduce the annual capital gains taxes that must be paid. (Should the delineation between long-term and short-term capital gains return to the tax code, dividend investors following this program would benefit due to the fact that no issue would be held for less than one year.)

Table A5.1.   Top Five and Top Ten Annual Portfolio Turnover

Year	Top Five	Top Ten
1958	40%	30%
1959	40%	30%
1960	40%	30%
1961	20%	20%
1962	20%	10%
1963	60%	30%
1964	20%	30%
1965	20%	20%
1966	20%	20%
1967	40%	30%
1968	40%	20%
1969	40%	10%
1970	40%	30%
1971	20%	30%
1972	60%	30%
1973	20%	40%
1974	60%	60%
1975	60%	50%
1976	60%	40%
1977	40%	20%
1978	60%	50%
1979	40%	30%
1980	60%	20%
1981	60%	30%
1982	60%	20%
1983	40%	40%
1984	20%	10%
1985	20%	20%
1986	40%	20%
1987	40%	30%
1988	40%	20%
1989	40%	40%
1990	40%	30%
1991	40%	
Average	40%	28%

Appendix 6

Variance Among the Yield Groups

Variance is a measure of fluctuation per unit time in a system. As it relates to investing, variance is a measure of the consistency of returns of an investment methodology, and as such is used by many investors as a proxy for risk. Lower variance would equate to lower risk, as the outcome of a particular investment methodology would be more predictable.

The data show that the high-yield groups, particularly the Top Ten, have lower variances than the market and the low-yield groups. The advantage of the high-yield groups is especially notable in bear market periods such as 1966 to 1974 and 1969 to 1978. In general, the Bottom Five and Bottom Ten displayed the worst levels of variance along with the lowest rates of return — a particularly bad combination. The variance of the leveraged Top Five was indeed the highest, but this is to be expected with a leveraged portfolio. The investor was rewarded for accepting the high variance in the leveraged Top Five by garnering what was by far the highest long-run rate of return.

Table A6.1.   Comparison of Portfolio Variances

TOTAL RETURN VARIANCES 1957 to 1990 (refer to Tables 3.5 and 11.3)	
Portfolio	Variance
Top 5	34.46
Top 10	27.88
Dow 30	28.33
Bottom 10	37.82
Bottom 5	48.12
Leveraged Top 5	102.96

TOTAL RETURN VARIANCES 1966 to 1981: Bear Market (refer to Tables 5.1 and 11.5)	
Portfolio	Variance
Top 5	40.68
Top 10	31.81
Dow 30	32.27
Bottom 10	47.40
Bottom 5	33.71
Leveraged Top 5	129.08

CAPITAL RETURN VARIANCES 1957 to 1990 (refer to Table 4.1)	
Portfolio	Variance
Top 5	33.14
Top 10	26.25
Dow 30	27.31
Bottom 10	37.13
Bottom 5	48.05

TOTAL RETURN VARIANCES 1966 to 1974: The Worst Case (refer to Table 5.3)	
Portfolio	Variance
Top 5	23.82
Top 10	20.75
Dow 30	25.77
Bottom 10	36.68
Bottom 5	30.30

TOTAL RETURN VARIANCES 1957 to 1972: The Early Period (refer to Table 6.1)	
Portfolio	Variance
Top 5	34.41
Top 10	27.73
Dow 30	23.20
Bottom 10	27.29
Bottom 5	35.54

TOTAL RETURN VARIANCES 1973 to 1990: The Later Period (refer to Table 6.2)	
Portfolio	Variance
Top 5	35.19
Top 10	28.22
Dow 30	34.27
Bottom 10	49.11
Bottom 5	59.99

Table A6.1 Continued

TOTAL RETURN VARIANCES 1959 to 1968: A "Normal" Market (refer to Table 6.3a)	
Portfolio	Variance
Top 5	26.05
Top 10	19.75
Dow 30	19.67
Bottom 10	30.06
Bottom 5	42.39

TOTAL RETURN VARIANCES 1969 to 1978: A "Bear" Market (refer to Table 6.3b)	
Portfolio	Variance
Top 5	55.20
Top 10	38.44
Dow 30	42.55
Bottom 10	60.42
Bottom 5	49.51

TOTAL RETURN VARIANCES 1979 to 1988: A "Bull" Market (refer to Table 6.3c)	
Portfolio	Variance
Top 5	12.35
Top 10	15.74
Dow 30	13.56
Bottom 10	26.29
Bottom 5	60.64

Index